The NATIONS, ISRAEL and the CHURCH in PROPHECY

D1617232

The Books of Dr. Walvoord . . .

The NATIONS, ISRAEL and the CHURCH in PROPHECY

John F. Walvoord

Academie
Books Grand Rapids,
Michigan
Zondervan Publishing House

The Nations, Israel, and the Church in Prophecy
Copyright © 1967, 1962, 1964 by Zondervan Publishing House
Copyright Preface © 1988 by John F. Walvoord
Originally published in three volumes as
The Nations in Prophecy, Israel in Prophecy, The Church in Prophecy

ACADEMIE BOOKS is an imprint of Zondervan Publishing House,
1415 Lake Drive, S.E., Grand Rapids, Michigan 49506.

Library of Congress Cataloging in Publication Data

Walvoord, John F.
    The nations, Israel, and the church in prophecy / John F.
Walvoord.
        p.   cm.
    Reprint. (1st work). Originally published: The nations in
prophecy. 1st ed. Grand Rapids : Zondervan Pub. House, 1967.
    Reprint. (2nd work). Originally published: Israel in prophecy.
Grand Rapids : Zondervan Pub. House, c1962.
    Reprint. (3rd work). Originally published: The church in prophecy.
Grand Rapids : Zondervan Pub. House, 1964.
    Bibliography: p.
    Includes indexes.
    ISBN 0-310-34171-X
    1. Bible–Prophecies.   2. Bible–Prophecies–Jews.   3. Bible-
-Prophecies–Israel.   4. Bible–Prophecies–Church.   I. Title.
BS647.2.W33 1988
220.1'5–dc19   88-14772
                                                                    CIP

All rights reserved. No part of this publication may be reproduced, stored in a
retrieval system, or transmitted in any form or by any means—electronic,
mechanical, photocopy, recording, or any other—except for brief quotations in
printed reviews, without the prior permission of the publisher.

Printed in the United States of America

91 92 93 / AK / 10 9 8 7 6 5 4

CONTENTS TO
THE NATIONS IN PROPHECY

CONTENTS TO
ISRAEL IN PROPHECY

CONTENTS TO
THE CHURCH IN PROPHECY

PREFACE

With one-fourth of the Bible prophetically future when it was written, the interpretation of prophecy is one of the most challenging areas of biblical study. Too often preconceptions have led interpreters to draw from the biblical text doctrines that were quite removed from what the text actually states. Because prophecy is scattered from the early chapters of Genesis to the last chapter of Revelation and deals with so many different situations and subjects, interpreters of prophecy have too often abandoned any detailed interpretation and reached only general conclusions.

From the careful study of the prophetic Scriptures three main subjects emerge: (1) what the Bible teaches about the nations, (2) what the Bible teaches about Israel, and (3) what the Bible teaches about the church. Major prophecies concerning the person and work of Christ and prophecies concerning the future activities of holy angels, as well as Satan and the demonic world, are related to these three primary subjects. When biblical prophecies are classified under this threefold approach, and hundreds of prophecies are related to these divisions, the pattern for the future becomes clear.

Combining in one volume prophecies concerning the nations, Israel, and the church gives the reader a broad interpretation of the entire prophetic Word, avoiding the confusion that often exists when mingling these prophetic strains. Publication in this form will provide the reader with an understandable statement of what the Bible teaches about the future.

The study of man as told in history and prophecy is the most exciting drama ever written. It reveals the omnipotent God unfolding his purpose for the nations in measured movements designed to demonstrate his own sovereignty, wisdom, and power. Though in the original creation man was made in the image and likeness of God, in the fall the image is marred. Nevertheless man was destined to be the channel of divine revelation. The history of the human race as recorded in Scripture was designed to demonstrate both the inadequacy of the creature and the sufficiency of the omnipotent Creator. Earth was to be the divine stage and man the actor, but there can be no question that human destiny remains in the hands of the unseen God even if at times he seems to work behind the scenes.

In the twentieth century when history seems to be moving rapidly toward its destiny, the study of history and prophecy in Scripture is especially appropriate. Only the Bible can provide a divine interpretation of history and the revelation of the prophetic future of nations. However, one of the most neglected areas of biblical prophecy is that of the predictions concerning the nation Israel, beginning with God's declared purpose for Abraham and extending throughout the rest of the Old Testament and the New Testament. The establishment of the new state of Israel in the Middle East in 1948 raised the question whether the future restoration of Israel was beginning. Although there has been a tendency to ignore specific prophecies of the future in biblical interpretation and especially prophecies concerning Israel, the literal return of thousands of Israelites to their homeland provides a proper basis for a fresh look at Scripture.

Before the eyes of the entire world the seemingly impossible has occurred. A people scattered for almost two millenniums are now firmly entrenched in the land of their forefathers. What has often been denied as impossible now provides a new emphasis to the study of prophecy concerning Israel.

The interpretation of prophecy concerning Israel has been a major cause of prophetic confusion. Some have attempted to make these prophecies conditional and therefore never to be fulfilled. Others have attempted to take them in a nonliteral sense and apply them to the church.

Although the nation Israel is a comparatively small part of the world's population, from the standpoint of biblical doctrine the divine plan for Israel can justly claim a place of central importance. Prophecies concerning Israel are pervasive throughout both Testaments, and understanding them is necessary for the interpretation of all Scripture. From the standpoint of clarifying confusion in the interpretation of prophecy the proper interpretation of Israel's role in the past, present, and future is a crucial issue.

The material in *Israel in Prophecy* was originally delivered as lectures to the student body and faculty of Western Conservative Baptist Theological Seminary in Portland, Oregon, and is published with some alterations. Some of the material in *The Church in Prophecy* was given in lecture form at Grace Theological Seminary in 1963.

The study of prophecy relating to the church is a fitting capstone to the previous discussion of prophecy relating to the nations and Israel, revealing as it does the major undertaking of God in the present age.

Christ himself introduced this major revelation of prophecy when he declared to Peter in his previous conversation with him, "I tell you that you are Peter, and on this rock I will build my church, and the gates of Hades will not overcome it" (Matt. 16:18). In a peculiar way the Gospel of Matthew blends the past with the present and the future, introducing for the first time prophecy relating to the church. The Gospel of Matthew primarily is a bridge from the Old to the New Testament explaining Christ's fulfillment of prophecies of his first coming. In the final message of Christ in the Upper Room (John 13–17) Christ revealed in detail for the first time the distinct character of the church. This revelation is introductory to the prophetic hope of the church in its theology, ethics, and distinctive character as unfolded in the epistles. The consummation of prophecies relating to the nations, Israel, and the church are revealed in the Book of Revelation.

The study of prophecy relating to the church is essential to revealing the distinctive purpose of God in the present age. This subject was not revealed in the Old Testament. In the interpretation of prophecy concerning the church the same general principles of exposition of the Word of God are followed as in previous discussions of the nations and Israel, that is, the Scriptures are taken in their normal or literal meaning unless there is clear ground for assigning another meaning. As such the church is distinguished from the saints in the Old Testament whether Jews or Gentiles, distinguished from the nation of Israel, and distinguished also in its prophetic future. Although there are similarities in prophecies concerning Israel and the church, the distinction continues throughout the eternal future in the New Jerusalem.

In these present closing years of the twentieth century, evidence is pointing to the fulfillment of end-time events leading up to the second coming of Christ. Most important is the revelation of the special purpose of God to catch up the church in the rapture before the final drama runs its course. The hope of the church today is the imminent return of Christ to take his own from the world to heaven while great world events consummate and fulfill many prophecies relating to the nations and Israel. With the second advent of Christ prior to the millennial kingdom the separate course of fulfillment relating to the nations, Israel, and the church is continued. If this study in these major fields of prophecy is helpful to students and encourages their expectation for prophetic fulfillment for the end of the church age, the purpose of this presentation will be fulfilled.

John F. Walvoord

The NATIONS in PROPHECY

CHAPTER I

THE NATIONS IN CRISIS

The world today faces an international crisis unparalleled in all the history of man. A tremendous revolution is under way in the international scene, in science, in economics, in morals, in theology, and in the religious structure of the church. The world is aflame with the raw passions of men ambitious for power and desperate to be freed from poverty and frustration. An ominous cloud hangs over the hearts of men and nations. The nations are indeed at the crossroads, and impending events cast their shadow on every aspect of human life. The world is moving faster and faster like a colossal machine out of control whose very power and momentum inevitably will plunge it into ultimate disaster.

Apart from the Bible, the world does not have a ray of hope. Our most brilliant leaders have not found an answer. World leaders, whether in Moscow or Washington, are troubled by the great issues which face the world today. President John F. Kennedy before his untimely assassination expressed the viewpoint of western civilization when he said, "I speak today in an hour of national peril, and of national opportunity. Before my term has ended, we shall have to test anew whether a nation organized and governed such as ours can endure. The outcome is by no means certain. The tide of events has been running out, and time has not been our friend."

The present world crisis is not a result of any one factor, but a concurrence of causes and effects which combine to set the world stage for a conflict which may quickly bring an end to hundreds of years of progress in western civilization and establish new centers of international power. Whatever the future holds, it is going to be dramatically different than the past. In this dark picture only the Scriptures chart a sure course and give us an intelligent explanation of world-wide confusion as it exists today. The present world crisis in the light of the Scriptures reveals the existence of remarkable components in almost every area which may lead to a dramatic climax of world history. The present crises in every area of human life all point to the same conclusion, that disaster awaits the nations of the world.

SPIRITUAL CRISIS

The twentieth century has witnessed a gathering spiritual crisis. The history of the church to some extent has paralleled the intellectual progress of the world since apostolic days. For many centuries Christianity was largely obscured in the darkness of the Middle Ages. The vigorous evangelical movement of the church largely sprang from the Protestant Reformation and political freedom which permitted the proclamation of the Gospel. During the last century an unprecedented missionary effort has been witnessed. Thousands of missionaries carried the Gospel to distant lands and the Bible was published in hundreds of tongues. Through the printed page and through radio the Gospel has reached most of the civilized world to some extent, and more individuals are within potential reach of the Gospel than ever before.

Although there are many encouraging aspects to contemporary missionary efforts, it should be obvious even to the most sanguine observer that the proclamation of the Gospel is not even keeping up with the population explosion, much less overcoming opposition engendered by the nationalism of small nations and the vigorous growth of communism in many lands. As far as numbers of converts are concerned, communism as well as some of the non-Christian religions of the world are far exceeding Christianity in its present outreach. Even in so-called Christian United States of America, Biblical truth has had realistic application to only a small segment of the population and has not materially influenced our national policies whether in politics, business, or educational areas of national activity.

The spiritual crisis is pinpointed by the rejection of Jesus Christ as Saviour and Lord by the masses of world population in every nation. In Europe, the cradle of Protestantism, only a small fraction of the total population has an intelligent belief in Jesus Christ and nowhere in the world is the Christian faith a dominant influence. It is obvious that a projection of the contemporary efforts to further the Christian faith and to introduce people to Jesus Christ will fall far short of any realistic goal. The world has plunged into an age where the great majority do not know the facts about Jesus Christ, and if they did, would probably not receive them sympathetically.

THEOLOGICAL CRISIS

If the historic Christian faith embodied in the great creeds of the church and expressed by the Protestant reformers are taken as the standards, it is evident that the church today is in a major theological crisis. Central in this controversy is the rejection of the Bible as the inerrant Word of God. In spite of the fact that more facilities are available than ever before to print, translate, and proclaim Scriptural truth, the educated people of the world have not turned to the Scriptures in faith. Within the walls of the professing church unbelief in the Scriptures has come in like a flood until many so-called Biblical scholars assume that the historic faith in the Bible as God's holy Word is now outmoded and not even worthy of debate. Substituted for Biblical faith is confidence in spiritual experience — either natural or supernatural, and in the promotion of ritualism, moralism, and rationalism.

Man has once again assumed the impossible task of defining and proclaiming infinite truth apart from God's divine revelation, an effort which history has demonstrated is doomed to failure. Churches and institutions of learning which are standing with the Protestant Reformers in fundamental doctrines are all too few and are an evident minority in the great mass of contemporary Christendom.

While in our day some of the extremes of liberalism have been rejected, there is no observable trend toward the absolute standard of accepting the Bible as the inerrant Word of God. There does not seem to be any hope of reclaiming this doctrine for the majority of the church. Organized Christendom today is like a ship without a rudder and an anchor, at the mercy of the winds of chance and bound for no certain port. The ultimate end can only be disaster for the ship and all those who put their trust in it.

MORAL CRISIS

It is only natural that spiritual crisis and theological crisis should have its ultimate end in the moral crisis of our day. Never before in the history of the world has there been more organized and deliberate immorality in defiance of Biblical ethics. The new liberal theology has bred a new morality. That such immorality should be true of the heathen world is to be expected. That it should come from cultured, educated, and liberated people is certainly an omen that only divine judgment can deal with this situation. Even in lands where Christianity has been widely taught, the basic morality of honesty and decency, the sanctity of marriage and the home, and related ethical standards are dragged into the mire of a civilization devoted to every sinful pleasure and to ridiculing any return to decency.

Such a situation is plainly treated in II Peter 2 as a natural result stemming from departure from the doctrine of the person and work of Christ. The immorality of our day is the inevitable fruit of departure from Christ and the Word of God. For it there can only be divine judgment such as the Scriptures clearly predict.

ECCLESIASTICAL CRISIS

The trend away from Biblical theology and Biblical morals has precipitated in the modern church a desire to organize all Christendom in one centrally governed body. In this way the church can achieve a powerful role in the world not dependent upon its theology or spiritual power. Although motivated in many cases by a sincere desire to advance the cause of Christ, the ecumenical movement has emerged in the modern scene as a colossus embracing all Christendom in a gigantic organization responsible to its leaders but not to its laity. This centralization of power is no substitute for the spiritual unity accomplished by the indwelling power of the Holy Spirit.

Because the majority of the organized church are committed to theological and spiritual doctrines which differ from historic Christianity, progress in the ecumenical movement can only result in the throttling of evangelical activity true to the Gospel. Both on the mission field and in the homeland its influence has tended to make the way difficult for those who still proclaim the old orthodoxy. Most important in understanding our times is the suggestion that the creation of an ecumenical church is a foreshadowing and preparation for a new world religion which in the prophetic future will be completely devoid of spiritual truth related to Christianity. The present demand for conformity to the organized church could end in the throttling of freedom of speech and conscience which would threaten any future spiritual progress for the church at large.

SCIENTIFIC CRISIS

One of the major elements in our modern world is the rapid rise of science whether in the field of electronics or the atomic structure of matter. Incredible advances are being achieved in one year which more than equal the advance in whole centuries of the past. The modern world has been brought together by rapid communication and transportation. The atomic bomb has greatly increased the ability of evil men to destroy or control. The race to command space is driven by the fear of some breakthrough which would give one nation a dominant position of power over the entire world. To the horrors of war already conceived are added the possibilities of bacteriological or chemical warfare which could well wipe out whole civilizations and drastically change the face of the earth.

The scientific colossus is such that increased knowledge brings only increased fear, and those in the best position to know have the greatest dread of that which the future may hold. The scientific advance has contributed tremendously to the accumulated evidence that the world is facing a showdown, that history in the future will not be as it was in the past, and that some gigantic crisis looms on the horizon.

RACIAL CRISIS

Among the tensions contributing to the international scene are growing racial tensions evident not only in the United States but throughout the world. It is evident that people wrongly oppressed in some cases are not content with equality and redress, but want supremacy. The down-trodden masses of the world regardless of race often find in the racial issue a springboard from which to launch their claims.

From a Biblical standpoint, antisemitism in the Middle East is a matter of major significance. The people of Israel now restored to their ancient land, although small in number, are regarded as a thorn in the side of the non-Jewish world and constitute one of the major tensions in a pivotal area of the world.

From the standpoint of prophecy this issue looms large in the present day and in the prophetic future, and Israel's restoration is by divine appointment. Israel as the chosen people is destined to a prominent place in future world affairs, but not before enduring much hardship and persecution. The racial issue, however, is not limited to the Middle East, and almost every nation under the sun has serious racial tensions on a plane never before realized in the entire history of the world.

ECONOMIC CRISIS

Those living within the United States of America have an unusual platform from which to view the economic situation of the entire world. Prosperity has swept America to a degree never before realized, and its average citizen has more money, more pleasure, more luxuries than ever before. But the United States is an island in a world of desperate economic need. Millions of the masses of the world who are oppressed and deprived of any fair share of economic wealth are clamoring to be heard. In many nations there is no middle class, but only the extremely rich and the extremely poor. The tensions raised by such a situation cannot forever lie dormant. The word *revolution* will undoubtedly be prominent in the days ahead, as oppressed people are exploited by communists as well as ambitious politicians and encouraged to rebel with empty promises of improvement in their situation.

While certain areas of the world are experiencing unprecedented prosperity, other portions are still laboring in desperate need of the basic material things of life with millions who are in constant danger of starvation and for whom the simplest shelter and provision of clothing is often lacking. The mushrooming population of the world has only aggravated the situation until major sections of the earth can no longer support themeslves. The resulting pressures inevitably will affect future world history and continue to erupt until the whole earth is caught in a world crisis combining all of these several elements.

POLITICAL CRISIS

One of the most evident areas of crisis is in the international scene with nations motivated by communistic principles attempting to wrest control from the noncommunist world. Never before in history have such dramatic changes taken place as have occurred in the last twenty-five years. During these years major countries have been freed from control of other nations and many small nations have emerged as independent states. The immaturity of the new countries and their lack of economic resources and wise leadership already have produced an erratic course which does not portend a glorious future. The world-wide struggle between communism and the noncommunist nations is moving relentlessly in favor of communism, and the question which many thoughtful leaders raise is how long will this struggle continue. For those interested in freedom of conscience, freedom of enterprise, and freedom of speech, these are indeed dark hours, and no one humanly speaking dares to predict what another generation will face.

CRISIS IN PROPHETIC FULFILLMENT

The many factors which contribute to world crisis in our day have tremendous significance as compared to the Scriptures. The amazing fact is that these factors fit into a prophetic pattern which describes the end of the age. The Bible anticipates that a world crisis would precede the coming of Christ to establish His millennial kingdom (Matthew 24:15-24). Before the final world crisis comes to its head Christ will come to take those who believe in Him out of the world in the rapture of the church (I Thessalonians 4:13 - 5:11).

In describing end-time events, the Bible makes plain that the world crisis will eventually result in a world government headed by an evil world dictator (Revelation 13:1-10). The United Nations of our present world built on the assumption that world government is the only way to world peace may well be a part of the preparation for world-wide acceptance of a world dictator as the only way out. In preparation for the formation of this world empire, the Bible seems to anticipate a revival of the ancient Roman Empire, a formation of a United States of countries in the Mediterranean area. From this will come a temporary solution of the Israel-Arab controversy by means of a covenant with the people of Israel (Daniel 9:27).

This preliminary stage, however, is only the forerunner of a final world government in which the world dictator assumes supreme control and demands that all worship him in recognition of a new world religion of which he is the head (Revelation 13:8). Israel as well as those who name the name of Christ in that day will become the objects of fearful persecution. Divine judgments in an unprecedented way will fall upon the earth (cf. Revelation 6 - 19). These and many other developments will tend to make this period a time of great tribulation. This tremendous movement will climax in a great world war and the second coming of Jesus Christ to establish His earthly kingdom.

The significance of the present world crisis is that it contains practically all the elements which are a natural preparation for the end of the age. The raging of the nations (Psalm 2:1) is the forerunner to the Son of God establishing His government in Zion (Psalm 2:6; Isaiah 2:2-4). The present generation may witness the dramatic close of the "times of the Gentiles" and the establishment of the kingdom of heaven upon the earth, thus bringing to fulfillment one of the great themes of prophecy — the divine program for the nations of the world.

CHAPTER II

THE BEGINNINGS OF THE NATIONS

THE BEGINNING OF CREATION

The Bible is a book of beginnings. The reader of the Scriptures is introduced in the very first verse of the Bible to the sweeping statement "In the beginning God." The eternal God who knew no beginning is the source of all the beginnings which follow. In the original creation, the material universe was brought into being with all its complexity and natural law seen today in the organic and inorganic world. In this universe of mass and motion were introduced the first moral creatures, the holy angels. Each angel was the object of immediate creation. They were moral agents with moral will and intelligence capable of serving God. Some of these left their first estate in rebellion and headed by Satan became fallen angels (Isaiah 14:12-15; Ezekiel 28:12-15).

CREATION OF MAN

The holy angels and the fallen angels, those who left their first estate, were not created in the image and likeness of God. Adam and Eve were created to fulfill this lofty purpose here on earth, and were designed to be morally like God. There is some evidence that the world of Adam and Eve was a re-creation and not the original creation of the heavens and the earth. The introduction of man, however, was something new and was the beginning of the divine purpose in which ultimately God would become man in Christ.

FROM ADAM TO NOAH

The early history of man from Adam to Noah is summarized in a few short chapters which graphically picture the introduction of sin into the human race through Satanic temptation and man's choice to disobey God. The downward course of humanity was rapid. Genesis 6:5-7 depicts God observing the great wickedness

21

of man, "that every imagination of the thoughts of his heart was only evil continually," and God declared His purpose, "I will destroy man whom I have created from the face of the earth; both man, and beast, and the creeping thing, and the fowls of the air" (Genesis 6:7). The only bright spot in the unrelieved depravity of man was that "Noah found grace in the eyes of the LORD" (Genesis 6:8). Of the many thousands which populated the earth at that time only Noah and his wife and three sons and their wives were worth saving from the flood which God declared would compass the earth.

THE FLOOD

The story of the flood must have been important in the eyes of God for more space is given to it in Genesis than the whole story of creation and more than the whole history from Adam to Noah. This was another new beginning, a wiping out of that which was spoiled and impossible of restoration, and a beginning with a godly family which, in the midst of universal corruption, had found faith and grace and manifested a determination to do the will of God. Noah lived to the ripe old age of 950 years, one of the oldest men in the Bible, exceeded only by Methuselah who lived 969 years. Most important, however, is the historic fact that Noah became the father of the entire human race. His three sons born before the flood, Japheth, Ham, and Shem were to be the progenitors of mankind subsequently born on the earth. There is no record of any other sons of Noah, and his three sons who shared with him the task of building the ark and who survived the flood were to be the means by which God repopulated the earth.

INTRODUCTION OF HUMAN GOVERNMENT

The new beginning with Noah and his sons also marked the progression and the unfolding of the divine purpose in human history. In Noah and his family for the first time were exercised the prerogatives of human government, the right of man to rule his fellow men. Adam had been given the charge to "subdue" the earth (Genesis 1:28), but he did not properly execute his responsibility. The commission, therefore, was renewed with enlargement to Noah in Genesis 9:1-6 embodied in the dictum, "Whoso sheddeth man's blood, by man shall his blood be shed: for in the image of God made he man" (Genesis 9:6).

The sword of divine retribution was placed in the hand of man in an attempt to control the natural lawlessness of the human heart. The principle of government thus introduced is reinforced throughout the Scriptures and is reiterated in Romans 13:1-7. In Romans the political ruler is declared to be "ordained of God" (Romans 13:1) and "the minister of God, a revenger to execute wrath upon him that doeth evil" (Romans 13:4). The human conscience proved unreliable when operating individually and thus the corporate responsibility of human government was introduced.

The place of human government in the world looms large in much of the history of the race as well as in prophecy of the end time. God has declared His concern for governments which God has recognized and with whom He is going to deal. The ultimate human government will be that of Christ Himself as He rules in the millennium and in its eternal form in the new heaven and the new earth. Earthly governments though ordained of God have largely been in rebellion against Him. As the psalmist said, "Why do the heathen rage?" and, "The kings of the earth set themselves, and the ruler take counsel together, against the LORD, and against his anointed" (Psalm 2:1, 2). God's answer is, "Yet have I set my king upon my holy hill of Zion" (Psalm 2:6).

PROPHECY CONCERNING NOAH'S SONS

Early in the history of the race prophecy begins to cast its guiding light upon the course of future human events. God promised that never again would the waters of the flood destroy all flesh (Genesis 9:15). The rainbow was made a symbol of this covenant (Genesis 9:13-17).

The most important prophecy relating to the nations which has laid the guidelines for all subsequent human history was the aftermath of a dark chapter in the life of godly Noah when he drank wine from his newly planted vineyards and became drunk (Genesis 9:20, 21). The irreverence of Ham in comparison to the respect of Shem and Japheth as they dealt with their father in his weakness led to Noah's solemn words recorded in Genesis 9:25-27, "And he said, Cursed be Canaan; a servant of servants shall he be unto his brethren. And he said, Blessed be the LORD God of Shem; and Canaan shall be his servant. God shall enlarge Japheth, and he shall dwell in the tents of Shem; and Canaan shall be his servant."

This prophetic utterance reveals that the human race would

be divided according to the natural divisions stemming from the three sons of Noah. Canaan or the descendants of Canaan, the youngest son of Ham, were to be cursed, a servile people. By contrast Shem is to be the master of Canaan and "blessed of the LORD God." It was through Shem that God's divine revelation was to come, the Scriptures were to be written, Israel to be chosen, and ultimately the Saviour and Redeemer was to appear. The contrast between Canaan and Shem is a prophetic one, not an exhortation or justification to mistreat the descendants of Ham. These broad prophecies were to characterize the people as a whole. It was not to prevent those who sought the Lord among the descendants of Ham from enjoying His blessing nor was it to assure those who were descendants of Shem that they would avoid the righteous judgment of God so largely written in God's dealings with Israel in the captivities and similar chastisements.

The immediate history that followed Noah's prophetic utterances does not constitute evidence that the curse or the blessing was necessarily immediately administered to any particular generation or individual, for many hundreds of years after Noah the descendants of Ham seemed to have flourished, and by contrast the children of Israel, the descendants of Shem, became slaves in Egypt. But, the principle laid down has subsequently been justified and constitutes God's ultimate purpose in dealing with these broad divisions of humanity.

By contrast Japheth is promised enlargement. Enlargement was not immediately evident in subsequent history of the race, but eventually the promise was fulfilled. In the history of the world since the time of Christ, the descendants of Japheth have become the principal custodians of Gentile power and have spread over the world in their power and wealth. The original prophecy indicated that Japheth would somehow inherit the blessings stemming from Shem. It has been fulfilled in that many among the Gentiles have participated in the redemption provided by Christ of the line of Shem. These original prophecies, broad in their scope and extensive in their fulfillment, will provide the framework of the history of the nations as well as the prophetic picture of that which will constitute the nations in the end of the age.

THE DESCENDANTS OF NOAH

One of the great chapters in the Bible often neglected in casual Bible study is Genesis 10, with its chronicle of the descendants of

Noah. It is obvious from the study of this chapter that here we have the background of nations which ultimately emerged and what is recorded here as history is the framework for prophecy. The compilation of the descendants of Noah is not simply a genealogy, but is designed to account for the great nations which later covered the inhabited earth.

The record of Genesis 10 is more than an ethnography, that is, a description of origin of races, but it is a profound introduction to ethnology, having to do also with the distribution, relationship, and significance of the descendants of Noah in history. Genesis 10 is one of the most remarkable historical records of this kind to be found anywhere in ancient literature, and all studies of anthropology and related sciences must begin with the facts given here. It is possible that Moses had before him documentary evidence which he used in writing the chapter, but in any case the Spirit of God guided him in selection, correction, and accurate expression of that which was far more important to subsequent history than even Moses imagined.

Broadly speaking, humanity is divided into three great divisions, that of Shem, the most important from the Biblical point of view, issuing into the Semitic family; that of Ham, sometimes referred to as the Turanian; and that of Japheth, the Aryan. That these peoples intermarried and often lived side by side in early history is evident, but the broad streams of their posterity nevertheless are still distinguishable today.

The relationship and probable identification and geographic location of the sons of Noah and their descendants are indicated in the tables provided for quick reference. The discussion which follows each table provides further detail.

TABLE OF THE SONS OF JAPHETH
Genesis 10:2-5

Gomer — Ancient Cimmerians, the Gimirray of the Assyrians, Western Russia (Gen. 10:2, 3; I Chron. 1:5, 6; Ezek. 38:6).

Ashkenaz — Originally north of the Black Sea and the Caspian Sea (Gen. 10:3; I Chron. 1:6; Jer. 51:27). The name is evidently connected with cuneiform *Ashguza*, "Scythians."

Riphath — Location unknown, but probably included in modern Russia (Gen. 10:3; I Chron. 1:6).

Togarmah—Originally in Southwest Armenia, immigrating north

and west (Gen. 10:3; I Chron. 1:6; cp. Ezek. 27:14; 38:6). This is Tegarama in cuneiform texts near Carchemish.

Magog — Probably the ancient Scythians, probably now in modern Russia (Gen. 10:2; I Chron. 1:5; Ezek. 38:2, 6; Rev. 20:8).

Madai — More commonly known as the Medes, originally south of the Caspian Sea (Gen. 10:2; I Chron. 1:5; cp. II Kings 17:6; 18:11; Ezra 6:2; Esth. 1:3, 14, 18, 19; Isa. 13:17; 21:2; Jer. 25:25; 51:11, 28; Dan. 5:28, 31; 6:8, 12, 15; 8:20; 9:1; 11:1; Acts 2:9).

Javan — Hellenists, Ionians, generally the Greek people, modern Greece (Gen. 10:2, 4; I Chron. 1:5, 7; Isa. 66:19; Ezek. 27: 13, 19; Dan. 8:21; 10:20; 11:2; Zech. 9:13).

Elishah — Inhabitants of Cyprus (Gen. 10:4; I Chron. 1:7; Ezek. 27:7). Corresponds to cuneiform *Alashiya,* Cyprus.

Tarshish — Location uncertain, but possibly inhabited Spain (from Tartessus in Spain) and Western Mediterranean (Gen. 10:4; I Chron. 1:7; cp. I Kings 10:22; 22:48; II Chron. 9:21; 20:36, 37; Pss. 48:7; 72:10; Isa. 2:16; 23:1, 6, 10, 14; 60:9; 66: 19; Jer. 10:9; Ezek. 27:12, 25; 38:13; Jonah 1:3; 4:2).

Kittim or Chittim — The Ionians, Greeks, and inhabited islands and coasts of Mediterranean Sea (Gen. 10:4; I Chron. 1:7; cp. Num. 24:24; Isa. 23:1, 12; Jer. 2:10; 25:22; 47:4; Ezek. 27:6; Dan. 11:30).

Dodanim — Lived in Illyricum and Troy, the entire region known as Dalmatia in modern times, i.e., Southeastern Europe (Gen. 10:4; I Chron. 1:7). Some prefer reading of Rodanim, hence Island of Rhodes.

Tubal — Identified with ancient Scythians originally in Eastern Asia Minor, and later probably immigrating further north to modern Russia (Gen. 10:2; I Chron. 1:5; Isa. 66:19; Ezek. 27:13; 32:26; 38:2, 3; 39:1).

Meshech — Originally in Eastern Asia Minor, later farther north in modern Russia (Gen. 10:2; I Chron. 1:5; Ezek. 27:13; 32:26; 38:2, 3; 39:1).

Tiras — Originally in Eastern Asia Minor, later in modern Russia (Gen. 10:2; I Chron. 1:5).

The sons of Japheth were more prolific in number than any of the other sons of Noah, and world history since the birth of Christ has largely featured those who were descendants of the seven sons of Japheth.

Japheth's son Gomer (Genesis 10:3) first mentioned in the list, according to Herodotus was the forefather of the Cimmerians. As a family in their early history, they conquered Urartu (Armenia) coming from their original Ukranian home where they lived before 800 B.C. They first appear in historical records as among the early enemies of Assyria and are mentioned prophetically in Ezekiel 38:6. There seems to be some evidence that they emigrated north ultimately out of Armenia into what today is known as Russia.

The three sons of Gomer are mentioned in Genesis 10:3 and also in I Chronicles 1:6, namely, Ashkenaz (cp. I Chronicles 1:6; Jeremiah 51:27), usually identified with the Scythians who lived north of the Black Sea and the Caspian Sea and spread over inner Asia. Others believe, however, that the Scythians are better identified as related to Magog. Riphath was another son of Gomer (cp. I Chronicles 1:6), but little is known about his descendants. Togarmah (cp. I Chronicles 1:6; Ezekiel 27:14; 38:6) appears occoccasionally in both history and prophecy. Descendants of Togarmah can be located in the fourteenth century B.C. as inhabiting Southwest Armenia. They are mentioned as furnishing horses, horsemen, and mules to Tyre (Ezekiel 27:14). Prophetically they are included in the invading host of Ezekiel 38:5, 6. Speaking generally, the descendants of Gomer inhabit the area north of the Holy Land and eventually emigrated north and east.

The second son of Japheth, Magog (cp. I Chronicles 1:5), is probably to be identified with the ancient Scythians (cp. discussion of Ashkenaz, above). Little mention is made of them historically except in these genealogies. Prophetically they are included in the invading horde of Ezekiel 38:2, 6 and again in Revelation 20:8. Speaking in general, they seem to have inhabited the area north of the Holy Land and could be one of the major elements in the population of Russia.

The third son of Japheth called Madai (cp. I Chronicles 1:5) is known more familiarly by the title given his descendants, the name *Medes,* who lived in Media south of the Caspian Sea bordered on the east by Hyrcania and Parthia, on the west by Assyria and Armenia and by Persia and Susiana on the south. The Medes are mentioned frequently in the Bible (II Kings 17:6; 18:11; Ezra 6:2; Esther 1:3, 14, 18, 19; Isaiah 13:17; 21:2; Jeremiah 25:25; 51:11, 28; Daniel 5:28, 31; 6:8, 12, 15; 8:20; 9:1; 11:1; Acts 2:9).

The Medes formed an important division of the times of the

Gentiles as prophesied by Daniel. They occupy a large share in the prophetic program of the Old Testament leading up to Christ. The height of the power of the Medes, after several centuries of struggle, was reached in the sixth century B.C. when the kingdom of the Medes was merged with that of Persia under Cyrus. Their notable triumph was the conquering of Babylon in 539 B.C. as recorded in Daniel 5. The Medes flourished for two centuries thereafter until the time of Alexander the Great.

The fourth son of Japheth known as Javan (cp. I Chronicles 1:5, 7) was the forefather of the Ionians or the Greeks. Descendants of Javan are mentioned in inscriptions of Assyria and Achaemenia. They were the Hellenists and the word *Javan* is so translated in the Septuagint. The descendants of Javan are mentioned frequently in the Bible (Isaiah 66:19; Ezekiel 27:13, 19; Daniel 8:21; 10:20; 11:2; Zechariah 9:13). The descendants of Javan inhabited Libya, and Caria, the Aegean Islands and the area known in modern history as Greece. As early as the eighth century B.C. Assyrian records mention a naval battle with the Greeks.

The four sons of Javan, Elishah, Tarshish, Kittim, and Dodanim do not appear as major elements in subsequent history. The descendants of Elishah seem to have inhabited Cyprus, referred to as the "isles of Elishah" (Ezekiel 27:7). They exported purple and scarlet fabrics to the market at Tyre, the purple dye being derived from shells rich in this color on the Aegean coasts.

The name *Tarshish* is found in the Phoenician language, meaning *smelting plant* and is closely associated with the smelting and transportation of smelted ores from distant places such as Spain in the Western Mediterranean and Solomon's copper smelting works in Southern Arabia. As ships were used to carry the smelted ore, frequent mention is made to ships of Tarshish (cp. I Kings 22:49, 50; II Chronicles 20:36, 37). Some believe the term also applies to any large ship regardless of geography (Psalm 48:7; Isaiah 23:1; 60:9; Ezekiel 27:25). It is therefore not clear whether the name *Tarshish* as the description of a descendant of Javan is the proper meaning in these many references and there may be no racial connection.

Kittim (sometimes spelled Chittim), another son of Javan, seems also to refer to the Ionian or Greeks. Although the name with various significations is found in a loose way to refer to the islands and coasts of the Mediterranean without specifying any particular geographic location, the name Kittim occurs with varied spellings elsewhere in the Old Testament (cp. Numbers 24:24; Isaiah 23:1, 12; Jeremiah 2:10; 25:22; 47:4; Ezekiel 27:6; Daniel 11:30). It is not clear to what extent Kittim is related to these references.

Dodanim (Genesis 10:4; I Chronicles 1:7), the fourth son of Javan, is regarded as the progenitor of those who lived in Illyricum and Troy and were closely associated with Kittim. They are relatively unimportant in subsequent Scriptures.

The three remaining sons of Japheth are named without posterity, signifying that their descendants did not form an important segment of the human race. Tubal (Genesis 10:2; I Chronicles 1:5) seems to be related to the Scythians. Their normal home seems to be near the Black Sea in Eastern Asia Minor. They are subsequently mentioned in the prophets (Isaiah 66:19; Ezekiel 27:13; 32:26; 38:2, 3; 39:1). Prophetically they will join with the invading army of the land of Israel in the last days recorded in Ezekiel 38 - 39. It is probable that their modern descendants now live in Russia.

Meshech appears in history as early as the twelfth century B.C. when his descendants lived to the north of Assyria in the Black Sea area. In Ezekiel 27:13, the descendants of Meshech had commercial dealings with Tyre, selling slaves and vessels of bronze. Prophetically, Meshech has a place in the last days as recorded in Ezekiel 32:26; 38:2, 3; 39:1 and is included in the invading army.

Tiras the last son of Japheth is mentioned only in the genealogies (I Chronicles 1:5) and it is generally believed that his descendants became the Thracians who inhabited the Aegean coast.

The descendants of Japheth spread out to the north, east, and west, and are probably the progenitors of most of the Northern Europe lands and, hence, of all countries derived from Europe such as the United States and Canada. They formed the major part of the Gentiles or the nations and will have their important role in the chapters of world history which will bring the times of the Gentiles to conclusion.

TABLE OF THE SONS OF HAM
Genesis 10:6-20

In general the sons of Ham inhabited all of Asia except the north, and lived in Southern Europe and Northern Africa.

Cush — Southern Egypt, Abyssinia, Nubia, and Ethiopia (Gen. 10: 6-12).

Seba — Ancient Sabeans (Gen. 10:7; I Chron. 1:9; Ps. 72:10; Isa. 43:3; cp. "Sabeans," Job 1:15; Isa. 45:14; Ezek. 23:42; Joel 3:8; also "Sheba," I Kings 10; II Chron. 9; Job 6:19; Ps. 72:10, 15; Isa. 60:6; Jer. 6:20; Ezek. 27:22, 23; 38:13).

Havilah — Modern Yemen (Gen. 10:7; I Chron. 1:9; cp. Gen. 2:11; 10:29; 25:18; I Sam. 15:7; I Chron. 1:23).

Sabtah — Located East of Yemen (Gen. 10:7; I Chron. 1:9).

Raamah — His sons, Sheba and Dedan, and their descendants, inhabited Southwest Arabia (Gen. 10:7; I Chron. 1:9; Ezek. 27:22).

Sabtechah — Inhabited the eastern side of the Persian Gulf (Gen. 10:7; I Chron. 1:9).

Nimrod — Famous progenitor of inhabitants of Mesopotamia, Asshur, Nineveh, and Babylon. Also related to Erech, Accad, Calneh, Rehoboth, Calah, and Resen (Gen. 10:9-12; I Chron. 1:10; Micah 5:6). Some of these may be descriptive nouns rather than names of cities.

Mizraim — Egypt and East of Egypt (Gen. 10:13, 14; I Chron. 1: 11, 12; cp. all references to Egypt). All these names are plural emphasizing their ethnic character.

Ludim — Not yet identified but may be Libyans, North Africa (Gen. 10:13; I Chron. 1:11).

Anamim — Northern and Middle Egypt (Gen. 10:13; I Chron. 1:11).

Lehabim — Related to Libyans (Gen. 10:13; I Chron. 1:11).

Naphtuhim — Northern Egypt, Thebes, and Memphis (Gen. 10:13; I Chron. 1:11).

Pathrusim — Same location as Naphtuhim or may be Upper Egypt (Gen. 10:14; I Chron. 1:12).

Casluhim — Originally in Nile delta in Egypt, possibly inhabited Philistia later (Gen. 10:14; I Chron. 1:12). Some identify them as from Crete (cp. Deut. 2:23; Jer. 47:4; Amos 9:7).

Caphtorim — Origin same as Casluhim, possibly inhabited Philistia (Gen. 10:14; I Chron. 1:12).

Phut or Put — Generally Egypt, and Libya (Gen. 10:6; I Chron. 1:8; Isa. 66:19; Jer. 46:9; Ezek. 27:10; 30:5; 38:5; Nah. 3:9).

Canaan — At the time of the conquest all the land designated as

Palestine, west of the Jordan (Gen. 10:15-18; I Chron. 1:8,
13-16; etc., over 150 Old Testament references).

Sidon — Ancient Phoenicia, city of Sidon (Gen. 10:15; I Chron.
1:13; etc., about 40 Old Testament references and 12 New
Testament references).

Heth — The ancient Hittites, a major civilization in Asia Minor
(Gen. 10:15; I Chron. 1:13; etc., about 60 Old Testament
references).

Jebusite — Original inhabitants of Jerusalem (Gen. 10:16; Josh.
15:63; Judg. 1:21; II Sam. 5:6, 8; 24:16, 18; I Chron. 1:14;
11:6; 21:18; Ezra 9:1; Neh. 9:8; Zech. 9:7; etc., about 35
Old Testament references).

Amorite — Located originally west of the Dead Sea (Gen. 10:
16; I Chron. 1:14; etc., about 100 Old Testament references).

Girgashite — Located in Southern Palestine West of Jordan
(Gen. 10:16; 15:21; Deut. 7:1; Josh. 3:10; 24:11; I Chron.
1:14; Neh. 9:8).

Hivite — Northern Palestine, Shechem (Gen. 10:17; I Chron.
1:15; etc., about 25 Old Testament references).

Arkite — North of Sidon (Gen. 10:17; I Chron. 1:15).

Sinite — North of Lebanon (Gen. 10:17; I Chron. 1:15).

Arvadite — Located on an island off the coast of Phoenicia,
familiar in Assyrian records (Gen. 10:18; I Chron. 1:16;
Ezek. 27:8, 11).

Zemarite — West of Galilee (Gen. 10:18; I Chron. 1:16; cp. Josh.
18:22; II Chron. 13:4).

Hamathite — Upper Syria, at the foot of Lebanon (Gen. 10:18;
I Chron. 1:16; etc., over 35 Old Testament references).

The sons of Ham occupy a large portion of the Genesis 10
record (10:6-20; cp. I Chronicles 1:8-16). Four sons of Ham are
mentioned in Genesis 10:6: Cush, Mizraim, Phut, and Canaan. Unquestionably the large space given to the sons of Ham was due
to their ultimate relationship to the subsequent history of Israel and
the purposes of God in the Middle East.

First mentioned of the sons of Ham is Cush whose descendants
are enumerated as Seba, Havilah, Sabtah, Raamah, and Sabtechah.
Special mention is made of the sons of Raamah, namely, Sheba
and Dedan. The most prominent son of Cush, however, is Nimrod
mentioned in Genesis 10:8-12.

In general the descendants of Ham occupy all of Asia except

the northern part, and settled in Southern Europe, and Northern Africa. They may be the forefathers of the American Indians who are believed to have originally entered the American continent through Alaska, having come up the east coast of Asia. The descendants of Cush seem to have inhabited Southern Egypt and the land to the south and east of Egypt, including ancient Abyssinia, Nubia, and Ethiopia. Because of the close proximity of the Semitic race, the Ethiopian language eventually became Semitic even though the racial origin was otherwise.

The five sons of Cush seem to refer to various peoples in the general geographic area of Egypt. Some of them reached all the way to the Persian Gulf and some mention is made of most of them in various Scriptures: Seba (cp. I Chronicles 1:9; Psalm 72: 10; Isaiah 43:3; cp. references to Sabeans, Job 1:15; Isaiah 45:14; Ezekiel 23:42; Joel 3:8; and references to Sheba, I Kings 10; II Chronicles 9; Job 6:19; Psalm 72:10, 15; Isaiah 60:6; Jeremiah 6: 20; Ezekiel 27:22, 23; 38:13). Havilah seems to refer to Southwestern Arabia known in modern times as Yemen (Genesis 10:7; I Chronicles 1:9; cp. Genesis 2:11; 10:29; 25:18; I Samuel 15:7; I Chronicles 1:23). Little is known of Sabtah except that probably it is to the east of Yemen (Genesis 10:7; I Chronicles 1:9). The descendants of Sabtah lived east of Yemen. The descendants of Raamah (Genesis 10:7; I Chronicles 1:9) are mentioned in Ezekiel 27:22 as famous traders and according to inscriptions were located geographically in Southwest Arabia adjacent to the Persian Gulf. Sabtechah (Genesis 10:7; I Chronicles 1:9) may have lived on the eastern side of the Persian Gulf.

The two sons of Raamah, namely, Sheba and Dedan are usually mentioned together and there is some confusion between Sheba and Seba (cp. Seba, above). Both lived in the general area of Arabia.

The special mention of Nimrod (Genesis 10:9-12; I Chronicles 1:10; cp. Micah 5:6) as a descendant of Cush is occasioned by the fact that he is the originator of Babel later known as Babylon and apparently was an energetic man who with his posterity built the Mesopotamian area and such famous spots as Asshur and Nineveh (Genesis 10:11). Nimrod was unquestionably the Napoleon of his day and the head of one of the earliest empires subsequent to Noah recorded in Scripture. His government seems to have occupied most of Western Asia and has left many monuments. The politi-

THE BEGINNING OF THE NATIONS 33

cal might symbolized in Nimrod and his empire was ended subsequent to the divine judgment at the tower of Babel when their one language was confounded.

The second son of Ham, Mizraim, was the progenitor of the major population of Egypt and usually the term is translated *Egypt* (about 87 times) in its many instances in the Bible. It is generally agreed, however, that the desccndants of Mizraim, of which seven are named (Genesis 10:13, 14), migrated to the east and this accounts for the similarity between those who inhabited the area adjacent to the Indian Ocean to the Egyptians. Ludim apparently refers to the Libyans of Northern Africa. Anamim is mentioned only in the genealogies (Genesis 10:13; I Chronicles 1:11) but probably lived in Northern or Middle Egypt. Lehabim is also mentioned only in the genealogies (Genesis 10:13; I Chronicles 1:11) and they also have been related to the Libyans. Naphtuhim and Pathrusim (Genesis 10:13, 14; I Chronicles 1:12) seem to be related to Northern Egypt and especially the area around Thebes and Memphis. Casluhim and Caphtorim (Genesis 10:14; I Chronicles 1:12) were in the Nile Delta area of Egypt. In general Mizraim is therefore to be identified with Egypt, but its people migrated extensively to the east. As one of the important nations related to Israel, they figure largely in subsequent prophecy and form one of the great prophetic themes of the Old Testament which will be the subject of later discussion.

The third son of Ham, Phut or Put, is mentioned a number of times in the Bible (Genesis 10:6; I Chronicles 1:8; Isaiah 66:19; Jeremiah 46:9; Ezekiel 27:10; 30:5; 38:5; Nahum 3:9). From these references it is clear that the people who descended from Phut were Africans closely associated with the descendants of Mizraim. Their exact geographic location, however, is not clear and it may be that they were scattered. Most probable identifications are that they lived in Libya and other considerations have led some to think that they lived south of Egypt or east of Egypt around the Red Sea. Phut is mentioned in Isaiah 66:19 (spelled "Pul") along with other nations to whom God will send a sign at the beginning of the millennial kingdom. In Jeremiah 46:9 where the Hebrew *Put* is translated "Libyans," they are the objects of God's judgment along with Egypt. Mercenary soldiers from Phut were used by Tyre (Ezekiel 27:10) and by Egypt (Jeremiah 46:9). They are again associated with the fall of Egypt in Ezekiel 30:5 where they are described as from "Libya." Prophetically they are included in the host which invade Israel in Ezekiel 38:5 where they are again described as coming from Libya. According to Nahum 3:9 their mercenary soldiers also helped Nineveh. The fact that the descendants of Phut are not described would indicate that they do not occupy a major role among the Gentiles.

The last son of Ham, Canaan, is obviously important to Biblical history and to the nation Israel. Eleven branches of descendants are mentioned in Genesis 10:15-18, "And Canaan begat Sidon his firstborn, and Heth, And the Jebusite, and the Amorite, and the Girgasite, And the Hivite, and the Arkite, and the Sinite, And the Arvadite, and the Zemarite, and the Hamathite."

The firstborn of Canaan, Sidon, is prominent in Scripture and descendants of Sidon probably formed the inhabitants of the ancient Phoenician city of Sidon or Zidon located some twenty miles north of Tyre. His descendants are first mentioned in the Amarna letters about 1400 B.C. and are prominent in Biblical history from the time of the conquest (Joshua 19:28). It became a city located in the territory of Asher and later was given the modern name of Saida. The city and its inhabitants are mentioned about forty times in the Old Testament and a dozen times in the New Testament. Its history is bound up with that of the Phoenicians from the eleventh and the eighth centuries B.C. and there is constant mention of them throughout the history of the Old Testament. On at least one occasion Christ preached in this area (Mark 7:24, 31) and condemned the sins of its inhabitants (Matthew 11:21-24). Paul also visited the city on his way to Rome (Acts 27:3). The prophets Isaiah, Jeremiah, and Ezekiel, all pronounced solemn judgments upon Sidon (Isaiah 23:2-12; Jeremiah 25:22; 27:3; 47:4; Ezekiel 27:8; 28:20-24; cp. Joel 3:4; Zechariah 9:2). Their prominence in Biblical history and prophecy is undoubtedly due to their geographic location and their close proximity to Tyre which was the special object of divine wrath.

Heth, the second son of Canaan, was the progenitor of the Hittites who figure prominently in Old Testament history. The Hittites are mentioned forty-seven times by this name in the Old Testament and fourteen times as the sons of Heth. Abraham's dealings with them are mentioned in Genesis 23 and the desire of Rebekah to avoid intermarriage with them is indicated in Genesis

27:46. The Hittites are included among the heathen nations with whom the Israelites had to deal in the conquest of the land. Even in David's time Uriah the Hittite is mentioned as the husband of Bathsheba, indicating the intermarriage of the Hittites with Israelites.

The center of the Hittite civilization, now uncovered by archaeologists, was in Asia Minor, and there is evidence that they had an important civilization and extensive literature and times of unusual political power especially during the period 1400-1200 B.C. Some have classified the Hittites as third in importance in the Middle East, with the Egyptians and the inhabitants of Mesopotamia surpassing them. The Hittites do not seem to be vitally connected with the prophetic program of Scripture.

The remaining descendants of Canaan each had their important influence on Biblical history. The Jebusites originally inhabited Jerusalem itself (Joshua 15:63) and their military might was indicated in the fact that the tribes were not able to dislodge them completely, and for many years they continued to live on the border between Judah and Benjamin (Joshua 15:63; Judges 1:21). They do not seem to have loomed large in the history of Israel although there is occasional mention throughout the Old Testament (cp. II Samuel 5:6, 8; 24:16, 18; I Chronicles 11:6; 21:18; Ezra 9:1; Nehemiah 9:8; Zechariah 9:7; and a number of other references).

The Amorites are prominent in Biblical history, being mentioned almost a hundred times in the Old Testament. They were one of the principal nations conquered by Israel in the conquest of the land and lived originally west of the Dead Sea. Their history is recorded, not only in the Scriptures, but in the inscriptions in which they were known as the Ammuru, with a history that extends from before Abraham. Their importance is mostly historical and they do not figure in prophecy except in predictions which were fulfilled in the conquest.

The Girgashites, living west of Jordan, also were one of the nations dispossessed by Israel in the time of the conquest. They are mentioned only seven times in the Old Testament (Genesis 10:16; 15:21; Deuteronomy 7:1; Joshua 3:10; 24:11; I Chronicles 1:14; Nehemiah 9:8). They have no role in the prophetic future.

The Hivites were also significant as a nation dispossessed by

Israel in the conquest. They seem to have lived in the northern part of the Holy Land, and they are mentioned about twenty-five times in the Old Testament usually in connection with other heathen countries whom Israel conquered. At one time they inhabited Shechem (Genesis 34).

The descendants of Canaan described as Arkites can be located some eighty miles north of Sidon and their name has been perpetuated in modern times by the city Tell Arka. This locality had a long history recorded outside the Bible as early as 1400 B.C., but is mentioned in the Bible only in Genesis 10:7 and I Chronicles 1:15 in the genealogies.

The Sinites are referred to only in Genesis 10:17 and I Chronicles 1:15. No definite identification is possible, but it is probable that they are located in the northern part of Lebanon where Strabo refers to "*Sinna*" as a fort in the mountains. Several other obscure references are found to it in ancient literature.

The Arvadites, mentioned only four times in Scripture (Genesis 10:18; I Chronicles 1:16; Ezekiel 27:8-11), were inhabitants of the island Arvad located two miles from the shore off the coast of Phoenicia. Its modern name is Ruwad.

The Zemarites are cited in Genesis 10:18 and I Chronicles 1:16 and lived in the area west of Galilee between Arvad and Hamath. Other locations have been mentioned, such as Emessa, modern Hums, with others finding them at Sumra, or in the area of Mount Zemaraim (cp. Joshua 18:22; II Chronicles 13:4).

The Hamathites inhabited the city-state of Hamath in upper Syria, referred to about thirty-five times in the Old Testament. At one time an important Canaanite colony (Genesis 10:18), it was captured by the Assyrians in the time of Hezekiah (II Kings 18:34). Located at the foot of Lebanon, it had a long history and came under the control of Assyria, then a province of Syria, and eventually came under the government of Persia in Nehemiah's time. Undoubtedly the descendants of Canaan spread over considerable territory — from Sidon to Gaza and eastward as far as the area east of the Dead Sea as indicated in the mention of Sodom, Gomorrah, Admah, Zeboim, and Lasha in Genesis 10:19.

Taken as a whole, the sons of Ham lived in an extensive geographic area and were the original inhabitants of the land given by God to Israel.

TABLE OF THE SONS OF SHEM
Genesis 10:21-31

Elam — Eastern neighbor and traditional rival of Mesopotamian states, settled in a portion of Persia (Gen. 10:22; I Chron. 1:17; cp. Gen. 14:1, 9; Isa. 11:11; 21:2, 6; Jer. 25:25; 49: 34-39; Ezek. 32:24; Dan. 8:2).

Asshur — To be identified with Assyria (Gen. 10:22; I Chron. 1:17; cp. Num. 24:22, 24; Ezra 4:2; Ps. 83:8; Ezek. 27:23; 32:22; Hos. 14:3; and about 140 Old Testament references to Assyria).

Arphaxad — Located originally north and east of Nineveh (Gen. 10:22, 24, 25; 11:11-27; I Chron. 1:17-24; cp. Luke 3:36).

  Salah — Also spelled Shelah (Gen. 10:24; 11:12-15; I Chron. 1:18; Luke 3:35).

    Eber — Father of Hebrew race (Gen. 10:21, 24, 25; 11:14-17; I Chron. 1:18, 19, 25).

      Peleg — Progenitor of Abraham (Gen. 10:25; 11:16-19; I Chron. 1:19, 25).

      Joktan—His thirteen sons were progenitors of the Arabs (Gen. 10:25, 26, 29; I Chron. 1:19, 20, 23).

Lud — Associated with both Asiatic and African people, possible reference to Lydians of Anatolia, location uncertain (Gen. 10:22; I Chron. 1:17; Isa. 66:19; Ezek. 27:10).

Aram — Inhabited wide area in Syria and Mesopotamia (Gen. 10:22, 23; I Chron. 1:17; cp. also about 65 Old Testament references to Syrians, another name for descendants of Aram).

  Uz — Occupied Arabian desert west of Babylon (Gen. 10:23; I Chron. 1:17; cp. Job 1:1; Jer. 25:20; Lam. 4:21).

  Hul — Probably located near Lake Merom, north of Sea of Galilee (Gen. 10:23; I Chron. 1:17).

  Gether — Location unknown (Gen. 10:23; I Chron. 1:17).

  Mash — Also known as Meshech, location unknown (Gen. 10:23; I Chron. 1:17).

The third major division of the children of Noah were descendants of Shem, mentioned in Genesis 10:21-31. These were also known as "all the children of Eber" (Genesis 10:21). By this is meant that the children of Eber, who were descendants of Shem through Arphaxad and Salah, were descendants of Shem, but the term is not properly applied to all of the descendants of Shem. They were the more important descendants of Shem. It was from this line that Abraham and the children of Israel came (cp. Genesis 11:10-27).

Five sons of Shem are mentioned in Genesis 10:22. The descendants of Elam (Genesis 10:22; I Chronicles 1:17), seemed to have settled in that portion of Persia which bears their name (cp. Genesis 14:1, 9; Isaiah 11:11; 21:2, 6; Jeremiah 25:25; 49:34-39; Ezekiel 32:24; Daniel 8:2).

Asshur is mentioned second (Genesis 10:22; I Chronicles 1:17; cp. Numbers 24:22, 24; Ezra 4:2; Psalm 83:8; Ezekiel 27:23; 32:22; Hosea 14:3; and about 140 Old Testament references to Assyria). The descendants of Asshur lived in Assyria. They were the forerunners of the later mighty Assyrian Empire, having come originally from Babylon and having a close connection with the Babylonians throughout their subsequent history. As Assyria held a prominent place in the history of the ancient world from the ninth to the seventh century B.C., they had an important place in prophecy which has already been fulfilled.

Arphaxad (Genesis 10:22, 24, 25; 11:11-27; I Chronicles 1:17-24; cp. Luke 3:36) is important as progenitor of the line which led to Abraham and to Christ in the genealogies introduced in Genesis 10:24, 25 and amplified in Genesis 11:13-27. One of the important descendants of Arphaxad was Eber (Genesis 10:21, 24, 25; 11:14-17; I Chronicles 1:18, 19, 25), son of Salah, or Shelah (Genesis 11:12-15; I Chronicles 1:18, 24), who had two prominent sons, Peleg and Joktan. From Peleg (Genesis 10:25; 11:16-19; I Chronicles 1:19, 25) descended the line to Abraham. Joktan (Genesis 10: 25, 26, 29; I Chronicles 1:19, 20, 23) had thirteen sons (Genesis 10: 26-29). Almodad was the founder of one of the Arab tribes. Sheleph had descendants who probably settled in Sulaf. Hazarmaveth settled in a portion of Arabia; Jerah was another Arabian tribe. Hadoram was another Arabian tribe impossible to identify. Uzal is often connected with Sanaa, a city in Yemen. Diklah was the progenitor of a people who settled in Yemen; Obal fathered another Arabian tribe called Ebal in I Chronicles 1:22, whose location is unknown. The founder of an Arab tribe known as Mael was Abimael. Sheba was the forerunner of an important kingdom in Southern Arabia known as the kingdom of Sheba. Nothing seems to be known about Ophir. Havilah probably populated a portion of Southern Arabia. Jobab is the name of another Arabian tribe concerning whom little is known. The descendants of Joktan according to Genesis 10:30 lived in the area from Mesha unto Sephar, the area to the west and south of Babylon corresponding with Arabia Petraea.

Lud, the fourth son of Shem (Genesis 10:22; I Chronicles 1:17; Isaiah 66:19; Ezekiel 27:10), seems to have become associated with Ludim, descendants of Mizraim. Both Lud and Ludim are associated with peoples of Africa and Asia, but their precise location is not clear. One explanation is that the term may have referred to mercenary soldiers who because of the character of their work were scattered. They were employed by Egypt.

Aram (Genesis 10:22, 23; I Chronicles 1:17), the last named of the children of Shem, was the progenitor of a large offspring which inhabited a wide area of Syria and Mesopotamia. The word *Aram* is translated *Syrian* more than 65 times in the Old Testament. Uz (Genesis 10:23; I Chronicles 1:17; cp. Job 1:1; Jeremiah 25:20; Lamentations 4:21), a son of Aram, seems to have settled in Arabia west of Babylon, the scene of the Book of Job. Hul (Genesis 10:23; I Chronicles 1:17) and his descendants probably lived near Lake Merom on the Jordan north of Galilee. The location of Gether and Mash (Genesis 10:23; I Chronicles 1:17), who is also known as Meshech in I Chronicles 1:17, is unknown.

Important to the history of Israel is the fact that the wives of Jacob were Aramaic or Syrian (Deuteronomy 26:5). By the time of King Saul the Aramaeans had occupied several districts adjacent to Israel including the land between the Tigris and Euphrates; Damascus (I Kings 11:23, 24); Zobah (II Samuel 8), north of Hamath; Maachah (Joshua 12:5; 13:11), east of Jordan near Mount Hermon; Geshur (Deuteronomy 3:14; II Samuel 15:8; 13:37), east of the Sea of Galilee; Beth-Rehob (cp. Numbers 13:21; Judges 18:28), near Geshur; and Ish-tob (II Samuel 10:6), also east of Jordan.

From a Biblical standpoint, the descendants of Shem were most important because through them is traced the line of the Messiah, Abraham, and Israel. It is probably for this reason that they are mentioned last in the genealogy in contrast to the fact that they are mentioned first in Genesis 10:1.

The genealogies of the nations provide a framework of Biblical prophecy. While many of the nations do not figure largely or prominently, the outworking of the divine purpose inevitably stems from these early progenitors of the human race. The fact that they are itemized in Scripture indicates that from the divine viewpoint these constitute the outline of the divine purpose in human history.

CHAPTER III

ISRAEL AND THE NATIONS

The selection of Abraham as the progenitor of a new division of humanity was a dramatic milestone in the history of mankind. It may be compared to the creation of Adam and Eve following the prehistoric fall of some of the holy angels led by Satan, and was similar to the new beginning with Noah after the destruction of the rest of humanity by the flood. The sovereign choice of Abraham marked a new and significant development in the progressive unfolding of God's purpose in the world.

The fact that Genesis itself devotes only eleven chapters to the whole history of the universe up to Abraham and then uses the remainder of almost forty chapters to trace the life of Abraham, Isaac, and Jacob, in itself demonstrates the tremendous significance of this new development. From Genesis 11:10, where the genealogy of Abraham is given, to the last book of the Bible, Revelation, the seed of Abraham is constantly in the foreground, and the Gentiles are introduced only as they are related to the history of Israel. No approach to a proper understanding of Scripture can ignore this obvious divine emphasis upon the numerically small people who descended from Jacob. The explanation is not in any peculiarity of the people of Israel, but rather in the sovereign choice of God in selecting them to fulfill His purpose. Three major areas tell the story of the relation of Israel to the nations.

THE DIVINE PURPOSE IN REDEMPTION

Unquestionably one of the principal reasons for the selection of Abraham and his posterity was the divine purpose to fulfill the promise given to Adam and Eve that the seed of the woman would bruise the head of the serpent (Genesis 3:15). The divine intention to fulfill this through Abraham's posterity is embodied in the promise, "in thee shall all families of the earth be blessed" (Genesis 12:3). The primary importance of Israel rests in the fact that

41

through them God would fulfill His purpose to reveal His grace and provide redemption in Christ. Through this provision not only would God redeem the nation of Israel, but also those in all of the nations who would turn to God and Christ in faith. The spiritual seed of Abraham according to Galatians 3:7 are all those who like Abraham trust in God.

No philosophy of history is complete unless it includes recognition of God's redemptive plan from the standpoint of eternity. The important factor in every life as well as in every nation is the fulfillment of God's redemptive purpose to save those by grace who believe. Life becomes meaningless except as it is related to Jesus Christ as Saviour and Lord and as it is related to eternity by receiving eternal life in time. If it were not for God's redemptive purpose, life as well as history would be a hopeless puzzle without motivation and objective, and God and His purposes would be an unsolvable enigma.

THE DIVINE PURPOSE IN REVELATION

Important as is the divine purpose in salvation, however, this is only one aspect, although a major aspect, to be found in God's selection of Abraham and his posterity. If the major reason for God creating the universe and man is to use the world as a means of declaring His own ineffable glory, then the selection of Abraham also assumes major importance because through Abraham's seed God purposed to reveal Himself. This revelation came first through prophets, such as Abraham himself, through whom God spoke. Most important were the writers of Scripture such as Moses and those who succeeded him. Most if not all of the Bible was written by those who were physical descendants of Abraham. It was through Abraham that not only Christ came, but also the prophets. Although God on occasion spoke through Gentiles, as in the dreams of Nebuchadnezzar, these were incidental rather than central in God's usual method of revealing Himself through history.

The final and climactic revelation was of course in the person of Jesus Christ who in the incarnation not only became man, but revealed God through human flesh. Christ was not only the way of salvation, but He was also the way of revelation. All of this was included in the purpose of God in divine revelation in selecting Abraham and his descendants. The choice of Abraham as the channel through which both redemption and divine revelation should come introduces another important factor often overlooked in the theological analysis of God's promises to Abraham and their fulfillment.

THE DIVINE PURPOSE IN THE HISTORY OF ISRAEL

God was not only going to use Israel as a means of redemption and a means of revelation, but their very history and prophecy were to be a cameo which would reveal God in His dealings with mankind in general. The history of Israel in the Old Testament in their relationship to the Gentiles is also a spiritual analysis of human experience as the people of God seek to live in a temporal world. The careful recital of Israel's failures and successes and the principles which guided their rise or fall according to Romans 15:4 "were written aforetime . . . for our learning, that we through patience and comfort of the scriptures might have hope."

The relationship of Israel to the nations therefore forms not only an important background for understanding "the times of the Gentiles" (Luke 21:24) and God's dealings with nations other than Israel, but also makes clear the role of the Gentiles in God's purpose in history. It was to be in the context of their relationship to the nations that Israel was to reveal their particular qualities as a people of God. In this they illustrated the timeless spiritual principles that are involved in a people of God living in a world which is basically anti-God. The history of Israel in relation to the nations prior to the times of the Gentiles and the Babylonian captivity may be divided into seven subdivisions.

Israel in Egypt. Abraham, Isaac, and Jacob, although promised the land as a perpetual possession of their seed, never actually possessed the Promised Land. Instead, as God predicted in Genesis 15:13, 14, "Know of a surety that thy seed shall be a stranger in a land that is not theirs, and shall serve them; and they shall afflict them four hundred years; And also that nation, whom they shall serve, will I judge: and afterward shall they come out with great substance." This prophecy of Israel's relationship to Egypt was fulfilled in Genesis 46 when Jacob and his family followed Joseph to the land of Egypt to avoid the famine in the Promised Land.

The sojourn of the children of Israel in Egypt for 430 years (1876-1446 B.C.) increased the people of Israel from 70 to approximately 3,000,000. Their rapid increase in numbers and wealth aroused the opposition of the Egyptian kings. Israel soon became an enslaved people first under the Hyksos rulers who displaced the native Egyptian kings in the period 1730-1580 B.C., and later when the Egyptian kings were able to resume control at which time the iniquitous law requiring the killing of all male children in Israel was imposed. During the reign of Amenhotep II (1447-1421 B.C.), after the imposition of the ten plagues upon Egypt, the nation of Israel was finally expelled from Egypt and the Exodus began. This probably occurred in 1446 B.C., although some critical scholars favor a date as late as 1290 B.C. During the years of their growth in Egypt, God had marvelously begun the preparation of the Promised Land for their occupation. Now, however, it was necessary to temper and discipline the nation Israel for their new role as a separate people inheriting the promises of God.

Israel in the wilderness wanderings. During the forty years in which Israel wandered in the wilderness, they were the objects of God's special care in a way that no people had ever previously experienced. The Exodus from Egypt had been preceded by the miraculous intervention of God in the plagues inflicted upon the Egyptians. This had been supported by the great deliverance from the hosts of the Egyptians at the Red Sea when a miraculous strong wind permitted the Israelites to cross the sea as on dry land, but the Egyptians were engulfed by the returning waters when they attempted to follow.

In the first year of their wilderness wanderings at Mount Sinai, Israel was introduced to the covenant of the law which involved for them not only the obligation to keep a particular rule of life, but to be "a kingdom of priests, and an holy nation" (Exodus 19: 6). The comprehensive revelation given to Moses of Israel's moral, ceremonial, and social law as well as the order of worship and the details of the construction of the Tabernacle and its furniture was a tremendous disclosure of God which was greeted almost immediately by rebellion on the part of the people as recorded in Exodus 32.

It was subsequent to this preliminary failure that Israel, after sending out spies to survey the land for forty days, accepted the unfavorable report of the ten spies that the land could not be conquered. Because of their spiritual immaturity and lack of faith, Israel rebelled against God and was saved from extermination only by Moses' intercession (Numbers 14). The subsequent disciplinary judgment of God declared that all the adults would die in the wilderness during forty years of wandering, whereas their little ones whom they said would fall prey to the enemy would inherit the promise of possession of the land (Numbers 14:28-34).

During the wilderness wanderings, for the most part, Israel did not engage in fighting with existing tribes, but their few contacts with other nations were unhappy chapters in the years of their wandering. In Numbers 20:21 Edom, the descendants of Esau, Jacob's twin brother, refused to let Israel pass through their territory. This began a history of long enmity between Israel and Edom which will continue throughout the times of the Gentiles.

Another traditional enemy of Israel was Sihon of Heshbon, an Amorite, and a descendant of one of the eleven sons of Canaan who also opposed the children of Israel. His opposition, however, was used of God to destroy him as the children of Israel took all of his cities and destroyed them utterly from Aroer to Gilead, that is, most of the land east of Jordan from Galilee to the Dead Sea. Their subsequent contacts with Og King of Bashan, another division of the Amorites, resulted in a similar disaster for Og and his people. They too were exterminated, and the children of Israel occupied this territory, the land to the east of Galilee and somewhat to the north. These preliminary victories at the close of the years of wandering were the forerunner of the conquering of the land west of Jordan. Also illustrated is the spiritual conflict be‐ tween a people of God and those who are anti-God as represented in their enemies.

The conquering of the Promised Land. With the death of Moses, Joshua succeeded him as the leader of Israel, and the book that bears his name records the subsequent conquest of the land. Most of the territory west of Jordan was nominally under the control of Egypt whose King Amenhotep III reigned from approximately 1412-1376 B.C. He had neglected Palestine to the point that its political government was largely conducted by city-states over which there was only lax supervision. They were accordingly ill-prepared to resist an aggressive, co-ordinated attack from the nation Israel.

Israel crossed the Jordan through a miraculous stopping of the waters during the flood state probably in the spring of 1406 B.C. Their conquest of Jericho was aided by a supernatural destruction of the walls subsequently. After an initial defeat, in a second attack they conquered Ai with the result that the larger city Bethel (Joshua 8) was likewise conquered. The southern portion of the land west of Jordan was possessed first by Gibeon who through trickery secured a treaty and then by the defeat of the alliance of five Amorite kings who had besieged Gibeon (10:1-27). Their victory was aided by the supernatural long day of Joshua 10:12-14. The conquest of other kings including Jabin, King of Hazor (Joshua 11:1-11) resulted in the bulk of the land falling to Israel during the first six years of the conquest. Joshua, now approaching old age, arranged for the division of the land even though many of the Canaanites still retained potential for opposition, and some of the land had not yet been possessed. The victory, although tremendous and allowing living space for Israel, was far short of what God had promised if they would truly possess the land by faith (Joshua 1:2-5). They failed to carry out the command of Moses to exterminate completely the Canaanites. The utter immorality and false religions of the Canaanites were to prove so damaging to the people of Israel that it led to the extended period of political anarchy and moral decay which characterized the period of the judges.

The period of the Judges. The early verses of Judges record some of the preliminary victories against the Canaanites. But even before the end of the first chapter the sad record is given: "The children of Benjamin did not drive out the Jebusites that inhabited Jerusalem" (Judges 1:21). Nor did the children of Manasseh conquer the Canaanites that dwelt in their area, but rather put them under tribute (1:27, 28). Similar failure of other tribes is recorded in verses 29-36. This disobedience of the express command of Moses (Deuteronomy 7:2) set up the situation for Israel's spiritual and political decay.

For more than three centuries Israel was ruled by judges often local in their influence and sometimes contemporary. The lesson repeatedly given, however, was that when Israel sinned, God would use the Gentiles to inflict disciplinary punishment and overlordship upon them. When they genuinely repented, God would raise up a judge or leader to deliver them from their enemies. Their subsequent deliverance, however, was often short-lived, and they drifted back into the old sins. The book of Joshua is a spiral, but a spiral downward, and Israel's moral situation at the close of Judges was one of total anarchy ethically, religiously, and politically. Israel never sank lower than in the closing chapters of Judges. Such is the clear lesson of what happens to a nation with initial spiritual power when it joins socially and religiously as well as politically with the world totally debased and devoid of moral purity.

As in the later history of Israel, God used the Gentiles to inflict punishment upon the children of Israel. Among the more important enemies of Israel were the Hittites who lay to their north and the Egyptians who were to the south. Also prominent in the period were the Moabites, descendants of Lot, and Amalek, descendants of Esau (Judges 3:12-14). The Canaanites led by Jabin (Judges 4:1-3) were another who oppressed Israel.

In the time of Gideon, the Midianites were the instrument of oppression. Although their origin is obscure, they probably were descendants of Midian a son of Abraham by Keturah (Genesis 25: 1-6) who had inhabited much of the land east of Jordan and the Dead Sea. In the time of Moses they had accumulated considerable wealth as nomads (Numbers 31:22, 32-34). They did not figure largely in history outside the Bible and have long since disappeared. The remarkable deliverance by Gideon's three hundred is one of the bright chapters of Judges.

Among the other oppressors of Israel were the Philistines, an ancient people who inhabited the coastal region along the Mediterranean west of the Dead Sea. The Philistines had a long history, having apparently invaded the Middle East from the sea and engaged Raamses III (1195-1164 B.C.), ruler of Egypt, in a series of battles. The Philistines who survived settled in southeast Palestine and eventually gave the entire area the name Palestine, the Greek form of Philistia. The name Philistine appears in the Bible over two hundred times and in more than seventy different chapters.

In many respects the relationship of Israel to the Philistines was their spiritual barometer. When Israel was in the dominant position, it was a token of God's blessing. When they were in oppression by the Philistines, it was a sign of spiritual declension. Much of the closing material of Judges relates to the Philistines. It was not until the time of Samuel that Israel was rescued from forty years of domination by the Philistines (Judges 13:1).

Samuel and Eli the priest were the last two of the fourteen judges which prefaced the appointment of Saul as King. It was through Samuel that the crushing defeat of Israel at Ebenezer (I

Samuel 4), in which Eli and his sons died, was turned into a victory in a later battle recorded in I Samuel 7. Another attempt was made by the Philistines to gain power in the battle which resulted in the death of Saul and Jonathan (I Samuel 31). The period of the Judges was completely indecisive as far as victory for Israel is concerned, but is a record of human failure, contrasted to divine grace extended to a people when repentant. God's forgiveness was a demonstration of the faithfulness of God to a people who deserved judgment rather than mercy. The sovereign purpose of God in the nation Israel, though obscure in Judges, emerges more clearly in the period of the kingdoms.

The kingdoms of Saul, David, and Solomon. When Israel rejected the theocratic rule of God through judges and demanded that a king be appointed, God made clear that they were inviting oppressive rulers who would make slaves of their children and who would demand a large portion of their income. Their desire to be like the Gentiles was obviously born of the flesh rather than of the Spirit. In granting their request, however, prophecy was being fulfilled, for God had said to Abraham, "Kings shall come out of thee" (Genesis 17:6).

The first king to be appointed was Saul, anointed privately by Samuel, then later named publicly and finally confirmed after the victory at Jabesh-Gilead (I Samuel 11). Saul proved, however, to be an inept ruler, foolishly proud of his sovereignty and position, and jealous of David who had become a national hero by conquering Goliath. The fulfillment of the prophecy of his death in battle is recorded in the closing chapter of I Samuel and the first chapter of II Samuel. David immediately was proclaimed king over his own tribe of Judah (II Samuel 2:4). After a period of civil war and the death of Ish-bosheth the ruler of the ten tribes, he became king over all Israel about 1003 B.C. Among the first achievements of his reign was the complete rout of the Philistines.

The reign of David occurred at a time in which neighboring nations were in a weakened or inefficient state and unable to counter his rising power. The Hittites to the north had been broken by Barbarian invasions and rendered ineffective. Assyria likewise was in a weakened state, and Egypt was in a battle of power between the priests and merchants who alternately ruled from 1100 B.C. on. The reign of David was a glorious achievement of a man whom God had blessed and who was gifted as a warrior, general, and king. His power extended from the Euphrates River to the northeast, to the Mediterranean to the west, and the Red Sea to the south.

His long reign was not without its complications. His lax discipline of his sons, the product of multiple marriages, his crime in relation to Uriah and Bathsheba, and his sin in numbering the people were blots on his record. God nevertheless assured to him that his son would have a glorious reign, and in due time Solomon succeeded David.

In contrast to the experience of his father, Solomon's reign was one of peace and luxury, and social and cultural advance. He exceeded his father in multiple marriages, many of them with heathen women, with the result that his children were not brought up in the knowledge of the Lord (cp. Deuteronomy 17:17). He likewise violated the law in his reliance upon many chariots and military strength, instead of depending upon God (Deuteronomy 17:16). His luxurious living and demand for many buildings resulted in increased oppression and taxation which in turn led to the divided kingdom after his death.

The period of Saul, David, and Solomon was, from an outward standpoint, undoubtedly one of the most glorious in the history of Israel. Its outer glory, however, did not hide many spiritual failures which ultimately resulted in the captivities and the destruction of the monuments erected by David and Solomon.

The divided kingdoms of Judah and Israel. After the death of Solomon in 930 B.C. his son Rehoboam, who succeeded him, foolishly continued the oppressive taxation with the result that the ten tribes withdrew and formed the northern kingdom of Israel. Although endowed with many advantages over the kingdom of Judah, the kingdom of Israel from the start was a record of spiritual failure. Their reliance upon idols, commercial prosperity, and the fertility of the soil in their area led them to depart from God and to neglect the sanctuary in Jerusalem. The golden calves introduced by Jeroboam, their first king at Dan and Bethel, were blasphemous substitutes for the true worship of God.

The kings of Israel without exception were ungodly men, and the course of Israel was downward for the next two centuries ending in the captivity of the ten tribes by Assyria 721 B.C. The period was marked with warfare between Israel and Judah and at times both kingdoms were dominated by outsiders such as the Syrian domination 841-790 B.C. Although there were periods of prosperity and strength, as under Jeroboam II, when outside oppression was at a minimum, the path of the kingdom of Israel was downward.

The nation of Judah, composed of the two tribes Judah and Benjamin in and around Jerusalem, had the advantage of the spiritual strength of being the religious center of the nation. Although some of its kings were wicked men, there were periods of revival as under Hezekiah and Josiah. They only temporarily, however, and somewhat superficially brought the children of Israel back to God. Ultimately the two remaining tribes fell to the invading Medes and Babylonians, as prophesied by Nahum (3:18, 19). The Babylonian defeat of the Egyptians at Carchemish in 605 B.C. introduced the period of Babylonian domination which continued for more than a half century and made possible the captivity of the two remaining tribes, many of whom were carried off into ancient Babylon. The kings who would fight their enemies, which Israel had demanded of God, had brought only temporary prosperity. Morally, the period of the kings, especially the kings of Israel, was no better than the period of the judges. Israel had yet to learn the lessons that under the law blessing could be secured only by obedience. Although God was a gracious God who welcomed a repentant people, there was a high price to pay for neglect of the law and for worship of idols.

Post-captivity. In the captivity of Israel by Assyria and the captivity of Judah by the Babylonians, most of the population were carried off into captivity. The ten tribes suffered a series of deportations beginning in the reign of Pekah, king of Israel, when Tiglath-pileser III about 740 B.C. carried off the tribes to the east of Jordan to Assyria (I Chronicles 5:26) and some of those in Galilee (II Kings 15:29). In 721 B.C. Samaria was captured and more than 25,000 of the population went into captivity. Before the Babylonian captivity even began, it is estimated that 200,000 captives were taken from the ten tribes as well as the cities of Judah.

The Babylonian captivity began with the fall of Jerusalem 606 B.C. when selected captives including Daniel were carried off to Babylon. This was followed by a major deportation in 597 B.C. when 10,000 of the leaders of Judah were deported. Another major deportation took place in 586 B.C. when Jerusalem itself was destroyed.

The captivities continued until 538 B.C. when Cyrus issued a decree for a return of some of the pilgrims to their ancient land (Ezra 1:2). With the time taken to organize the expedition and return to their ancient land, the predicted seventy years was consumed between 606 B.C. and 536 B.C. in fulfillment of the prediction of seventy years of captivity (Jeremiah 25:11, 12; 29:10). The returning pilgrims, after some delay, were able to build the temple, completed about 516 B.C. or exactly seventy years after Jerusalem itself was laid desolate and the previous temple destroyed (Daniel 9:2).

The number of the returning pilgrims in the first expedition were 42,360 (Ezra 2:64). Their servants brought the total number to approximately 50,000. Most of these were from the tribes of Judah and Benjamin and Levi, but included some from other tribes. Some of those carried off in the Assyrian captivities returned as they were able, until all twelve tribes were represented. A later expedition led by Ezra (Ezra 7-10) further swelled the number of returning pilgrims. Under the leadership of Nehemiah the walls of the city were rebuilt and a plan for the rebuilding of the city itself was adopted and put into effect.

As the Old Testament closes, the children of Israel are back in the land, but always under some form of Gentile supervision and authority. The remaining centuries which led up to Christ were unhappy ones for Israel especially under the fearful persecutions of the Romans who according to Josephus slaughtered more than 1,000,000 Israelites in the siege of Jerusalem alone in A.D. 70. In the second century following Christ. Palestine was almost devoid of Jews, who had been scattered to the four winds. It was not until the twentieth century that Israel was restored to their ancient land and re-established as a nation there.

In the history of God's dealings with Israel He revealed His attributes in a way in which He did not reveal them to the Gentile world. To Israel, God had made many wonderful and everlasting promises. They were to be a people who would continue forever (Jeremiah 31:35-37). They were to have a king forever of the line of David (II Samuel 7:16). They were to have title to the land forever (Genesis 17:8).

These promises, though unfulfilled to generations which neglected the Word of God and trusted in idols made with hands, nevertheless manifest God's faithfulness in dealing with an erring people. Even in the midst of their apostasy and sin, when the prophets of God thundered warnings of divine judgment, there is the recurring note of God's unfailing purpose, of God's faithfulness to Abraham, Isaac, and Jacob. The certainty of the ultimate fulfillment of the promises is made clear as they are repeated again and again in the Old Testament Scriptures.

The relationship of the Gentiles to Israel is always that of a supporting role. God's sovereignty and divine power are again and again manifested in His dealings with the nations, but this is always subordinated to His purpose for Israel and the fulfillment of the spiritual promises to all who would trust in the God of Israel. The eternal shines again and again through the temporal, and the immediate actors on the stage are never allowed to forget that behind the scenes God is still directing the panorama of history to His desired and prophesied end. Prophecy concerning the Gentiles, accordingly, although more expansive in its character and worldwide in its significance, is always presented in Scripture in relation to God's purposes for Israel. World history which is not related to this is usually omitted in Scripture. The Biblical point of view, therefore, is quite different from that of the world in general to whom Israel was an insignificant people. From the standpoint of God's divine election, Israel is instead the key, and through Israel God was to fulfill His purpose whether redemptive, political, or eschatological.

Chapter IV

WORLD HISTORY IN OUTLINE

The study of Daniel is an indispensable introduction to the Biblical foreview of world history. Through Daniel came the revelation of the major events which would mark the progress of what Christ referred to as "the times of the Gentiles" (Luke 21:24). Christ defined this as the period during which "Jerusalem shall be trodden down of the Gentiles," i.e., from Nebuchadnezzar 606 B.C. until the second advent of Jesus Christ.

No system of philosophy or theology which attempts to arrive at the meaning of history can ignore this divine analysis of the progress of human events. The broad prophetic program for the nations when viewed alongside the prophetic program for Israel and the program of God in the present age for the church answers the major question of the divine purposes of God in history in which God reveals His glory.

In God's program for Israel, He has revealed His faithfulness, His love, and His righteousness. In His program for the church, the grace of God is supremely revealed. In the program of world history as a whole, God's dealings with the nations reveal His sovereignty, power, and wisdom. The nations may foolishly rage against God (Psalm 2:1), but God nevertheless shall triumphantly place His Son as King in Zion (Psalm 2:6).

Daniel the Prophet

Daniel the prophet was born in the ill-fated days just preceding the captivity. As a lad he was apparently separated from his parents and carried captive to far away Babylon. There, because of his unusual intelligence and promise, he was trained along with his companions for service in the court of the king. It was only after Daniel had successfully completed this course of training and had demonstrated his wisdom and understanding (Daniel 1:20) that he faced the supreme test recorded in Daniel 2.

NEBUCHADNEZZAR'S DREAM

Nebuchadnezzar, the king of Babylon, had had a rapid rise to power, heading what is known in secular history as the Neo-Chaldean Empire. His father Nabopolassar had founded the empire in 625 B.C. His son Nebuchadnezzar had won an outstanding victory over Necho of Egypt at Carchemish in 605 B.C. and in the process of his conquest had conquered and later destroyed Jerusalem, carrying off many of the Jews as captives. According to Daniel 2:29, the king had pondered the practical question of "what should come to pass hereafter." What would be the end result of his great victories and magnificent kingdom? It was in such a state of mind that God gave to Nebuchadnezzar a prophetic dream.

Aware of the fact that the dream had tremendous significance, but unable to recall its details, he called in his wise men and demanded that they show him the dream and its interpretation. Brushing aside their protest that this was an unreasonable request, when they were unable to comply, the king commanded that all of the wise men should be slain (Daniel 2:13). Daniel and his companions, who had not been in the king's court, were included in the sweeping order.

When the matter was known to Daniel, he requested time of the king and promised that he would give the interpretation of the dream. Then with his three companions, Hananiah, Mishael, and Azariah, Daniel went to prayer to God who alone could reveal the secret. When the dream was made known to Daniel, he recognized the profound character of the divine revelation. His hymn of worship and praise is recorded in Daniel 2:20-23:

> Blessed be the name of God for ever and ever: for wisdom and might are his: And he changeth the times and the seasons: he removeth kings, and setteth up kings: he giveth wisdom unto the wise, and knowledge to them that know understanding: He revealeth the deep and secret things: he knoweth what is in the darkness, and the light dwelleth with him. I thank thee, and praise thee, O thou God of my fathers, who hast given me wisdom and might, and hast made known unto me now what we desired of thee: for thou hast now made known unto us the king's matter.

DANIEL'S DESCRIPTION OF THE DREAM

When brought before the king, Daniel made no claim for insight or wisdom of his own, but declared plainly:

The secret which the king hath demanded cannot the wise men, the astrologers, the magicians, the soothsayers, shew unto the king; But there is a God in heaven that revealeth secrets, and maketh known to the king Nebuchadnezzar what shall be in the latter days (Daniel 2:27, 28).

Daniel then recited the details of Nebuchadnezzar's great dream (Daniel 2:31-35):

Thou, O king, sawest, and behold a great image. This great image, whose brightness was excellent, stood before thee; and the form thereof was terrible. This image's head was of fine gold, his breast and his arms of silver, his belly and his thighs of brass, his legs of iron, his feet part of iron and part of clay. Thou sawest till that a stone was cut out without hands, which smote the image upon his feet that were of iron and clay, and brake them to pieces. Then was the iron, the clay, the brass, the silver, and the gold, broken to pieces together, and became like the chaff of the summer threshingfloors; and the wind carried them away, that no place was found for them: and the stone that smote the image became a great mountain, and filled the whole earth.

FOUR GREAT WORLD EMPIRES

Having declared the dream, Daniel then gave the interpretation. Four great world empires were to succeed each other, to be climaxed by a kingdom which comes from heaven. Nebuchadnezzar was identified as the head of gold, the supreme ruler of the civilized world of his day. Two other kingdoms are mentioned briefly by Daniel in Daniel 2:39, "And after thee shall arise another kingdom inferior to thee, and another third kingdom of brass, which shall bear rule over all the earth." These two kingdoms are represented in the body of the image.

Major attention, however, is directed to the fourth empire as being of supreme, prophetic importance, preceding as it does the final kingdom which comes from God. The fourth kingdom is represented by the legs and feet of the image:

And the fourth kingdom shall be strong as iron: forasmuch as iron breaketh in pieces and subdueth all things: and as iron that breaketh all these, shall it break in pieces and bruise. And whereas thou sawest the feet and toes, part of potters' clay, and part of iron, the kingdom shall be divided; but there shall be in it of the strength of the iron, forasmuch as thou sawest the iron mixed with miry clay. And as the toes of the feet were part of iron, and part of clay, so the kingdom shall be partly strong, and partly broken. And whereas thou sawest iron mixed with miry clay, they shall mingle themselves with the seed of men: but they shall not cleave one to another, even as iron is not mixed with clay (Daniel 2:40-43).

THE FOURTH EMPIRE

Although the first three kingdoms are clearly identified in Daniel in subsequent chapters, namely, Babylon, Medo-Persia (chapter 5), and Greece (8:21), the fourth kingdom is not named. There can be little doubt, however, that it refers to the Roman Empire, the greatest of all the world empires of history and one which had a larger effect upon subsequent posterity than any of the preceding empires. Even to modern times, there has never been an empire equal to that of the ancient Roman Empire.

The description given of it is typical of the Roman Empire. It is described as "strong as iron" (Daniel 2:40) and as an empire which breaks in pieces all that opposes it. This is, of course, precisely what the Roman armies did as they swept almost irresistibly into country after country, first of all conquering the western portion of the empire and then later the eastern portion. Although the division of the Roman Empire into western and eastern portions did not come until late in its history, it is anticipated in the fact that the image has two legs.

Major attention, however, is directed to the weakness in the feet and the toes described in verses 41-43. It is obvious that this is a matter of major importance. The feet and toes of the image are described as being part of pottery or clay and part of iron. This is interpreted as revealing in part its strength and at the same time its weakness in that the pottery was brittle and easily and quickly broken. Further, in verse 43 attention is called to the fact that iron and clay do not adhere one to the other and do not properly bond.

Whether this difference in material reflects differences in political ideology such as democracy versus absolute rule, differences in culture or race, or differences in economic situations, it is clear that the feet of the image are an area of weakness which leads to its complete downfall. In the light of the prophecy which follows, the feet stage of the image is best understood to refer to a form of the Roman Empire which is yet future, namely, the time just before "the God of heaven" shall "set up a kingdom, which shall never be destroyed" (2:44).

Many attempts have been made to find in the history of the Roman Empire a stage which corresponds to the toes of the image which may be presumed to be ten in number corresponding to the ten horns of the later vision in Daniel 7:7. It should be observed, first, that this situation demands a period in which the Roman Empire is divided into precisely ten kingdoms. There is no such period in the history of the Roman Empire. Although in its latter stages it was divided up into separate kingdoms, there never was a time when there were precisely ten such kingdoms, and no event followed such as is depicted in Daniel 2:44, 45. For the prophetic vision, therefore, to be completely fulfilled, there must be a future fulfillment.

THE FIFTH KINGDOM FROM HEAVEN

The prophecy of the destruction of the image is embraced in Daniel 2:44, 45:

> And in the days of these kings shall the God of heaven set up a kingdom, which shall never be destroyed: and the kingdom shall not be left to other people, but it shall break in pieces and consume all these kingdoms, and it shall stand for ever. Forasmuch as thou sawest that the stone was cut out of the mountain without hands, and that it brake in pieces the iron, the brass, the clay, the silver, and the gold; the great God hath made known to the king what shall come to pass hereafter: and the dream is certain, and the interpretation thereof sure.

It is clear that the stone cut out of the mountain without hands smites the image on the feet — that is, its last stage — with the result that the entire image is completely destroyed. The destruction cannot be properly compared to the advance of Christianity within the bounds of the ancient Roman Empire; that action was a gradual permeation which never assumed catastrophic character and never vitally changed the political aspect of the Roman Empire. History is clear that the Roman Empire was destroyed not by Christianity, but by its own inherent weaknesses and immorality.

What is demanded in fulfillment of this prophetic interpretation is a sudden catastrophic event which destroys all vestige of Gentile power and replaces it with the kingdom which God Himself establishes. The stone represents a divine agency rather than human, indicated in the fact that it is cut out without hands and is a proper representation of Jesus Christ as the crushing stone of judgment at His second advent. The Christian Gospel to the present hour has never had power to destroy Gentile government in the world and replace it with spiritual government, and there is no prospect that it will. Only divine intervention in the human scene and a display of the omnipotence of God could possibly break up the power of this world and convert it into the kingdom of heaven.

PROPHECY FULFILLED IN HISTORY

The prophetic foreview of world history afforded in the dream of Nebuchadnezzar was remarkably fulfilled except for the consummation. The kingdom of Babylon was indeed the first of the great world empires. Although not the most extensive or powerful in many respects, it was the most glorious. This is anticipated in the gold which represents the Babylonian Empire. After the death of Nebuchadnezzar in 562 B.C., it rapidly deteriorated until on the fateful night described in Daniel 5 on October 13, 539 B.C., Babylon was conquered and the decline of the great city began. The rule of the Medes and the Persians, though less glorious than that of Babylon, was much longer in duration and continued for over two hundred years to 332 B.C. when Alexander the Great conquered Babylon without a battle.

After Alexander's death, the Seleucidae controlled Babylon from 312 to 171 B.C. and were succeeded by the Parthian Empire which successfully resisted Rome and controlled Babylon from 171 B.C. to A.D. 226. Babylon continued to be inhabited in some form or other as late as A.D. 1000. In control of the Holy Land, however, Alexander was succeeded by the Roman Empire. The deterioration in the value of the metals depicted in the image had the compensation of increase in strength, and Rome until the time of the Barbarian invasion was truly characterized by the strength of iron.

As is frequently the case in the Old Testament, the prophecy of Daniel takes no notice of the many years separating the first and second advent of Christ. It anticipates a future empire in the Mediterranean area which will correspond to the ancient Roman Empire and which, from the divine viewpoint, will be a continuation of it. This fourth empire will be succeeded by the kingdom of heaven, begun with a sudden judgment upon Gentile power.

The final world power described in Daniel 2:44, 45 is obviously different in character than the preceding four empires. It is subsequent to these four empires and cannot be brought in until their total destruction. It is a kingdom which is established by the God of heaven rather than by human agency. In contrast to the other empires which had their rise and fall, the kingdom which God establishes will never be destroyed. It shall break in pieces and consume all other powers and shall stand forever.

That the dream was interpreted properly and that the interpretation should be considered factual is brought out in Daniel 2:45 where it is stated: "The great God hath made known to the king what shall come to pass hereafter: and the dream is certain, and the interpretation thereof sure." In the light of the literal and graphic fulfillment of prophecy relating to the first four kingdoms, except for the portion of the fourth which is yet future, it is natural to conclude that the fifth kingdom is also to be literally and factually fulfilled in God's future program.

The grandeur of this panorama of human history and the important place that it assigned the kingdom of Babylon as the first of the succession of world empires so impressed King Nebuchadnezzar that in spite of his high office and absolute rule it is recorded in Daniel 2:46, "Then the king Nebuchadnezzar fell upon his face, and worshipped Daniel, and commanded that they should offer an oblation and sweet odours unto him." King Nebuchadnezzar also gave testimony that the God of Daniel is "a God of gods, and a Lord of kings, and a revealer of secrets, seeing thou couldest reveal this secret." The elevation of Daniel to a prominent place in the government of the Babylonian Empire testifies to the profound impression made upon King Nebuchadnezzar. The experience of Nebuchadnezzar ultimately resulted in his turning to the God of Israel in faith (Daniel 4).

The revelation given in Daniel 2 of world history in its panoramic form constitutes the essential framework for all prophecy related to the nations. Subsequent details in Daniel and elsewhere in Scripture are amplification and added details and explanations. The Scriptures give special emphasis to the latter stage of the fourth empire and concerning this a great body of prophetic Scripture fills in the total picture.

The guidelines, however, for future fulfillment are found in the past. A study of Babylon, Medo-Persia, and Greece, as prophecies relating to them have been fulfilled, provides an important background for that which is yet future. The geographic area of these kingdoms is involved in the final chapters of world history. Babylon has perpetuated itself religiously and to some extent is reproduced politically in the last stage of the fourth kingdom. A study of prophecy relating to these kingdoms as well as historic fulfillment is, then, the Biblical introduction to the nations in the end of the age.

CHAPTER V

THE RISE AND FALL OF BABYLON

EARLY HISTORY OF BABYLON

The early history of Babylon is shrouded in mystery. First mentioned in the Bible is the record of Genesis 10:8-10 which names Nimrod, the grandson of Ham, as the founder of the city in the dim prehistoric past. Its name was derived from a later experience revealed in Genesis 11 where the inhabitants of the land of Shinar, the southern portion of Mesopotamia, are recorded as building a tower designed to reach the heavens. This may have been the beginning of a practice of building towers with religious significance. Such a tower is known as a ziggurat, designating an artificial mound of brick and soil elevated above the surrounding terrain.

The Biblical description of the tower is in keeping with the characteristics of the area. Lacking stones, they made brick and used slime or bitumen native to the area in the construction of the tower. According to Scripture, the inhabitants had said,

> Go to, let us make brick, and burn them thoroughly. And they had brick for stone, and slime had they for mortar. And they said, Go to, let us build us a city and a tower, whose top may reach unto heaven; and let us make us a name, lest we be scattered abroad upon the face of the whole earth (Genesis 11:3, 4).

The Scriptures record that the Lord judged the people and confounded their language with the result that the city and the tower were left unfinished (Genesis 11:5-8). The place according to Genesis 11:9 was "called Babel; because the LORD did there confound the language of all the earth: and from thence did the LORD scatter them abroad upon the face of all the earth." It seems probable that the name given to the city in Genesis 10:10 actually supplanted the original name at this time, and this incident contributes to the long history of Babylon as a center of religious significance, and as a source of false religion and rebellion against the true God.

Although the city of Babylon does not rise to prominence until 1830 B.C., the area in which it is located, called Babylonia, had a long history. Early civilization near the site of ancient Ur in lower Babylonia dates from the fourth millennium B.C. and successive civilizations have been traced from 2800 B.C. The period of the early dynasties (2800-2360 B.C.) recorded an advanced civilization including great temples, canals, and other construction. The old Akkadian period (2360-2180 B.C.) included the extensive empire of Sargon from Persia to the Mediterranean. This was followed by the Neo-Sumerian period (2070-1960 B.C.), in which time Abraham was born. The land was sacked by the Elamites and Amorites in the period 1960-1830 B.C.

The history of Babylonia proper, known as the Old Babylonia period (1830-1550 B.C.), included the brilliant reign of Hammurabi (1728-1686 B.C.) whose famous Code was discovered in 1901. Babylonia was next invaded by the Kassites in the period 1550-1169 B.C. This was followed by Dynasty II of Isin (1169-1039 B.C.), whose kings were native Babylonians. In the period from 1100 to 625 B.C. the land suffered various invasions including that of Assyria. In 729 B.C. Tiglath-pileser became king of Babylon and later in 689 B.C. attacked by Sennacherib, Babylon was destroyed by fire. It was rebuilt by Esarhaddon, and was finally wrested from Assyria around 625 B.C. when the Neo-Babylonian Empire was founded by Nabopolassar, the father of Nebuchadnezzar. With the help of the Medes, Nineveh was destroyed in 612 B.C. Necho of Egypt was defeated in 605 B.C. The stage was now set for the brilliant reign of Nebuchadnezzar which included the earlier conquering of Jerusalem in 606 B.C., the ultimate captivity of its inhabitants, and the destruction of the city itself.

THE PROPHECIES OF ISAIAH CONCERNING BABYLON

Apart from a reference to a "Babylonish garment" in Joshua 7:21, there is no Biblical reference to Babylon after Genesis 11 until the great prophecies of Isaiah, Jeremiah, Ezekiel, and Daniel unfolded God's plan for the ancient city. Most of the Biblical prophecies relating to Babylon are in relation to the captivity and God's

revelation to Jeremiah, Ezekiel, and Daniel concerning the ultimate end of the captivity both for Israel and for Babylon. Most
remarkable, however, are the prophecies of Isaiah delivered a century before Babylon had risen to power and recorded at a time
when Babylon was still in obscurity with no indication of its coming greatness. Outstanding chapters in Isaiah's predictions are
13, 14, and 47 with scattered references elsewhere (21:9, 39:1, 3,
6, 7; 43:14; 48:14, 20).

The predictions of Isaiah have to do with Babylon's ultimate
destruction in the Day of the Lord. The near and the far view are
often mingled as in chapter 13. The destruction of Babylon is
pictured in Isaiah 13:1-11 as part of God's program to punish the
entire world (cp. 13:11). The historic conquering of Babylon by
the Medes and the Persians is mentioned specifically in Isaiah 13:
17-19.

> Behold, I will stir up the Medes against them, which shall not regard
> silver; and as for gold, they shall not delight in it. Their bows also
> shall dash the young men to pieces; and they shall have no pity on
> the fruit of the womb; their eye shall not spare children. And Baby-
> lon, the glory of kingdoms, the beauty of the Chaldees' excellency,
> shall be as when God overthrew Sodom and Gomorrah.

The prophet seems to refer to the far view, that is, the destruction of Babylon in relation to the second coming of Christ in 13:
20-22. Here it is declared:

> It shall never be inhabited, neither shall it be dwelt in from genera-
> tion to generation: neither shall the Arabian pitch tent there; neither
> shall the shepherds make their fold there. But wild beasts of the
> desert shall lie there; and their houses shall be full of doleful creatures;
> and owls shall dwell there, and satyrs shall dance there. And the
> wild beasts of the islands shall cry in their desolate houses, and dragons
> in their pleasant palaces: and her time is near to come, and her days
> shall not be prolonged.

As far as the historic fulfillment is concerned, it is obvious from
both Scripture and history that these verses have not been literally
fulfilled. The city of Babylon continued to flourish after the Medes
conquered it, and though its glory dwindled, especially after the
control of the Medes and Persians ended in 323 B.C., the city continued in some form or substance until A.D. 1000 and did not ex-

perience a sudden termination such as is anticipated in this prophecy.

Interpretation has been made more difficult by the varied meanings of Babylon itself. Sometimes the term (in the Hebrew *Babel*) refers to the city whose history continued and was flourishing even during the Apostolic period when it became a center of Jewish learning after the destruction of Jerusalem. Sometimes the term is used in reference to the political power of Babylon which obviously fell in one night when the Medes and the Persians took control of Babylon. Sometimes it is used in a religious sense, for Babylon has been the fountain of many of the pagan religions which have competed with Judaism and Christian faith ever since. The interpretation of Isaiah 13:20-22 is inevitably determined by the meaning assigned to Revelation 17, 18.

Many interpreters agree that Babylon in its religious and political sense will be revived at the end of the age. Debated is the conclusion that the city itself will have a physical revival to become the capital of the world at the end of the age. Such a rebuilding of the ancient city would make possible a literal fulfillment of the prophecy of complete and sudden destruction as predicted in Isaiah 13:19-22.

Isaiah 14 seems to confirm that the ultimate destruction in view is one related to the second advent of Christ and the Day of the Lord. The satanic power behind Babylon addressed as "Lucifer, son of the morning" (14:12) is portrayed both in his original rebellion against God and in his ultimate judgment. The destruction of Babylon is related to the judgment upon "all the kings of the nations" (14:18).

Another massive prophecy against Babylon is found in Isaiah 47. Here a prediction of Babylon's utter humiliation is given, and the foreview seems to relate primarily to the capture of Babylon by the Medes and the Persians. The sad pronouncement is made at the conclusion of the passage, "None shall save thee" (Isaiah 47:15). The major attention given to Babylon in Isaiah's prophecies confirm Babylon's importance in prophecy relating to the nations.

THE PROPHECIES OF JEREMIAH CONCERNING BABYLON

The prophet Jeremiah like Isaiah devotes two long chapters to the prediction of Babylon's ultimate judgment and destruction

(Jeremiah 50, 51). If the prophecies of Isaiah are remarkable for their anticpation of Babylon's rise to power and the captivity of Judah a hundred years before it actually occurred, the prophecies of Jeremiah are notable because they were delivered at the peak of Babylon's power when it seemed most unlikely that the great nation would fall. Babylon is pictured as being punished because of its cruel treatment of Israel (50:17, 18; 51:24, 49).

Practically all of the predictions of Jeremiah seem to relate to the fall of Babylon by the attack of the Medes and the Persians. Only occasionally does there seem to be a reference to a future ultimate destruction as in Jeremiah 51:62-64. The prophecies of Jeremiah predicting the fall of Babylon at the hands of the Medes and the Persians were graphically fulfilled approximately sixty-five years later, as recorded in Daniel 5.

Major attention is devoted to the captivity of Judah in the prophecies of both Jeremiah and Ezekiel. There is almost constant reference to the Babylonian captivity of Judah in Jeremiah beginning in chapter 20; numerous references are also found in Ezekiel. Much of Jeremiah's ministry was to his own generation as he predicted the downfall of Jerusalem and the victory of the Babylonian armies. Jeremiah is seen as the true prophet of God in contrast to the false prophets who had predicted victory over Babylon (cp. Jeremiah 28:1-17). Jeremiah's prophecies were largely ignored. The first copy of his book was destroyed by the king (36:23). Jeremiah himself suffered affliction and imprisonment (37:15—38: 13). With the capture of Jerusalem, the prophecies of Jeremiah were fully vindicated.

Most important were Jeremiah's prophecies concerning the duration of the captivity, designated as seventy years in Jeremiah 25:11 and 29:10. It was this prophecy which was read by Daniel which led to his prayer for the return of the captives to Jerusalem (Daniel 9:2).

A prominent theme of Jeremiah's prophecies were predictions against Egypt in which he anticipated that Nebuchadnezzar would conquer Egypt. As a traditional enemy of Israel, Egypt was thus to experience God's judgment in the form of coming under the power of Babylon. Jeremiah devotes considerable Scripture to this theme, including 43:10-13; 44:30; 46:1-26. In chapter 44 Jeremiah sends a message to the Jews in Egypt in which he predicts that their attempt to escape the power of Babylon would only result in their own destruction.

THE PROPHECIES OF EZEKIEL CONCERNING BABYLON

Ezekiel echoes the prophecies of Jeremiah relating to the Babylonian captivity (Ezekiel 17:12-24) and like Jeremiah predicts the conquering of Egypt (29:18, 19; 30:10-25; 32:1-32). Added is the prediction of the destruction of Tyre in Ezekiel 26:7 - 28:19.

It is obvious from these many passages in the prophets that Babylon occupies a large place in the prophetic program of the Old Testament for the nations surrounding Israel. It is with this context that Daniel the prophet takes up the theme and relates God's dealings with Babylon to His ultimate purpose of bringing all nations into subjection unto the Son of God.

THE PROPHECIES OF DANIEL CONCERNING BABYLON

Daniel's first recognition of Babylon prophetically was in his interpretation of Nebuchadnezzar's dream. Babylon was represented in the great image by the head of gold, and Daniel recognized the importance of Nebuchadnezzar:

Thou, O king, art a king of kings: for the God of heaven hath given thee a kingdom, power, and strength, and glory. And wheresoever the children of men dwell, the beasts of the field and the fowls of the heaven hath he given into thine hand, and hath made thee ruler over them all. Thou art this head of gold (Daniel 2:37, 38).

After the death of Nebuchadnezzar, Daniel's vision recorded in chapter 7 includes much added revelation. In his description of the first beast which represents Babylon, Daniel states, "The first was like a lion, and had eagle's wings: I beheld till the wings thereof were plucked, and it was lifted up from the earth, and made stand upon the feet as a man, and a man's heart was given to it" (Daniel 7:4).

Babylon was indeed like the lion, the king of beasts, and had eagle's wings like the king of birds. That the wings would be plucked and the beast would stand as a man with a man's heart was the divine portrayal of Nebuchadnezzar's experience in Daniel 4 as well as an anticipation of the ultimate humiliation of the Babylonian rulers in Daniel 5. In Daniel's interpretation of the tree vision of Nebuchadnezzar in Daniel 4, he had predicted Nebuchadnezzar's humiliation in which he suffered seven years of insanity before his reason returned. Nebuchadnezzar was ready then to give praise to God as he does in Daniel 4:2, 3, 34-37. The prophecies of Daniel were meticulously fulfilled.

THE FALL OF BABYLON

The fall of the Babylonian Empire came suddenly when the Medes and the Persians overran the city of Babylon in a night attack in 539 B.C. Prior to this event, the Babylonian Empire had already fallen on evil days. When Nebuchadnezzar died in 562 B.C., he was succeeded by his son Amel-Marduk who was assassinated only two years later. In 560 B.C. Neriglissar took the throne. When he died in 556 B.C. after only four years of reign, he was succeeded by his son who was assassinated shortly after he came to the throne. Nabonidus then assumed power appointing his son Belshazzar as co-ruler. It was this Belshazzar who held the ungodly feast of Daniel 5 and perished at the hands of the Medes and Persians.

At the time of the downfall of the city of Babylon recorded in Daniel 5, the city was still a monument to the genius of Nebuchadnezzar. According to Herodotus, the city was approximately 14 miles square with the Euphrates River bisecting it north and south. Two sets of walls inner and outer protected the city and, according to standards of the day, rendered it safe from attack from without. If Herodotus can be believed, the walls were indeed formidable being 350 feet high and 87 feet thick. Walls also lined the river on either side and 150 gates of solid brass protected the entrances. On the wall were some 250 watchtowers, 100 feet higher than the wall itself. The outside wall had a deep water moat some 30 feet wide.

During the height of its power, provisions were stored in Babylon supposedly sufficient for twenty years of siege and designed to discourage anyone attacking it. Within the walls the city was laid out in square blocks with beautiful houses lining the streets usually three and four stories in height. The city also included great parks and gardens, some of which, such as the hanging gardens described by Diodorus, were outstanding wonders in the ancient world. The gardens were built on terraces and supported large trees. A great bridge some 660 feet long and 30 feet wide bridged the Euphrates River and connected the eastern and western halves of the city. Notable buildings were also found such as the palace of the king, the temple of Bel over eight stories in height, and many other buildings of less importance.

It was this city, proud of its supposed invulnerability, which had ignored the rapidly expanding power of the Medes and the Persians. Media as a separate kingdom had matched the rise of the Babylonian Empire. After the Medes had captured Asshur in 614 B.C. under alliance with the Chaldeans, they had also captured Nineveh. The downfall of the Assyrian Empire, marked by these events, paved the way for the rise in power of Media which was in alliance with Nebuchadnezzar during most of his reign. Persia was also rising in power, however, and under Cyrus II Media was conquered by the Persians about 549 B.C. Media and Persia were united in a common government which lasted until Alexander the Great in 331 B.C. Their armies had proceeded to conquer much of the territory around Babylon before the fateful night in 539 B.C. (Daniel 5).

Setting siege to the large city of Babylon, the Medes had dug a canal diverting the water that flowed under the city wall. At the very time of Belshazzar's impious feast, they were entering the city on the dry channel underneath the mighty walls. The drinking feast celebrated by the one thousand lords apparently was shared by other inhabitants so that the normal watch kept on the walls was not observed, allowing the invaders valuable time in conquering the city before their presence was fully known. At the very time the Medes were pouring into the city, the handwriting appeared on the wall (Daniel 5:5, 24-28). Daniel correctly interpreted the writing as spelling the doom of the Babylonian Empire and the beginning of the empire of the Medes and the Persians (Daniel 5:28, 31). Thus ended the fabulous reign of the Babylonian Empire, the symbol of Gentile glory and moral and religious wickedness.

CONTINUED INFLUENCE OF BABYLON

Although the fall of Babylon marked the end of political rule of Babylonian rulers, much of the Babylonian culture, its pagan religions, and its ideology were continued in the kingdoms which followed. Babylonian influence was perpetuated down through the centuries especially in ancient pagan religions. Babylon, the symbol of religious confusion, was to appear again in the apostate church of Revelation 17, and its political power was to be revived in the final form of the Roman Empire as depicted in Revelation 18. Even if literal Babylon is not rebuilt as a city in the last days and subjected to the sudden destruction described in Revelation 18, Babylon as an influence for evil politically and religiously will not be terminated until Jesus Christ comes in power and glory to reign.

Chapter VI

THE MEDES AND THE PERSIANS

The history of the rise and fall of the Medes and the Persians forms an important background for over two hundred years of Biblical history. Located in the area south of the Caspian Sea and east of the Zagros Mountains, its original domain stretched for 600 miles north and south, and 250 miles east to west. The nation first came into prominence in the ninth century B.C. and is mentioned in inscriptions concerning Shalmaneser III (about 836 B.C.). Though under the domination of Assyria until the seventh century B.C., their rise in power was contemporary with the decline of the Assyrian Empire and in 614 B.C. the Medes captured Asshur, the capitol city of Assyria. Later in 612 B.C. in alliance with the Chaldeans they captured Nineveh resulting in the downfall of the Assyrian Empire. In the years which followed they were an important ally of Babylonia and formed various alliances and intermarriages. Toward the end of the reign of Nebuchadnezzar, the Persians began to become a powerful force and under Cyrus II Media was conquered in 549 B.C. and was combined with the empire of the Persians to form Medo-Persia. The combined strength of the Persians and the Medes led to conquest of Babylon in 539 B.C., with the resulting extension of their empire over much of the Middle East until the conquest of Alexander the Great in 331 B.C.

EARLY PROPHECY CONCERNING THE MEDES

First mention of the Medes in Scripture is found in the prophetic utterance of Isaiah when he declared 175 years before it was fulfilled, "Behold, I will stir up the Medes against them, which shall not regard silver; and as for gold, they shall not delight in it" (Isaiah 13:17; cp. 21:2). In succeeding verses the downfall of Babylon is predicted, "And Babylon, the glory of kingdoms, the beauty of the Chaldees' excellency, shall be as when God overthrew Sodom and Gomorrah" (Isaiah 13:19).

Jeremiah includes the Medes as one of many nations which will be punished by God (Jeremiah 25:25). Jeremiah also states that the Medes will be used of God to destroy Babylon: "Make bright the arrows; gather the shields: the LORD hath raised up the spirit of the kings of the Medes: for his device is against Babylon, to destroy it; because it is the vengeance of the LORD, the vengeance of his temple" (Jeremiah 51:11; cp. 51:28). Thus long before Babylon fell it was predicted that the Medes would be God's avenging instrument.

PROPHECY OF DANIEL

It was given to Daniel the prophet, however, to give the Medes and the Persians their proper place in the panorama of future history. The Medes and the Persians are anticipated in the expression in Daniel 2:39, "And after thee shall arise another kingdom inferior to thee." This refers to the chest of silver in the image of Daniel 2, where the two arms anticipated the dual kingdom of the Medes and the Persians. More detail is given in the vision of Daniel recorded in 7:5 where Daniel describes the second beast in these words, "And behold another beast, a second, like to a bear, and it raised up itself on one side, and it had three ribs in the mouth of it between the teeth of it: and they said thus unto it, Arise, devour much flesh."

The kingdom of the Medes and the Persians is described as a bear which raises itself on one side (referring to Persia being greater than Media) and has three ribs in its mouth. No explanation is given of this, but the strength of a bear is a good symbol of the empire of the Medes and the Persians. The three ribs may refer to the principal elements of the kingdom, namely, the Medes, the Persians, and Babylonia. The exhortation to "Arise, devour much flesh," is encouragement to the new empire to expand as it did in its conquests to the north and to the west.

A further prophetic picture of the empire of the Medes and the Persians is given in Daniel 8 where the ram with two horns which is destroyed by the goat is an obvious reference to the kingdom of the Medes and the Persians. The two horns represent the Medes and the Persians. Daniel's description of it in Daniel 8:3, 4 is characteristic of the two centuries of the rule of the Medes and the Persians,

> Then I lifted up mine eyes, and saw, and, behold, there stood before the river a ram which had two horns: and the two horns were high;

but one was higher than the other, and the higher came up last. I saw the ram pushing westward, and northward, and southward; so that no beasts might stand before him, neither was there any that could deliver out of his hand; but he did according to his will, and became great.

The lower horn apparently refers to the kingdom of the Medes and the higher horn that came up later to the kingdom of Persia, which dominated Media. The fourth verse describes their conquests westward, northward, and southward which characterize the history of this empire as there was no considerable progress eastward. All of this prediction is precisely fulfilled in later history. Only by divine revelation could Daniel know in advance that the conquests of the Medes and Persians would be to the north, south and west, but not to the east — in contrast to the Macedonian conquests which were mainly to the east, as indicated in subsequent verses in the activities of the he goat.

ISRAEL'S RESTORATION UNDER MEDES AND PERSIANS

While the prophetic record concerning the Medes and the Persians is clear and its fulfillment is confirmed by history, its principal importance is historical rather than prophetic. In contrast to the Babylonian Empire which is significant for its destruction of Jerusalem, the city of God, beginning Gentile dominion over Israel which will not culminate until Christ comes in His second advent, the rise of the Medes and the Persians is important as forming the background of Israel's partial restoration.

Three of the historical books, namely, Ezra, Nehemiah, and Esther and three of the minor prophets, Haggai, Zechariah, and Malachi have their context in the reign of the Medo-Persian Empire. During this period the captives of Judah were permitted to go back to Jerusalem and restore their ancient city and its temple. The key to the Babylonian Empire is Gentile dominion over Jerusalem. The key to the Empire of the Medes and the Persians is restoration of Jerusalem.

Daniel gives a whole chapter to the account of his being cast into the lions' den. This important episode in the life of Daniel, while affording many spiritual lessons of God's care over His prophet as well as foreshadowing God's protection over the people of Israel as a whole, illustrates the beneficent attitude of the Medes and the Persians to the people whom they had conquered. Their deference to individual religious faith is manifested in the attitude of Darius to Daniel and his earnest desire that Daniel might be delivered from the lions.

Darius himself, described in Daniel 5:31 as "Darius the Median," is properly identified as Gobryas or Gubaru, a governor of Babylon appointed by Cyrus the supreme monarch of the empire of the Medes and the Persians. (Cyrus II or Cyrus the Great reigned from 559 B.C. until he was killed in battle in 530 B.C.) Darius the Mede is mentioned a number of times in Daniel (6:1, 6, 9, 25, 28; 9:1; 11:1). Darius seems to have reigned under Cyrus in governing the southern portion of the kingdom known as the Fertile Crescent. The statement that "Daniel prospered in the reign of Darius, and in the reign of Cyrus the Persian" (Daniel 6:28) must therefore be interpreted as the reign of Darius under the contemporary reign of Cyrus.

It was in the first year of the reign of Cyrus that permission was given to the children of Israel to return to reconstruct their temple in Jerusalem (II Chronicles 36:22, 23; Ezra 1:1-4). More than a century before the remarkable prophecy of Isaiah about Cyrus (Isaiah 44:28) had anticipated the Israelites return. The generous permission and encouragement of Cyrus for Israel to restore their ancient worship was in line with the official policy to allow captive people freedom of religion. The temple, however, was not finally completed until the reign of Cambyses II (530-522 B.C.) who succeeded his father Cyrus and is referred to in Ezra 4 as Artaxerxes.

Artaxerxes was a common name ascribed to many kings. Others given this title include Artaxerxes of Ezra 7:1, known as Artaxerxes I Longimanus who reigned 465-425 B.C., and Ahasuerus or Xerxes of Esther 1:1 who reigned 486-465 B.C. The appeal to Darius the king mentioned in Ezra 6:1 is a reference to Darius I, known as Darius the Great who reigned 522-486 B.C., and should not be confused with the Darius the Mede of Daniel's prophecy.

The more important kings of the Medo-Persian Empire are again the subject of prophecy in Daniel 11:2 where Daniel is told: "Behold, there shall stand up yet three kings in Persia; and the fourth shall be far richer than they all: and by his strength through his riches he shall stir up all against the realm of Grecia." The first of the three kings which were to follow Darius the Mede (Daniel 11:1) can be identified as Cambyses II. He was followed by

Smerdis, a usurper who reigned for eight months. (Some think he is the ruler mentioned in Ezra 4:7-24 instead of Cambyses.) After the murder of Smerdis a Darius the Great (522-486 B.C.) appeared. He is referred to in Ezra 4:24. It was under Darius that the authority to complete the temple was received.

The king designated as "the fourth" in Daniel 11:2, who used his great riches to attack the realm of Grecia, was undoubtedly Xerxes (486-465 B.C.) referred to as Ahasuerus in Esther 1:1. His celebrated attempt to conquer Greece ended in miserable failure. This attack can be placed chronologically between the first and the second chapter of Esther. In fact, the great feast of Esther 1 was a part of the preparation for the organization of the campaign against Greece which occurred in the third year of Xerxes' reign. Esther 2, recording his marriage to Esther, did not occur until four years later after his return and the crushing defeat and loss of his great army and naval force. From a prophetic standpoint, Xerxes was important as incurring the undying hatred of the Grecian people which forms the background of the conquest of Alexander the Great more than a century later.

The importance of Ezra, with its record of events which occurred under Persian rule, is that the temple was restored as the center of Israel's religious life. The record of Daniel 8 and 11 is also significant as forming the prophetic bridge from Babylon to Alexander and giving the background of Israel's history in this period. In Ezra 7:1 a successor to Xerxes is mentioned, namely, Artaxerxes I Longimanus, but he does not figure in Daniel's prophecy because he was not important to Daniel's revelation. The same is true of other rulers who followed in the Medo-Persian Empire prior to its downfall.

REBUILDING OF JERUSALEM

Nehemiah adds the important final chapter in Israel's reconstruction. Under Nehemiah's leadership during the reign of Artaxerxes I Longimanus the wall of Jerusalem was rebuilt with the encouragement and supply of materials from the king, and subsequently the debris of the city was cleared out and houses were built, thus repopulating the city of God. The two important steps of rebuilding the temple and rebuilding the city during the reign of the Persians mark this period as the time of Israel's partial restoration in preparation for the coming of their Messiah. The spiritual revivals under Ezra and Nehemiah are a corresponding spiritual restoration which the people thoroughly needed.

The prophetic writings of Haggai and Zechariah also fit into this period and are related to the prophetic encouragement of the people during the reconstruction of the temple of Ezra 5. Malachi gives the concluding chapter of the Old Testament before Israel was plunged into the so-called four hundred silent years before Christ came. The history of the Medes and the Persians, constituting as it does accurate and meticulous fulfillment of God's prophetic Word, is another important evidence supporting the hope that prophecies yet unfulfilled will have their day of fulfillment in the consummation of the age. The Medes and the Persians, however, belong to fulfilled prophecy and do not figure largely in events of the end time although Persia is mentioned in passing in Ezekiel 38:5.

CHAPTER VII

THE KINGDOM OF GREECE

The third world kingdom, which was to succeed that of the Medes and the Persians, was the empire created by Alexander the Great whose armies were victorious over the Persians in 331 B.C. Only occasional reference to this empire is found by name in the Bible. It does not seem to have attracted the attention of the great prophets Isaiah and Jeremiah, and it does not coincide with Biblical history in that it fits into the period between Malachi and Matthew.

BIBLICAL BACKGROUND

The Hebrew does not actually use the word for *Greece* or *Grecia,* but the word *yawan* or its English equivalent *javan.* This name is derived from Javan of Genesis 10:2, one of the sons of Japheth and therefore a grandson of Noah. It is commonly believed, however, that Javan was the progenitor of the Greek race which inhabited not only Greece but the islands related to it and hence is properly translated by *Grecian* where it occurs (cp. Isaiah 66:19; Ezekiel 27:13, 19; Daniel 8:21; 10:20; 11:2; Joel 3:6; Zechariah 9:13).

PROPHECY OF DANIEL

According to the prophecy of Daniel in his interpretation of Nebuchadnezzar's image, the Grecian Empire was to be the third kingdom of brass (Daniel 2:39). Further light on the characteristics of this empire is given in Daniel 7:6 in the description of the third beast of Daniel's vision. Daniel describes the third beast as "like a leopard, which had upon the back of it four wings of a fowl; the beast had also four heads; and dominion was given to it." While Daniel's prophecies concerning Nebuchadnezzar and the kingdom of the Medes and the Persians were fulfilled in part in Daniel's lifetime, in his prediction of the empire of Greece he accurately foreshadowed an empire which did not come into existence until two hundred years later. It would have been impossible for Daniel by any natural insight to have anticipated that a small and insignificant Greek state, namely, Macedonia, should reach such great power and prestige and have such a rapid rise as that of Alexander's kingdom.

Conquests of Alexander the Great

History records how Alexander with the agility of a goat crossed the Hellespont, having previously conquered Greece, and began the march to revenge the humiliation inflicted upon Greece by Xerxes more than a century before. Conquering Troy, he first met Persian opposition at Granicus and after subduing all of Asia Minor proceeded to battle a host of one-half million Persians whom Darius had assembled. Meeting in the plain of Issus, he slaughtered the greatly superior Persian force and broke the back of Persian opposition. Proceeding southward, city after city yielded without a fight except for Tyre and Gaza where a siege was necessary before it was subdued.

Continuing south to Egypt, Alexander conquered the entire country without a fight and established the city Alexandria as the capital of the area, which soon became the largest city of the Hellenic world. Proceeding east he had still another battle with Darius at Issus and again defeated a greatly superior force. His armies reached India, but his troops, weary with battle, refused to go further.

Returning to Babylon, Alexander intended to make this the capital of his entire empire. While engaged in establishing his new organization, he died a victim of his profligate eating and drinking coupled with an attack of malaria. Brief as was his domain, the fact that he carried Greek culture with him and often established new cities on a Hellenic pattern had the effect of leaving his mark upon the civilized world of his day and indirectly prepared the area of his conquest to receive the Gospel later which was largely preached in Greek. The extent of his conquest is all the more remarkable because it was foreshadowed in such a clear way in Biblical prophecy.

The description of the leopard, one of the swiftest of beasts, characterizes the lightning-like attack of Alexander's armies which with unprecedented speed swept the world of his day into its power. The four wings on the back of the leopard not only represent the idea of speed, but also symbolize the historic fact that Alexander's empire was controlled after his death by four principal generals, also, anticipated in the four heads of the beast. The accuracy of this prophecy is so evident that liberal scholars who consider detailed prophecy an impossibility are forced to postulate that the entire book of Daniel is in fact a forgery written by a pseudo-Daniel who lived after these events of Alexander's conquest had already taken place. This unwilling confession of the accuracy of Biblical prophecy is in itself most significant and a testimony to the accuracy of prophecy as a whole.

THE PROPHECY OF DANIEL 8

Unlike the kingdoms of Babylon and that of Media and Persia, there is little prophecy concerning Alexander and his empire outside of Daniel. It does not seem to have attracted the attention of any of the other prophets, although bare mention is made as previously indicated. More detail is given in Daniel about the Alexandrian Empire, however, than any of the preceding kingdoms. The entire eighth chapter is devoted to portraying the rise of the third empire and further details are given in chapter 11.

In a vision given to Daniel before the fall of Babylon, the conquest of the kingdom of the Medes and the Persians by Alexander was depicted in the destruction of the ram with two horns by the goat with the important horn between its eyes. After describing the conquest of the ram, which portrays the power of the kingdom of the Medes and the Persians, Daniel records the destruction of the Persian Kingdom by Alexander in these words:

> And as I was considering, behold, an he goat came from the west on the face of the whole earth, and touched not the ground: and the goat had a notable horn between his eyes. And he came to the ram that had two horns, which I had seen standing before the river, and ran unto him in the fury of his power. And I saw him come close unto the ram, and he was moved with choler against him, and smote the ram, and brake his two horns: and there was no power in the ram to stand before him, but he cast him down to the ground, and stamped upon him: and there was none that could deliver the ram out of his hand (Daniel 8:5-7).

This description accurately predicted the conquest of the Persian Empire by Alexander and his armies which brought to a close more than two hundred years of the illustrious political power under the Persians. The interpretation of these verses is plainly given in Daniel 8:20, 21, "The ram which thou sawest having two horns are the kings of Media and Persia. And the rough goat is the king of Grecia: and the great horn that is between his eyes is the first king."

DIVISION OF GRECIAN EMPIRE

As history records, however, Alexander the Great, while able to conquer the world, was not able to conquer himself. When at the pinnacle of his power, Alexander died in a drunken feast and his conquests were peaceably divided between his four generals. This is anticipated in Daniel 8:8: "Therefore the he goat waxed very great: and when he was strong, the great horn was broken; and for it came up four notable ones toward the four winds of heaven." This is interpreted in Daniel 8:22 as being the four kingdoms into which the Grecian Empire was divided, headed up by the four generals of Alexander. Ptolemy was given Egypt and adjacent territories. To Seleucas was given Syria, Asia Minor, and the East. Lysimachus took control of Thrace and adjoining territories. Cassander ruled over Macedonia and Greece itself. Eventually Macedonia and Thrace were joined, resulting in the emergence of three strong kingdoms, Macedonia, Syria, and Egypt. Political rule was therefore divided until the Roman Empire arose to provide a new unifying political factor.

ANTIOCHUS EPIPHANES

Daniel is primarily concerned in his prophetic foreview in Daniel 8 with what constituted a relatively unimportant aspect of the total picture from the standpoint of world history, but what was to be quite important in its relationship to the people of Israel. In Daniel 8:9-14, Daniel records the emergence of "a little horn, which waxed exceeding great, toward the south, and toward the east, and toward the pleasant land."

The subsequent description of the little horn indicates that it is a man who opposes God (8:10), exalts himself in opposition to God, and takes away the daily sacrifice (8:11, 12). A question is then raised in Daniel 8:13 as to how long the desolation of the sanctuary shall continue and is answered in 8:14, "Unto two thousand and three hundred days; then shall the sanctuary be cleansed."

The vision is subsequently interpreted to Daniel and the revelation is recorded in Daniel 8:15-26. Daniel is informed that the

vision relates to "the time of the end" (8:17). Similar expressions
are found in 8:19, "the last end of the indignation" and "the time appointed the end" (8:19), and "in the latter time of their kingdom,
when the transgressors are come to the full" (8:23). In the interpretation, the ram with the two horns is stated to be "the kings of Media
and Persia" (8:20), and the rough goat is stated to be "the king
of Grecia" (8:21). The great horn of the rough goat is declared
to be "the first king" (8:21). According to 8:22, the four horns
which replaced the single broken horn are "four kingdoms" which
shall appear, but which shall not have the power of the great horn.

The little horn of 8:9 is described in 8:23, 24 as "a king of fierce
countenance, and understanding dark sentences" whose "power
shall be mighty, but not by his own power: and he shall destroy
wonderfully, and shall prosper, and practise, and shall destroy the
mighty and holy people." He is described also as opposing the
Prince of princes, but it is declared that "he shall be broken without hand" (8:25). Students of prophecy have recognized in this
description first of all the anticipation of an immediate fulfillment
in connection with the Macedonian Empire.

The most probable interpretation of this little horn is that it
concerns Antiochus Epiphanes, a ruler in the kingdom of Syria
about 170 B.C. His terrible persecution of the Jews which inspired
the Maccabean revolt is a matter of history. Through his instru-
mentality the sacrifices of the Jews were stopped and their temple
desecrated. With an army of some 22,000 men he attacked Jerusalem on a Sabbath day massacring the men and making captives
of the women and children. He issued a decree commanding that
all should worship only according to the religion of the prevailing
political power. The resulting revolt of the Jewish people was
ultimately resolved only after long struggle and by the ascendance
of the Roman Empire.

The reference to 2300 days (literally 2300 mornings and evenings) is best understood as 2300 ordinary days, during which the
sanctuary remained desecrated. Historically it was approximately
this length of time before a restoration was accomplished. It has
been computed that the sanctuary was cleansed on December 25,
165 B.C. by Judas Maccabaeus. This will allow a period from 171
B.C. to 165 B.C. as the period of desecration. However, as the altar
was not actually desecrated until December 168 B.C., some have
suggested the twenty-three days were actually 1150 mornings plus

1150 evenings, i.e., 2300 mornings and evenings together or approximately 3½ years. In any case, there is no excuse for the interpretation that the 2300 days are years and that this marks the year A.D. 1844 as a prophetic date as one cult has taught. An adequate explanation is found in a literal rendering of this period of time. It is, therefore, properly considered a reference to an important and heroic chapter in Israel's history which is probably the most significant event during the period in which Alexander's successors rule as history is viewed from a Biblical standpoint.

ANTIOCHUS THE FORESHADOWING OF THE FUTURE PRINCE

Many consider the desecration of the Jewish temple by Antiochus Epiphanes a foreshadowing of a still future desecration that will be fulfilled in the time of the great tribulation (cp. Daniel 9:27; Matthew 24:15-22). The references in the interpretation to "the end" and the description given of the king seem in some respects to go beyond Antiochus Epiphanes. In this case the description would apply to the ultimate world ruler previously described in the little horn of Daniel 7 and concerning whom further revelation is given in Revelation 13:1-10. If so, this is another instance of dual fulfillment of prophecy, the partial fulfillment foreshadowing the ultimate fulfillment.

PROPHECIES OF DANIEL 10, 11

Further detail and amplification of this period is found in the remarkable prophecies recorded in Daniel 10, 11. A whole chapter, Daniel 10, is devoted to the introduction in which Daniel is informed that the angelic messenger had been engaged in conflict with demonic powers for three weeks and thus delayed in bringing his message to Daniel (cp. Daniel 10:13). Daniel then records in Daniel 11:1-35 one of the most detailed prophecies to be found anywhere in the Word of God. It has been estimated that one hundred thirty-five prophecies are contained in these thirty-five verses and that all of these prophecies have already been fulfilled.

Details concerning the persecutions of Antiochus Epiphanes are given in Daniel 11:21-35. Most of the passage describes his conflict with Egypt, "the king of the south." Antiochus himself is described as "a vile person, to whom they shall not give the honour of the kingdom: but he shall come in peaceably, and obtain the kingdom by flatteries" (Daniel 11:21).

At the height of his power he was forced by the rising power of the Roman Empire to give up Egypt. Turning his attention to his own land, he began the persecution of the Jews as previously described in Daniel 8:11-14. In the process it is declared, "They shall pollute the sanctuary of strength, and shall take away the daily sacrifice, and they shall place the abomination that maketh desolate" (Daniel 11:31). The persecution of Israel is indicated in the words, "they shall fall by the sword, and by flame, by captivity, and by spoil, many days" (Daniel 11:33). This is an accurate description of the terrors of the Maccabean persecutions.

After describing the role of Antiochus the prophecy leaps to the end of the age in Daniel 11:36 to describe "the king" who "shall do according to his will." This is probably a reference to the final world ruler of whom Antiochus Epiphanes is a foreshadowing. The portion of the prophecy already fulfilled has had its graphic realization in history and stands as another testimony to the accuracy of the prophetic Word. The prophetic vision of Daniel, beginning in verse 36 of the chapter, still remains to be fulfilled in the time of great tribulation of which the trials and persecutions of Antiochus Epiphanes were an anticipation.

GRECIAN EMPIRE A PREPARATION FOR ROME

The precise fulfillment of prophecy in the Grecian Empire sets the stage for the fourth and final Gentile world power, that of Rome, which dominated the scene at the time Christ was born in Bethlehem. It is this empire which figures largely in the history of the church as well as in prophecy of things to come and constitutes the framework of prophecy related to the nations in the end of the age.

CHAPTER VIII

THE RISE AND FALL OF ROME

Long before Antiochus Epiphanes had fulfilled the prophecies of Daniel 8:23-25 and 11:21-35, the fourth empire of Daniel's prophecy was already in the making in the rising power of Rome. Roman power was manifested first in the conquering of Italy except for the far north. Rome then proceeded to challenge Carthage which at that time was the absolute master of all Northern Africa. Carthage had been founded by Phoenicians from Tyre and Sidon centuries before, but in the divided power of the Macedonian Empire it was possible for Carthage not only to conquer Northern Africa, but many islands in the Mediterranean including Sicily.

The expanding power of Rome was first manifested in conquering Sicily in 242 B.C., and Carthage had to recognize this conquest in the following year. Although Carthage continued to meet success in conquering Spain and under Hannibal made remarkable progress in extending its power into Gaul, these victories were short lived. It was not long until Rome attacked Spain, and in 202 B.C. at the battle of Zama in North Africa Carthage came under Roman control as a tributary and was eventually destroyed completely in 146 B.C.

THE RISE OF ROMAN POWER

With the beginning of the second century B.C., the western Mediterranean became a Roman lake. The Roman Empire also extended in the north to the Alps, but the next major move was to the east. One by one the nations fell, first Macedonia, then Greece, then Asia Minor. Countries conquered were often allowed to have local government for a time which later would be replaced by Roman rulers. The prophetic description of Rome as a monster with great iron teeth which trod underfoot its opponents (Daniel 7:7) was fulfilled again and again. People seized in conquered countries were sold by the hundreds and thousands, and all menial tasks were performed by these slaves. Such was the power of Rome that Antiochus Epiphanes who had previously been compelled to surrender Egypt to Rome barely survived the threat of Roman domination until his death in 164 B.C., but thereafter Syria also became Roman. Roman conquest continued with the conquering of Palestine under the Roman general Pompeius who subdued Jerusalem in 63 B.C. Thus it was that our Lord was born in Bethlehem where Joseph had gone in obedience to a Roman order for registration.

Meanwhile Roman power was being extended throughout middle Europe including what is today Great Britain, Switzerland, France, and Belgium, with all the territory south of the Rhine and the Danube in Roman hands as well as some territory to the north. The march of Rome continued until by the end of the second century A.D. most of Mesopotamia and the area up to the Euphrates River was under Roman control. Everywhere as country after country fell under the heel of Rome, thousands were carried off into slavery and extreme brutality became the order of the day.

The glory of Rome was built on the misery of its conquered peoples. Thus were the prophecies of the fourth kingdom accurately fulfilled as in Daniel 2:40, "And the fourth kingdom shall be strong as iron: forasmuch as iron breaketh in pieces and subdueth all things: and as iron that breaketh all these, shall it break in pieces and bruise." Daniel's prophecies thus far have been graphically fulfilled in history.

PROPHESIED END OF ROME NOT FULFILLED

It is essential to the understanding of prophecy relating to the fourth empire to discern, however, that the final state of this empire described in Daniel 2:42-45 has never been fulfilled. In like manner, the description of the beast as having ten horns and the further development of the emergence of a little horn by which three of the first horns were uprooted (Daniel 7:7, 8) has never been fulfilled. It is also evident that there has been no literal fulfillment of the fifth kingdom which was to succeed the fourth, namely, the kingdom described as that of the Son of Man which is everlasting in its character and which can only come when the fourth kingdom is destroyed.

In contrast to the first three beasts who according to Daniel 7:12 "had their dominion taken away: yet their lives were prolonged for a season and time," the fourth beast according to Daniel 7:11 "was slain, and his body destroyed, and given to the burning flame." The fourth beast according to these prophecies was violently and dramatically to be broken at the time of the institution of the kingdom given to the Son of Man.

THE FALL OF ROME IN HISTORY

Nothing should be clearer from the subsequent history of the Roman Empire than that there has been no fulfillment of this last stage of the Roman Empire. The growth of the Roman Empire took almost four centuries, in contrast to the rapid rise of the three preceding empires. It was also slow to disintegrate.

As the history of the Roman Empire makes clear, the western half from which its power originated was the first to go down. The details of this need only be mentioned in a general way. It began with the division of the empire into the eastern and western parts in A.D. 364 by the Emperor Valentinian I. In the fifth century, barbarians from the north such as the Goths, originating in northeastern Germany, conquered most of southwestern Europe and a large part of Spain. Much of France was also occupied and Roman troops had to leave Great Britain as early as A.D. 409.

Eventually the barbarians invaded Italy itself and, under Attila, the Huns not only conquered much of Europe, setting up a rival kingdom to the eastern half of the Roman Empire, but invaded Italy in A.D. 451. Italy was also attacked by the Vandals and Moors in A.D. 455 who invaded Italy by sea from North Africa, taking off many of the objects of wealth to Carthage, including the vessels from the temple at Jerusalem captured by Titus in A.D. 70. All of these tremendously significant movements in Europe and in North Africa tended to wrest power from the western half of the Roman Empire.

It is most important, however, to note that none of these movements correspond in the slightest to what the Scriptures anticipate as the last stage of the Roman Empire, namely, the ten nations anticipated in the ten horns of Daniel 7:7 or in the toes of the image in Daniel 2:42. Even if they had, it would not have provided any explanation of the continuance of the eastern half of the Roman Empire, which from a Biblical standpoint was probably more important, inasmuch as it related to the Holy Land.

The destruction of the Roman Empire in its eastern division

was accomplished only after the western Roman Empire had been practically destroyed. This was effected largely by the rising tide of the followers of Mohammed (A.D. 570-632) who had as their goal the conquering of the eastern aspect of the empire. After the death of Mohammed, his successor conquered Persia. Later leaders gained control over Syria, Palestine, and Egypt, extending their power over all of North Africa and into Spain. The rapid rise of the empire of the followers of Mohammed, however, lacked a cohesive force and soon various portions of it declared their independence.

The political weakness of Mohammedanism paved the way for the conquest of the Turks who had originally come from Central Asia. The Turks rapidly conquered Persia, Armenia, and Asia Minor. Although opposed by the Crusaders who attempted to conquer Palestine and free it from the Turks as well as the Saracens (followers of Mohammed), the Turks, nevertheless, although opposed by the Mongols in the thirteenth century, consolidated their power in Asia Minor. Under the Ottomans, they succeeded in conquering all the area around the Black Sea including Constantinople and Greece, as well as Northern Africa and Egypt, also extending their power into the Mesopotamia valley.

In A.D. 1453 Mohammed II conquered Constantinople, installing Moslem worship. In the process, the Roman Empire, for all practical purposes, ceased to exist with the death of the last of the Roman emperors who was killed in the battle. The decline of the Turkish Empire began shortly before the seventeenth century, but in the twentieth century they still controlled Asia Minor, the Holy Land, and the Mesopotamian valley. One of the important results of World War I was the freeing of the Holy Land from Turkish domination.

THE FUTURE DESTRUCTION OF ROME

It should be evident from this brief historical survey that nothing corresponding to the complete destruction of the image of Daniel 2 or the beast of Daniel 7 occurred in the gradual deterioration of the Roman Empire. More than 1,500 years elapsed from the beginning of the Roman Empire to its final complete destruction, A.D. 1453. A more gradual process could hardly be imagined, nor is it true that the empire was destroyed by Christians or by the power of the Gospel as some postmillenarians teach. Rather, the normal courses of war and superior military might took its toll. With its decline the Roman Empire left unfulfilled that of which prophecy had spoken, namely, the sudden destruction of the feet stage of the image of Daniel 2 and the ten-horn stage of the beast of Daniel 7:7.

Inasmuch as the first portion of the prophecy concerning the Roman Empire was so graphically fulfilled in history just as other prophecies relating to the preceding empires of Babylon, Medo-Persia, and Greece, it is most reasonable to conclude that the final stage of the Roman Empire will also have its precise fulfillment. At that future time the stage will be set for its complete destruction and the bringing in of the fifth kingdom, by the Son of Man, which will occur at the second coming of Christ.

Chapter IX

THE REVIVAL OF ROME

The Middle East the Center of World History

For careful students of history the possibility of revival of the ancient Roman Empire has long been considered plausible. The history of the world for the last 2,500 years has had its principal center of interest in Southern Europe, Northern Africa, and Western Asia. It is only in the last millennium that Northern Europe and Great Britain have become principal actors, and still more recent is the rise of power in the United States of America. While world population in Asia has always exceeded the population of the other continents, somehow they have not figured as largely in the major events of the last millennium.

The Middle East as the geographic hub of three major continents is by its location as well as its long history destined to play an important part in the future. Predictions are not wanting even from non-Christian writers that the Middle East would once again in the future be the center of world political and economic interest. In such a context the revival of the ancient Roman Empire does not seem to be as unlikely as would first appear.

Unfulfilled Prophecy Concerning the Times of Gentiles

For the Biblical expositor, however, the principal reason for believing in the revival of the ancient Roman Empire is the fact that prophecies dealing with the latter part of this empire have not been fulfilled, in contrast to the specific and detailed fulfillment which occurred in connection with the first three empires — Babylon, Medo-Persia, and Greece — and the first stage of the fourth empire of Rome. Inasmuch as fulfillment of the first portion of this prophecy concerning the times of the Gentiles has been so minute, as illustrated for instance in Daniel 11:1-35, it is logical to assume that the latter portion of the prophecy will have a similar fulfillment. It is for this reason that careful expositors, who fully honor the Word of God as an infallible record and who assume therefore that prophecies of the future are just as authentic as records of history, have concluded that there is yet to appear on the stage of world history a revival of the ancient Roman Empire in the form anticipated in unfulfilled prophecy relating to the times of the Gentiles. The anticipated revival of Rome is related, first, to its geography, second, to indications of its political character, and, third, relationship of the political revival to the last form of apostate religion which will appear before the second advent of Christ.

Geographically the ancient Roman Empire at the height of its power extended from the Euphrates River to the east across Northern Africa and Southern Europe and included a portion of Great Britain. It is obviously not necessary in contemplating such a revival to require that all of this territory should be incorporated in the revived empire in its first stage. It is reasonable to assume, however, that the revived empire would include the ancient capital, Rome, and would be located in a portion of the territory once under Roman control.

THREE FUTURE STAGES OF THE ROMAN EMPIRE

As far as it is possible to understand the prophetic foreview of this revived empire, it appears that geographically it will go through three stages. First, there will appear a confederacy of ten kingdoms within the ancient Roman Empire which will constitute the first phase of its revival. Second, there will appear a strong man who will consolidate these ten nations into a united kingdom and probably extend its borders in various directions. Third, there is the final stage of the Roman Empire when its power extends to the entire earth. The final or third stage may be in a state of partial disintegration at the time of the second coming of Christ as indicated by the very fact that there is warfare and rebellion against the Roman ruler.

THE FUTURE TEN-NATION CONFEDERACY

The Scriptural background for these conclusions is found first in Daniel 2:41-43 where the feet-and-toes stage of the image is described. The Roman Empire, previously divided into eastern and western divisions as indicated by the legs of the image, in its last stage will be represented by the feet of the image, which is divided into ten kingdoms represented by the ten toes, assuming that the toes of the image correspond to the characteristics of man. Daniel chapter 2 does not specifically state that there are ten toes.

The corresponding revelation given in Daniel 7:7, 8 is to some extent more specific and has the advantage of the divine commentary in Daniel 7:17-27 which interprets the characteristics of the fourth beast. The final stage of the Roman Empire is clearly defined in the expression, "it had ten horns" (Daniel 7:7). This is interpreted in Daniel 7:24 as ten kings, "And the ten horns out of this kingdom are ten kings that shall arise."

There have been many attempts to identify these ten nations specifically, but the Scriptures do not give sufficient information. In the study of prophecy it is well on the one hand to take seriously what the Scriptures do reveal, and on the other hand to respect the silence of Scripture. The identity of the nations has not been revealed and with this we may be content. The probability is, however, that the ten nations will include not only portions of Southern Europe and Northern Africa, but also some nations in Western Asia, inasmuch as the revived Roman Empire to some extent is viewed as including the three preceding empires which were largely Asiatic. As the Holy Land is the center of Biblical interest, it would only be natural for the empire to include this area, especially when it is taken into consideration that the Holy Land becomes a part of the area of influence of the Roman Empire as demonstrated in the covenant with Israel (Daniel 9:27) and in the later warfare described as being in this area (Ezekiel 38, 39; Daniel 11:40-45; Zechariah 14:1-3).

Although the identity of the ten nations cannot be determined, there has been much speculation concerning the materials which form the toes of the image described in Daniel 2:41-43 as being partly of iron and partly of pottery or dried clay. In the prophecy attention is called to the fact that iron does not mix with the clay and therefore that the feet of the image are the weakest portion of the entire structure. According to Daniel 2:41, 43, "the toes of the feet were part of iron, and part of clay, so the kingdom shall be partly strong, and partly broken. And whereas thou sawest iron mixed with miry clay, they shall mingle themselves with the seed of men: but they shall not cleave one to another, even as iron is not mixed with clay."

It is clear that inasmuch as the legs of iron represent the strength of the ancient Roman Empire further described in the "great iron teeth" of Daniel 7:7 the clay must in some sense be an area of political weakness. A common interpretation is that the clay is democracy in contrast to the absolute government of the Roman Empire. This, however, seems to be a superficial conclusion as the Roman Empire had during a portion of its history at least a form of democracy.

Another suggestion has been that the clay represents the people of Israel who by their religious and racial characteristics are not easily absorbed in a Gentile government and constitute a difficulty rather than a strength within the revived Roman Empire. This again, however, is conjecture and not without its difficulties.

Probably a safe interpretation is that the clay mixed with iron represents the diverse elements, whether they be racial, religious, or political, that are included in the confines of the revived Roman Empire and contribute to its ultimate downfall. This view may be supported by the fact that the Roman Empire when it does reach its world stage immediately begins to encounter difficulties that result in the final world conflict which is underway when Christ returns. Again it is difficult to be specific where the Word of God does not give us the precise interpretation of the symbolism involved in the clay. The revelation of the fourth empire in Daniel 7 does not mention this weakness.

THE COMING ROMAN PRINCE

That the ten-nation confederacy is a Roman confederacy and a revival of the Roman Empire is brought out in the second stage of the development, not mentioned in Daniel 2, but is revealed in Daniel 7:8. Here according to the Scriptures, out of the ten horns or the original ten kings who formed the first phase of the Roman confederacy another little horn appears representing a ruler who conquers three of the kings and apparently secures the subjection of the others: "I considered the horns, and, behold, there came up among them another little horn, before whom there were three of the first horns plucked up by the roots: and, behold, in this horn were eyes like the eyes of man, and a mouth speaking great things" (Daniel 7:8).

As the prophecy indicates, the little horn is described as a man in that he has eyes like the eyes of a man and a mouth speaking great things such as a man would speak. In the interpretation of the vision in Daniel 7:24 he is described in the words, "Another shall rise after them; and he shall be diverse from the first, and he shall subdue three kings." It is quite obvious that this character is a man who conquers three of the kings by war with the implication that the others submit to him. His blasphemous character is indicated in Daniel 7:25 and his destruction will occur at the second advent in Daniel 7:26, 27.

The fact that he is a Roman prince is a deduction from Daniel 9:26, 27. According to this Scripture in the chronology of Daniel's seventy-sevens of years, the Messiah was to be cut off in the interval between the sixty-ninth seven and the seventieth seven. This refers, of course, to the death of Christ. The prophecy continues, "And the people of the prince that shall come shall destroy the city and the sanctuary" (Daniel 9:26). The most sensible interpretation of this reference is that it concerns the destruction of Jerusalem under the Roman general Titus in A.D. 70 which also occurred in the interval between the sixty-ninth seven and the beginning of the seventieth seven.

The peculiar expression "the people of the prince that shall come" must be interpreted as referring to the Roman people for they were the ones who destroyed the city. It then follows that "the prince that shall come" is also Roman. Inasmuch as he is able to make the political covenant because of his political power, it follows that if he is Roman, then the empire also is Roman. This is, of course, confirmed by the very continuity of the fourth empire linking the last stage with the first stage which was obviously Roman.

As the destruction of Jerusalem came approximately forty years after the Messiah was cut off, it demonstrates clearly that the last seven years of Daniel 9:27 in which a covenant is made with the people of Israel must be subsequent to the destruction of Jerusalem. Therefore, the chronology requires a time period between the sixty-ninth seven and the seventieth seven which has extended to the present day. The prophecy of Daniel 9:27 can only be fulfilled when the Roman prince appears who will make the covenant and when he is in a postion of power to do so. It would therefore follow that the covenant will be signed only after the little horn of Daniel 7 has conquered the ten kings and has reached a place of political supremacy over them. The revival of Israel in the form of the Israeli nation in the twentieth century may be a preparation for the fulfillment of this prophecy and one of the indications that world history may be moving into its final stage.

The possibility of the formation of such a ten-nation confederacy headed by a dictator in the form of "the prince that shall come" has long been predicted by students of prophecy. Until the period following World War II, however, humanly speaking it seemed a remote possibility, although there had been forerunners of such an idea. As early as 1914, a committee was formed for the promotion of a European Federation which anticipated political, economic, and legal ties. The movement toward such a European Federation emerged after World War I in the League of Nations, an organization which failed, however, to gain sufficient support to endure.

With World War II, and its reminder to the nations of the world that war is not the best way to settle disputes, the United Nations was formed, thus embodying for the first time a world government in principle.

More significant, however, to the possibility of a revival Roman Empire was the emergence of the European Common Market. Under agreements between the principal nations of continental Europe, a gradual reduction in tariffs was achieved, allowing a free flow of goods from one country to another and unhindered transfer of available labor. The resulting prosperity of Europe under this arrangement has brought forth many predictions of an ultimate United States of Europe which could eventually include not only Europe itself, but the Mediterranean world. Whether the Common Market in its present form is prophetically significant or not, it silences critics of the idea of a revived Roman Empire who had previously claimed that such a union was impossible because of the diverse political, economic, and racial factors which had separated the European nations for centuries. With the economic feasibility of such a union already demonstrated, it is a relatively short step to a common banking system and political ties which would bind various nations together while allowing them freedom on a larger scale than that afforded by the individual states of the United States of America.

How the ten-nation confederacy will arise is too early to predict. Many prophecies anticipate that nations will find themselves in distress and perplexity at the end of the age (cp. Luke 21:25, 26). The beast of Revelation 13:1 is said to come up out of the sea, a figure often used of the nations of the world as in Isaiah's prophecy in Isaiah 17:12, 13, where the rushing of the nations is compared to the rushing of mighty waters. The empire will be the child of its times, a result of political, economic, and military pressures.

THE WORLD EMPIRE OF ROME

The final state of the revived Roman Empire politically is described as being an empire which embraces the entire world. This third stage in development is brought out specifically in Daniel 7:23 where the fourth beast is predicted to "devour the whole earth, and shall tread it down, and break it in pieces." This picture of world-wide dominion is confirmed by the companion prophecy found in Revelation 13. Here it is specifically said of the beast that "power was given him over all kindreds, and tongues, and nations. And all that dwell upon the earth shall worship him" (Revelation 13:7, 8).

This final stage where the Roman Empire becomes a world empire is most naturally understood to coincide with the beginning of the great tribulation, a term referring to the last three and one-half years leading up to the second advent of Christ. The Scriptures do not directly explain how the Roman Empire becomes a world empire, but a plausible explanation may be found in the battle of Gog and Magog described in Ezekiel 38, 39.

Here is predicted the destruction of the northern kingdom which apparently challenged the Roman Empire by attacking Israel. With the northern kingdom destroyed there is no major political force standing in the way of the Roman Empire, and the world empire is achieved by proclamation. The apparent invincibility of the Roman ruler, supported as he is by Satanic power, is intimated in the question of Revelation 13:4, "Who is like unto the beast? who is able to make war with him?"

The fact that this world empire begins at the mid-point in Daniel's last seven years leading up to the second advent is supported by Revelation 13:5 where it states that "power was given unto him to continue forty and two months." Inasmuch as the power of this character is broken by the second advent of Christ, it fixes the beginning of his world empire as exactly forty-two months prior to the second advent.

The political character of this world empire is such, however, that it is not firmly established. This paves the way for rebellion of major sections of the world described as leading up to the battle of the great day of God almighty, a world conflict which is brought to an abrupt close by the second coming of Christ and destruction of the contending armies (Revelation 19:11-21).

THE WORLD RELIGION OF ROME

The geographic and political characteristics of the revived Roman Empire form the background for the religious character of the revival of Rome. According to prophetic Scriptures which describe the religious character of the period preceding the second advent of Christ, two major phases can be observed. The first is the apostate church described under the symbolism of the wicked woman of Revelation 17. The present theological apostasy which has engulfed so large a segment of the professing church will in that day, after the true church has been raptured, become a part of the world church movement and apparently will be successful in combining all the unsaved remnant of the professing church left behind at the rapture into a gigantic ecclesiastical organization of tremendous wealth, prestige, and political importance.

The Apostle John was introduced to this ecclesiastical organization symbolized by the woman in Revelation 17. He was invited by the angel, "Come hither; I will shew unto thee the judgment of the great whore that sitteth upon many waters: With whom the kings of the earth have committed fornication, and the inhabitants of the earth have been made drunk with the wine of her fornication" (Revelation 17:1, 2). John thus carried by the Spirit into the wilderness according to Revelation 17:3 beheld the woman who is described as sitting "upon a scarlet coloured beast, full of names of blasphemy, having seven heads and ten horns" (Revelation 17:3).

The beast thus described as blasphemous is unquestionably the same as that in Revelation 13:1 which has seven heads and ten horns and "the name of blasphemy." This beast is the revived Roman Empire in its political character as it will appear in the end of the age. The fact that the woman rides the beast indicates symbolically that the political and religious character of the Roman Empire work closely together with the woman in a dominant position and the beast as supporting the woman.

The traditional interpretation of this passage has identified the woman with the Roman Catholic Church. It should be observed, however, that this is a picture which is prophetically future and describes not the Roman church alone, but all Christendom combined under the Roman banner in that future day. It is most natural to assume that there would be an alliance between the Roman church, including all Christendom, and the revived Roman Empire.

The description of the woman in Revelation 17:4 is in keeping with the religious trappings of ceremonial Romanism where the purple and the scarlet color accompanied by gold, precious stones, and pearls are all too common. As this alliance of the woman with the political power constitutes spiritual fornication, she is described as guilty of this abomination.

Most significant is the title written on her forehead described as a mystery, namely, BABYLON THE GREAT, THE MOTHER OF HARLOTS AND ABOMINATIONS OF THE EARTH. The religious impact of ancient Babylon upon subsequent religions, including Romanism, is all too evident to students of the history of religion. It was in Babylon that the idolatrous worship of nature first was developed into an extensive religious system which has been traced to Nimrod and his queen Semiramis (Genesis 10:8-10). From this stemmed many of the false religions which swept the ancient world including the worship of Baal and the custom of worshiping the queen of heaven and her supposedly miraculously born son (cp. Jeremiah 7:18; 44:17-25). In ancient religions the queen of heaven and her worship is incorporated in the religions of the Greeks as Aphrodite, among the Romans as Venus, in Egypt as Isis, as Diana in Ephesus, and as Astarte in Syria.

From the standpoint of the history of Christianity, it is important to trace the influence of Babylon upon Rome especially. The cult of the woman and the child was expelled by the Medes and the Persians under Cyrus from Babylon in 539 B.C. as it was considered detrimental to the religious convictions of the Medo-Persians. The priests and priestesses of the cult, therefore, fled to Pergamos in Asia Minor where they were welcomed. Later the center of their religion was transferred by Julius Caesar to Rome in an attempt to combine their false religion with his dictatorship and introduce a religious element into his government. It was by these steps that Babylon became identified with Rome religiously and justifies the term "mystery" meaning that it should be understood in its religious rather than its historical character. With the establishment of the western branch of the Roman church in Rome, the pagan influences of the cult which originated in Babylon soon became manifested in various rites and ceremonies of the Roman Church.

That which has been historically true will reach its maximum in the future period under the revived Roman Empire. The world church of that day, almost entirely devoid of any true Christian or Biblical elements, will be the final form of apostate Christendom. As such, it will persecute any who in that day in defiance of the church follow true faith in the Lord Jesus Christ. The persecutions of Christians in the past under the power and authority of the church will be eclipsed by this future world church described as this wicked woman "drunken with the blood of the saints, and with the blood of the martyrs of Jesus."

The political power in alliance with the religious power is described in Revelation 17:8-14 in a passage which has confounded expositors, but concerning which the main elements are clear. The beast representing the political power is described as that which "was, and is not; and shall ascend out of the bottomless pit, and go into perdition" (Revelation 17:8). Later in the same verse the beast is described as "the beast that was, and is not, and yet is" [better translated, "that was, and is not, and shall be"] (Revelation 17:8). The beast is further described by the declaration of Revelation 17:9 that "The seven heads are seven mountains, on which the woman sitteth." The explanation continues in Revelation 17:10, "And there are seven kings."

Much has been written in the debate as to whether the seven mountains here describe the city of Rome often known as the city of seven hills. Many have concluded that this passage is declaring that the seat of authority for both the political and the ecclesiastical aspects of the revived Roman Empire will be the city of Rome. The passage is, however, by no means clearly a reference to the city of Rome, as the seven kings of verse 10 seem to be an exposition of what is meant by both the seven heads and the seven mountains. If the kings are the mountains and the heads, then they do not refer to the geographic situation of the city of Rome. Some nevertheless feel that the description is such that it includes both ideas.

The seven heads seem to refer to successive stages of the Roman Empire as personified in its principal rulers. In describing the seven kings in Revelation 17:10, the passage continues, "Five are fallen, and one is, and the other is not yet come; and when he cometh, he must continue a short space." This is followed by the statement in Revelation 17:11, "And the beast that was, and is not, even he is the eighth, and is of the seven, and goeth into perdition." If the eighth beast is a person heading up a political government such as the revived Roman Empire, it would naturally follow that the seven heads which precede him are also men following in chronological order and symbolizing the principal steps in the history of the ancient Roman Empire.

It has been suggested that these five heads may refer to ancient Roman rulers who had an untimely end, but who in life were worshiped as gods. Among these could be Julius Caesar, Tiberius, Caligula, Claudius, and Nero. Some have suggested that the expression "the one is" of Revelation 17:10 refers to Domitian, the last of the Caesars, and living at the time the Apostle John wrote this book. He was to be followed by a seventh who would be a forerunner to the eighth and final ruler who will appear in the period of the revived Roman Empire prior to the second advent of Christ.

In contrast to the seven kings, which seems to refer to chronological succession of rulers, are the ten kings represented by the ten horns who reign at the same time as the eighth beast. These are described as minor rulers supporting the rule of the one who is over them. In the end they fight God and perish in the final battle of Revelation 19 (Revelation 17:13, 14; 19:17-21).

In Revelation 17:15 the narrative returns to consideration of the wicked woman who is described as sitting upon many waters in Revelation 17:1 which is here interpreted as "peoples, and multitudes, and nations, and tongues." This introduces, however, the dramatic end of the world church. According to Revelation 17:16, 17, "And the ten horns which thou sawest upon the beast, these shall hate the whore, and shall make her desolate and naked, and shall eat her flesh, and burn her with fire. For God hath put in their hearts to fulfil his will, and to agree, and give their kingdom unto the beast, until the words of God shall be fulfilled." Probably at the beginning of the last three and a half years (the great tribulation preceding the second coming of Christ), the super-church which up to this time has worked with the political powers to gain control over the entire world is then suddenly destroyed. The world church has served its purpose. It has helped to place the entire world in the hands of the world political ruler. Its wealth, prestige, and organization are now at his disposal and he uses them to support his world power.

THE WORSHIP OF THE WORLD RULER

The last stage religiously of the times of the Gentiles will feature the worship of the world ruler. Concerning this, many Scriptures make a contribution. In Daniel 11:36-45 a description is given of the last days preceding the second advent of Christ. In this section described as "the time of the end" (Daniel 11:35), a king will appear who is described as an absolute monarch. Expositors have not been entirely agreed as to the particular identity of this king. Some have regarded him as a ruler in the Holy Land, possibly of Jewish background. A more likely interpretation, however, is that this king is none other than the prince that shall come of Daniel 9:26 and the same as the little horn of Daniel 7:3, who at the beginning of the great tribulation will take the role of world ruler.

The description of the king reveals him as an absolute ruler. According to Daniel 11:36, "The king shall do according to his will; and he shall exalt himself, and magnify himself above every god, and shall speak marvellous things against the God of gods, and shall prosper till the indignation be accomplished: for that that is determined shall be done." The fact that he is described as an absolute ruler and that none is greater than he would seem to identity him clearly as the world ruler. He is also described as magnifying himself above God and taking the place of God which is also an accurate description of this world ruler during the time of the great tribulation. It would therefore seem unlikely that he would be a subordinate ruler who would not be in a position of power to accomplish either absolute political government or to demand that people would recognize him as God.

Much has been written on Daniel 11:37, 38 where the statement is made concerning him, "Neither shall he regard the God of his fathers, nor the desire of women, nor regard any god: for he shall magnify himself above all. But in his estate shall he honour the God of forces: and a god whom his fathers knew not shall he honour with gold, and silver, and with precious stones, and pleasant things."

The expression that he shall not regard "the God of his fathers" has been interpreted by some as indicating a Jewish background. The characteristic Hebrew, however, for this expression in the entire Old Testament is the "Jehovah of his fathers" rather than the "Elohim of his fathers" as it is here. The term *Jehovah* is used only of the God of Israel, but the term *Elohim* is used both of the God of Israel and of heathen gods, and it also lends itself to translation as a term which is plural. The better translation is, "He shall not regard the gods of his fathers." This means that he will disregard whatever religion his forefathers followed. He also disregards "the desire of women" referring to the desire of women to be the mother of the Messiah. He puts aside the Messianic hope of a Saviour and Deliverer for Israel. Then to make it plain Daniel continues to record the message of the angel that this character will not regard any god, but shall consider himself above all deities. The world ruler who heads the revived Roman Empire will require the entire world to worship him.

In Daniel 11:38 he is described as worshiping "the God of forces." This is better understood as "the God of fortresses" or symbolically the worship of the power of military might. This indicates that this ruler, on the one hand, requires all to worship him as God, and, on the other hand, has respect only for military might. By this means he puts aside any recognition of the true God, any consideration of the supernatural sovereignty of God, and relying on satanic power attributes to himself all the prerogative of both God and supreme ruler of the entire world.

The description thus given in Daniel 11 is supported by New Testament additional revelation. According to II Thessalonians 2: 3, 4 in the future day of the Lord there will appear a lawless one or "man of sin" who will be "the son of perdition; Who opposeth and exalteth himself above all that is called God, or that is worshiped; so that he as God sitteth in the temple of God, shewing himself that he is God." This passage prophesies that the world ruler who attributes to himself the prerogatives of deity, having desecrated the temple set aside for Jewish worship under the covenant of Daniel 9:27, probably through the form of an idol will demand that people worship him. The universal worship of the world ruler is stated explicitly in Revelation 13:8, "And all that dwell upon the earth shall worship him."

THE FUTURE WORLD RELIGIOUS LEADER

The future world ruler is supported in his efforts to gain the worship of the entire world by the second beast of Revelation 13:

11-18 who originated as the supreme religious head of the world church and when this was destroyed is perpetuated in power as a supporting personage in the efforts of the beast to gain the worship of the entire world.

According to Revelation 13:11-15 he has remarkable powers attributed to Satan. He causes fire to come down from heaven and performs other miracles including an apparent ability to simulate life, or breath, in the idol of the world ruler to deceive men into thinking that the image has life. The expression in Revelation 13: 15, "And he had power to give life unto the image of the beast," is better translated, "And he hath power to give breath unto the image of the beast." The appeal to universal recognition of the beast as God, supported as he is by the second beast or the false prophet, is enforced by the edict that all shall be put to death who do not worship the image. Economic pressure is also put upon the entire world in that all receive the mark of the beast, namely, some token indicating that they are a worshiper of the beast as an identifying symbol to permit them to buy and sell.

The satanic power of this period exceeds that of any previous time and men are put in complete bondage to the worship of the beast except for those who in that day, in spite of the difficulties and even martyrdom, do come to Christ in salvation and resist the pressures to worship the world ruler. In this way the supreme power of the final world ruler and the empire which he creates is used by Satan to enslave the souls of men and bring upon the world deception of a religious character which will blind the eyes of the great majority of the world to the true facts concerning Jesus Christ.

The extreme deceptive character of this total program centering as it does in the world ruler is pictured graphically in II Thessalonians 2:8-12 where he is described as working with satanic power, deceiving those who would not receive the love of the truth. The Scriptures solemnly conclude, "And for this cause God shall send them strong delusion, that they should believe a lie: That they all might be damned who believed not the truth, but had pleasure in unrighteousness" (II Thessalonians 2:11, 12).

When the great opportunity in this present age of grace of receiving Christ as Saviour, accompanied as it is by the convicting work of the Spirit, is spurned it leads into this period during which satanic deception will reach new heights and the great mass of the world's population will blindly follow their leader to their doom. The political and spiritual warfare attributed to the beast in Daniel 7:21, 25 will have its literal fulfillment.

These great prophecies predicting the rise of the ten-nation confederacy headed by a Roman ruler who ultimately will gain control over this entire world are the major prophetic program of the period between the rapture and Christ's second coming to the earth. Into this context fit many other prophetic Scriptures such as the great battle of Ezekiel 38 and 39 and the final conflict in which the king of the south, kings of the east, and the king of the north are engaged in deadly struggle with the head of the Roman Empire at the very time that Christ returns in power and glory. Because of its strategic importance in the sequence of the events of the end time, the great battle of Ezekiel 38 and 39 will next be considered.

CHAPTER X

THE KING OF THE NORTH:
THE NORTHERN CONFEDERACY

In the warfare that characterizes the end of the age, the Scriptures predict a great world conflict which eventually involves all the nations of the earth. In the Scriptures that portray these stirring events, three major crises may be observed. First, a crisis in the Mediterranean area leads to the formation of the revived Roman Empire composed of a ten-nation confederacy. This is occasioned by the rise of the Roman "prince that shall come" (Daniel 9:26) who subdues three of the kings and secures the submission of the seven remaining rulers. His successful conquest of these ten kingdoms, outlined in Daniel 7:23-26, makes the Roman ruler supreme in his control of this revived form of the ancient Roman Empire.

The second phase of the struggle is recorded in Ezekiel 38 and 39. The great battle there described may be the forerunner of the expansion of the Roman Empire from domination of the Mediterranean area to the role of a world empire embracing all nations of the earth (cp. Daniel 7:23; Revelation 13:7, 8). The third phase of the world struggle is at the end of the great tribulation period just before the second coming of Christ, when major sections of the world rebel against the Roman ruler as their leader. A gigantic world war ensues with the Holy Land as its focal point (Daniel 11:40-45; Revelation 16:12-16).

Expositors are by no means agreed as to the precise details of these events or their place in the sequence. It is possible, however, to be sure about such facts as the geographic origination of military forces which converge upon the Holy Land, described as coming from the north, the east, and the south. All of these forces seem to be in opposition to the Roman ruler who may be called the king of the west, although the Scriptures never assign him this title.

The prophet Daniel in his summary of the world struggle which ends the age declares: "And at the time of the end shall the king of the south push at him: and the king of the north shall come against him like a whirlwind, with chariots, and with horsemen, and with many ships; and he shall enter into the countries, and shall overflow and pass over" (Daniel 11:40). The reference to the king of the north in this passages raises the question concerning Russia and other countries to the north of the Holy Land which figure in this final world struggle. A major contribution to this subject is found in the prophecies of Ezekiel concerning a great invastion of the Holy Land from the north in the end time.

THE RISE OF RUSSIA IN THE TWENTIETH CENTURY

One of the significant aspects of modern life which all have observed in the last quarter of a century is the remarkable rise of Russia to a place of world prominence. At the close of World War II, Russia as a nation was crushed, its manpower destroyed, its cities in ruin. It was a nation that would have been utterly defeated if it had not been for American help. Since World War II, Russia has recovered and has become a prominent nation with world-wide influence which few nations have ever achieved. Today, Russia is one of the principal competitors of the United States of America for world fame and world leadership. Through the instrument of communism and nations which share Russia's convictions on communism, almost half of the world's population is in some sense or other in the Russian orbit. Such a phenomenal rise of a nation so godless and blasphemous must have some prophetic significance.

DOES THE BIBLE CONTAIN PROPHECY ABOUT RUSSIA?

In the study of prophecy, care must be taken not to create doctrine without proper Scriptural support. Many aspects of prophecy in the Bible may be understood only partially. There are great themes of prophecy, however, which do not rest on isolated texts, but upon extended portions of the Word of God. As these Scriptures are studied, some settled conclusions can be reached regarding the main movements of God in the prophetic future.

The word *Russia* is not found in the English Bible, and at first glance it would seem that there is nothing in the Bible that would give any information about Russia. A more careful investigation, however, reveals that there are two long chapters in the Bible which seem to concern themselves with the nation Russia, with certain other portions of Scripture which cast added light upon the subject. Not only has the Bible something to say about Russia, but what it reveals is of tremendous significance in God's prophetic program.

In Ezekiel 38 and 39, a description is given of a war between Israel and a nation which many have identified as Russia. The two chapters mentioned describe the invasion of the land of Israel by the armies of Russia and the nations that are associated with her. The Scriptures are plain that this is a military invasion and reveal many details about the situation existing at the time of that invasion. The dramatic outcome of the battle is the utter destruction of the' army that invades the land of Israel. Written by the prophet Ezekiel, who himself was in exile from the land of Israel, this prophecy was inspired by the Spirit of God. A natural question can be raised, however, inasmuch as this was written some twenty-five hundred years ago, whether this passage has already been fulfilled.

The land of Israel has been the scene of many wars, and invasions have come from various parts of the world, north, east, and south. Many times the march of soldier's feet has been heard crossing the little nation of Israel. The Bible records some of these wars and some of them have occurred since the canon of Scripture was closed. It would be difficult to examine the details of all these wars; however, if one did, he would find that none of them correspond to this prophecy. There never has been a war with Israel which fulfills the prophecies of Ezekiel 38 and 39. If one believes that the Bible is the Word of God and that it is infallible and must be fulfilled, the only logical conclusion is that this portion of Scripture, like many others, is still due a future fulfillment.

THE IDENTIFICATION OF RUSSIA

In beginning the study of this chapter, it is necessary to establish beyond any question that this passage deals with the nation Russia, inasmuch as the term itself does not occur. There are a number of important factors which lead to the conclusion that the only nation which could possibly fulfill the specifications of these two chapters is the nation Russia. In the study of this chapter the American Standard Version will be used because of its clarification of certain difficult passages.

First of all, it is important to note the geographic description which is given. The terms "king of the north" and "king of the south" were used in Daniel 11:5-35 to describe the rulers to the north and south of Palestine who engaged in constant warfare in the second and third centuries B.C. This is now fulfilled prophecy. The king of the north and king of the south of Daniel 11:40-45, however, are future rulers involved in warfare in the end time. This is still unfulfilled prophecy. Ezekiel 38 and 39 fit into this future picture.

According to Ezekiel, the invading armies come to the land of Israel from "the uttermost part of the north" or as we would put it from the far north. In the Authorized Version the expression is translated merely "from the north," but in the more literal translation of the Hebrew found in the American Standard Version it is rendered, "the uttermost parts of the north," i.e., the extreme north. The important point is that it designates not merely the direction from which the army attacks Israel, but specifies the geographic origination of the army from a territory located in the far north. The house of Togarmah, one of the nations that is associated with Russia in this invasion, also comes from "the uttermost parts of the north" (Ezekiel 38:6).

A similar statement concerning the invader is made in verse 15, "Thou shalt come from thy place out of the uttermost parts of the north, thou, and many peoples with thee, all of them riding upon horses, a great company and a mighty army" (ASV). Again in Ezekiel 39:2, God says to them, "I will turn thee about, and will lead thee on, and will cause thee to come up from the uttermost parts of the north; and I will bring thee upon the mountains of Israel" (ASV). Three times in these chapters this army is stated to come from the extreme north.

If one takes any map of the world and draws a line north of the land of Israel he will inevitably come to the nation Russia. As soon as the line is drawn to the far north beyond Asia Minor and the Black Sea it is in Russia and continues to be in Russia for many hundreds of miles all the way to the Arctic Circle. Russia today spreads east and west some 6,000 miles, and one cannot escape Russia if he goes north of the Holy Land. On the basis of geography alone, it seems quite clear that the only nation which could possibly be referred to as coming from the far north would be the nation Russia. The suggestion that the nation is ancient Assyria revived is rendered improbable by the geographic description.

As the Scriptures are further examined, not only geographic data but also some confirming linguistic evidence is discovered. In the opening portion of Ezekiel 38, in verses 1 through 6, some names are mentioned which identify the invaders. This portion indicates that the Word of the Lord came to Ezekiel saying,

> Son of man, set thy face toward Gog, of the land of Magog, the prince of Rosh, Meshech, and Tubal, and prophesy against him, and say, Thus saith the Lord Jehovah: Behold, I am against thee, O Gog, prince of Rosh, Meshech, and Tubal: and I will turn thee about, and put hooks into thy jaws, and I will bring thee forth, and all thine army, horses and horsemen, all of them clothed in full armor, a great company with buckler and shield, all of them handling swords: Persia, Cush and Put with them, all of them with shield and helmet; Gomer, and all his hordes; the house of Togarmah in the uttermost parts of the north, and all his hordes; even many peoples with thee (ASV).

Most of the terms in this portion of Scripture are quite strange to us and do not immediately connote anything relating to Russia. Certain facts are discovered as the passage is examined more particularly. This portion of Scripture is a message from God delivered by the prophet Ezekiel, directed to a person whose name is Gog, who is described as of the land of Magog and apparently the ruler of this land. The term "Magog" is mentioned in Genesis 10:2. There we learn that Magog was the second son of Japheth, the son of Noah.

Magog is best identified with the Scythians, a people descended from Magog. The ancient historian Josephus makes that identification and we have no reason to question it. The Scythians apparently lived immediately to the north of what was later to be the land of Israel, then some of them emigrated north, going all the way to the Arctic Circle. In other words, their posterity was scattered precisely over the geographical area that today is called Russia.

In Ezekiel 38 Gog is described as "the prince of Rosh" (ASV). The Authorized Version expresses it as the "chief prince." The translation, "the prince of Rosh," is a more literal rendering of the Hebrew. "Rosh" may be the root of the modern term, Russia. In the study of how ancient words come into modern language, it is quite common for the consonants to remain the same and the vowels to be changed. In the word "Rosh," if the vowel "o" is changed to "u" it becomes the root of the modern word, Russia, with the suffix added. In other words, the word itself seems to be an early form of the word from which the modern word, Russia, comes. Genesius, the famous lexicographer, gives the assurance that this is a proper identification, that is, that Rosh is an early form of the word from which we get Russia.

The two terms, "Meshech" and "Tubal," also correspond to some prominent words in Russia. The term "Meshech" is similar to the modern name Moscow, and "Tubal," obviously, is similar to the name of one of the prominent Asiatic provinces of Russia, the province of Tobolsk. When this evidence is put together, it points to the conclusion that these terms are early references to portions of Russia, and therefore, the geographic argument is reinforced by the linguistic argument and supports the idea that this invading force comes from Russia.

As the prophecy is examined further it becomes obvious that the invaders utterly disregard God, because any nation that attacks the nation of Israel by so much is disregarding the Word of God. The godlessness of the invading army attacking Israel also points the finger to the nation Russia. On the basis of these three arguments, the geographic argument, the linguistic argument, and what might be called the theological argument, it may be concluded that the reference is to the nation Russia. In fact, there is no other reasonable alternative. Russia is today the only nation which seems to fit the picture.

A number of nations are associated with Russia in the invasion, but not too much is known about them. Persia, of course, is in that general area. Cush is another name for Ethiopia, which poses a problem because today Ethiopia is to the south. The term *Cush* may have been applied to other geographic areas, including that to the north of the land of Israel. The term, "Put," is a difficult expression about which little is known. In verse 6 the term, "Gomer," is identified by most as referring to the ancient Cimmerians, a portion of whom lived in what today is called southern or western Germany. Togarmah is commonly recognized as referring to the Armenians, who at one time lived immediately north of the land of Israel, and they, too, to some extent emigrated to the north. The nations which accompany Russia, for the most part, fit properly into the picture of assisting Russia in this invasion of the land of Israel.

THE PREDICTED INVASION OF ISRAEL

The actual invasion is described in Ezekiel 38:8-12. Some of the distinctive facts mentioned about the particular situation which will exist when this war begins are of utmost significance in the light of the world situation today. In this passage the "thou" refers throughout to Russia or to Gog. The term "they" is used to refer to Israel. Beginning in verse 8 and continuing through verse 16, the passage reads as follows:

> After many days thou shalt be visited: in the latter years thou shalt come into the land that is brought back from the sword, that is gathered out of many peoples, upon the mountains of Israel, which have been a continual waste; but it is brought forth out of the peoples, and they shall dwell securely, all of them. And thou shalt ascend, thou shalt come like a storm, thou shalt be like a cloud to cover the land, thou, and all thy hordes, and many peoples with thee.
>
> Thus saith the Lord Jehovah: It shall come to pass in that day, that things shall come into thy mind, and thou shalt devise an evil device: and thou shalt say, I will go up to the land of unwalled villages; I will go to them that are at rest, that dwell securely, all of them dwelling without walls, and having neither bars nor gates; to take the spoil and to take the prey; to turn thy hand against the waste places that are now inhabited, and against the people that are gathered out of the nations, that have gotten cattle and goods, that dwell in the middle of the earth. Sheba, and Dedan, and the merchants of Tarshish, with all the young lions thereof, shall say unto thee, Art thou come to take the spoil? hast thou assembled thy company to take the prey? to carry away silver and gold, to take away cattle and goods, to take great spoil?
>
> Therefore, son of man, prophesy, and say unto Gog, Thus saith the Lord Jehovah: In that day when my people Israel dwelleth securely, shalt thou not know it? And thou shalt come from thy place out of the uttermost parts of the north, thou, and many peoples with thee, all of them riding upon horses, a great company and a mighty army; and thou shalt come up against my people Israel, as a cloud to cover the land: it shall come to pass in the latter days, that I will bring thee against my land, that the nations may know me, when I shall be sanctified in thee, O Gog, before their eyes (ASV).

INVASION AFTER ISRAEL'S REGATHERING

Some highly significant facts are given in the above passage concerning the precise situation existing when the invasion takes place. There are a number of references to the fact that the people of Israel are back in their ancient land. This of course is of tremendous importance because it is only in our generation that the people of Israel have gone back to their ancient land. In A.D. 70, Titus, the Roman general, conquered Jerusalem, utterly destroyed it, and killed up to a million of the Jews. Roman soldiers later systematically went throughout the entire land of Israel destroying every building, sawing down or uprooting every tree, and doing everything they could to make the land totally uninhabitable. The result was that the land of Israel lay in waste for several generations. The children of Israel from that day to this have been scattered over the face of the earth.

At the close of World War II the children of Israel began to return to their ancient land in large numbers. Some had gone earlier, but they were few in number. They built up their strength and numbers until finally they were recognized as a nation in May, 1948. At that time one million Jews were back in their ancient land, the largest return since the days of the Exodus. In the years since, their number has doubled, and today there are two million Israelites under their own flag, speaking the Hebrew language, and reviving and restoring their ancient land to a scene of fertility, wealth, and prosperity. These facts are tremendously significant, for the return of Israel has occurred in our generation.

Ezekiel's prophecy obviously could not have been fulfilled prior to 1945, for the nation Israel was not regathered to their ancient land. Until our generation, Israel's situation did not correspond to that which is described in Ezekiel's passage. Ezekiel's prophecy of twenty-five hundred years ago seems to have anticipated the return of Israel to their ancient land as a prelude to the climax of this present age.

INVASION AFTER REBUILDING OF CITIES

Another important aspect of the prophecy is found in verse eleven where it states that the people of Israel will be dwelling "securely, all of them dwelling without walls, and having neither bars nor gates." It was customary in ancient times, whenever a city prospered, to build a wall around it. One can go to ancient lands and see the ruins of walls around most important cities. They would, at least, have a fortress with a wall around it to which they could retire if the houses themselves were scattered and a wall about the houses was impracticable. In other words, it was customary to build walls about cities. In our modern day, this custom has been discontinued for the obvious reason that a wall is no protection against modern warfare.

If one goes to Israel today, though one can see many fabulous cities being built and marvelous developments taking place, one will not find a single new city with a wall built around it. They are cities without walls. How did Ezekiel know that at a future time the war situation would be such that cities would be built without walls? Of course, the answer is a simple one. He was guided by the inspiration of God, and it was not a matter of his own wisdom. But in this scene he is describing a modern situation, something that could not and would not be true back in the days of old, before Christ. This detail is very important because unwalled villages point to Israel's situation today.

INVASION AT A TIME OF ISRAEL'S PROSPERITY

A third feature may also be observed. This portion of Scripture is explicit that one of the reasons why Russia wants to conquer the land of Israel is that it had become a land of great wealth. Russia comes to take a prey, to take silver and gold, and the wealth that has been accumulated (cp. Ezekiel 38:12, 13). Until our generation, the geographic area of the land of Israel was anything but something to be prized. It did not have any wealth; it was a land that was strewn with stones; a land that was backward as far as civilization is concerned. Many of the areas that at one time were fruitful in Bible times were unused prior to Israel's reclamation. The land was eroded and useless as far as agriculture is concerned.

Since the Israelites have gone back to their ancient land, they have done fabulous things. They have taken rocky fields, gathered the stones in piles along the edge, and cultivated and irrigated the ground and made it to bring forth abundantly. They have reclaimed swamps where mosquitoes and malaria made civilization impossible before. In fact, the first people that tried to do something about it lost their lives because of the unhealthy situation. These former swamps are today one of the richest areas of farm land in the entire world. It is almost incredible what has occurred there since 1948. They have spent money, they have put forth extreme effort, and from one end of Israel to the other tremendous progress is in evidence. The result is today that Israel is beginning once again to be a nation that has wealth. A great deal is being exported to other countries, and money is beginning to flow back to the little nation of Israel.

In addition to agricultural wealth, there are some factors that Ezekiel did not know which we know today. One factor is that to the east of the land of Israel are tremendous oil reserves. One of the largest and richest oil fields in the entire world is in the Middle East. It is outside the present geographic area of Israel, but the nation that wants to control that oil land must control the nation Israel. It is obvious that the tremendous oil reserves of the Middle East are one of the prizes that Russia wants to secure.

Another aspect of wealth which has come to light in modern times is the chemical value of the Dead Sea area, where water has evaporated for centuries, leaving its mineral deposit. Israel has established a plant at the south end of the Dead Sea and is reclaiming the chemicals. Millions of dollars of those chemicals are being shipped, and they have just begun to tap this wealth. Ezekiel anticipated the time when the land of Israel would be fabulously wealthy.

MILITARY IMPORTANCE OF ISRAEL

In addition to all these factors, it is obvious that the geographic location of the Middle East, being as it is a hub between three major continents — Europe, Asia, and Africa — is of tremendous strategic importance to any nation that wants to dominate the world. The geographic significance of the Middle East alone would be worth a real effort on the part of Russia to have this portion of the world under its control. Again Ezekiel anticipates today's situation.

THE DESTRUCTION OF THE INVADING ARMY

When the Russian army comes down upon this land they are met with complete and utter destruction. Strange to say, as we examine the Scriptures, we do not find them being destroyed by an opposing army, but rather it seems to be by divine intervention. Somehow God by His own power destroys the army. In Ezekiel 38:19, 20 a description is given of earthquakes, mountains falling, and other disturbances which hinder their progress.

Then God declares:

> And I will call for a sword against him unto all my mountains, saith the Lord Jehovah: every man's sword shall be against his brother. And with pestilence and with blood will I enter into judgment with him; and I will rain upon him, and upon his hordes, and upon the many

peoples that are with him, an overflowing shower, and great hailstones, fire, and brimstone. And I will magnify myself, and sanctify myself, and I will make myself known in the eyes of many nations; and they shall know that I am Jehovah (Ezekiel 38:21-23, asv).

The army's destruction is portrayed in Ezekiel 39:4 ff. God declares: "Thou shalt fall upon the mountains of Israel, thou, and all thy hordes, and the peoples that are with thee: I will give thee unto the ravenous birds of every sort, and to the beasts of the field to be devoured." In other words, the army is completely destroyed, and the means used are earthquakes, hailstones, fire and brimstone. It seems also that parts of the army begin to fight each other, so that every man's sword is against his brother.

Some natural questions are raised about this. Some have suggested that the description of hailstones, fire and brimstone might be Ezekiel's way of describing modern warfare, such as atomic warfare. There is a possibility that Ezekiel was using terms that he knew to describe a future situation for which he did not have a vocabulary. The language of Scripture indicates, however, that the victory over this invading horde is something that God does. It is God, Himself, who is destroying the army.

In any case, regardless of the means, the army is completely destroyed and chapter 39 goes on to describe the aftermath. For months thereafter they have the awful task of burying the dead. For a long period after that men are given full-time employment as additional bodies are discovered, and the process of burial continues. Attention is also directed to the debris of the battle. It is used as kindling wood for some seven years. The general character of this battle and its outcome seems to be quite clear, even though we may have some questions and problems about the details.

Time of the Invasion

One of the principal questions one could ask about this battle is, When is the battle going to occur? It has not occurred in the past. What indication do we have in this portion of Scripture that the battle will occur at a specific time? Unfortunately, varying opinions have been offered by capable Bible scholars on this point, and there has been considerable disagreement. Some have felt that the battle will take place before the rapture, others believe it will take place in connection with the battle of Armageddon, or the battle of the Great Day of God Almighty, at the end of the great

tribulation. Some place it at the beginning of the millennium, as an
act of rebellion against Christ. Some find it at the end of the millennium, for there is a reference to Gog and Magog in Revelation 20.
Others put it in the earlier part of Daniel's seventieth week, just
before the great tribulation.

It will not be possible to consider all these views in detail,
but there are some hints that provide a good clue as to when this
battle will take place. One of the hints given is that the battle takes
place at a time when Israel has been regathered into their ancient
land, and are dwelling securely and at rest. There are not too many
times when Israel is at rest in God's prophetic program. They have
been scattered and persecuted over the face of the earth, and not
even in the future will Israel have many periods of rest.

Certainly Israel is not at rest today. Israel is an armed camp,
living under a truce with their Arab neighbors about them. Their
enemies would drive every Israelite into the Mediterranean Sea
and kill them if they could. The reason that they do not is because,
humanly speaking, Israel has a good army which is more than a
match for its neighbors. Today an armed truce and a no-man's land
separate Israel from their enemy.

Every young Israeli man is required to have two and one-half
years of military training and every young woman two years of
military training. While the women are trained for jobs that are
not necessarily of combatant type, they also learn to use weapons,
so that if they need to fight, they can. After military training, many
of them are settled in villages near the border, where they can serve
a double purpose — following their occupation, whatever it is, and
serving as guards for the border of Israel. Israel's state of unrest
does not correspond to Ezekiel's prophecy. If Russia should invade
the Middle East today, it would not be a fulfillment of this portion
of Scripture. That has to take place when Israel is at rest.

One point at which Israel will be at rest is in the millennial
kingdom. But we are told expressly that, in the millennial kingdom,
there will be no war (Isaiah 2:4), and only when the rebellion
occurs at the end of the millennium when Satan is let loose (Revelation 20:7-9) does war break out. Certainly Israel is not going to
be at rest under these circumstances either, once Satan is let loose.

Some have suggested that Israel will be at rest in the period of
great triblulation, and that the prophecy of Russia will be fulfilled
at that time. In the time of great tribulation, Israel will not be at

rest, for Christ told them to flee to the mountains to escape their persecutors. Therefore the invasion described by Ezekiel could not be a part of the battle of Armageddon, or the battle of the Great Day of God Almighty.

There is only one period in the future that clearly fits this description of Ezekiel, and that is the first half of Daniel's seventieth week of God's program for Israel (Daniel 9:27). After the church has been raptured and saints have been raised from the dead and the living saints have been caught up to be with the Lord, a confederacy of nations will emerge in the Mediterranean Sea. Out of that confederacy will come a strong man who will become its dictator (discussed in previous chapters). He is described in Daniel 9:26 as "the prince that shall come." He will enter into a seven-year covenant of protection and peace with the people of Israel (Daniel 9:27).

Under that covenant, Israel will be able to relax, for their Gentile enemies will have become their friends, apparently guaranteed their borders and promised them freedom. During that first three and one-half years, we have the one time when regathered Israel is at rest and secure. Apparently Russia will invade the land of Israel during that period, possibly toward its close, and the Scripture will then be fulfilled.

PROBLEMS OF INTERPRETATION

There are some other problems in the passage which merit study. A reference is made to bows and arrows, to shields and chariots, and to swords. These, of course, are antiquated weapons from the standpoint of modern warfare. The large use of horses is understandable as Russia today uses horses a great deal in connection with their army. But why should they use armor, spears, bows and arrows? This certainly poses a problem.

There have been two or more answers given. One of them is this that Ezekiel is using language with which he was familiar — the weapons that were common in his day — to anticipate modern weapons. What he is saying is that when this army comes, it will be fully equipped with the weapons of war. Such an interpretation, too, has problems. We are told in the passage that they used the wooden shafts of the spears and the bow and arrows for kindling wood. If these are symbols, it would be difficult to burn symbols. However, even in modern warfare there is a good deal of wood used. Possibly this is the explanation. We are not in a position today to settle this problem with any finality.

A second solution is that the battle is preceded by a disarmament agreement between nations. If this were the case, it would be necessary to resort to primitive weapons easily and secretly made if a surprise attack were to be achieved. This would allow a literal interpretation of the passage.

A third solution has also been suggested based on the premise that modern missile warfare will have developed in that day to the point where missiles will seek out any considerable amount of metal. Under these circumstances, it would be necessary to abandon the large use of metal weapons and substitute wood such as is indicated in the primitive weapons. Whatever the explanation, the most sensible interpretation is that the passage refers to actual weapons pressed into use because of the peculiar circumstances of that day.

THE FUTURE OF RUSSIA

The general character of the passage, the nature of the war, the invasion when it comes, and the outcome is, however, perfectly clear. What significance does it have to the modern scene? First of all, if we understand the passage correctly, Russia, instead of being a nation which is going to dominate the whole world, is headed for a tremendous military defeat. It is not possible to predict what is going to happen between now and the time this battle takes place, but the Bible seems quite clear that there is no room for a Russian-dominated world empire. The Bible prophesies only four world empires. The empire of the great tribulation period which will come as a form of the revived Roman Empire, is the final form of the fourth empire of Daniel, not a Russian Empire. This, in turn, will be succeeded by the millennial reign of Christ.

The passage seems to confirm that Russia, instead of becoming a world power that is going to dominate the whole world, is instead headed for an awful defeat, a judgment from God because of its blasphemy and ungodliness. If this becomes true during the time of the seventieth week of Daniel, it may explain something that otherwise might be difficult.

THE EMERGENCE OF A WORLD EMPIRE

We know that in the last half of Daniel's seventieth week there will be a world government headed by the ruler of the Mediterranean confederacy. The question is, how does he forge this world empire so quickly and so easily, and apparently without fighting for it? We learn in Revelation 13:4 that the question is asked, "Who is able to make war with him?" i.e., with the Beast. The answer is that nobody is able to make war with him. It should be obvious that if Russia and her satellites are destroyed as military powers, the other side of the balance of power, represented by the Mediterranean confederacy, is then in a position to dominate the whole world. Nobody is able, for at least a time, to contest their right to rule.

The destruction of the Russian army may be the preface to the world government which will sweep the world during the last half of Daniel's seventieth week and be in power at the time Christ comes back to establish His millennial kingdom. These two portions of Scripture, while they concern themselves with a future war, are of tremendous significance as we face the present world scene and the dominance of Russia as a military power. We can trust that God, in due time, and perhaps sooner than we think, will bring these Scriptures to their sure conclusion and fulfillment.

THE EMERGENCE OF A WORLD RELIGION

There is another aspect of the problem that is worthy of careful consideration. What is the relation of all this to what we today call communism? It must be recognized that communism and Russia are not synonymous, for there are nations which are communistic which are not necessarily following Russia's leadership. Communism is a form of political philosophy; it is a form of religion. It is an ideology which is not limited to the Russian nation even though Russia has provided the major spark for it.

Communism is an atheistic religion — a religion denying that God exists, a religion denying that there is anything that is supernatural, a religion that recognizes only material force. If these facts are kept in mind, it becomes a most significant fact that in the false religion which will sweep the world during the time of the great tribulation there are precisely the same elements present.

The false religion at the tribulation time is described in Daniel 11:36-38. This portion of Scripture describes the king who shall do according to his will, i.e., an absolute ruler. The king is believed by many to be the future world ruler of which the Scriptures speak, as indicated in previous discussion. He may be "the prince that shall come" of Daniel 9:26. In Daniel 11:37, it states of this ruler, "Neither shall he regard the gods of his fathers, nor the desire of women, nor regard any god; for he shall magnify himself above all" (ASV). In other words, this ruler will push aside any previous kind of religion, any god which had been previously worshiped, and in their place he will put himself as the object of universal worship.

In explanation of this, it states in Daniel 11:38, "But in his place shall he honor the god of fortresses" (ASV). In the Authorized Version it is translated, "the god of forces," but the word "forces" represents military forces. It is a recognition of the power to make war. This Scripture reveals, in a word, that the only deity this man will recognize and respect is the power to make war. He is an absolute atheist, an absolute materialist.

It should be clear that the rapid rise of communism in our generation has swept within its folds almost half of the world's population, a phenomenon without parallel in the history of the world. While the ultimate false religion will not be communism in the form we know it today, communism may very well be the forerunner and preparation for the future world religion that will sweep all the world during the time of the great tribulation.

Millions of young people today are being systematically taught atheism, denying that any God exists. They are taught to give their complete allegiance to their political leaders, and to die, if need be, for the cause that this represents. Certainly, as they are being conditioned, brainwashed, trained to think this way, the ground is being prepared for the future atheistic, blasphemous worship of Satan's man — Satan's substitute for Christ who alone has the right to rule as King of kings and Lord of lords.

In the rise of communism, something different from the rise of Russia can be seen. While the Scriptures seem to indicate that Russia as a political power will go down, the philosophy and the godlessness and the atheism which it has spawned in our modern day seem to be just the beginning of that which some day will sweep the entire world.

Those who have put their trust in the Lord Jesus can certainly have a wonderful refuge in the Word of God in facing these facts. We believe that the Lord Jesus Christ is coming first to take His body, the church, out of the world in the translation of the living and resurrection of the dead in Christ before these things come to their consummation, before Russia attacks the land of Israel, before this godless religion sweeps the world. But the very fact that these forces are in the world today, Russia, a great nation, poised to the north of the Holy Land, Israel in its place, already a nation of wealth and significance and a prize to be sought, indicates that the end may be near. Ezekiel described the building of cities without walls and anticipates a time when Israel would be secure and at rest. We see today the remarkable preparation for events which will take place after the rapture of the church. God is setting the stage in Israel, in Russia, and in communism for world events that will end the age.

We certainly must realize that this situation is not going to remain static, that it is rapidly moving to a consummation. In that consummation we believe the first important event will be Christ's coming for His own. If there ever was a generation of Bible-believing Christians who had a right to look forward to the coming of the Lord momentarily day by day, on the basis of what they see in the world, it is our present generation. Even unbelievers are telling us today that things cannot go on as they are much longer.

An interesting commentary on the widespread expectation of a coming world climax is found in the present tension between Israel and the Arab world. The efforts of Israel to secure a peace have been unavailing because of fanatical opposition on the part of the Arab world to any sort of a settlement with Israel. Any Arab ruler who would attempt to negotiate with Israel would be in danger of assassination even as one king of Jordan has already been killed. Jewish leaders, however, are still longing for the day when peace can be consummated. One of their leaders made the statement in the hearing of the writer to this effect, "Sooner or later there will rise someone who will make a covenant with the people of Israel, and as soon as he does it, while he may be very unpopular before he does it, he will be hailed as a hero and as a leader in the Middle East."

In Daniel 9:26 there is the prophecy of "the prince that shall come" who will make a covenant with Israel. We cannot presume that the covenant Israel hopes for today is necessarily Daniel's covenant, but it might be. When this Israeli leader was asked when this might come about, he replied, "It could be any day." This coming from the lips of one who is not of the Christian faith and who does not know the prophetic Scriptures was certainly almost prophetic in its character. The hour of the Lord's return may indeed be very, very near.

The rise of Russia and the widespread power and influence of communism are two important factors pointing to the conclusion that the stage is being set for the end of the age. The future invasion from the north obviously fits into our contemporary scene and adds its important evidence that time is running out and that the nations will soon move into their final crisis.

The invasion pictured in Ezekiel 38 and 39 is probably, however, not the last invasion of the king of the north. As previously indicated in Daniel 11, there is evidence that the king of the north will again come upon the Holy Land. According to Daniel 11:40 a series of actions will take part in the great battle and world struggle which will be under way at the very time that the Lord Jesus Christ returns in power and glory. As this event takes place several years after the debacle of Ezekiel 38 and 39, it appears that the king of the north is able by that time to put another army in the field and again becomes a factor in the struggle with the Roman ruler. Details of the second invasion are not given, however, except the mention in Daniel 11 and intimations that an army comes from the north in the very last days of the age.

Chapter XI

EGYPT AND THE KING OF THE SOUTH

For more than three thousand years before the birth of Christ, Egypt was one of the greatest civilizations of the ancient world. Although much of its history was shrouded in mystery until the last century, the careful research of archaeologists has now provided almost limitless material for Egyptology, the science of the history and culture of this great nation of the past. Both from the standpoint of world history as well as the Biblical point of view, no other nation in Africa has had such an impact upon the world as a whole. Long before Babylon became great or Greek civilization came into flower, Egypt was already a great nation with a culture, history, and literature of its own. Nourished by the rich Nile valley, a delta a dozen miles wide and extending more than 500 miles in length, the land of Egypt early became one of the important factors in Biblical history and a great political power in the Mediterranean scene.

First mention of Egypt is under its ancient name of Mizraim, one of the sons of Ham in Genesis 10:6. The name itself is in a dual number which some believe refers to the natural division of the country into upper and lower Egypt. The modern name Egypt is thought to have been derived from a king by the name of Egyptus who reigned in 1485 B.C. However, this conclusion is challenged. The Egyptians themselves referred to their land as Kemet which has the meaning, "the black land." In the Bible it is also referred to as "the land of Ham" referring to the Hamitic origin of the Egyptians.

First mention of Egypt in the history of the Old Testament occurs in Genesis 12 where it is recorded that Abraham, because of the famine in the land of Canaan, went to Egypt (Genesis 12:10). There he attempted to hide the fact that Sarah was his wife and called her his sister — a partial truth. Only by intervention of God who plagued Pharaoh was Sarah rescued from the possibility of being taken as a wife of Pharaoh, and Abraham and his wife were sent out of Egypt.

The subsequent fruit of this ill-fated venture into Egypt was that he brought Hagar back with him. She ultimately became the mother of Ishmael (Genesis 16:1-6) who became the progenitor of the Arabian tribes who caused Israel so much trouble in the years that followed. Isaac was forbidden to go down into the land of Egypt as Abraham had done (Genesis 26:2), but Ishmael guided by his mother took a wife from Egypt (Genesis 21:21). It was not until the time of Joseph that the children of Israel again entered the land of Egypt.

ISRAEL'S SOJOURN IN EGYPT

The first prophecy concerning Egypt in Scripture is found in the important fifteenth chapter of Genesis where God confirms His covenant with Abraham. This chapter becomes the cornerstone of fulfillment of the Abrahamic covenant as it relates to possession of the land ultimately to be possessed by Israel, defined as the area "from the river of Egypt unto the great river, the river Euphrates" (Genesis 15:18). The expression "the river of Egypt" is probably a reference to the small river which is the boundary between Egypt and Palestine known as Wady-el-Arish. Apart from its reference to Egypt the chapter is important for its vision of God as "a burning lamp" which some have taken as the first instance of the Shekinah glory, and for its enumeration of the important nations adjacent to Israel or occupying its land in ancient times. Ten nations are named in Genesis 15:19-21.

Of major importance in relation to prophecy relating to Egypt, however, is the statement made to Abraham in Genesis 15:13, 14: "Know of a surety that thy seed shall be a stranger in a land that is not their's, and shall serve them; and they shall afflict them four hundred years; And also that nation, whom they shall serve, will I judge: and afterward shall they come out with great substance." Although Egypt is not named, it is inescapable that this is the reference intended by the term "land that is not theirs." Thus long before the children of Israel went down into Egypt, it was predicted that they would sojourn there and be afflicted for 400 years.

Considerable attention has been given to the question of the 400 years as historical data does not necessarily support this idea.

If Israel left Egypt at the time of the Exodus about 1440 B.C. as most conservative scholars have agreed, they actually were in Egypt approximately 210 years. How can this be explained?

On the basis of the chronology of Galatians 3:17 where it is stated that the law came 430 years after the promise, a reasonable chronology is provided by beginning the 430 years at the time that Abraham left Ur of Chaldees. From that point to the birth of Isaac was a period of approximately 30 years. From the birth of Isaac to the birth of Jacob was another 60 years. From the birth of Jacob until Jacob went down into Egypt was another 130 years. This computation provides at least one good explanation for this reference to 400 years in Genesis 15. This is confirmed by the Septuagint rendering of Exodus 12:40, 41 where the children of Israel are said to have sojourned in the land of Egypt and in the land of Canaan for 430 years. This early reference to the children of Israel sojourning in the land of Egypt is one of the important milestones in prophecy in the Old Testament.

The story of how Jacob and his family went to Egypt is given in detail in Genesis, chapter 37 to chapter 50. The story's importance in the history of Israel is demonstrated in the fact that Genesis, which devotes only two chapters to the whole creation narrative and only one chapter to the entrance of sin into the human race, uses fourteen chapters to trace the history of Israel from the time of Joseph being sold as a slave until the time of his death. Egypt was to be the matrix in which Israel would grow from a family of 70 to a great nation of several million.

THE EXODUS FROM EGYPT

The history of Israel and of Egypt makes clear that the affliction or servitude mentioned in Genesis 15:13 was not always severe. However, during the latter portion of their sojourn in Egypt, there was a change in dynasty of the "Shepherd Kings" known as the Hyksos who dominated the scene for two hundred years, 1750-1570 B.C., and were in power at the time that Joseph came to Egypt. Their expulsion and the formation of the new empire beginning with Dynasty XVIII set the stage not only for Israel's period of great glory and the construction of vast buildings, but also the slavery of the people of Israel. Thutmose III, who reigned 1482-1450 B.C., conquered all of Palestine, and defeated the Hittites. Thutmose III was followed by Amenhotep II (1450-1425 B.C.), the Pharaoh with whom the children of Israel had to deal in connection with the Exodus. The subsequent decline of Egypt and her loosening grip on Palestine ultimately made possible the conquest of the land by the children of Israel without Egyptian interference.

Contributing to the confusion which arose in the reign of Amenhotep II were the series of plagues inflicted upon the Egyptians recorded in the early chapters of Exodus. The story of Israel's deliverance from Egypt and the destruction of the Egyptian host in the Red Sea marks the close of the Egyptian bondage and the beginning of Israel as a separate nation.

The subsequent history of Egypt included constant contact with the children of Israel. The large part that Egypt played in the Old Testament is borne out by more than 700 references to Egypt in the Old Testament contrasted to less than 30 in the New Testament. Most of these are reminders to Israel that they were "brought up out of the land of Egypt" and this recurring phrase occurs approximately 125 times.

Commercial relationships with Egypt reached a high point during the reign of Solomon. According to I Kings 3:1, "Solomon made affinity with Pharaoh king of Egypt, and took Pharaoh's daughter, and brought her into the city of David." I Kings 10:28 records that Egypt was the source of the horses Solomon used in his host of chariots for which he was famous. Solomon had 12,000 horsemen and 1400 chariots with both the horses and the chariots purchased out of Egypt (I Kings 10:26, 29). Other commodities such as linen yarn were bought in Egypt. The commercial alliance with Egypt and Solomon's host of horses and chariots were in violation of the Word of God (Deuteronomy 17:16) and were a part of the secularization in Solomon's reign which led to Israel's spiritual downfall after his death.

Along with Assyria and Babylon, Egypt was one of the great nations of the past and is destined to have its important place in prophetic fulfillment at the end of the age. Egypt, however, was not the benefactor, but traditionally the enemy of Israel. This is seen in the sad commentary which forms a footnote to Solomon's relationships to Egypt recorded in the reign of Rehoboam, his successor, when Shishak king of Egypt conquered Jerusalem in the fifth year of the reign of Rehoboam and took away all of the treasures of the king's house and of the house of the Lord (I Kings 14: 25, 26). Egypt, under the able leadership of the Egyptian ruler

Pharaoh-Necho (609-593 B.C.), once again conquered Palestine during the reign of King Josiah (631-608 B.C.). The Egyptian bondage, however, was soon to end and be replaced by the Babylonian captivity with the rise of Nebuchadnezzar and the conquering of Jerusalem in 606 B.C. Jeremiah the prophet of the exile was carried against his will to Egypt where he died. The Old Testament history does not record anything further of importance concerning Egypt.

Where Biblical history stops, however, the prophetic narrative begins. Egypt was destined to have an important place in subsequent history as related to Israel and the Promised Land. The prophetic narrative concerning Israel is found in the great prophecies of Isaiah, Jeremiah, Ezekiel and Daniel with echoes in the minor prophets Joel, Hosea, Micah, and Zechariah. To this the New Testament adds little of importance, but these great prophecies not only trace the subsequent history of Egypt, much of which has now been fulfilled, but also paint the picture of the final chapter in relation to the second coming of Christ.

THE PROPHECIES OF ISAIAH CONCERNING EGYPT

The prophecies of Isaiah include one of the more important chapters of prophetic utterance concerning Egypt. The main section of this prophecy is found in the nineteenth chapter beginning with the ominous phrase, "the burden of Egypt." The chapter is preceded by prophecies relating to Egypt's neighbor Ethiopia and is followed in chapter 20 by the prediction that Assyria would conquer Egypt and Ethiopia and lead them off as captives.

The nineteenth chapter of Isaiah is of special interest because it provides a rather comprehensive picture of God's plan and purpose for Egypt. The first half of the chapter predicts divine judgment upon Egypt. This will be fulfilled by the destruction of their idols (verse 1), destruction by civil war followed by the rule of "a cruel lord" and "a fierce king" (verses 2-4), judgment on the Nile River with attending economic distress (verses 5-10), and confusion of their wise men (verses 11-15), accompanied by a dread of Jehovah (verse 16). Divine judgment can well be associated with events of the Old Testament period, although it may be a foreshadowing also of future judgments.

Beginning with verse 16, however, the thought seems gradually to change to that which will be fulfilled in the future. Although they will experience fear of Judah (verses 16-18), it is predicted that there will be "an altar to the Lord in the midst of the land of Egypt, and a pillar at the border thereof to the Lord" (verse 19). The passage which follows seems to anticipate a time of blessing which may have its ultimate fulfillment in the millennial reign of Christ. The thought is summarized in verse 22 in the phrase, "And the Lord shall smite Egypt: he shall smite and heal it: and they shall return even to the Lord, and he shall be intreated of them, and shall heal them." It is predicted that Egypt and Assyria will be associated with Israel as the three primary nations of that period and that a highway will connect them (verses 23, 24). The prophecies which follow in chapter 20 refer to the historic invasion of Egypt by Assyria fulfilled largely in Isaiah's day. Because of the ultimate downfall of Egypt, Israel is exhorted not to trust in Egypt as a refuge against other enemies (Isaiah 30:2, 3; 31:1; 36:6, 9). These prophecies assure God's continued attention to the nation Israel and His divine judgment upon them for their sins. From the standpoint of unfulfilled prophecy, the most important passage in Isaiah is found in 11:10-16. Here Egypt is mentioned as one of the nations from which Israel will be regathered (11:11).

One of the interesting predictions is found in Isaiah 11:15 where it states, "And the Lord shall utterly destroy the tongue of the Egyptian sea; and with his mighty wind shall he shake his hand over the river, and shall smite it in the seven streams, and make men go over dryshod." The passage then goes on to mention the highway between Assyria and Egypt also mentioned in Isaiah 19:23.

The interpretation depends largely on the question as to whether prophecy is to have literal fulfillment. Numerous attempts have been made to spiritualize these prophecies as referring to the progress of the church and conversion of the heathen. The more probable interpretation, however, is to take these as geographic terms and the events as those which will be related to the future Messianic kingdom. The tongue of the Egyptian Sea is clearly the northern end of the Red Sea. The prophecy then predicts that in this future time the topography of this land will be changed and what is now water will become dry land. This apparently is connected with the prophecy of a highway between Egypt and Israel for which this may be a preparation.

This passage with its prediction of Israel's future place is set in the midst of prophecy that refers to the future millennial kingdom on earth. The first part of chapter 11 deals with Christ's reign on earth in perfect righteousness and equity. Chapter 12 refers to the joy and blessings that will characterize worship in this kingdom. It must be concluded therefore not only that Israel will be revived and that a future kingdom on earth will be realized, but that many of the ancient nations mentioned in the Bible will have their future revival as well. As Isaiah the prophet makes so plain in chapter 2, Jerusalem will be the capital of the world and the nations surrounding Israel will be subordinate but nevertheless blessed of God in that day. Taken as a whole, the prophecies of Isaiah set the pattern for other portions of the Word of God in tracing precise fulfillment of many prophecies in the past already fulfilled and establishing the main outline of Israel's future in relationship to the earthly kingdom of the Messiah.

THE PROPHECIES OF JEREMIAH CONCERNING EGYPT

Most of the prophecies of Jeremiah concern Jeremiah's own generation and the struggles of the kingdom of Judah with the contending powers of Babylon and Egypt. The possibility of a Babylonian conquest precipitated the choice of either casting their lot with Egypt or submitting to the Babylonian armies. It was in this situation that Jeremiah the prophet delivered his prophetic message. The good king Josiah had been succeeded by his son Jehoiakim who was on the throne during the period in which Nebuchadnezzar was attempting to subdue Tyre — more than a dozen years. When Jehoiakim died, he was succeeded by his son Jehoiachin, who after three months was succeeded by Zedekiah, another son of Josiah and Jehoiachin's uncle. At this time Egypt was applying great pressure on the kingdom of Judah to cast their lot with them. When Jeremiah the prophet was consulted after receiving a message from God, he delivered his pronouncement as contained in Jeremiah 42. The substance of his reply was that they should not go down into Egypt and that if they did they would be destroyed. The advisors of king Zedekiah were intent, however, on going to Egypt and they rejected Jeremiah's prophetic warning and added insult to injury by forcing Jeremiah to accompany them as indicated in Jeremiah 43. While in Egypt Jeremiah delivered a further message to the Jews (chapter 44) predicting their destruction except for a small remnant that would escape and return to Israel. The eloquent and moving plea of Jeremiah is prophetic literature at its best and is highly significant because it embodies also complete and literal fulfillment.

Jeremiah continues his prophetic utterances concerning Egypt in the series of prophecies against the Gentiles beginning in chapter 46 and concluding with the great section against Babylon in chapter 50 and 51. In these predictions he anticipates the defeat of Egypt by Nebuchadnezzar and the destruction of their great cities. The section on Egypt concludes in chapter 46:27, 28 with another reminder to Israel that Jacob need not be afraid, that Israel would return from their captivity and ultimately be at rest and ease in their own land. As Jeremiah concluded, "Fear thou not, O Jacob my servant, saith the LORD: for I am with thee; for I will make a full end of all the nations whither I have driven thee: but I will not make a full end of thee, but correct thee in measure; yet will I not leave thee wholly unpunished" (Jeremiah 46:28). Taken as a whole, Jeremiah does not contribute much to the future of Egypt except to assure God's continued and providential direction of this nation to the fulfillment of His purpose to bring Israel into their ancient land and establish them in the millennial kingdom.

THE PROPHECIES OF EZEKIEL CONCERNING EGYPT

The prophecies of Ezekiel include four long chapters dealing with Egypt, beginning with the prophecy against Pharaoh in chapter 29. Most of these predictions are concerning the domination of Egypt by Babylon and Nebuchadnezzar viewed as a divine judgment of God upon Pharaoh for claiming to be God and taking the credit for the fertility of the Nile Valley. With great prophetic eloquence, Ezekiel declares that Egypt is going to fall even as Assyria fell more than a century before. Most of chapter 31 is devoted to the analogy between the fall of Assyria and the fall of Egypt. The concluding prophecy concerning Egypt is a lamentation contained in chapter 32 in which Egypt is compared to a young lion trapped with a net and destroyed.

In a similar way miscellaneous other prophecies in Ezekiel relate to the downfall of Egypt. In the parable of the great eagle in Ezekiel 17 and its interpretation, Ezekiel declares that the king of Babylon has conquered Jerusalem and will judge those who flee to Pharaoh for refuge. The foolishness of relying on Egypt is again mentioned in Ezekiel 19:4. Israel is likewise denounced for their wickedness in idol worship in Egypt in the parable of Aholah and

Aholibah representing Samaria and Jerusalem. God's judgment upon them for this is declared.

Of these many prophecies most of them related to the contemporary situation of Ezekiel's day. The opening portion of chapter 30 of Ezekiel, however, referring as it does to the day of the Lord, has been interpreted as having a dual fulfillment, first, in the conquest of Egypt and Ethiopia by Babylon and, second, the future conquest of Egypt in the world struggle which will end the age. The main burden of the prophecy, however, seems to relate to Nebuchadnezzar and his conquest as indicated in Ezekiel 30:10. Taken as a whole, Ezekiel is an enlargement of the prophecies of Isaiah and Jeremiah depicting the judgment upon Egypt in his day, but assuring the people of Israel of their ultimate restoration and deliverance.

THE PROPHECIES OF DANIEL CONCERNING EGYPT

To the prophet Daniel was committed the major task of tracing the prophetic program of the four great world empires, namely, Babylon, Medo-Persia, Greece, and Rome. This in the main is the times of the Gentiles, constituting one of the major programs of God. Under the circumstances, it is surprising that Daniel has so little to say specifically about Egypt.

In Daniel 9:15 there is an allusion in Daniel's prayer to the deliverance of the people of Israel out of the land of Egypt, a constantly recurring thought in the Old Testament. In Daniel 11:8 there is mention of captives being carried into Egypt, a reference to the supremacy of Egypt during the reign of Ptolemy III Euergetes (246-222 B.C.).

The two other references to Egypt are found in Daniel 11: 42, 43, and these relate to the future struggle among the nations at the end of the age still to be fulfilled.

The few direct references to Egypt, however, are misleading as Egypt figures in a large way in the events both historic and prophetic described in Daniel chapter 11. Instead of referring to Egypt by name reference is made instead to "the king of the south," an expression which occurs in Daniel 11:5, 6, 9, 11, 14, 15, 25, 29, 40, a total of ten references including the double reference in 11:25. Instead of referring to only one ruler, however, the expression in all probability concerns seven different kings of Egypt, six of them in the past and one still to come.

The period of history described in Daniel 11:5-20 was the tangled period subsequent to the death of Alexander the Great which deals with the struggles of Egypt with the lands to the north, principally Syria. The accuracy of the prophecy given by Daniel more than two hundred years before it was fulfilled is so minute that liberal scholars reject the idea that Daniel could possibly have written it and claim it was written by a pseudo-Daniel after the events had actually taken place. Evangelical scholarship, however, has been agreed that this is genuine prophecy and another illustration of the accuracy of the prophetic Word.

The king of the south mentioned in Daniel 11:5 was probably Ptolemy I Soter (323-285 B.C.) who was associated with the famous Seleucus I Nicator (312-281 B.C.) who was king of Babylon. Their alliance succeeded in defeating Antigonus and Seleucus I Nicator became the ruler of the entire area from Asia Minor to India and hence was stronger than Ptolemy I Soter, his associate.

The king of the south mentioned in Daniel 11:6 was probably Ptolemy II Philadelphus (283-246 B.C. who gave his daughter Berenice to Antiochus II Theos (261-246 B.C.) who was the third in the line of Seleucid kings.

Reference to another king of Egypt is found in verses 7 and 8. He was probably Ptolemy II Euergetes (246-222 B.C.) referred to as the king of the south in Daniel 11:9. The king of the south of Daniel 11:11 was Ptolemy IV Philopator (222-203 B.C.). The king of the south mentioned in verse 14 and referred to under the term "the arms of the south" in verse 15 was Ptolemy V Epiphanes (204-181 B.C.) who was an infant at the time of his accession. As Daniel 11:13-16 indicates, he was crushed by the great army of Antiochus III the celebrated ruler of Syria to the north in a battle at Paneiom in 198 B.C. The result was that Egypt lost its hold upon the Holy Land and it was transferred to the Seleucids. This set the stage for the activities of Antiochus Epiphanes described in Daniel 11: 21-35 (previously discussed) which constitutes such a significant foreshadowing of the coming man of sin and world ruler in the end time. Antiochus III was followed by his son Seleucus IV Philopator (187-175 B.C.) to whom reference is made in Daniel 11:20 as a raiser of taxes. He was followed in turn by Antiochus Epiphanes.

The exact fulfillment of these many prophecies, including that of Antiochus Epiphanes in Daniel 11:21-35, sets the stage for the climactic prophecy beginning in Daniel 11:36 which leaps the centuries to the end of the age and the final king of Gentile power.

Daniel 11:36-45 concerns itself with the military and political struggles of the end of the age with special reference to the great tribulation the last three and a half years before the second coming of Christ to the earth. The period is described as "the time of the end" in verse 35 and again in Daniel 11:40. The description of the warfare which characterizes the period of Daniel 11:40-45 speaks of a future king of the south, namely, of Egypt engaging in a military campaign against the king of Daniel 11:36 who is most probably identified as the world ruler of the end time. At the same time there is an attack by the king of the north, namely, Russia and her associates as they contend with the world ruler for control of the Holy Land.

It is reasonable to assume from the description of a series of battles that this is not just one single military encounter, but a series of military maneuvers which come at the very end of the great tribulation. Earlier there may have been other wars such as that of Ezekiel 38 and 39 which led up to the world empire directed by the head of the revived Roman Empire. With the defeat of Russia described in Ezekiel 38 and 39, however, the Roman ruler becomes a world ruler. His empire accomplished by proclamation and because there was no suitable military force to contend against him does not stand indefinitely, however, and begins to fall apart with a major rebellion developing as the great tribulation closes. This is the scene described in Daniel 11:40 and following.

According to Daniel 11:40-42 the preliminary struggle results in the Roman ruler being victorious and conquering Egypt and putting down the king of the south. In the process, however, of assuming "power over the treasures of gold and of silver, and over all the precious things of Egypt" (Daniel 11:43) he receives word of additional problems of a military force coming from the east and from the north. This apparently refers to the great host coming from the Orient described first in Revelation 9:13-21, an army of two hundred million and then again in a later phase in the invasion described in Revelation 16:12-16. The great invasion from the east therefore follows the attack of the king of the south. Daniel 11, however, makes plain that in the preliminary struggle the Roman ruler is victorious as indicated in Daniel 11:45. However, at the very time of the second coming of Christ according to Zechariah chapter 14:1-3 a military struggle is going on in the city of Jerusalem itself and the armies of the world are gathered in the Holy Land with the valley of Megiddo referred to as Armageddon (Revelation 16:16) as its marshalling center.

From this entire context it is evident that the king of the south, namely, Egypt, has a part in end-time events and participates in the world struggle leading up to the second coming of Christ.

However, a final chapter is written in Egypt's future in which it is pictured that Egypt will have a spiritual revival (cp. Isaiah 19:18-24) and Israel will be regathered.

PROPHECIES OF EGYPT IN THE MINOR PROPHETS

The few scattered references to Egypt in the minor prophets do not contribute much to the total picture. Hosea has the most references, including the Messianic statement in Hosea 11:1: "When Israel was a child, then I loved him, and called my son out of Egypt." This reference to the Exodus is interpreted as having a dual meaning in that it prophesies that Jesus would come out of Egypt (cp. Matthew 2:15). Other references to Egypt in Hosea either predict destruction of those who go to Egypt as in Hosea 7:11-16 or contain warnings concerning returning to Egypt as in 8:13; 9:3, 6; 11:5. Joel 3:19 predicts that "Egypt shall be a desolation." This seems to be a general reference to God's judgment on Egypt largely already fulfilled although it is found in a passage dealing with Israel's millennial blessings.

Micah in one reference (7:12) predicts the regathering of Israel from Assyria and from "the fortress." This is best interpreted as a reference to Egypt and hence the prediction is that the children of Israel will be gathered from Assyria, the cities of Egypt ("the fortified cities"), and from Egypt ("the fortress") even to the river (the Euphrates). This reference to regathering from Egypt may presume an influx of Jews into Egypt which is not true today or it may refer to the few that are there as being subject to regathering.

The subject of regathering is brought up again in Zechariah 10:10 where it is stated concerning Israel, "I will bring them again also out of the land of Egypt, and gather them out of Assyria." Zechariah 10:11 refers to the fact that both Assyria and Egypt will be afflicted under divine judgment in contrast to God's blessing upon Israel.

The final reference in the Old Testament to Egypt is found in

Zechariah 14:18, 19, where in the future millennial kingdom it is stated, "And if the family of Egypt go not up, and come not, that have no rain; there shall be the plague, wherewith the LORD will smite the heathen that come not up to keep the feast of tabernacles. This shall be the punishment of Egypt, and the punishment of all nations that come not up to keep the feast of tabernacles." From these verses it may be concluded that God will continue to discipline Egypt even in the coming millennial kingdom if they have failed to obey Him and observe His feast.

SUMMARY

Taking the Scriptural prophecies concerning Egypt as a whole, it is easily seen that Egypt has had a great role as one of the principal neighbors of Israel in centuries past. The fact that Israel sojourned in Egypt, grew to be a great nation there and subsequently had so many dealings with Egypt forms a large part of the Old Testament prophetic narrative.

The Scriptures, however, reveal that Egypt will also have a place in the future. Egypt will be one of the nations which figure in the final world conflict and will be the leader of the African forces in contending against the Roman ruler who is attempting to maintain a world empire. The role of Egypt will continue in the millennial kingdom after the searching divine judgments which attend the second coming. The last word of the Old Testament pictures the continued discipline of Egypt in the millennium if they fail to observe the rule of the king.

CHAPTER XII

THE KINGS OF THE EAST:
THE ORIENTAL CONFEDERACY

One of the significant developments of the twentieth century is the political and military awakening of the Orient. The great nations of Asia east of the Euphrates River, slumbering for centuries, are now beginning to stir and to become a major factor in the international situation. The geographic immensity and the millions of humanity involved make it inevitable that any future development embracing the entire world must take the Orient into consideration.

In our twentieth century the major nations of Asia have thrown off the yoke of political overlordship of western civilization. Red China with its population approaching one billion is flexing its muscles not only against the United States of America, but even against its associate in communism, Russia. India, now independent of Great Britain, is likewise beginning to feel its strength. Japan is experiencing a great industrial revolution where the comforts and manufacturing techniques of western civilization are now an integral part of Japanese life. Lesser nations also are beginning to assert themselves, hoping for a large role in world affairs. Most of this has taken place in the last twenty-five years and developments continue to be rapid. Even if there were no Scripture bearing on the place of the Orient in end-time events, it would be only natural to expect them to be part of the world-wide scene.

The great nations of Eastern Asia have had no important part in the history of Israel. Far removed in geography and interests, there is no record of any past war between Israel and the nations beyond the Euphrates. Alexander the Great penetrated as far as India with his armies, but he left no permanent imprint upon the oriental world. The future, however, in view of modern rapid communications and transportation and the world-wide character of any military effort in the missile age, will be a different story.

The western world was rudely awakened to the power of the Orient by the Japanese attack on Pearl Harbor on December 7, 1941. During the months that followed, the Japanese army, navy, and air force dominated the Asiatic scene. It was only when the full force of American military power was brought into play that Japan went down along with its ally, Germany. The downfall of Japan, however, was followed by the emergence of Red China and independent India. The conflict between the United States and Viet Nam, although not large in extent, symbolizes that Asia is the number one problem of the world today.

In World War II the Japanese Yamamoto was quoted as boasting, "I shall not be content merely to occupy Guam, the Philippines, Hawaii, and San Francisco. I shall look forward to dictating peace to the United States in the White House at Washington." Although today this is an idle boast, Red China and Russia are still dreaming of world conquest by means of communistic philosophy. No one takes lightly the possibility of a world-wide conflict sparked by the belligerence of Red China and other communistic nations. In this confused situation that has so many omens of future disaster for western civilization, a student of the Scriptures may well ask whether prophecy has any sure word concerning the role of Asia among the nations of the world in the end time.

CHINA IN PROPHECY

Scriptures rarely go outside the confines of the ancient Roman Empire in predicting future events. An exception to this is the statement found in Isaiah 49:12 relating to the ultimate regathering of the nation Israel, "Behold, these shall come from far: and, lo, these from the north and from the west; and these from the land of Sinim." Although it is not possible to be dogmatic as to the precise reference of "the land of Sinim," conservative scholarship has generally agreed that the most probable explanation is that this refers to the ancient land of China.

It is known that China for centuries was a great nation and had its own culture and extensive history long before Christ was born in Bethlehem. It is possible to trace some commercial relationships with China in ancient days as far as the Mediterranean and there is also evidence that some of the history of the Old Testament was known in China. Even if the Chinese had not penetrated as far west as the Mediterranean, the world-wide scattering of the people of Israel would inevitably have brought some of them to the great land of China. Under these circumstances, the prophecy assumes a logical and natural interpretation, namely, that in the end time some of the Jews who will be regathered will come not only from the north and the west, the more important directions of concentration of Jewish population, but also from the east. Although this prophecy is not related to events which concern the nations, it does indicate that the Scriptures recognize the existence of the Far East in relation to the Holy Land.

THE MAGI FROM THE EAST

One of the most familiar Biblical references to the Far East is related to the visit of the Magi as they brought gifts to the Christ child. According to Matthew 2:1, 2, "Now when Jesus was born in Bethlehem of Judaea in the days of Herod the king, behold, there came wise men from the east to Jerusalem, Saying, Where is he that is born King of the Jews? for we have seen his star in the east, and are come to worship him."

It has been commonly held from the times of the early church fathers that these strange visitors came from the area east of the Euphrates and probably from ancient Persia. The Persian origin of the Magi was suggested by such men as Clement of Alexandria, Diodorus of Tarsus, Chrysostom, and Cyril of Alexandria. Somehow the Messianic hope had been transmitted in some form even to this distant land. The star appearing over Bethlehem prompted their journey and inquiry concerning the birth of the King of the Jews. The fact that they wanted to worship Him and recognized Him as the King of the Jews reveals that the basic facts concerning the Old Testament were more widely known than is commonly realized. As in the case of the reference to the land of Sinim, the story in the New Testament gives added support to the conclusion that the Bible includes the Orient in its world-wide view.

DANIEL'S PROPHECY OF A MILITARY INVASION FROM THE FAR EAST

In Daniel's prophecy of "the time of the end" beginning in Daniel 11:35, a king is pictured in the Mediterranean area who engages in a military conflict with the king of the south, the king of the north, and a military force from the east. Although identification of this king is difficult, the most plausible explanation is that he is the head of the revived Roman Empire who at this point has assumed the role of a world dictator. In the period just prior to the second coming of Christ in the latter part of the great tribulation, major portions of the world will rebel against him. This explains the military conflict with armies pushing against him from the south, the north, and from the east.

In the prophecy it is stated in Daniel 11:44, "But tidings out of the east and out of the north shall trouble him: therefore he shall go forth with great fury to destroy, and utterly to make away many." Although the information given is meager, in the light of the context it appears that these tidings concern a military invasion from the Orient. This is probably the first word of trouble in the Orient in relation to his world-wide empire and comes as an added blow to insurrection in the north and the south. It appears that he is victorious in his preliminary battles with the north and the south, as it states in Daniel 11:44, "therefore he shall go forth with great fury to destroy, and utterly to make away many." But that the conflict is not completely resolved, is borne out by the fact that at the time of the second coming of Christ a great war is under way in which the armies are deployed over much of the Holy Land with the valley of Armageddon as its focal point. The statement in Daniel, however, introduces a subject concerning which there is additional revelation given in the New Testament that lends support to the concept that the Orient will have a place in the great world conflict of the end time.

THE GREAT ARMY FROM THE ORIENT

Two important passages in Revelation, namely, 9:13-21 and 16:12-16 contribute to the conclusion that one of the large armies employed in the final world conflict will be a military force of great power which comes from the Orient. The first intimation of this is found in Revelation 9 where it is recorded that John

> heard a voice from the four horns of the golden altar which is before God, Saying to the sixth angel which had the trumpet, Loose the four angels which are bound in the great river Euphrates, And the four angels were loosed, which were prepared for an hour, and a day, and a month, and a year, for to slay the third part of men. And the number of the army of the horsemen were two hundred thousand thousand: and I heard the number of them (verses 13-16).

The passage goes on to describe the character of this army and the conclusion that one-third of the men were killed in the resulting military struggle.

Although all of the details are not entirely clear, the most reasonable explanation of this prophecy, related as it is to the great river Euphrates which forms the eastern boundary of the ancient Roman Empire, is that the army comes from the Orient and crosses the Euphrates River in order to participate in the struggle that is going on in the land of Israel. The information that it is prepared for "an hour, and a day, and a month, and a year, for to slay the third part of men" means simply that it is an army especially prepared for the day of battle which follows.

A most staggering statistic is the fact that the number of the horsemen is declared to be two hundred thousand thousand or two hundred million. Never in the history of the human race until now has there been an army of this size. The total number of men under arms in World War II on both sides of the conflict together never was more than fifty million. Accordingly, it has been the custom for expositors to spiritualize the number or to regard the army as demonic rather than human. The statistics of two hundred million horsemen must have been especially astounding to the Apostle John for at that time the total world population did not exceed this number. With the twentieth century and its attendant population explosion, however, the number of an army of two hundred milion men becomes increasingly a possibility and with modern transportation and means of supply, for the first time in history such an army is plausible. It is at least of more than passing interest that Red China alone claims to have a man and woman militia engaging in serious training numbering two hundred million (*Time,* May 21, 1965, page 35), precisely the figure mentioned in Revelation 9:16.

Although their militia includes the home guard which under present circumstances would not be thrown into a battle such as the one in Revelation, it at least introduces the possibility that the number should be taken literally. If so, this is an imposing statistic of the power and influence of the Orient in the final world war. The deadly character of the army is revealed in their slaughter of one third, a figure mentioned in Revelation 9:15 and again in Revelation 9:18. Although it may not be intended to consider this as one third of the entire world's population, the implication is that many millions of people are involved.

THE KINGS OF THE EAST

A later development in prophetic fulfillment is portrayed in the sixth vial described in Revelation 16:12-16. There it is recorded, "And the sixth angel poured out his vial upon the great river Euphrates; and the water thereof was dried up, that the way of the kings of the east might be prepared" (Revelation 16:12). Revelation 16:14 reveals that this movement is part of a world-wide gathering of "the kings of the earth and of the whole world" in order that they might participate in "the battle of that great day of God Almighty." The focal point of the gathering is mentioned as Armageddon in Revelation 16:16.

Many interpretations have arisen concerning the meaning of the phrase "the kings of the east." These interpretations may be divided into two classes, those that take this phrase literally, and those who find in it a nonliteral meaning. If the nonliteral interpretation be followed there is no end to the possible interpretation. The kings of the east have been connected with almost every important set of characters in the world. The bewildering array of conflicting opinions is its own refutation.

The kings of the east have been identified with the Dacians who conquered Rome and the Euphrates is then taken to represent the Danube. Others relate the kings of the east to the Parthians who contended against Rome at the Euphrates. Some have referred it to the people of Israel returning to their ancient land or identified it with the kingdom of God or Christianity. Some think it refers to the ten kings of Revelation 17:12; others have related it to the Apostles or to the four angels of Revelation 9:14, 15. Still other explanations have been given such as relating it to Vitringa, or Constantine the Great, or to Gog and Magog, or Turkey, and still other interpretations too numerous to mention. A method of interpretation yielding so many different results is obviously wrong in principle.

The most simple and suitable explanation is to take the passage literally. The Euphrates River then becomes the geographic boundary of the ancient Roman Empire. The kings of the east are kings from the east or "of the sunrising," that is, monarchs who originated in the Orient. The battle which ensues is therefore a genuine military conflict.

THE DRYING UP OF THE EUPHRATES RIVER

The interpretation of this difficult passage, if taken literally, provides an important segment of information concerning the final world conflict. The prophecy begins with a reference to the Euphrates River and the declaration that "the water thereof was dried up." Just what is meant?

From the standpoint of Scripture, the Euphrates River is one of the important rivers of the world. The first reference is found in Genesis 2:10-14 where it is included as one of the four rivers having its source in the garden of Eden. The Euphrates River is mentioned a total of nineteen times in the Old Testament and twice in the New Testament. In Genesis 15:18 it is cited as the eastern boundary of the land promised to Israel. An army, therefore, which crosses the Euphrates River from the east to the west by this act invades the Promised Land.

The Euphrates River is important in some of the major events of the Bible. Although not mentioned by name in Daniel 5, it was the diversion of the Euphrates River from its normal course through the midst of Babylon that left the river channel dry and permitted the armies of Darius the Mede to take the city by storm on the memorable night of Belshazzar's feast (Daniel 5). Therefore the drying up of the Euphrates contributed to the downfall of Babylon. There seems to be a connotation in that the drying of the Euphrates River in Revelation 16:12 will lead to the downfall of the revived Roman Empire which spiritually and politically is also identified with Babylon.

The drying up of the Euphrates, however, is probably best interpreted as a literal but miraculous drying up of the Euphrates River thereby permitting easy access of the military hordes from the Orient to cross its dry river bed. The Euphrates River has long been an important geographic barrier and in the ancient world was second to none in importance. Its total length was some seventeen hundred miles, and it was the main river of southwestern Asia dividing the land geographically much as the Mississippi River divides North America. Not only from the standpoint of prophecy, but historically, geographically, and biblically the Euphrates River is the most important in the ancient world. To take it literally is therefore not a strange or an unnatural conclusion.

The drying up of the Euphrates is pictured as an act of God. This has inspired all sorts of nonliteral interpretations as symbolizing some great victory of God. In the past this has been suggestive of the declining power of Turkey, or as anticipating a future decline in the Roman Catholic Church. Although Turkey has receded in power, there is no evidence that this applies to Rome or any other ecclesiastical organization. It is rather a physical act permitting the army to cross the Euphrates much as was enacted in God drying up the waters of the Red Sea and of the Jordan to permit the passage of the children of Israel without difficulty. Inasmuch as such a literal interpretation makes a great deal of sense and there is no agreement as to the spiritualized meaning of the passage, the literal interpretation is obviously to be preferred.

If the drying of the Euphrates River is to be taken literally, then what can be understood by the reference to "the kings of the east"? Here again the literal view is to be preferred. Inasmuch as it would be most natural in a world war culminating in the Middle East to have the Orient represented, the interpretation that views the kings of the east as the political and military leaders of Asiatic forces east of the Euphrates is a satisfactory solution.

There has been some tendency to take the expression "the kings of the east" — literally, "the kings of the sunrise" — as referring specifically to Japan where the rising sun is a symbol of its political power. However, it is more natural to consider the term "rising sun" as a synonym for east, and therefore the army would include all the nations of the Orient. If the army is literally two hundred million, it would hardly be possible for Japan alone to staff, maintain, and move such a gigantic force without help from China, India, and other great nations of the Orient.

CONCLUSION

The ultimate explanation is therefore relatively a simple one. By an act of God the Euphrates River is dried up. This makes easy the descent of the tremendous army of two hundred million men upon the land of Israel to participate in the final world conflict. If such an army is to be raised up, it would be natural to conclude that it would come from Asia, the great population center of the world. Although they seem to come in opposition to the Roman ruler and his power, it is clear that this invasion springs from unbelief and these armies like the others gathered "to the battle of that great day of God Almighty" forget their individual conflicts to oppose the coming of Jesus Christ in power and glory from heaven.

The fact that the rise of Asia has occurred in our twentieth century with so many rapid and unexpected developments is another evidence that the world is moving toward its final climax and the end of the times of the Gentiles. In Asia, as in other parts of the world, the stage is being set for the final drama in which the kings of the east will have their important part.

CHAPTER XIII

ARMAGEDDON AND THE SECOND COMING OF CHRIST

The dramatic conclusion of the "times of the Gentiles" is described in prophecy as a gigantic world war which is climaxed by the second coming of Christ. The war that brings to a close the times of the Gentiles, which already has embraced twenty-five hundred years of history, is also the final effort of Satan in his strategy of opposition to the divine program of God. The second coming of Christ is God's answer. Some of the major elements of this conflict have already been considered and now need only to be related one to the other.

THE BEGINNING OF THE FINAL WORLD CONFLICT

The great world war which will engulf the Middle East at the end of the age is an outgrowth of the world situation during the time of the great tribulation. The Roman Empire formed earlier has now extended its power "over all kindreds, and tongues, and nations" (Revelation 13:7). The world government formed at the beginning of the great tribulation is scheduled in prophecy to endure for forty-two months or three and a half years (Revelation 13:5). At its beginning there is no serious challenge of the power and authority of the world ruler, and he is able to assume supreme power not only in the political field, but also receives recognition and worship as God and controls the economic power of the entire world. His reign is afflicted, however, by a series of great judgments of God described in the breaking of the seals, the blowing of the trumpets, and the outpouring of the vials of the wrath of God (Revelation 6:1—18:24). The disruptive force of these judgments is keenly felt throughout the world and it soon becomes evident that the promised utopia which his rule was designed to produce is not going to be fulfilled.

THE TRINITY OF EVIL

Many students of prophecy have noted the "trinity of evil" which characterizes the end time. In some respects this trinity corresponds to the Trinity of the Godhead. The ultimate source of power and evil in the end time is none other than Satan himself, referred to as "the great dragon," and as "that old serpent, called the Devil, and Satan" (Revelation 12:9). The political as well as the religious power which dominates the world is unquestionably Satan, and for this reason it is stated in Revelation 13:4 that the world "worshipped the dragon which gave power unto the beast." Satan assumes much the same power and prerogatives as God the Father.

The world ruler, who is Satan's masterpiece as a counterfeit of Christ, is the actual supreme dictator of the entire world and in a sense is Satan incarnate. He is undoubtedly a brilliant man intellectually and a dynamic personality, but he is completely dominated by Satan. In keeping with the satanic approach of imitation and counterfeit of God's program, the world ruler is Satan's king of :ings and lord of lords. Many students of Scripture assign the term antichrist" to this person for this reason, although in the Bible ione of the references to antichrist clearly indicate the personage .n view (cp. I John 2:18, 22; 4:3; II John 7).

The third member of the unholy trinity is the "beast coming up out of the earth" (Revelation 13:11) who assists the world ruler, performing satanic miracles and causing all men to worship the image of the beast (Revelation 13:12-15). He apparently also is instrumental in linking the economic and religious life of the world in that only those who worship the beast can buy or sell (Revelation 13:16). This personage is undoubtedly the same as "the false prophet" (Revelation 19:20) and in every respect he is the right-hand man and expediter for the world ruler. In his activities he corresponds to some extent to the ministry of the Holy Spirit on behalf of Christ and thus forms the third member of the trinity of evil. The world situation is therefore firmly in the grasp of Satan, Satan's man who is the world dictator, and the false prophet who heads up the satanic world religion of the great tribulation. In spite of the satanic control of the world by divine plan (Revelation 16:16), as the great tribulation moves on to its close, major sections of the world rebel against their ruler, and this sets the stage for the final great world war.

THE GATHERING OF THE ARMIES OF THE WORLD

The armies of the world which converge upon the Middle East according to Revelation 16:13 are induced to engage in the final conflict by satanic influences. This is introduced in the statement of John the Apostle: "I saw three unclean spirits like frogs come out of the mouth of the dragon, and out of the mouth of the beast, and out of the mouth of the false prophet. For they are the spirits of devils, working miracles, which go forth unto the kings of the earth and of the whole world, to gather them to the battle of that great day of God Almighty" (Revelation 16:13, 14).

There has been endless speculation as to the identity of the three unclean spirits like frogs. The passage itself indicates plainly that they are spirits of devils or demons and unquestionably are fallen angels under the command of Satan who are sent forth to draw the kings of the world into this final conflict. Humanly speaking, they are gathering to wrest the world rulership from the Roman ruler. In the satanic purpose, however, the armies of the world are gathered to fight the armies of heaven which will accompany Christ at His second coming. As in so many undertakings of Satan, such as is supremely illustrated in the crucifixion of Christ, the very program of Satan is its own destruction, and although Satan is inevitably impelled to gigantic opposition to Christ, he only sets the stage for the triumph of God. It is to facilitate the gathering of these armies that the Euphrates River is dried up that the armies from the east may converge without difficulty upon the Middle East.

Three major armies are mentioned in the Bible, namely, the army from the north, the army from the east, and the army from the south. These three armies are combining their efforts to wrest power from the Roman ruler who may be considered as the king of the west, although this title is never given to him in the Scriptures. The focal point for their gathering is declared in Revelation 16:16 to be "a place called in the Hebrew tongue Armageddon." Although various explanations have been given of this title, it seems to refer to the valley of Esdraelon also known as the valley of Jezreel located to the east of Megiddo in northern Israel. The word *Armageddon* actually means Mount of Megiddo from *har* meaning mount and Megiddo.

The broad valley that is here described is approximately fourteen miles wide and twenty miles long and historically has been the scene of many great battles of the past. In modern times the area became a great swamp, but with the revival of the area under the state of Israel the water has now been drained, and it is a fruitful and beautiful plain well suited for a great army. It is obvious, however, that this is only the central staging area for the war as actually the size of the armies involved preclude the possibility of confining them to this valley. As Scripture indicates, the war rages for some two hundred miles north and south thereby engulfing the entire Holy Land.

THE EARLY BATTLES OF THE FINAL WORLD WAR

Scripture does not provide much detail on the characteristics of the final world conflict. The main significance is that they are assembled in the Holy Land at the time of the second advent and oppose Christ in His return to the earth. However, some indication of the nature of the battles preceding the second coming of Christ is given in Daniel 11:40-45. If the order of introduction of events is taken chronologically, it appears that the first stage of the battle is an attack by the king of the south. According to Daniel 11:40, "And at the time of the end shall the king of the south push at him."

In rapid succession an attack also comes from the north which apparently is successful. The Scriptures state that "the king of the north shall come against him like a whirlwind, with chariots, and with horsemen, and with many ships; and he shall enter into the countries, and shall overflow and pass over." This king of the north may be Russia. The force of his invasion is such that he proceeds through the Holy Land and conquers Egypt at least temporarily. (Some expositors, however, interpret the passage beginning in Daniel 11:42 as referring to the Roman ruler who is naturally to the north of Africa, rather than to Russia as the king of the north, i.e., north of Palestine, as this seems to be the main theme of the passage.) The warfare brought about by the invasion of the king of the north and the king of the south, however, is now followed by another phase, namely, the arrival of the host from the east.

According to Daniel 11:44, "Tidings out of the east and out of the north shall trouble him: therefore he shall go forth with great fury to destroy, and utterly to make away many." The arrival of the forces from the Orient described as an army of two hundred million in Revelation 9:16 brings on the last phase of the world struggle, and at the time of the second coming of Christ the war is raging in a number of areas.

At least four geographic locations are mentioned in the Bible as figuring in the final struggle. The center, of course, is Armageddon where the main forces are located. Another focal point for the battle is the city of Jerusalem itself. According to Zechariah 12: 2-10 a siege will be declared against the city of Jerusalem. Jerusalem apparently will be defended to some extent by the power of God by miraculous intervention, for the armies of the world have great difficulty in subduing the city. It is stated in Zechariah 12:3, "And in that day will I make Jerusalem a burdensome stone for all people: all that burden themselves with it shall be cut in pieces, though all the people of the earth be gathered together against it." The passage goes on to say how the horses are smitten with blindness and the riders with madness.

At the time of the second coming of Christ, however, Jerusalem has finally been entered and is in the process of being subdued at the very moment that the glory of Christ in the heavens in His second advent appears. This is stated in Zechariah 14:2, 3: "For I will gather all nations against Jerusalem to battle; and the city shall be taken, and the houses rifled, and the women ravished; and half of the city shall go forth into captivity, and the residue of the people shall not be cut off from the city. Then shall the LORD go forth, and fight against those nations, as when he fought in the day of battle." From this description it is clear that the nations are engaged in active warfare in relation to Jerusalem at the time of the second advent.

Another geographic location is that of the valley of Jehoshaphat mentioned in Joel 3:2, 12. Although there is some dispute as to its location, it appears to be a valley immediately east of Jerusalem. Here, according to Joel, God declares: "I will also gather all nations, and will bring them down into the valley of Jehoshaphat, and will plead with them there for my people and for my heritage Israel, whom they have scattered among the nations, and parted my land." This valley is the scene of the divine judgment mentioned in Joel 3:12. Whether this gathering has to do with the battle for Jerusalem or is a subsequent event to the second advent, is not entirely clear.

Still another geographic location mentioned is that of Edom in Isaiah 34:1-6 and 63:1-6. Again it is not entirely clear, however, whether this is part of the battle or a subsequent judgment of God. In Daniel 11:41 Edom, Moab, and Ammon are specifically mentioned as escaping the full brunt of the battle.

The awful bloodshed stemming from this conflict is indicated in Revelation 9:18 where one-third of the armies are declared to be destroyed by the army from the east and the statement in Revelation 14:20 that "blood came out of the winepress, even unto the horse bridles, by the space of a thousand and six hundred furlongs." This is a distance of approximately two hundred miles and seems to indicate the extent of the bloody battle as these armies converge upon the Holy Land.

Although the exact deployment of the forces and the precise character of the successive battles which precede the second coming of Christ are not indicated in Scripture, it is sufficient for us to know that the Holy Land will be crowded with the armies of the world in preparation for the dramatic second advent of Christ. This is the final showdown of Gentile power dominated by Satan in blasphemous opposition to the Lordship of Jesus Christ.

The Second Coming of Christ and the Annihilation of the Armies

As the armies of the world are engaged in struggle for power throughout the Holy Land and in the very act of sacking the city of Jerusalem, the glory of the Lord appears in heaven and the majestic procession pictured in Revelation 19:11-16 takes place. At the head of the procession is Christ, described as riding on a white horse coming to judge and make war. His eyes are as a flame of fire and on His head are many crowns. His vesture is dipped in blood. Accompanying Him are the armies of heaven also riding on white horses and clothed in fine linen. In verse 15 it is stated of Christ, "Out of his mouth goeth a sharp sword, that with it he should smite the nations: and he shall rule them with a rod of iron: and he treadeth the winepress of the fierceness and wrath of Almighty God."

In contrast to His lowly birth in Bethlehem where He was laid in a manger, this advent is the triumphant King of kings and Lord of lords coming to claim the world for which He died and over which He is now going to exercise His sovereign authority in absolute power. The verses which follow invite the fowls of the earth to feed upon the carnage of the flesh of kings and mighty men and of their horses (Revelation 19:18).

According to Revelation 19:19 the armies of the world, which have previously been fighting each other, forget their differences and unite to fight against Christ in His second advent to the earth. John writes: "I saw the beast, and the kings of the earth, and their armies, gathered together to make war against him that sat on the horse, and against his army." Their struggle against such an adversary, however, is useless. It is apparent that they are put to death not by ordinary military struggle, but by the word of authority proceeding out of His mouth described as "a sharp sword" (Revelation 19:15). All the armies and their horses apparently are put to death at one stroke, but the beast (the world ruler) and the false prophet (the religious ruler of the world) are taken alive, and according to Revelation 19:20, "These both were cast alive into a lake of fire burning with brimstone." However, the doom of the rest is sealed in Revelation 19:21: "And the remnant were slain with the sword of him that sat upon the horse, which sword proceeded out of his mouth: and all the fowls were filled with their flesh."

Thus ends in one dramatic blow the power of the Gentiles which had controlled Jerusalem from the time of Nebuchadnezzar, 606 B.C. Thus ends also the satanic control of the Gentiles who had been a demonstration of satanic power, guilty of blasphemy and of the blood of countless martyrs, especially in oppressing the nation Israel.

Satan, their unseen leader, is also dealt with, and according to Revelation 20:1-3 he is cast into the abyss where he is rendered inactive for the entire period of the thousand-year reign of Christ on earth. Then he is destined to join the beast and the false prophet in the lake of fire (Revelation 20:10). The Gentile population of the world as a whole is judged at a separate judgment which follows and is a part of the establishment of Christ's kingdom on earth.

The inglorious end of Gentile power is precisely that which was anticipated in Daniel 2 where the great image disintegrates into chaff when struck by the stone cut out without hands. The same dramatic end is contemplated in the destruction of the beast (Daniel 7:11) followed by the inauguration of the everlasting kingdom in Daniel 7:13, 14. Jerusalem was no longer to be trodden under the feet of the Gentiles and once again Israel was to be exalted.

CHAPTER XIV

THE JUDGMENT OF THE NATIONS

In the broad program of divine dealings with the Gentiles, the sovereignty of God over creation is revealed in an unusual way. Although God in His sovereign grace has allowed Gentiles to assume great power and in the words of Christ, "Jerusalem shall be trodden down of the Gentiles, until the times of the Gentiles be fulfilled" (Luke 21:24), the consummation of this program inevitably brings the Gentiles before God for much-deserved divine judgment.

The history of the world has demonstrated that mankind is not judged once but many times. God has already exercised His judgment upon angels, Adam and Eve, and many particular judgments have fallen upon individuals, cities, and nations. In the flood of Noah the entire world was subject to disciplinary judgment. Towering above all judgments in history is the fact that Christ on the cross was judged as the sin bearer for mankind and that there Satan also was judged and defeated (John 16:11). Christians in this present age of grace also experience the disciplinary judgment of God (I Corinthians 11:32). Throughout the whole period of the tribulation and especially in the great tribulation judgment after judgment is poured out upon the world.

In this sequence the judgment of the nations assumes great significance and is one of the important milestones in divine dealing with a wicked world. That it is not the final judgment is evident, for other judgments will follow at the end of the millennium and the final judgment of all will be at the Great White Throne. The judgment of the nations, however, is important as bringing to a close one of the major phases of divine dealings, namely, the times of the Gentiles, and in a preliminary way anticipates the judgment of all unsaved men which will occur a thousand years later. The confusion which has arisen in the attempt to make this

151

the judgment of all men, including both the resurrected and translated saints as well as the wicked, is corrected by careful attention
to the exact text of Matthew 25:31-46 where the details of the
judgment are given.

THE TIME OF THE JUDGMENT

The passage is introduced by a time clause indicating when
the judgment will take place in the tremendous sequence of events
related to the second coming: "When the Son of man shall come in
his glory" (Matthew 25:31). The context indicates that this is the
coming of Christ to the earth in connection with the establishment
of His earthly kingdom. The judgment, therefore, is distinguished
in time from judgments that relate to the judgment seat of Christ
occurring in connection with the rapture of the church, and from
all historic judgments that precede as well as the many judgments
that are poured upon the earth during the great tribulation. It
follows the second coming of Christ to the earth, and precedes and
is a preparation for His reign on earth for a thousand years. Therefore it is also distinguished from any judgments on rebellion during
His kingdom reign and from the final judgment of the Great White
Throne at the end of the millennium.

THE PLACE OF THE JUDGMENT

From the context it is also clear that the place of the judgment
is earth, not heaven. The phrase, "the Son of man shall come in his
glory, and all the holy angels with him," is a picture of Christ and
the angels coming from heaven to the earth. This is substantiated
by another time clause, "Then shall he sit upon the throne of his
glory" (Matthew 25:31). This is not the throne of God in heaven,
but rather the earthly throne predicted by the prophets. It is the
beginning of the fulfillment of Jeremiah's prophecy, "Behold, the
days come, saith the LORD, that I will raise unto David a righteous
Branch, and a King shall reign and prosper, and shall execute judgment and justice in the earth" (Jeremiah 23:5). The place of this
judgment, therefore, is the millennial earth not heaven.

THE SUBJECTS OF THE JUDGMENT

In Matthew 25:32 the subjects of this divine judgment are
clearly declared to be "all nations." The passage could be translated "all Gentiles" as the Greek word is *ethne*. This is a common

word found frequently in the Bible and generally used of non-Jewish races. Although occasionally used of the Jews themselves (cp. Luke 7:5; 23:2; John 11:48, 50, 51, 52; 18:35; Acts 10:22; etc.), the more common meaning is to refer to Gentiles as distinguished from Jews, for instance in the references in Romans 11:13; 15:27; 16:4; Galatians 2:12. In some passages the Gentile character of the word is the main thought as in Romans 3:29; 9:24.

The context here indicates that the nations or the Gentiles should be viewed as the non-Jewish population of the world. In the narrative they are contrasted to "my brethren" (Matthew 25:40) who in the passage are distinguished from both the sheep and the goats, which comprise the entire mass of the Gentiles. In order to maintain the distinctions, it is best to understand it as referring to the non-Jewish peoples of the world. However, a similar judgment awaits the Jewish people (Ezekiel 20:34-38) and the issue is not whether both Jews and Gentiles are judged, but rather whether this passage concerns itself primarily with the Gentiles. In view of the fact that this is the climax of the times of the Gentiles, it seems appropriate that a special judgment should be applied to these who have oppressed Israel throughout their history.

From the English word *nations* some have inferred that what is dealt with here are political entities or countries as such. This is not at all indicated by the word *ethne,* a racial rather than an organizational term, and the details of the prophecy are such that they can be applied only to individuals and not to groups. The expression "all nations" therefore is best understood as referring to all Gentiles and more specifically all Gentiles who are living on earth at this time. It should be understood that many Gentiles at the time of the second coming of Christ were also already judged in the very act of divine wrath being poured on the armies gathered in the Middle East according to Revelation 19:17-21. As this is an earlier event in connection with the second advent, it must be assumed that we have here living Gentiles who were noncombatants or not involved in this great struggle.

THE BASIS OF THE JUDGMENT

This passage in Matthew 25 is a remarkable one in that works are prominent. According to the Scriptures, as all Gentiles are gathered before Christ to be judged they are divided into two classes, one described as "sheep" and the other designated "goats."

According to Matthew 25:33, "he shall set the sheep on his right hand, but the goats on the left." Having made this arbitrary division, He then justifies what He is doing by addressing Himself first to the sheep. In graphic language Christ in His role as "the King" declares to the sheep on his right hand: "Come, ye blessed of my Father, inherit the kingdom prepared for you from the foundation of the world: For I was an hungred, and ye gave me meat: I was thirsty, and ye gave me drink: I was a stranger, and ye took me in: Naked, and ye clothed me: I was sick, and ye visited me: I was in prison, and ye came unto me" (Matthew 25:34-36).

The declaration by Christ is remarkable because attention is called to certain rather ordinary works such as feeding the hungry, giving the thirsty drink, clothing the naked, visiting the sick and those in prison. Furthermore, Christ declares that they who have done these things have done them to Him personally.

The righteous accordingly answer Him with the question, "Lord, when saw we thee an hungred, and fed thee? or thirsty, and gave thee drink? When saw we thee a stranger, and took thee in? or naked, and clothed thee? Or when saw we thee sick, or in prison, and came unto thee?" (Matthew 25:37-39).

In reply Christ as "the King" states, "Verily I say unto you, Inasmuch as ye have done it unto one of the least of these my brethren, ye have done it unto me" (Matthew 25:40).

In contrast to this, Christ then turns to those on the left hand described as goats and declares, "Depart from me, ye cursed, into everlasting fire, prepared for the devil and his angels: For I was an hungred, and ye gave me no meat: I was thirsty, and ye gave me no drink: I was a stranger, and ye took me not in: naked, and ye clothed me not: sick, and in prison, and ye visited me not" (Matthew 25:41-43). In like manner the goats replied asking when they had neglected these works of mercy. The judgment then is pronounced upon the goats by Christ, "Verily I say unto you, Inasmuch as ye did it not to one of the least of these, ye did it not to me. And these shall go away into everlasting punishment: but the righteous into life eternal" (Matthew 25:45, 46).

This passage has troubled expositors for it seems to indicate that the sheep go into life eternal because of their righteous works whereas the wicked are condemned because of their failure to do these prescribed deeds of kindness. The question is naturally raised whether a person can be saved by works. If any passage in the Bible seems to imply it, this would be the passage.

When other Scriptures are brought to bear upon the question of whether people can be saved by works, it soon becomes evident that salvation by works is an impossibility under any circumstances. Although grace may be revealed in different degrees in different dispensations, it is evident from the very doctrine that all men are sinners, that all men are spiritually dead, and that no amount of good works can reverse the sentence of death or change the sinful nature of man. Works can never be the ground of man's salvation. There can be no cure for depravity, Adamic sin, and obvious human failure found in every life, other than the grace of God. Hence, while there may be different dispensations with varying rules of life there can be only one way of salvation, namely, through Christ and His provided redemption. The question remains then how this passage in its plain emphasis on works can be justified.

The answer is first of all found in the fact that in every dispensation works are not the ground of salvation, but rather they are the evidence of salvation. It is always true that "faith without works is dead" (James 2:26). This does not mean that a man is saved by works, but it does mean that one who really trusts God and is the recipient of divine grace will manifest this fact in a changed life. Humanly speaking, it is proper to challenge faith that does not manifest itself in some way. The passage then should be added to all others that emphasize the importance of works, not as the basis for salvation, but as the evidence of it.

A question still remains, however, concerning the precise character of these works. Is it always true that those who are kind to others and feed them and clothe them are necessarily Christians? The obvious philanthropy of many non-Christians in our modern world would seem to indicate that this cannot be taken normally as an indisputable evidence of eternal life.

The answer to the problem is found in the peculiar circumstances which form the background of the judgment. The people who are here being judged as Gentiles are those who have survived the horrors of the great tribulation. In this period which Jeremiah refers to as "the time of Jacob's trouble" (Jeremiah 30:7), anti-semitism will reach an all-time high. It is evident from the warning of Christ in Matthew 24:15-22 that the Jewish people will be hounded to the death especially in the Holy Land, and possibly throughout the world. Satanic hatred will be manifested to a degree never before achieved and will be part of the world-wide satanic deception which will cause men to believe a lie. In the words of II Thessalonians 2:11, "God shall send them strong delusion, that they should believe a lie."

Under these peculiar circumstances, under the strain and stress of satanic hatred of God and compulsion to worship the world ruler, anyone who would befriend a Jew would be a marked man. It is almost inconceivable that one who would be a true worshiper of the beast would ignore the world-wide command to exterminate the Jew. For a Gentile under these circumstances to befriend one who is designated as "my brethren" would be phenomenal and could be motivated only by a realization that the Jewish people are indeed the people of God and that their Messiah is indeed the Saviour of all who believe in Him. A simple work of kindness such as is here described therefore becomes highly significant, and in the context of this judgment one who would perform deeds of kindness would inevitably be a believer in the Lord Jesus Christ. Hence, while the works are not the ground of their salvation, which inevitably must be the grace of God and the sacrifice of Christ, works are nevertheless the evidence of salvation and to this our Lord points.

It is still true that salvation is "not of works, lest any man should boast" (Ephesians 2:9) but rather by faith and by grace.

The importance of works in the final judgments of mankind here has another divine revelation. The sheep who have manifested their faith in Christ under trying circumstances by befriending a Jew are now rewarded by being ushered into the millennial kingdom with its blessings of Christ's righteous rule and beneficent care over all who trust in Him. By contrast, the goats who followed the course of this world and undoubtedly participated in the persecution of the Jewish people as well as neglecting their acts of kindness now come under the divine judgment which they justly deserve, and are cast into everlasting fire.

THE JUDGMENT

The purpose of the judgment of the Gentiles is obviously one of separation of the righteous from the unrighteous in preparation for the millennial kingdom (cp. Matthew 24:40, 41). It is a fulfillment of that which was anticipated in the parables of Matthew

13 where it was predicted that in the end the wheat and the tares would be separated, the good and the bad fish would be dealt with, and the bad fish destroyed. The millennial kingdom will begin with the entire adult population of the world limited to those who have put their trust in Christ. It will be a new beginning comparable to that following the flood when Noah and his immediate family formed the entire population of the earth.

From this context it is also evident that this is not a final judgment of the individuals concerned. Those ushered into the millennial kingdom in this judgment still are in their natural bodies, still have a natural life to live, and ultimately will either die or be translated and have their life reviewed in finality. Although there is no specific revelation of this fact, the general truth of Hebrews 9:27, "as it is appointed unto men once to die, but after this the judgment," it may be concluded that the sheep will be subject to ultimate reward for their works even though at this time they are assured of eternal salvation in that they possess eternal life. In a similar way the casting of the wicked into everlasting fire should not be confused as a final judgment in which they are cast into the lake of fire which does not occur for another thousand years. It is rather that they move into a state of divine judgment described by the word "everlasting fire" such as is true both in Hades, the temporary abode of the wicked dead, and the lake of fire, the final state of the wicked. Their judgment in a word is that they are put to death physically, but subject to future judgment and final resurrection at the Great White Throne judgment. This judgment accordingly ends the times of the Gentiles and begins the millennial rule of Christ.

Chapter XV

THE NATIONS IN THE MILLENNIUM AND
THE ETERNAL STATE

The divine purpose of God for the Gentiles comes to its natural conclusion at the end of the times of the Gentiles which is marked by the second coming of Jesus Christ. The millennial reign of Christ primarily concerns the nation Israel and their restoratio to their ancient land. Most of the prophecies dealing with the millennial kingdom describe Israel's day of glory and prominence with Christ as their king and David resurrected from the dead as the prince.

There are, however, numerous prophecies that indicate that the Gentiles also will participate in the millennial reign of Christ and will inherit many of the blessings which characterize this period. As the reign of Christ is from sea to sea it necessarily goes far beyond the borders of the Promised Land, outlined so long ago to Abraham as extending from the River of Egypt to the Euphrates (Genesis 15:18). Outside the Promised Land, but often adjacent to it are the millennial counterparts of the ancient peoples who in one way or another were related to Israel's long history.

EXTENT OF GENTILE PROPHECY

In addition to the major nations which had a large part in the history of Israel such as Babylon, Assyria, and Egypt, a number of important prophecies are found in the Old Testament relating to minor nations. While such prophecies are scattered throughout the Old Testament, three major passages are found in Isaiah 13-23, Jeremiah 46 - 51, and Ezekiel 25 - 32. Seven major nations are mentioned in Isaiah to which can be added prophecies concerning the cities of Tyre and Damascus. Jeremiah adds additional prophecies relating to five of these plus a passage on the Ammonites (Jeremiah 49:1-6) and a short prophecy about Kedar and Hazor (49:28-31). Ezekiel offers additional prophecies concerning five

of these nations and adds a prophecy about Zidon (Ezekiel 28:
20-24). As special attention has already been directed to the prophecies relating to Babylon, the most prominent nations in these
prophecies to be considered here are the remaining nations, namely,
Assyria, Egypt, Philistia, Moab, Damascus, Ethiopia, Edom or
Dumah, Arabia, the city of Tyre, the Ammonites, Kedar and Hazor,
and Zidon.

The great prophecies of Isaiah, Jeremiah, and Ezekiel treat the
predictions concerning the nations in the context of Israel's coming
day of restoration and glory. Unquestionably the main theme in
the prophet's mind, whether it is stated or not, is that Israel in contrast to the nations which surround them is destined for glory and
honor in God's ultimate kingdom on earth. This tremendous truth
has been blurred by the unfortunate tendency to spiritualize these
prophecies in the attempt to make them describe the glory of the
church. If they are taken literally, however, they provide a pattern
of fulfilled prophecy in the past and a program of unfulfilled prophecy in the future which is tremendously significant in unfolding the
great purposes of God for the nations of the world.

The prophet Isaiah for instance portrays the glories of the
coming kingdom in Isaiah 11–12 before turning to the prophecies
relating to the nations in chapter 13 and following. It is clear that
from the prophetic viewpoint the importance of these prophecies
relating to the nations can be discovered only in the contrast to the
prophecies relating to Israel, many of which are yet unfulfilled.

In a similar way the prophecies of Jeremiah emphasize Israel's
restoration and coming glory. Often these prophecies are set in
the midst of prophecies relating to the nations and are presented
as sharp contrasts to the destined doom of the other nations and
God's divine judgment upon them.

The major portion of Jeremiah's section on prophecy concerning the nations occurs late in the book in chapters 46–51 preceded
by the historical and prophetical matter describing the stirring
relationship of Jeremiah to his contemporary situation coupled with
many prophecies concerning Israel in the latter days.

Ezekiel by contrast presents the prophecies concerning the nations first in chapters 25–32 and then follows in chapters 33 and 34
with predictions concerning the coming kingdom. Then after additional prophecies concerning Mount Seir, Israel's future is again
depicted in the latter portion of chapter 36. The vision of the valley

of dry bones in chapter 37 foreshadows Israel's ultimate restoration. Then before the great section beginning in chapter 40 there are the prophecies concerning Gog and Magog related to Israel's restoration in chapters 38 and 39. It is clear in Ezekiel as in the other prophecies that Israel's future is set into the context of God's dealings with the surrounding nations in the past as well as in the future. A survey of prophecies of these nations can well begin with an examination of prophecy relating to Assyria.

ASSYRIA

The importance of Assyria is borne out by more than 140 references in the Bible to this ancient people and more than 20 references to its principal city Nineveh. First mention is found as early as Genesis 2:14 where Moses in describing the Hiddekel River, later known as the Tigris, stated concerning this river, "that is it which goeth toward the east of Assyria." Moses of course was alluding to Assyria as it existed at the time he was writing Genesis. A similar reference is found in Genesis 25:18.

According to archaeologists, Assyria had a long history. As early as 2900 B.C. colonists, probably from Babylon, settled in a small area between the rivers Tigris and Zab southeast of the Armenian Mountains. Racially they were closely related to the people of Babylonia and mixed with the Sumerian people who were the earlier residents of this area. The Assyrians are generally classified as belonging to the Semitic race. Their language, similar to that of the Babylonians, was written mostly in ideograms on clay and stone by a wedge-shaped instrument, and hence is known as cuneiform.

Assyria first became a great city state under Shamshi-Adad I (1748–1716 B.C.) and increased in power as Babylon declined. Its greatest period, however, began with Tiglath-Pileser I (1114–1076 B.C.) when it extended its borders westward to the Mediterranean Sea and embraced a considerable area. Its power rose and fell for a number of centuries following and it was in this period that Assyria came in contact with Israel. Shalmaneser III (858-824 B.C.) is recorded as fighting Ahab in 853 B.C. and accepted tribute from Jehu, the son of Omri. These incidents, however, are not mentioned in the Bible.

A later ruler, Tiglath-Pileser III, according to II Kings 15:19, conquered Israel and exacted tribute from Menahem and carried off many of the children of Israel as captives. His successor Shal-maneser V (726-722 B.C.) attacked Hoshea of Israel who had re-volted against him. His successor, Sargon II (721-705 B.C.), men-tioned only in Isaiah 20:1, conquered the capital of Samaria (II Kings 17:3-41). Sennacherib (704-681 B.C.) is recorded as attempt-ing to conquer Jerusalem, but was thwarted by the slaying of his army by the angel of the Lord (II Kings 19:1-37) and was suc-ceeded by his son Esar-haddon. With the rising power of Babylon, Nineveh, capital of Assyria, fell in 612 B.C. under a collation of Babylonian, Median, and Scythian armies. With this event Assyria came abruptly to the end of its career and in a remarkably short time Assyrian civilization was completely destroyed. Its great cities became mounds of debris and for centuries were lost until finally recovered by archaeologists and identified in the nineteenth cen-tury.

From the standpoint of prophecy, the history of Assyria is im-portant because along its path numerous prophecies were fulfilled. Isaiah the prophet, for instance, solemnly warned the children of Israel of the coming invasion of the Assyrians and their ultimate captivity (Isaiah 7:17-20; 8:4-7) and predicted that Assyria would be punished in due time and brought down (Isaiah 11:12-16). The entire book of Nahum relates to the downfall of Nineveh, and the book of Jonah records the remarkable experience of repentance of the people of Nineveh at the preaching of Jonah which delayed their ultimate destruction one hundred and fifty years.

Most of the prophecies concerning Nineveh have already been fulfilled. A few references, however, are subject to fulfillment in the millennial reign and events relating to it.

One of the prophecies concerning the destruction of Assyria is found in Micah 5:5, 6 where the context seems to indicate a mil-lennial situation. Some expositors have identified "the Assyrian" of Micah 5:5 as the little horn of Daniel 8 and conclude that the future world ruler who will head the Roman Empire will be an Assyrian. This identification, however, is doubtful, and it is more probable that Micah, living in the period of Assyria's ascendancy, is merely contrasting here the future glory of Israel with the destruction of Nineveh and of Assyria which actually took place in the seventh century B.C.

That Assyria is to be recognized in the millennial situation, however, is indicated in several passages. According to Isaiah 11:

11, 16, the regathering of Israel at the beginning of the millennium will be from Assyria as well as from other nations, and a highway will stretch from Egypt to Assyria through the land of Israel as a major transportation link in the millennial kingdom. A similar prophecy is found in Isaiah 19:23-25 in reference to the future millennial kingdom: "In that day shall there be a highway out of Egypt to Assyria, and the Assyrian shall come into Egypt, and the Egyptian into Assyria, and the Egyptians shall serve with the Assyrians. In that day shall Israel be the third with Egypt and with Assyria, even a blessing in the midst of the land: Whom the LORD of hosts shall bless, saying, Blessed be Egypt my people, and Assyria the work of my hands, and Israel mine inheritance."

It is evident from this passage that Israel's two most important neighbors in the millennial kingdom will be the peoples who inhabit the area of ancient Assyria to the northeast and Egypt to the southwest. In that day both Assyria and Egypt will be blessed along with Israel. The fact that Israel is called "third" in the light of other prophecies should not be interpreted, however, as meaning that Israel is less than these nations, but rather that it will be spoken of in the same breath as a prominent world power of that day. Another reference to Israel's regathering from Assyria is found in Isaiah 27:13. Zechariah adds his contribution in Zechariah 10:10, 11 where the destruction of the pride of Assyria and the scepter of Egypt is predicted and the regathering of Israel from these lands is anticipated. Assyria, the great nation of the past which antedated the Babylonian Empire and successive dominions of the Gentiles, will have its echo in the prophetic future and its place in the divine program of the millennial kingdom.

EGYPT

In the millennial situation, Egypt likewise is to have a prominent place as already illustrated in passages cited concerning Assyria. Israel will be regathered from Egypt to their Promised Land, but Egypt will be a prominent nation in the millennial situation. That Egypt will be blessed is mentioned specifically in Isaiah 19:25 and that it will be a prominent nation along with Israel and Assyria is indicated in the same passage. Egypt is singled out for special warning in Zechariah 14:18, 19; God will punish them unless they keep the feast of tabernacles in the millennial kingdom. What is revealed in respect to Egypt has reference to the world-wide rule of Christ and indicates that all people will necessarily be required to serve Him.

PHILISTIA

The prominence of the Philistines in the history of Israel is demonstrated by approximately 270 references to them in the Old Testament. Most of these concern historic events depicting the constant struggle between Israel and the Philistines. A few references to the Philistines contain prophecies of their doom or defeat at the hands of Israel already fulfilled. References such as Jeremiah 47:1; Ezekiel 25:15, 16; Amos 1:8; Zephaniah 2:5; and Zechariah 9:6 are probably best interpreted as already fulfilled.

A few references to the Philistines, however, are found in a context of the future millennial kingdom and imply that the territory of the Philistines and the inhabitants in that future day will have a relationship to the kingdom. According to Isaiah 11:14 Israel will have domination over the Philistines in that day. Again in Obadiah 19 the house of Jacob shall possess the Philistines. In both of these prophecies it may be presumed that the writer of Scripture is referring to the territory known to them at that time as possessed by the Philistines and to the future inhabitants of that area. It means simply that Israel will be victorious over their ancient enemies and possess their territory.

MOAB

Of the more than 180 references to Moab in the Old Testament, the great majority deal with historic events. They had many contacts with the children of Israel during the Exodus as well as in the period of the judges. The fact that Ruth was a Moabitess and in the lineage of David sets this people apart.

The first important prophetic utterance relative to Moab is recorded in Numbers 24:17 where Balaam predicted concerning the Messiah, "I shall see him, but not now: I shall behold him, but not nigh: there shall come a Star out of Jacob, and a Sceptre shall rise out of Israel, and shall smite the corners of Moab, and destroy all the children of Sheth." The reference is, of course, to the Davidic line of which Christ is the ultimate fulfillment, and the prophecy anticipates not only the conquering of the Moabites under David and his successors but the ultimate possession of the land by Israel in the coming kingdom.

In Isaiah 11:14 a similar reference is found where the children of Israel are predicted to conquer Edom and Moab as well as the Philistines and the children of Ammon. This too refers to the possession of the land by Israel in the millennial kingdom.

Still another allusion to the Moabites in the future is included in the prophecies of the final world war described in Daniel 11: 40-45. In Daniel 11:41 Moab along with Edom and the children of Ammon is said to escape the warfare between the king of the north and the king of the south with the Roman world ruler. This will have its fulfillment in the days just preceding the second coming of Christ.

The more extensive prophecies relating to Moab seem to have their primary fulfillment in history. These prophecies anticipate that Moab will be punished by God for their sins and for their opposition to the children of Israel. Some of them, like Isaiah 25:10, may have a future reference like those previously considered and will be fulfilled in the millennial kingdom. But the great prophetic passages such as Isaiah 15:1–16:14, Jeremiah 48:1-47, and Ezekiel 25:8-11, although describing in detail the downfall of Moab, seem to have their primary fulfillment in events of the past. Although they may foreshadow, as prophecy often does, the ultimate triumph of the children of Israel, the two important prophetic references to Moab in the minor prophets, namely Amos 2:1, 2 and Zephaniah 2:8, 9, refer to judgments already fulfilled.

Although the unfulfilled prophecies relating to Moab do not seem to be a large proportion of the total material provided in Scripture, they add their evidence to the total picture of the future kingdom in which Israel will be restored and triumphant over her traditional enemies.

DAMASCUS

Damascus was one of the most ancient cities of the Middle East and one of the few to have a continuous history down to modern times. First mentioned in Genesis 14:15, it continued to have a relationship to Israel throughout the Old Testament period where there are more than forty references and in the New Testament where it is mentioned fifteen times. The more extended prophecies as found in Isaiah 17:1-14 and Jeremiah 49:23-27 have all been fulfilled as well as the occasional references found in Isaiah 7:8; 8:4; Amos 1:3-5; 3:12; 5:27. In Ezekiel 47:16-18 and 48:1 reference is made to Damascus as being in existence in the coming kingdom and furnishing identification for the borders of the land of Israel. No events are predicted and the reference seems to be to geography rather than to people who inhabit the land at that time. It is of interest that Damascus, which has had such a long history, apparently will continue its existence into the millennial kingdom.

THE ETHIOPIANS

The Ethiopians were so named by the Greeks and the Romans and refer to those known as the children of Cush in the Hebrew. They were descendants of Ham and occupied the area south of Egypt. Although most of the references to Ethiopians seem to concern events already fulfilled or historic in connection with the Ethiopians, some of the statements seem to be prophetic. The extended prophecy of Isaiah 18:1-7, while largely fulfilled, seems to go beyond the past, such as in the prediction of Isaiah 18:7 where it is stated that the Ethiopians shall be brought as a subdued people to the Lord of hosts in Mount Zion. Isaiah 45:14 may also be interpreted as picturing the triumph of Israel over the Ethiopians in the kingdom period, although the reference may be to historic fulfillment. The predictions of Isaiah 20:3-5 and 43:3 seem to have had adequate fulfillment in the past. The prophecies of Ezekiel 30:4, 5 relating as they do to the Day of the Lord may well have some future fulfillment. The reference to Ethiopia in Ezekiel 38:5, because it describes a northern invasion, has been taken by some to refer to another people, but in any event it is future and a part of the great northern invasion of Israel yet to be fulfilled.

Several other future references to Ethiopia seem to be found in the prophets. In Daniel 11:43 Ethiopia is mentioned as one of the countries that escaped warfare in the final world struggle which apparently reaches Egypt, but does not go farther south. In Psalm 68:31 it is predicted, "Ethiopia shall soon stretch out her hands unto God." This seemingly refers to the future millennial kingdom, although the prophecy of Zephaniah 2:12 of destruction at the hands of the Lord probably was fulfilled in the past. The prediction of Zephaniah 3:10, that the Ethiopians will come as suppliants to the Lord, fits best into the future millennial kingdom.

Taken as a whole, the references to Ethiopia recognize their continued significance in God's program and their ultimate destiny as one of the Gentile nations which will be subordinate to Israel when Christ reigns on earth.

EDOM

The descendants of Esau are frequently mentioned in the Old Testament under various designations, but usually as the Edomites. Many of the prophecies relating to Edom have already been fulfilled, such as the extended predictions of Jeremiah 9:26; 25:21; 49:7-22; Lamentations 4:22; Ezekiel 25:12-14; Joel 3:19; Amos 1:6, 9, 11; 2:1. Some of these may be a foreshadowing of ultimate subjugation of Edom in the millennial kingdom.

The prophecies concerning Esau and his descendants stem from the original prophecy of Isaac. After Jacob had stolen the blessing intended for Esau, Isaac pronounced the lesser blessing on Esau recorded in Genesis 27:39, 40. Esau is promised physical blessing, but is put under the dominion of Jacob, although it is predicted that he would break the yoke of Jacob from off his neck. The long history of the relationship of the children of Jacob to the descendants of Esau carried out the conflict anticipated here and the children of Edom continued to figure in prophecy up to and including the kingdom age.

Isaiah 11:14 mentions Edom as being subdued by Israel in the kingdom period. Isaiah 63:1 is a prophetic description of the coming of Christ in judgment at His second coming. He is described as coming "from Edom." Daniel 11:41 includes Edom as one of the countries which escape warfare in the final world conflict before the second coming.

The most extended prophecy concerning Edom is found in Obadiah which is entirely devoted to this subject. Verses 1 to 14 speak of the judgment of God upon Edom because of their sins in rejoicing over the captivity of the children of Judah. These prophecies had at least partial fulfillment. The passage, verses 15-21, which conclude the book, picture Edom in the Day of the Lord as having experienced divine judgment and being under the domination of the house of Jacob. The age-long controversy between Esau and Jacob will be resolved in Jacob's favor in keeping with the sovereign choice of God in which it was declared that the elder should serve the younger (Romans 9:12). Taken as a whole, the prophecies relating to Edom have already had amazing fulfillment in so far as God's judgment has fallen upon them in the past. The ultimate fulfillment awaits the second coming of Christ.

ARABIA

Of the comparatively few references to Arabia in the Bible, the principal prophecy is found in Isaiah 21:13-17. Although the passage is not entirely clear, it seems to have been already fulfilled in the past. The kings of Arabia are also mentioned as those who will drink of the divine judgment of God in Jeremiah 25:24, probably already fulfilled. In Isaiah 13:20 it is also mentioned that the Arabian will no longer pitch his tent in Babylon after its destruction. On the whole, these prophecies are brief and insignificant in the total program of God.

TYRE

The city of Tyre like Damascus is one of the ancient cities of the world. Its riches and commercial interests were renowned, and it figured largely in the history of the ancient world. Although assigned to the tribe of Asshur, it was not subdued by them, but through much of its history was in friendly relationship with Israel as during the time of the reign of Solomon. Because of a fortress on an island in the Mediterranean to which the people could retire when Tyre was under siege, Tyre was very difficult to subdue and was able to resist the Assyrian armies and stand off Nebuchadnezzar the king of Babylon for more than a dozen years. Alexander the Great had to construct a causeway from the mainland in order to conquer it, and in the process fulfilled many of the prophecies concerning the destruction of the city itself.

Most of the prophecies concerning Tyre have already been fulfilled, such as Isaiah 23:1-18; Jeremiah 25:22; 47:4; Joel 3:4-8; Amos 1:9, 10, and Zechariah 9:2-4.

The importance of Tyre prophetically stems largely from the great prophecy of Ezekiel where three long chapters are devoted to Tyre, namely, 26, 27, and 28. Chapter 26 of Ezekiel describes the judgment which is impending upon Tyre. The immediate occasion was Nebuchadnezzar's siege of the city, but it goes beyond the immediate situation to its ultimate destruction later at the hands of Alexander the Great. Then the remarkable prophecy of Ezekiel 26:14 was fulfilled which reads: "And I will make thee like the top of a rock: thou shalt be a place to spread nets upon; thou shalt be built no more: for I the LORD have spoken it, saith the Lord GOD." The city of Tyre was literally scraped to the rock in order to provide materials to build a causeway out to its island fortress. Visitors to Tyre today can see the evidence of this fulfillment.

Chapter 27 of Ezekiel is a long lamentation over the destruction of Tyre with its description of the riches which once characterized this city. The lamentation is extended to the prince of Tyre in Ezekiel 28:1-10. The prophecies to this point can probably best be interpreted as having been graphically fulfilled in the long history of Tyre.

The prophetic utterance of Ezekiel 28:12-15, while having a partial reference to Tyre, seems to go beyond the immediate human ruler to Satan himself in his original conflict with God. He is described as "the anointed cherub that covereth" who at one time was "perfect . . . from the day that thou wast created, till iniquity was found in thee." Many interpreters from Augustine to modern times have felt that this description is a revelation of the character of the original rebellion of Satan against God when he, according to the parallel description in Isaiah 14:12-15, sought to be like God and take the place of God in worship. The Ezekiel passage, however, beginning in verse 16 seems to return largely to a description of Tyre itself and predicts its utter destruction. The large place afforded Tyre in these three long chapters of Ezekiel indicate its importance from the prophetic standpoint as not only embodying divine judgment upon a wicked city which had exalted itself above God, but also upon its unseen ruler, Satan. The entire prophecy anticipates the downfall of Satan as well as the city of Tyre itself. As far as the prophetic program of God is concerned, Tyre does not seem to figure largely in end-time events, although the intimation is that it will be in existence in some form as a city in the time of the end.

MISCELLANEOUS PROPHECIES

Among the lesser prophecies concerning the nations is that concerning the Ammonites. Although the Ammonites are mentioned frequently in the Bible, they do not loom large in the prophetic narrative. One of the major passages is found in Jeremiah 49:1-6 where God's divine judgment and conquest of the Ammonites is pictured. A similar passage is found in Ezekiel 25:1-7 which prophesies the conquest of the Ammonites by "the men of the east." Other references to the Ammonites in prophecy now fulfilled are passages such as Jeremiah 25:21; Amos 1:13; and Zephaniah 2:8, 9.

The only reference clearly future is that of Daniel 11:41 where Ammon is said to escape some of the warfare at the end of the age. The dealings of God with the children of Ammon again illustrate His justice and the certainty of fulfilled prophecy.

A brief prophecy concerning Kedar and Hazor is contained in Jeremiah 49:28-33. It is a prediction of judgment upon them at the hands of Nebuchadnezzar king of Babylon. A similar judgment is pronounced upon Elam in Jeremiah 49:34-38. Other references to God's judgment on Kedar are found in Isaiah 21:16, 17. Only future reference relative to those of Kedar seems to be found in Isaiah 60:7 where it is indicated that "the flocks of Kedar shall be gathered together" as possessions of the coming Messiah.

Mention should also be made of Zidon also spelled Sidon, another ancient city on the eastern Mediterranean north of Tyre. In Ezekiel 28:20-24 it is predicted that Zidon will be subject to divine judgment of pestilence and warfare because of their sins. This has unquestionably been fulfilled already in history. Zidon is also mentioned as participating in the general judgment which falls upon Tyre in Isaiah 23:2, 4, 12 and is also associated with Tyre in other prophecies, such as Jeremiah 25:22; 47:4, and Joel 3:4. As a city it does not figure largely in prophecy.

A survey of the countries surrounding Israel demonstrate that prophecies of their coming judgment and subjugation to Israel are set in a context of Israel's exaltation in the kingdom age. Although in some cases the reference may be largely geographic rather than to the nations themselves, for racial continuity may be difficult to sustain, the language of Scripture is sufficiently clear to make plain that Israel will triumph over her enemies and in the process be restored to a place of glory and blessing under the rule of the Messiah. The fact that Israel is already in her place in the Middle East is a foreshadowing of these ultimate triumphs which await the second coming of her Messiah and Saviour.

THE NATIONS IN THE ETERNAL STATE

It is only natural that prophecies relating to the nations should be primarily concerned with the present earth rather than the eternal state. It is an error, however, to assume that national identity will be lost in eternity. Just as there will be individual identity, so also there will be racial identity, and individuals will inevitably carry throughout eternity an identification related to some extent to their place in the history of the world. Hence, Israelites will be Israelites throughout eternity and Gentiles will be Gentiles as well.

Although there has been some resistance to this idea, national identity seems a natural corollary to individual identity. If Abraham is to remain Abraham throughout eternity and David is to remain David, it is inevitable that they would be considered in their historical context in time. So also will it be with those who are saved among the Gentiles. There is no indication that nationality of individuals will be stressed, but the fact that they belong to a nation is revealed in the description of the New Jerusalem.

According to the revelation given to John, the New Jerusalem will include the angels (Revelation 21:12), the children of Israel (Revelation 21:12), the church as represented in the twelve apostles (Revelation 21:14) and the Gentiles (Revelation 21:24). This is anticipated in the itemization of those who will be related to the heavenly Jerusalem given in Hebrews 12:22, 23 where specifically the heavenly Jerusalem includes "an innumerable company of angels," the "church of the firstborn," and "the spirits of just men made perfect." This latter reference seems to be an inclusive one referring to all men who are saved who are not included in the previous itemization. Such a description obviously includes Gentiles who were saved. Hence, the reference to "the nations," better translated "the Gentiles," in Revelation 21:24 is not surprising.

Expositors are of course disagreed as to whether this description relates to the heavenly city in the millennial period or in the eternal state. In either case, however, the implication is that the same people who inhabit the eternal city in this description will continue to inhabit it throughout eternity. The conclusion is therefore sound and valid that the saved among the Gentiles will find their place in the eternal bliss which will characterize the saints in eternity to come as they dwell in perfect fellowship with God in the heavenly city, the New Jerusalem.

Although the pattern of Gentile prophecy and fulfillment is largely one of judgment upon their unbelief and blasphemous rebellion against God, it is another token of the grace of God that, in addition to His program for Israel and the church, the body of Christ, countless Gentiles in the Old Testament period as well as in the tribulation and the millennium will come to know Jesus Christ and His saving grace, and accordingly will be qualified to participate as individuals in the blessings which God has ordained for those who love Him. The majestic purpose of God for the nations is therefore crowned with this happy note of the triumph of grace in those among the Gentiles who turn to Jesus Christ.

Taken as a whole, the program of God for the Gentiles emphasizes His righteousness and His sovereignty which, though challenged for many centuries, ultimately has its clear declaration at the second coming of Jesus Christ. Throughout eternity, however, the presence of Gentiles who entered the eternal state is the reminder of the comprehensive character of the grace of God which provided Jesus Christ as a means of reconciling the world unto Himself. Their testimony will join with that of all other saints and the holy angels in the mighty symphony of worship and praise which will constitute the music of eternity.

Chapter XVI

AMERICA IN PROPHECY

One of the natural questions facing the world, but especially citizens of the United States of America, is the place of the United States in the unfulfilled prophetic program. In the last fifty years, the United States of America has become one of the most powerful and influential nations of all history. What does the Bible contribute to the question of the future of the United States?

In keeping with the principle that prophecy is primarily concerned with the Holy Land and its immediate neighbors, it is not surprising that geographic areas remote from this center of Biblical interest should not figure largely in prophecy and may not be mentioned at all. No specific mention of the United States or any other country in North America or South America can be found in the Bible. None of the rather obscure references to distant lands can be taken specifically as a reference to the United States. Any final answer to the question is therefore an impossibility, but nevertheless some conclusions of a general character can be reached.

The World Situation at the End Time

As previous study of prophecy has indicated, the Scriptures provide an outline of major events in the period beginning with the rapture of the church and ending with the second coming of Christ to establish His kingdom. Immediately after the rapture there will be a period of preparation in which the ten-nation confederacy in the Mediterranean will emerge and the little horn of Daniel 7 will be revealed as its eventual dictator. At the same time there will be the emergence of a world church as suggested in Revelation 17.

At the conclusion of this period of preparation the head of the Mediterranean confederacy, who will be the Roman "prince that shall come," will make a covenant with Israel (Daniel 9:27) which will introduce the second phase of the period, namely, a period of protection and peace for Israel. After enduring for three and a half years or one half of the projected seven-year period contemplated in the covenant, the Roman ruler will take the role of world dictator, assume the prerogatives of deity, and begin the great tribulation with its corresponding period of persecution for Israel and the emergence of a world religion with the world ruler as its deity. This third period will be climaxed by the second coming of Christ to the earth and its attending judgments.

THE RELATION OF THE UNITED STATES TO THESE WORLD EVENTS

Although the Scriptures do not give any clear word concerning the role of the United States in relationship to the revived Roman Empire and the later development of the world empire, it is probable that the United States will be in some form of alliance with the Roman ruler. Most citizens of the United States of America have come from Europe and their sympathies would be more naturally with a European alliance than with Russia or countries in Eastern Asia. It may even be that the United States will provide large support for the Mediterranean confederacy as it seems to be in opposition to Russia, Eastern Asia, and Africa. Actually a balance of power in the world may exist at that time not too dissimilar to the present world situation, namely, that Europe and the Mediterranean area will be in alliance with America in opposition to Russia, Eastern Asia, and Africa. Based on geographic, religious and economic factors such an alliance of powers seems a natural sequence of present situations in the world.

If the end-time events include a destruction of Russia and her allies prior to the final period of great tribulation, this may trigger an unbalance in the world situation that will permit the Roman ruler to become a world ruler. In this event, it should be clear that the United States will be in a subordinate role and no longer the great international power that it is today.

It has been suggested by some that the total absence of Scriptural comment on the United States of America in the end time is evidence that the United States previously has been destroyed by an atomic war or some other catastrophic means and therefore no longer is a voice in international affairs. Such a solution, however, overlooks the fact that not only the United States but all of the Americas are omitted from prophecy, and the same is true of

Australia. The fact is there are few references to any country at some distance from the Holy Land. The view, therefore, would be preferable that while the United States is in existence and possibly a power to be reckoned with in the rapidly moving events which characterize the end of the age, world political power will be centered in the Mediterranean area and necessarily the United States will play a subordinate role.

History has many records of great nations which have risen to unusual power and influence only to decline because of internal corruption or international complications. It may well be that the United States of America is today at the zenith of its power much as Babylon was in the sixth century B.C. prior to its sudden downfall at the hands of the Medes and the Persians (Daniel 5). Any realistic survey of moral conditions in the world today would justify a judgment of God on any nation, including that of the United States. The longsuffering God has offered unusual benefits to the United States both in a material and religious way, but they have been used with such profligacy that ultimate divine judgment may be expected. The question no longer is whether America deserves judgment, but rather why divine judgment has been so long withheld from a nation which has enjoyed so much of God's bounty.

A partial answer may be found in the fact that the United States of America in spite of its failures has nevertheless been a source of major Christian testimony in the world and has done more to promote the missionary cause in terms of money and men than any other nation. Although the United States numbers only five per cent of the total world population, in the last century probably more than fifty per cent of the missionaries and money spent has come from America. In view of the fact that it is God's major purpose in this present age to call out Jew and Gentile to faith in Christ and to have the Gospel preached in all nations, the prosperity which has been true of America has made possible this end and may have been permitted by God to accomplish His holy purposes.

Another important reason for delay in divine judgment upon America is the Abrahamic promise concerning his seed, "I will bless them that bless thee, and curse him that curseth thee" (Genesis 12:3). The United States for the most part has been kind to the Jew. Here the seed of Abraham has had religious freedom and opportunity to make wealth. Judgment on other nations has frequently been preceded by persecution of the Jew. So far in the United States the Jew has had equal treatment.

It is evident, however, that if Christ came for His church and all true Christians were caught out of this world, America then would be reduced to the same situation as other countries. The true church will be gone, and Israel may be persecuted. The drastically changed situation would no longer call for material or political blessing upon the United States. It would therefore follow that with the removal of the principal cause for withholding judgment, namely, the promotion of the missionary cause and befriending the wandering Jew, reason would no longer exist for maintaining America in its present standard of power politically and economically. It may well be that the United States, like Babylon of old, will lose its place of leadership in the world, and this will be a major cause in the shift of power to the Mediterranean scene.

Conclusion

Although conclusions concerning the role of America in prophecy in the end time are necessarily tentative, the Scriptural evidence is sufficient to conclude that America in that day will not be a major power and apparently does not figure largely in either the political, economic, or religious aspects of the world. America may well be at its zenith today both in power, influence, and opportunity. In view of the imminent return of the Lord, the time is short and the cause of evangelism is urgent. If prophecy has any one message as bearing on our times, it is that time and opportunity are short, and impending world conditions soon may close the door for further witness in many areas. What is true of America is true for the evangelical church throughout the world, and prophecy in general serves to emphasize the importance of the present task of bearing witness to the Gospel, beginning at Jerusalem and to the uttermost parts of the world.

The destiny of nations is in the hands of the omnipotent God. History is moving inexorably to its prophesied consummation. The divine program in all its detail will be fulfilled. The Son of God will reign in Zion. The nations will bow at His feet. Ultimately the present earth will be replaced with a new heaven and a new earth in which the New Jerusalem will be the home of the redeemed of all ages. All nations will continue throughout eternity to worship and adore the infinite Triune God whose majesty, wisdom, and power will be unquestioned. In that eternal day, God's love and grace will be supremely revealed in those among all nations who are redeemed by the blood of the Lamb.

ISRAEL
in
PROPHECY

Chapter I

THE NEW STATE OF ISRAEL

When Theodor Herzel announced in 1897 the purpose of the Zionist movement — "to create for the Jewish people a home in Palestine secured by public law" — few realized how dramatic would be the fulfillment. The Jews had dreamed for centuries of re-establishing themselves in their ancient land. Now this longing was translated into action. Few nations could point to a richer heritage as a basis for the hope of the restoration of the nation.

The History of Israel in the Old Testament

The history of Israel began more than thirty-five hundred years ago, when, according to the early chapters of Genesis, the divine call was extended to Abraham to leave his ancient land of Ur and proceed to a land that God would show him. After some delay, Abraham finally entered the land, and there the promised son Isaac was born.

Though God miraculously fulfilled the promise of a son in Isaac, Abraham himself never possessed the Promised Land but lived as a pilgrim and stranger. Rich in earthly goods, Abraham never fulfilled his hope of a homeland in his lifetime. His son Isaac shared a similar fate. Under Jacob, Isaac's son, the people of Israel forsook the Promised Land entirely and at the invitation of Joseph set up their homes in Egypt where they lived for hundreds of years. It was not until their very existence was threatened in Egypt by a hostile king that the day finally came for Israel's possession of the land. With Moses as their appointed leader, they began their momentous migration, one of the largest ever undertaken by any nation. After forty years of wandering in the wilderness, they finally completed their pilgrimage from Egypt to the land promised Abraham.

The book of Joshua records the conquest of Palestine and its partial occupation. The nation Israel, however, was doomed to generations of oppression and moral declension. They periodically were oppressed by Gentile nations about them with occasional cycles of spiritual and political revival, led by judges whom God raised up. The political anarchy which characterized the period of the judges was succeeded by the reign of the kings, beginning with Saul, and was followed by the glory and political power of the kingdoms under David and Solomon. Under Solomon, Israel reached its highest point of prestige, wealth, and splendor, and much of the land which God promised Abraham temporarily came under the sway of Solomon.

Again, however, moral deterioration attacked from within. Because of Solomon's disregard of the law against marriage to the heathen, many of his wives were pagans who did not share his faith in God. His children, therefore, were raised by their pagan mothers and they were trained to worship idols instead of the God of Israel. The resulting judgment of God upon Israel was manifested in the divided kingdoms of Judah and Israel. The ten tribes, united to form the Kingdom of Israel, persisted in complete apostasy from God, and idol worship became the national religion. In 721 B.C. the ten tribes were carried off into captivity by the Assyrians. The Kingdom of Judah, including the tribes of Benjamin and Judah, continued for a little more than another century until they too were taken captive by Babylonia. For a generation, the land of Israel was denuded of the descendants of Abraham.

The book of Ezra records the restoration of Israel which followed the captivities. In keeping with the promise given to Jeremiah that the captivity would continue for only seventy years (Jeremiah 29:10), the first expedition of the children of Israel, led by Zerubbabel, began their trek to their homeland. The book of Ezra records their early steps in restoring the land and building the temple. Nehemiah completes the picture with the building of the walls and the restoration of the city of Jerusalem itself. Once again Israel was in their ancient land, re-established as a nation.

The history of Israel from that point on was not without its serious problems. First, the warriors of Macedon under Alexander the Great swept over Palestine. Then they were subject to the rule of the Seleucian monarchs and later were controlled by Syrians. One of the sad chapters in Israel's history was the Maccabean revolt which occurred in 167 B.C. and which resulted in severe persecution of the people of Israel. In 63 B.C. Pompey established Roman control and from then on the land of Palestine, the homeland of Israel, was under Roman control for centuries. It was in this period that Jesus Christ was born in Bethlehem. During Christ's lifetime on earth, Israel was under the heel of Rome and Christ Himself was sent to the cross on the basis of Roman authority.

THE HISTORY OF ISRAEL SINCE CHRIST

The subsequent history of Israel was most unhappy. In A.D. 70, Titus, the Roman general, ordered Jerusalem and its beautiful temple destroyed, and a quarter of a million Jews perished. The remaining Jews continued to revolt and finally in A.D. 135 the desolation of Judea was ordered. Almost a thousand towns and villages were left in ashes and fifty fortresses razed to the ground. The people of Israel, except for a few scattered families who remained, were dispersed to the four winds.

From A.D. 135 to modern times, the nation Israel made their homes all over the world. In the eighth century the Abbasid Arabs took possession of Israel's ancient land. For a brief period the Frankish crusaders were established in Palestine only to be defeated by Saladin in 1187. The Ottoman Turks assumed power in 1517 and the land of Palestine continued as part of the Ottoman Empire until Turkey was defeated in World War I. The conquering of Palestine by General Allenby in 1917 and the British occupation of Palestine proved to be a dramatic turning point in the history of Israel.

The Return of Israel to the Land

Before control of Palestine was wrested from the Turks, the Zionist movement had already begun. As early as 1871 some efforts were made by the Jews to re-establish themselves in a small way, but in the entire area there was not one Jewish village and only the more learned were familiar with the Hebrew tongue. In 1881 modern Zionist resettlement began in earnest. At that time only 25,000 Jews lived in the entire area. The Zionist idea as stated in "The Basle Programme" was adopted by the first Zionist congress called by Theodor Herzl in 1897. Its published aim was to reclaim the land of Palestine as the home for Jewish people. By the outbreak of World War I, the number of Jews had swelled to 80,000.

The Zionist movement was given impetus during World War I when British Foreign Secretary Arthur J. Balfour instituted the Balfour Declaration on November 2, 1917, in which he stated: "His Majesty's Government views with favor the establishment in Palestine of a national home for the Jewish people. . . ." This declaration, though welcomed by the Jews, was opposed by the Arabs and little came of it. Meanwhile a British mandate given over the land of Palestine by the League of Nations became effective, but through a desire of the British to maintain friendship with the Arab nations, no progress was allowed in establishing a homeland for Israel.

In 1939, during the early portion of World War II, the British government issued a white paper which set forth the conditions for establishing an independent Arab state in Palestine. By that time, 400,000 Jews were in the country. The restrictions on Jewish immigration, however, were severe, and future immigration was subject to Arab consent. Only a small part of the land could be sold to the Jews.

During World War II, however, due to the world-wide sympathy aroused for the people of Israel because of the slaughter of six million Jews under Nazi domination, the feeling became widespread that Israel should have a homeland to which its refugees could come and establish themselves. An Arab league was formed in 1945 to oppose further Jewish expansion. After World War II the British government turned Palestine over to the United Nations and under the direction of this body a partition of Palestine was recommended with the division into a Jewish state and an Arab state. By 1948 Jewish population had risen to 650,000.

THE ESTABLISHMENT OF THE NEW STATE OF ISRAEL

On May 14, 1948, as the British withdrew control, Israel proclaimed itself an independent state within the boundaries set up by the United Nations. Before the day passed, however, Israel was attacked by Egypt, Jordan, Iraq, Syria, Lebanon, and Saudi Arabia, and open warfare broke out. Though both sides suffered heavily, a series of truces began. The first was on June 11 and was followed by a renewal of hostilities which ended in a final truce on July 17. On January 7, 1949, a general armistice was arranged in which Israel was allowed to retain the additional land secured during the hostilities. Israel itself was admitted to the United Nations. In the years that followed no adequate solution was found for the many difficulties attending a permanent peace. The Arab nations refused to recognize Israel and denied it the right of existence. Israel on her part adopted an unrealistic approach to the refugee problem which continued to be an open sore.

Since 1949, the nation Israel has made rapid strides until today it is well established. Though surrounded by enemies, Israel rests in its security of superior arms and effective military organization. Of significance is the unassailable fact, that for the first time since A.D. 70, the nation Israel is independent and self-sustaining, and is recognized as a political state.

The restoration of Israel to its ancient land and its establishment as a political government is almost without parallel in the history of the world. Never before has an ancient people, scattered for so many centuries, been able to return to their ancient land and re-establish themselves with such success and such swift progress as is witnessed in the new state of Israel.

POLITICAL AND MILITARY GROWTH OF ISRAEL

Of special significance is the fact that Israel is a recognized political state. In its original declaration on May 14, 1948, provision was made for the establishment of an ordered government in the form of a democratic parliamentary republic. The principal legislative body in Israel is the knesset, from a Hebrew word which means "assembly." The knesset meets in Jerusalem, which is the capitol of Israel, and temporarily occupies quarters adapted for this purpose. A government center is planned on an elevation which will face Mount Herzl where the founder of the Zionist movement is buried. The knesset has power to make and amend laws, and its approval is necessary before a government can take office. A new government must be formed at such times as the knesset votes no confidence in the existing government. Of its 120 members, the great majority are of Jewish background, but a few Arabs are included.

The constitution of Israel provides that any citizen over twenty-one may be elected, and each citizen over eighteen, without respect to sex, race, or religion, is entitled to vote for members of the knesset. Though most matters of law are handled by civil courts divided into three main categories — namely, magistrate courts, district courts, and the supreme court — a series of special courts corresponding to the religion of respective citizens have been established in regard to marriage, divorce, and similar matters. A Jew therefore is referred to the rabbinical courts, Moslems to the Moslem court, and Christians to the Christian court. All of the religious courts are under the control of the Ministry of Religion. The internal government of Israel allows considerable freedom to minority groups, and provides a proper legal basis for this enterprising nation to grow.

One of the important factors of Israel's progress has

been its highly efficient army. Formed under great difficulty during the early days of the state of Israel when they
were being attacked by enemies on all sides, through heroic
efforts, it was able to give a good account of itself and actually enlarge the area of Israel by some fifty per cent in
the resulting hostilities. The army is called in Hebrew
Tsahal, representing the initials of the defense army in
Israel known in Hebrew as the *Tseva Hagana Leisrael*. Included in its organization are forces equipped to fight on
land, sea, and air. The army has been trained by experienced officers from Europe and America and several military academies and a staff college have been created.

The corps of the army consists of volunteers who are
supplemented by reserves. Men on reaching the age of
eighteen serve for two and one half years. They are eligible
for service until they are forty-five. Single women are
also given two years of training. A system has been devised
by which reservists are settled in border areas and Israel
is reputed to have the fastest mobilization system of any
nation in the world. Along with the development of the
army itself has been the creation of an arms industry which
has enabled Israel not only to supply its own forces, but
to export in large quantities arms of various kinds, including one of the best automatic weapons available today.

Humanly speaking, it is because of the efficiency of their
army that Israel has enjoyed peace since the armistice of
1949 and was able to overrun the Gaza Strip in the hostilities which broke out in October, 1956. Though the nations
which surround Israel number some thirty million and con-
ceivably could overwhelm the small nation, the army of
Israel is more than a match for all of its enemies combined.
Because of this, the nation Israel today is in a high state of
confidence coupled with alertness.

DEVELOPMENT OF AGRICULTURE AND INDUSTRY

Probably the most astounding aspect of the restoration
of Israel is the rapid reclamation of the eroded land and
wasted resources which for centuries have characterized

the area which Israel now occupies. Travelers who visit Syria and Jordan first before coming to Israel are immediately impressed with the dramatic difference. Everywhere there is evidence of astounding progress in Israel.

One of the first problems which beset Israel was to reclaim the land strewn with rocks and seemingly hopeless as far as vegetation was concerned. By prodigious toil, often on the part of immigrants who had little knowledge of agriculture before, the land was cleared, terraced, and cultivated. In Israel, as in surrounding countries, the scarcity of water is a principal problem. Huge projects provided water for irrigation, not only for the northern portion of the nation, but also for the reclamation of the Negiv, the southern desert which forms a major portion of Israel's territory.

Travelers through Israel are introduced to field after field of cultivated crops on land that was hopelessly eroded just a few years before. By 1961, eighty million trees had been planted, and the continuing program eventually will make a major contribution in conserving water and providing timber. Orange trees have been planted in abundance, as well as other citrus fruits, and oranges have become a major export of the new nation. Crops such as cotton, sugar cane, grapes, peanuts, and sisal have become major productions. Just a few years ago eggs were closely rationed. By 1961 Israel was exporting almost a million eggs a day.

Though hampered somewhat by failure to conclude peace agreements with Arab nations which share the water available, by making the most of its own opportunities, Israel is building a gigantic irrigation system, drawing water from the Yarkon as well as from the Jordan and sending it south to the Negiv. Thousands of acres are being restored to fertility, and it is estimated that the reclaimed land will permit another one million immigrants during the next decade. Not only have desert lands been reclaimed, but one of the spectacular achievements was the draining of the swampland of the Valley of Esdraelon, the elimination of the mosquito menace, and the restoration of this broad area to cultivation, which has proved to be one of the most fertile areas in all Israel.

Progress in agriculture and reclamation of the land has been matched to some extent by establishment of industries. Textiles have now become an important part of Israel's production. The cutting of diamonds imported for this purpose, the manufacture of military weapons and arms, and the exploitation of the measureless chemical wealth of the Dead Sea are major factors of Israel's economy. Some oil has already been discovered as well as gas. One by one problems that beset Israel at the beginning are being solved.

The expanding economy has also furnished a basis for construction of fabulous new cities. The new city of Jerusalem, the capitol of Israel, has been beautifully constructed of stone with lovely streets and parks and by 1961 had attained a population of 160,000. Tel Aviv, the largest of the cities in Israel, has a population nearing 400,000, and offers every convenience of a modern city. Next to Tel Aviv is Haifa, with a population of 175,000. The growth of the cities has kept up with the growth in population which has almost tripled since 1948, reaching over two million in 1960.

EDUCATIONAL SYSTEM AND REVIVAL OF BIBLICAL HEBREW

One of the impressive sights in Israel is the spectacular rise of its educational system. Not only are new elementary schools built throughout the country to take care of the expanding population, but the Hebrew university with an enrollment in 1959-60 of seven thousand is one of the finest in the Middle East. In addition the Israel Institute of Technology has some twenty-five hundred students with training in various aspects of modern science. In the entire educational system Biblical Hebrew is used as the spoken and written language and has restored this ancient language to popular usage in Israel. New terms are being coined to meet modern situations. The revival of Hebrew inevitably ties the people of Israel to their ancient Scriptures in a way that otherwise would have been impossible.

The revival of Hebrew has also paved the way for a renewal of Biblical studies. Unlike American universities which neglect the Bible, the Old Testament is taught in public schools, including the universities, and is considered essential to any true education. Some four hundred study groups have been formed by the Israel Bible Study Association with a membership approaching twenty thousand. The reading of the Old Testament is popular, though often attended by little theological discernment. Even the New Testament is read as religious literature, though not considered on a par with the Old Testament by orthodox Jews. To some extent the new interest in the Bible has created an increased interest in the Jewish religion as such.

RELIGIOUS LIFE OF ISRAEL

It is to be expected with the rebirth of the nation and its renewed interest in the Bible that attendance at the synagogue has taken on new life in Israel. Visitors normally will find the synagogue crowded, though meeting in new and spacious buildings. It soon becomes evident, however, that the religious life of Israel is to some extent one of outer form. The religious exercises are devoted primarily to revival of their traditions, their reassurance of the general providence of God, and the application to some extent of moral standards. For Israel their religion is one of works rather than of faith, and their redemption is to be achieved by their own efforts.

The religious life of Israel is directed by some 430 rabbis who actively carry on their duties. It is to these leaders that Israel turns for direction. As a result of the revival of Judaism, the Sabbath is strictly enforced and everyone observes it, even those who never attend the synagogue. The religious life of Israel is largely in the hands of the orthodox, though the majority of ordinary Jews in Israel do not necessarily follow their leaders. The revival of interest, therefore, in the Jewish faith and the religious activities which characterize it, to some extent is an expression of patriotism and enthusiasm for the progress of the state rather than for theological or spiritual reasons. Nevertheless, the movement is a phenomenon without parallel in the modern history of Israel and is doing much to revive their ancient faith. The land of Israel which historically has been the cradle of Judaism, Christianity, and the Moslem faith is once again witnessing a revival of that which held sway for centuries.

POLITICAL AND PROPHETIC SIGNIFICANCE OF THE NEW STATE OF ISRAEL

The significance of the new state of Israel is bound up with the growing importance of the Middle East in international affairs. The land of Israel is located geographically in the hub of three major continents. Because of this strategic location, it is involved in the economic life of the world. Any major nation seeking to dominate the world would need to conquer this portion. Its military value is also obvious, for the Middle East is not only a channel of world commerce but is the gateway to the immense reserves in oil and chemicals found in that portion of the world. It is inevitable that any future world conflict would engulf this portion of the world as a primary objective. It is especially significant that from a Biblical standpoint the Middle East remains a center of interest. World events which are yet to unfold will find this area also its major theater. It is for this reason that students of the Bible, whether Jews or Christians, find the development of the new state of Israel one of the most important and significant events of the twentieth century.

The repossession of a portion of their ancient land by the new state of Israel is especially striking because of the promise given by God to Abraham of perpetual title to the land between Egypt and the Euphrates. As recorded in Genesis 15:18 the covenant of God with Abraham included the promise: "Unto thy seed have I given this land, from the river of Egypt unto the great river, the river Euphrates." This promise was subsequently repeated in Genesis 17:8

in these words: "And I will give unto thee, and to thy seed after thee, the land of thy sojournings, all the land of Canaan, for an everlasting possession; and I will be their God." Consideration will be given to these passages in later discussion, but their mention at this time demonstrates the great significance of the reoccupation of this area by the new state of Israel.

In the subsequent history of Israel neither Abraham nor his immediate posterity were able to possess the land and, as stated earlier, only at the time of the Exodus was the land ever actually possessed. Of great importance are the Scriptures which describe the dispersion of Israel in the captivities of Babylon and Assyria and the later scattering of Israel resulting from the persecution of the Romans. This will be followed by Israel's ultimate regathering. A study of some of the great promises relating to this future restoration of Israel to the land will be examined in detail later. The revival of Israel after these many centuries of dispersion introduces the major questions relating to the fulfillment of God's promise to Abraham and whether the creation of the new state of Israel is indeed a confirmation of Israel's continuance as a nation.

The return of Israel and the organization of the new state of Israel is especially significant in the light of prophecies to be examined concerning Israel's future time of trouble when Israel is pictured in the land, as for instance in Matthew 24:15-26. The predictions of the grand climax of the nation's history, given in Daniel 9:26, 27, when Israel is described as making a covenant with the future world ruler, is of special importance in the light of their renewed presence in their ancient land. Of the many peculiar phenomena which characterize the present generation, few events can claim equal significance as far as Biblical prophecy is concerned with that of the return of Israel to their land. It constitutes a preparation for the end of the age, the setting for the coming of the Lord for His church, and the fulfillment of Israel's prophetic destiny.

Chapter II

THE PROMISE TO ABRAHAM

In approaching the study of eschatology, the theology of Biblical prophecy, one is plunged immediately into a major division of divine revelation which is determinative in theology as a whole. Eschatology is the doctrine of last things, the word being derived from *eschatos,* meaning *last,* and *logos,* referring to theology as a rational science. In its larger dimension, it includes all that was prophetically future at the time it was revealed. This is subject to further subdivision into eschatology which has been fulfilled and eschatology which is still future or unfulfilled.

In modern theology this simple definition has become obscured. The modern concept of "realized" eschatology reduces its status to that of divine purpose. By so doing, it robs eschatology of its quality of specific prediction of the future. This point of view is based on the idea that it is impossible for anyone, even for writers of the Word of God, to predict the future.

Orthodox theology, however, has never submitted to such a limitation and throughout the history of the church it has been assumed that the Bible can speak authoritatively on things to come. Though there is evident difference of opinion as to how prophecy should be interpreted, the orthodox position does not question the authenticity of prophecy itself. In this discussion, it is assumed that the Bible in its original writings was given by inspiration of God and is an infallible revelation of His mind and purpose. The problem before us then is not one of demonstrating the validity of prophecy or the accuracy of the Scriptures. It is rather one of theological induction and interpretation of the revelation given in the Bible.

MAJOR DIVISIONS OF THE DIVINE PROGRAM

In order to approach the subject of eschatology intelligently, some principle of organization must be adopted in the interpretation of the broad and extensive field of Scriptural prophecy. Among a number of possibilities, two such principles may be mentioned by way of introduction.

First, the eschatological program of God may be considered in four major divisions: (1) The program for angels, including the present ministry and future blessedness of the elect angels and the present activity and future damnation of fallen angels, usually embraced in the branch of systematic theology called satanology. (2) The program of God for Gentiles embodied in the broad provisions of God's covenant with Adam and Noah and subsequently unfolded in the visions given to the Prophet Daniel in the book that bears his name. Included in God's program for the Gentiles is provision for the salvation of those who turn to God in true faith. (3) The divine program for Israel is unfolded in the Abrahamic, Palestinian, Davidic and new covenants and in a large measure is unfolded as the principal subject of the Old Testament beginning in Genesis 12. It includes all of God's dealings with Israel in the past and predicts a consummation in the future, when a time of great tribulation will befall the nation. The time of tribulation will be followed by Israel's regathering, restoration, and glory in the millennial kingdom. It is this division which will constitute our area of study. (4) The divine program for the church unfolded in the New Testament consisting in the divine program in the present age and its eschatological consummation in the translation of the church, its judgment, and reward. As presented in the New Testament, it falls into two broad areas: (a) the professing church, i.e. Christendom, destined to become a world religion of apostate character before its ultimate judgment by God at the second coming of Christ; (b) the calling out of the true church, the body of Christ, within the professing church, composed of Jew and Gentile alike on equal basis joined by the baptism of the Spirit, placed in Christ, born again of the

Spirit of God, and indwelt by the triune God. The salvation and sanctification of those who form the body of Christ is the central purpose of God in this present age and in some sense suspends the progress of God's dealings with the Gentile nations and Israel until God's purpose for the church has been realized.

ALTERNATE APPROACH OF COVENANT THEOLOGY

The fourfold division suggested for the program of God for His moral creatures is a comprehensive and illuminating approach to the tremendous mass of Scriptures which bear upon the divine purpose of God. An alternative to this is provided by a second approach, that of the so-called covenant theologians. It is not our purpose to deal in detail with this point of view, but its principal elements can be stated. It is the assumption of the covenant theologian that the major purpose of God is the salvation of the elect, embodied in a covenant of grace or covenant of redemption, and that all other purposes of God are subordinate to this. For this reason the divine revelation as it relates to angels is usually ignored as somewhat irrelevant. The contrast between God's program for Israel and the church is usually replaced by the concept that the church is a continuation of true Israel or that the church embraces all the saved of all ages.

At least two major objections can be mentioned opposing the covenant theologians' interpretation. First, the covenant theologian is guilty of the reductive error, namely, taking one facet of God's divine program and making it all-determinative. It leaves without adequate explanation the dealings of God with the natural world, and with the mass of unsaved humanity, which is regarded simply as an unfortunate context for God's major purpose. Second, the interpretation of Scripture required for covenant theology involves passing over the specifics of hundreds of prophecies in Scripture and taking these either in a spiritualized sense or ignoring them altogether.

Preferable is the point of view that regards God's

major purpose in the universe as that of self-manifestation. In this approach the *summum bonum* is the manifestation of the infinite perfections of God which constitute His glory. With this point of view, the natural world takes on wonderful meaning in that "the heavens declare the glory of God." The salvation of the elect in all dispensations is recognized as a major aspect of manifesting His glory, for in this alone can His infinite love and righteousness merge in grace, but other aspects of the divine program are not displaced. The separate programs of God for the angels, Gentiles, Israel, and the church each bring out different facets of God's infinite perfection such as righteousness in relation to the angels, faithfulness in relation to Israel, sovereignty in relation to the Gentiles, and grace and truth in relation to the church. Even the condemnation of the lost, pre-eminently demonstrating God's infinite righteousness and holiness, is seen in the context of divine love in that their hopeless estate was needless because Christ has died for them.

PRINCIPLE OF INTERPRETATION

In the broad approach of interpretation of prophecy attention needs to be given to two alternative principles of interpretation. That adopted in this study is the principle that Scripture should be interpreted in its normative, literal sense, except in such instances where a figurative or nonliteral interpretation is obviously indicated. In applying this principle no distinction needs to be observed between Scripture which is noneschatological and Scripture which is eschatological. The same hermeneutical principles which apply to any other portion of Scripture apply equally well to eschatology.

An alternative point of view was advanced by Augustine who suggested a dual hermeneutics, namely, that while all Scripture should be interpreted normally — that is, literally — prophecy or eschatology was to be understood in a figurative or nonliteral way. His principal reason for this dual hermeneutics was that a literal interpretation of prophecy would lead to chiliasm, or the premillennial interpretation.

Modern amillenarians have not improved much on Augustine's original dismissal of premillennialism. Their principal objection continues to be that the premillennial system is hopelessly confused and self-contradictory. The answer to this objection, while having many facets, is in the main a demonstration that premillennial interpretation is not only consistent with Scripture but consistent with itself and provides a program for eschatology which is not afforded in any other point of view.

It will be impossible within the confines of this study to debate in any satisfactory way the question of premillennialism versus amillennialism. This has been presented many times by competent scholars. Such works as J. Dwight Pentecost's *Things to Come;* Charles Feinberg's *Premillennialism or Amillennialism?;* Alva J. McClain's *The Greatness of the Kingdom;* Lewis Sperry Chafer's *Systematic Theology; The Basis of the Premillennial Faith* by Charles Ryrie; and my own volume, *The Millennial Kingdom,* set forth a sufficient answer for those who are willing to examine their pages.

The purpose of this study will be to examine Biblical prophecies relating to Israel and the theological implications arising from such an interpretation. The approach would be basically Scriptural and the reasonableness of the interpretation its own major defense. The best answer to the charge that there is no distinction between Israel and the church and similar amillennial dictums is to present what the Scriptures actually reveal. Fundamental to this whole point of view is the exegesis and interpretation of the Abrahamic covenant.

EXEGESIS OF THE ABRAHAMIC COVENANT

The first statement of the covenant of God made with Abraham, given in Genesis 12:1-3, was originally delivered to Abraham while still in Ur of the Chaldees and is stated in these words: "Get thee out of thy country, and from thy kindred, and from thy father's house, unto the land that I will show thee: and I will make of thee a great nation, and

I will bless thee, and make thy name great; and be thou a blessing: and I will bless them that bless thee, and him that curseth thee will I curse: and in thee shall all the families of the earth be blessed." God promised Abraham that subject to his obedience to the command to leave his own country and go to a land that God would show him, certain blessings would accrue to him.

First, certain promises were given to Abraham personally. Of Abraham, God would make a great nation. His divine blessing would rest upon Abraham. His name would be great. Abraham himself would be a blessing. In regard to Abraham, God promised a special circumstance in which He would bless those who blessed Abraham and would curse those who cursed him. The blessing promised through Abraham, according to verse three, was to extend to all families of the earth.

Second, though the Abrahamic covenant as given was directed primarily to Abraham as a person, it is obvious that out of it come two other major aspects of the covenant. Not only did God direct promises to Abraham himself, but the promise was given of the formation of a great nation out of Abraham. Third, the blessings falling on Abraham and his descendants would reach out unto all other families of the earth. Hence, an ordinary exegesis of the Abrahamic covenant in its original pronouncement involves (1) promises to Abraham; (2) promises to the nation, i.e., Israel; (3) promise of blessing to all nations, i.e., the Gentiles.

The prophecy of this Scripture is enriched by further revelation given later. In Genesis 12:7 God declared to Abraham: "Unto thy seed will I give this land." The promise of the land is reiterated in Genesis 13:14-17 where Abraham is exhorted to survey the land in all directions. In addition, Abraham's seed, destined to occupy the land, is described as being as numerous as the dust of the earth.

The dimensions of the land promised to the seed of Abraham are recorded in Genesis 15:18-20. The entire area from the river of Egypt unto the Euphrates river is

given to Abraham and his posterity as a perpetual possession. Further details are given concerning the promise to
Abraham in Genesis 17:1-8, including the fact that he would
have a multitude of seed, and would be the father of many
nations. In recognition of this his name is changed from
Abram, meaning "exalted father," to Abraham, meaning
"father of a multitude." It is further promised that he
would be exceedingly fruitful (17:6) and that kings would
descend from him. The covenant with Abraham is declared in verse seven to be everlasting and the promise of
possession of the land forever is reiterated in verse eight.
The Abrahamic covenant is subject to further elucidation
in Genesis 22:15-18 after Abraham's seed is limited to
Abraham's son Isaac in Genesis 21:12, in the words: "For
in Isaac shall thy seed be called." Taking into consideration
the fact that Isaac had two sons, Jacob and Esau, the promise
is further limited to Jacob and his descendants in Genesis
28:13, 14 in the revelation: "I am Jehovah, the God of
Abraham thy father, and the God of Isaac: the land whereon
thou liest, to thee will I give it, and to thy seed: and thy
seed shall be as the dust of the earth, and thou shalt
spread abroad to the west, and to the east, and to the north,
and to the south: and in thee, and in thy seed shall all the
families of the earth be blessed."

These many Scriptures dealing with the Abrahamic
covenant will be discussed more at length later, but their
mere itemization establishes the basic promises embodied in
the Abrahamic covenant which can now be summarized
as follows: (1) Abraham's name shall be great. (2) Abraham
shall personally have great blessing. (3) Whoever will
bless Abraham will be blessed and whoever will curse
Abraham will be cursed. (4) From Abraham will come a
great nation, innumerable as the dust of the earth. (5)
Abraham will be the father of many nations, not just one.
(6) Kings shall come from the line of Abraham. (7) Abraham's seed shall inherit the land from the river of Egypt to
the Euphrates river as an everlasting possession. (8) God
will be the God of Abraham and his seed forever. (9) Abra-

ham's seed shall conquer their enemies. (10) In Abraham's seed all the nations of the earth shall be blessed. (11) The covenant with Abraham shall be an everlasting covenant. (12) The promises to Abraham's seed are narrowed to the descendants of Isaac. (13) The promises to Abraham's seed are narrowed to descendants of Jacob, especially as pertaining to the land and the promise of blessing to all nations.

In arriving at these details, the plain language of Scripture and the promises of the Abrahamic covenant have simply been itemized. If the facts stand as they seem to be presented in the Scriptures, a massive presentation of the divine purpose of God for Abraham's seed is thus unfolded. It is a dramatic declaration of a new divine purpose quite different from His declared purpose for Gentiles as a whole. A particular rill of humanity has been sovereignly chosen to fulfill a divine purpose distinct in its character and in its fulfillment.

It is obvious, however, to any interpreter of Scripture that all will not agree on such a literal interpretation of these promises and it is therefore necessary to give attention not only to the exegesis but to the interpretation of the words and statements embodied in the Abrahamic covenant and its subsequent enlargement and repetition. Two major considerations confront the interpreter of the Abrahamic covenant: (1) Are these promises to be taken simply and literally, or are they to be interpreted in a nonliteral or figurative sense? (2) Are the promises embodied in the Abrahamic covenant sovereignly given or are they contingent upon subsequent obedience on the part of Abraham and his seed? In brief, the issue is literal versus spiritualized interpretation, and the question of whether the covenant is conditional or unconditional.

ARE THE PROMISES TO ABRAHAM LITERAL?

In approaching the interpretation of the Abrahamic covenant, one is faced with a determinative decision which goes far beyond the borders of specific promises of this covenant. The issue in a word is whether prophecy can be interpreted literally and normally or whether it should be understood in a figurative or spiritualized sense. The amillennial point of view requires extensive spiritualization of prophecy, whereas the premillennial interpretation is more literal. As related to the Abrahamic covenant, the question hinges on the interpretation of the expression, "the seed of Abraham," and the specifics that are promised. The problem has been somewhat confused by the fact that some premillenarians have tended to build their system upon an amillennial foundation and have not kept clearly in mind a proper basis for premillennial truth. In general, however, the premillennial point of view requires that the promises given to Abraham should be fulfilled by Abraham. Promises to Abraham's seed shall be fulfilled by his physical descendants, and promises made to "all families of the earth" will be fulfilled by Gentiles, i.e., those who are not physical descendants of Abraham. Hence, extreme care should be taken in determining precisely what promises are given to what peoples.

Guided by this principle, one can observe certain promises true only of Abraham, i.e., God's personal blessing upon him, the promise that his name shall be great, and that God will make a great nation of him. The promise given to all nations is limited to the idea that they shall be blessed through Abraham. This of course is subsequently enlarged in God's total program in grace for believing Gentiles in general and the church in particular. The crux of the interpretative problem, however, lies in the definition of the expression, "the seed of Abraham." How shall this expression be understood?

An examination of all references to the seed of Abraham in Scripture reveals that the expression is used in three distinct senses. First, there is the natural use, i.e., the natural seed of Abraham referring to those who are actual physical descendants of Abraham. Though there is a sense in which all natural descendants of Abraham are included, such as Ishmael and his descendants and Isaac and his descendants through Esau, it is clear that the particular promises of God to the seed are narrowed first to Isaac and then to Jacob and through Jacob to the twelve tribes of Israel. To them God promises in a special sense to be their God. To them was given the law of Moses, and the perpetual title to the Promised Land is given to them.

Second, the expression "the seed of Abraham" is used in special reference to the spiritual lineage coming from Abraham, that is, those in Israel who trusted in God, who kept the law, and qualified for many of the blessings of the covenant. It is evident, for instance, that all Israelites do not actually inherit the land and that only spiritual Israel will enter the future millennial kingdom and fulfill the promise. The distinction between natural Israel and spiritual Israel is revealed in such major passages as Romans 9-11 and specifically in Romans 9:6-8: "For they are not all Israel, that are of Israel: neither because they are Abraham's seed are they all children: but, in Isaac shall thy seed be called. That is, it is not the children of the flesh that are children of God; but the children of the promise are reckoned for a seed." It is evident then that the more particular promises of the Abrahamic covenant will not be fulfilled by all the natural seed, but by those in natural Israel who also qualify as spiritual seed. Further, the provision of divine sovereignty is that God apart from human merit determines the selection of Jacob instead of Esau (Romans 9:12, 13). In order to qualify, therefore, for the full promise of God to Israel, an individual had to be, first, of the natural seed of Abraham, i.e., a descendant of Jacob, and, second, one who trusted in God, thereby qualifying as belonging to the spiritual seed.

A third division, however, relating to the spiritual seed of Abraham is unfolded in Galatians 3:6-9 which reads as follows: "Even as Abraham believed God, and it was reckoned unto him for righteousness. Know therefore that they that are of faith, the same are sons of Abraham. And the scripture, foreseeing that God would justify the Gentiles by faith, preached the gospel beforehand unto Abraham, saying, In thee shall all the nations be blessed. So then they that are of faith are blessed with the faithful Abraham." Here we learn that there is also a spiritual seed of Abraham who are Gentiles, those who are not physical descendants of Abraham. Some, on the basis of this Galatians passage, have drawn the unwarranted conclusion that all distinctions between the natural seed of Abraham and the spiritual seed are thereby erased.

The passage itself, however, makes very clear that Gentiles who are recognized as the children of Abraham come under the promise given to the Gentiles and not under promises given to the physical seed of Abraham. The portion of the Abrahamic covenant which is quoted by Paul refers to the Gentiles in the words: "In thee shall all the nations be blessed." Paul's conclusion therefore is: "So then they that are of faith are blessed with the faithful Abraham." This means that they come under the blessing promised the nations, but it does not mean that they come under all the promises given to Abraham personally or to his seed in the physical sense. A Gentile in the present age is Abraham's seed because he is "in Christ Jesus" (Galatians 3:28). It is on this basis that Galatians 3:29 states: "And if you are Christ's, then are ye Abraham's seed, heirs according to promise."

A Gentile Christian therefore becomes the seed of Abraham not because of any physical lineage with Abraham himself nor simply by imitation of Abraham's faith, but because he is regarded by God as in Christ who is indeed a physical descendant of Abraham. The promises thereby assured are the promises given to Gentiles, not the particular promises given to Israel.

It may be concluded, therefore, that the seed of Abraham is used (1) of the natural seed of Abraham, more specifically the descendants of Jacob; (2) spiritual Israel, i.e., descendants of Jacob who trust in God; (3) Gentiles who are in Christ and are spiritual seed of Abraham, thereby qualifying for the promise of blessing to Gentiles in Abraham. Promises addressed to Abraham, therefore, can be apportioned according to the qualifying characteristic of each group. The promise given to Abraham that God would bless those who bless him, and curse those who curse him, has to some extent been extended to the entire nation of Israel, even to those who do not qualify as spiritual seed. History has demonstrated God's faithfulness in dealing with those who have oppressed His ancient people.

The realization of most of the promises, however, depends upon an individual Israelite being spiritual. Only thus will he ever enter into the future millennial kingdom, either as a survivor of the tribulation or as a resurrected saint. The blessings of God to Israel in this life as recorded in the Old Testament have been largely limited to spiritual Israel. Upon natural Israel in unbelief God has heaped His judgment and divine discipline. The promise to the spiritual seed of Abraham among the Gentiles is having a supreme demonstration in this present age in the calling out of the church composed largely of those who in their natural estate were Gentiles. The threefold distinction, therefore, in the seed of Abraham provides a solid basis for understanding eschatology as a whole while maintaining the proper distinction between Israel and the church and between Abraham's physical seed and Gentiles.

The principal opposition to this threefold distinction in the usage of the term "the seed of Abraham" arises from the amillennial interpretation and more particularly from those who embrace covenant theology. Illustrative of this amillennial point of view is the work, *The Seed of Abraham*, by Albertus Pieters. To him the term "the seed of Abraham" means only the spiritual seed of Abraham without distinction between Israel and Gentiles or between natural and spiritual. Pieters summarizes his point of view in these words: "The expression 'Seed of Abraham,' in biblical usage, denotes that visible community, the members of which stand in relation to God through the Abrahamic Covenant, and thus are heirs to the Abrahamic promise" (p. 20). He states further: "Whenever we meet with the argument that God made certain promises to the Jewish race, the above facts are pertinent. God never made any promises to any race at all, as a race. All His promises were to the continuing covenanted community, without regard to its racial constituents or to the personal ancestry of the individuals in it" (pp. 19, 20). He holds further that not only are the promises given only to the spiritual seed, but that the modern Jew of today has lost his lineage and there is no one qualified to inherit any promises given to the Jews as a race.

While it is not the intent here to provide a complete refutation of the amillennial exegesis of the Abrahamic covenant, certain important objections can be raised. First, the argument of Pieters rests on the assumption that there is no one today who is a physical descendant of Abraham. This extreme position is not shared by most amillenarians as it is faced by almost insuperable problems. The racial continuity of Israel, though marred by intermarriage with heathen, is recognized throughout the Scriptures. As late as the epistle of James, the twelve tribes are addressed (James 1:1). The Jews have been recognized by the world as a continuing people as manifested in the Zionist movement, the existence of the state of Israel today, the perpetuation of Israel's religion, and by almost universal recognition that the people of Israel are a distinct race. If the testimony of the book of Revelation may be introduced as evidence, one finds here again the twelve tribes of Israel specified by name as participating in the future great tribulation.

A notable weakness in the amillennial exegesis of the Abrahamic covenant is the fact that it does not take into consideration the specifics of God's revelation. Pieters for instance passes over Genesis 15:18-21 without even a word of comment, and the revelation that the covenant is everlasting and that the land is promised as an everlasting possession in Genesis 17:7, 8 is likewise given silent treatment. The fact is that any reasonable understanding of the terminology of these passages leads unmistakably to the conclusion that Abraham understood the promises as given to his physical seed, which forms the background of his special interest in Isaac and the promise of the land which evidently Abraham understood in a physical way. It is true that Abraham's faith went beyond the promise of the physical land to that of the heavenly city, the New Jerusalem in the eternal state, as indicated in Hebrews 11:10. But the promise of the land is obviously related to the temporal and will be fulfilled as long as the present earth lasts, whereas the promise of the eternal city had to do with the eternal state.

A spiritualized understanding of the promises of the land becomes ridiculous in that the land has to be made to mean heaven. The description given of the land in Genesis 15:15-18 as extending from the river of Egypt to the river Euphrates and including godless and pagan tribes is hardly a suitable terminology for the description of heaven. The efforts to understand the Abrahamic covenant in a specialized interpretation ultimately destroys any exegesis of these passages and changes the intended revelation to the point where the words used no longer have proper meaning. Premillenarians agree that there is a spiritual seed of Abraham, and that these inherit the appropriate promises addressed to spiritual Israel or spiritual Gentiles as the case may be. They deny that this requires spiritualization of the promises as pertaining to the physical seed of Abraham and the promises relating to the land. Further attention will be given these features later.

ARE THE PROMISES TO ABRAHAM CONDITIONAL?

The traditional amillennial interpretation of the Abrahamic promises tends to follow the method of spiritualizing them, thereby removing the element of specific and literal predictions. Another device, however, adopted by modern amillenarians, follows the argument that the promises are conditional. Under this approach a literal interpretation of the promise can be followed, i.e., it may be held that Israel was actually promised the land and other blessings, but it is charged that Israel failed to meet the conditions.

Therefore the promises are withdrawn. Such is the approach of Oswald Allis in his book, *Prophecy and the Church.*

Allis states his support of the conditional element in the Abrahamic covenant in these words: "It is true that, in the express terms of the covenant with Abraham, obedience is not stated as a condition. But that obedience was presupposed is clearly indicated by two facts. The one is that obedience is the precondition of blessing under all circumstances. . . . The second fact is that in the case of Abraham the duty of obedience is particularly stressed" (p. 33).

It is true that, in some cases in the Bible, promises are given in a conditional way. For instance, the Mosaic covenant contains many conditional promises, i.e., blessing for obedience, cursing or divine judgment for disobedience. However, it is not true that in Scripture obedience is always the condition of blessing. Allis, who is a Calvinist, has forgotten his doctrine of unconditional election. He has also forgotten the principle of divine grace in which God blesses those who are unworthy. The fact is that many of God's blessings fall upon those who are the least worthy of them. In such a doctrine as the security of the believer, which Allis would be the first to support, there is recognition of the principle that God makes promises which depend on Himself and His grace, not on human faithfulness. It certainly is not true that God's promises or that prophecy as a whole is conditioned upon human action. The major premise of Allis therefore, that obedience is always the condition of blessing, is a fallacy. God is able to make promises and keep them regardless of what men may do.

The second aspect of the position of Allis, that in the case of Abraham the duty of obedience is particularly stressed, is true in itself, but it does not affect the argument. In several instances in Abraham's life he was disobedient and in none of these instances did God withdraw the promise of the covenant. On other occasions when Abraham was obedient God reiterated the promise and added further details. But never was the promise made contingent upon later obedience. As a matter of fact, the history of Israel abounds in records of their disobedience, and yet the covenant of God given through Abraham is repeated in various ways and confirmed throughout the entire Old Testament.

There is, however, a partial validity to the point of view of Allis, namely, that under the covenant an individual Israelite would qualify for personal blessings by obedience which he would not receive if he were disobedient. For instance, when Israel was obedient they were blessed in the land. When they were disobedient they were removed and taken away into captivity. The ultimate fulfillment of the covenant with Abraham, however, was never in jeopardy as even in the midst of their apostasy they were given strongest assurances of being brought back into the land in subsequent generations and of their continuance as a nation.

Amillenarians are wont to bring up numerous problems, such as the conditional judgment pronounced upon Ninevah by Jonah, the judgment upon Eli's house, and limitation and application of blessings of the Abrahamic covenant to the spiritual scene. These have been answered in detail by premillenarians (cf. *The Millennial Kingdom* by the writer, pp. 154 ff). In a word, conditional promises under the Mosaic covenant do not affect the Abrahamic covenant. There is a proper answer to every amillennial objection, and the support of the concept that the Abrahamic covenant is unconditional is abundant.

The evidence that the covenant with Abraham is unconditional should be understood as supporting the idea that the complete fulfillment of the covenant was rendered sure when God gave it to Abraham in the first place. By using the word unconditional, it is not intended to imply that there were no human contingencies, but rather that God took all these contingencies into consideration when He made the promise. Further, it should be understood that the promise is not necessarily in all of its aspects fulfilled to every individual Israelite, but that some aspects of the promise are reserved for particular Israelites in a particular generation and limited to a large extent to those in Israel who are qualified as the spiritual seed of Abraham. The promise is not necessarily fulfilled therefore by *all* the seed of Abraham, but by *some* of the seed of Abraham.

The unconditional aspect of the Abrahamic covenant is confirmed by the fact that all of Israel's covenants are unconditional except the Mosaic. In the statement of the covenant itself no conditions are itemized. When confirmations are given, while these sometimes arise from some act of obedience or devotion, it is not implied thereby that the covenant itself is conditioned. Further, the covenant with Abraham was confirmed by the unqualified oath of God symbolized in the shedding of blood and passing between parts of the sacrifice as described in Genesis 15:7-21. While circumcision was required to recognize an individual as being within the covenant, it is not made the *sine qua non* of the fulfillment of the covenant. In fact, the Abrahamic covenant was given before the rite of circumcision was introduced. Not only was the covenant confirmed without conditions to Isaac and Jacob, but later it was reiterated to the people of Israel in times of disobedience and apostasy, the most notable case being that of Jeremiah, when the nation was promised that it would continue forever (Jeremiah 31:36). The New Testament declares the Abrahamic covenant immutable (Hebrews 6:13-18). A study of later covenants tends to support the unconditional character of the Abrahamic. The idea therefore that the Abrahamic covenant is suspended and inoperative because of sin in the lives of descendants of Abraham is untenable. If a literal interpretation of the promises is allowed, literal fulfillment can be expected.

SUMMARY

The prophetic program of God for Israel is therefore one of the four major programs revealed in the Bible: (1) The program of God for angels. (2) The program of God for Gentiles. (3) The program of God for the church.

(4) The program of God for Israel. This approach is far
superior to that of the covenant theologians as it compre-
hends all events of all classifications and relates them to the
total divine program in which God manifests His own infinite perfections to His own glory. It further permits a normal and literal interpretation of prophecy in the same way
as is used in interpreting other forms of Scriptural revelation.

The Abrahamic covenant contributes to the eschatology
of Israel by detailing the broad program of God as it affects
Abraham's seed. It includes promises to Abraham personally, promises to the nation as such, and promises of blessing through Israel to the Gentiles. Important in the Abrahamic covenant is the promise as directed to the seed which
is limited in subsequent Scripture to Isaac, and then Jacob,
and then the twelve sons of Jacob. The question of whether
the promises to Abraham should be interpreted literally
was shown to hinge on the question of literal interpretation of the expression "the seed of Abraham." It was shown
that this expression has a threefold use in the Bible —
first, to the natural seed of Abraham, that is, all of his physical descendants; second, to the seed of Abraham who followed Abraham's noble example of faith, i.e., the Israel who
trusted in God; and, third, the spiritual seed of Abraham,
that is, Gentiles who qualify for the promise given to the
nations. Evidence was adduced that the promises given to
Abraham's physical seed will be fulfilled in his literal descendants who qualify spiritually, whereas promises given
to the spiritual seed who are not physical descendants of
Abraham inherit the promises given to Gentiles. This approach allowed a normal and literal interpretation of the
Abrahamic covenant. The second leading question, namely,
are the promises given to Abraham conditional? was answered by pointing to Scriptures that affirm the unalterable
purpose of God that Israel should be a nation forever and
should possess the land forever. Amillennial arguments to
the contrary were considered and found without adequate
basis. It is not too much to say that the exegesis of the

Abrahamic covenant and its resulting interpretation is the foundation for the study of prophecy as a whole, not only as relating to Israel, but also for the Gentiles and the church. It is here that the true basis for a premillennial interpretation of the Scriptures is found.

CHAPTER III

ISRAEL'S FUTURE AS A NATION

One of the central questions in prophecy relating to Israel is whether Israel has any future as a nation. The question is by no means easily answered because there is a confusing number of answers to the question. These can be itemized as follows: (1) The point of view that denies that Israel exists today and therefore has no future as a nation, as illustrated in the book *The Seed of Abraham* by Albertus Pieters. In Pieters' opinion, Israel is nonexistent as either a race or a nation in the ordinary sense of the term. (2) The idea that Israel continues as a race but not as 'a nation. This concept is illustrated in conservative postmillennialism of the last generation in works like *Systematic Theology* by Charles Hodge and is held by some contemporary amillenarians such as William Hendriksen in his book *And So All Israel Shall Be Saved*. (3) The teaching of most premillenarians that Israel has not only continuity as a race, but a future as a nation in the millennial kingdom. This is the normal premillennial approach.

Variations in the statement of these three major points of view abound. The opinion of Albertus Pieters has already been discussed and the evident facts pointing to the continuance of Israel as a race have been stated. The formation of a political state in the Middle East in 1948 bearing the name Israel as well as the continuance of Judaism as a religion seems a sufficient answer to the first point of view. The principal question which remains is whether Israel continues merely as a race without a future or whether it has promises which can be fulfilled only by its continuance as a nation and its revival as a people in the political government of the millennial kingdom.

46

THE CONTINUANCE OF THE PHYSICAL SEED OF ABRAHAM

Though it is allowed by all conservative expositors of Scripture that Abraham had a physical seed, and in particular that Jacob was the father of the twelve tribes of Israel, an examination of this evidence serves to provide a basis for the theological implications which are based upon this fact. To be sure, modern liberals have asserted that the accounts of Abraham and his posterity are only traditional myths, but as this is done only by sweeping denial of the authority of Scripture, it does not require refutation in a discussion with orthodox scholars who accept the inspiration of the Bible. If the record of Scripture is valid, there can be little question concerning the fact that Isaac was born as a son to Abraham and Sarah when they both were past age, by miraculous intervention of God. Nor is there much question concerning the fact that Isaac had the twin boys Esau and Jacob. Much of the content of the book of Genesis deals with the story of Jacob, the birth of the twelve patriarchs, and the beginning of Israel's history as such. Even unbelievers in Scriptural revelation will acknowledge that the modern Jew is a descendant of Jacob and recognize the historical sequence which has brought Israel to the present hour.

It should also be evident from Scripture and history that Israel is more than just a race. From the time they left Egypt they assumed the proportions of a great nation and, though for a time they lived with little political unity during the period of the judges, there is abundant evidence to sustain the rise of the nation under Saul, David, and Solomon. Their moral deterioration, the Assyrian and Babylonian captivities, and the regathering and restoration of Israel recorded in the books of Ezra and Nehemiah and supported by Zechariah and Malachi provide a setting for the New Testament. When Christ was born, Israel was a nation even though it was under the heel of Roman oppression.

With the destruction of Jerusalem, however, and the scattering of the children of Israel, their national characteristics were blurred for many centuries. It is of tremendous significance, however, that the ties which bound together the race of Israel were of such character that in our modern day the nation Israel has once again returned to its ancient land, established itself as a political state, and is recognized as such by most of the civilized world. In any ordinary meaning of the term, Israel has continued as a nation and is in existence today in that capacity.

THE PROMISES TO ISRAEL AS A NATION

Much of the evidence which supports the concept of Israel as a nation is bound up in the promises which are given to her which will be discussed later. Sufficient for the present purpose, however, is to point out that the original Abrahamic covenant expressly promised that God would make a great nation out of Abraham's seed (Genesis 12:2). To this nation is given the promise of possession of the land, which implies national characteristics.

Relative to the express question concerning the perpetuity of Israel as a nation, the promise given to Abraham in Genesis 17:7, 8 is of special importance. Here the covenant with Abraham is declared to be an everlasting covenant, and the land is promised to Israel as an everlasting possession. It would be of course impossible for the covenant to be everlasting and the possession of the land to be everlasting unless the nation also continued forever. The Hebrew expression for "everlasting" is *olam*, meaning "in perpetuity." While it might not quite be the equivalent of the infinite term "everlasting," it would certainly mean continuance as long as this present earth should last. It is the strongest expression for eternity of which the Hebrew language is capable. Inasmuch as these promises are reiterated to Isaac and to Jacob and are constantly referred to throughout the Old Testament, the nature of these promises confirms the continuance of Israel as a nation.

The matter of Israel's regathering, judgment, and restoration still to be fulfilled will be the subject of later discussion, and only can be anticipated here. It follows, however, that if the Scriptures teach Israel is to be regathered, brought back to their ancient land, and actually possess the area promised by God to Abraham in Genesis 15:18-21, these predictions in their very character would demand Israel's continuance as a nation. Inasmuch as these promises do not rest on a few isolated texts, but on hundreds of prophecies in the Old Testament which directly or indirectly anticipate a future day of glory for Israel, it is hardly too much to say that there are few doctrines that are better attested in the Bible than that of the future of Israel, provided that these prophecies are interpreted in their normal and literal sense.

THE EXPRESS PROMISES OF ISRAEL'S PERPETUITY AS A NATION

In addition to the strong predictions of Genesis 17, the most pointed pronouncements are made elsewhere in the Old Testament concerning Israel's continuance as a nation. One of these, which should be decisive in itself, is that expressed by Jeremiah at a time of Israel's apostasy and captivity. In this context of Israel's disintegration Jeremiah predicts a new covenant with the house of Israel and the house of Judah (Jeremiah 31:31) which will replace God's covenant with them in the Mosaic law (Jeremiah 31:32). After defining the millennial situation in which this covenant will be fulfilled for the nation Israel, Jeremiah adds this word of assurance: "Thus saith Jehovah, who giveth the sun for a light by day, and the ordinances of the moon and of the stars for a light by night, who stirreth up the sea, so that the waves thereof roar; Jehovah of hosts is his name: If these ordinances depart from before me, saith Jehovah, then the seed of Israel also shall cease from being a nation before me for ever. Thus saith Jehovah: If heaven above can be measured, and the foundations of the earth searched out beneath, then will I also cast off all the seed of Israel for all that they have done, saith Jehovah" (Jeremiah 31:35-37).

In view of the fact that some amillenarians contend that the Abrahamic promise concerning Israel is conditioned on their obedience and therefore is set aside upon disobe-

dience, it is most significant that this strongest prophecy in
the Old Testament for the continuance of Israel is given in
a setting when Israel is manifestly in apostasy and about to
be carried off into captivity. It would be difficult to provide a setting anywhere which would make it clearer that
this is God's sovereign purpose entirely apart from Israel's
worthiness and the fulfillment is determined solely by God's
power and will. As long as the sun and moon endure and as
long as the heavens have not been measured, Israel will
continue as a nation. The divine purpose to continue the
nation Israel is supported by the continuance of these
elements of natural creation as long as the present earth
exists. It is not simply that they will continue as a seed,
but as Jeremiah expresses it, Israel shall not cease "from
being a nation before me for ever."

The promise of Israel's perpetuity in the new covenant
in Jeremiah 31 is supported by the provisions which are
itemized: (1) It is designated a covenant with "the house of
Israel, and with the house of Judah." The covenant is
therefore limited to the descendants of Jacob. (2) It is
a covenant designed to replace the Mosaic covenant also
made only with Israel. As such it will be written "in their
hearts" rather than on tables of stone. (3) The fulfillment
of the covenant may be expected after "the time of Jacob's
trouble" mentioned in Jeremiah 30:7. Jeremiah predicted
in 31:28: "And it shall come to pass that, like as I have
watched over them to pluck up and to break down and to
overthrow and to destroy and to afflict, so will I watch over
them to build and to plant, saith Jehovah." The time of
fulfillment is further identified as the time of Israel's regathering, indicated in Jeremiah 30:10 and Jeremiah 31:8
and following. (4) The time of its fulfillment is described
as a period when there will be universal knowledge of the
Lord. Jeremiah speaks of this in these words: "And they
shall teach no more every man his neighbor, and every
man his brother, saying, Know Jehovah, for they shall all
know me, from the least of them unto the greatest of them,
saith Jehovah" (Jeremiah 31:34).

Isaiah referred to this same time in Isaiah 11:9 when he predicted: "For the earth shall be full of the knowledge of Jehovah, as the waters cover the sea." This was an especially strong prediction in view of the fact that both Isaiah and Jeremiah lived in a day when ignorance of the Lord prevailed and apostasy characterized Israel. The new covenant therefore is related to the future day of Israel's glorious kingdom on the earth. (5) The period of its fulfillment will be one of great spiritual blessing. God will be publicly identified with Israel, and Israel will be God's people. Their sins will be forgiven, and they will be the beneficiaries of God's wonderful grace. It should be obvious to any student of premillennial interpretation that all of these prophecies fit naturally and easily into the context of the millennial hope.

The new covenant is frequently mentioned elsewhere in the Old Testament. In Isaiah 61:8, 9, in a similar context speaking of Israel's tribulation followed by regathering and blessing, it is affirmed that the covenant will be everlasting. Jeremiah himself reaffirms the covenant in 32:37-40 and mentions its everlasting character and fulfillment in the time of Israel's regathering.

The Prophet Ezekiel repeats all the familiar elements found in earlier statements of the covenant, namely that Israel is to be regathered, to be reunited in one kingdom, to be ruled by one king, is to be forgiven and cleansed from idolatry, and will dwell forever in the land of their covenant of peace (Ezekiel 37:21-28). God is going to be present with them, and Israel will be known all over the world as a nation blessed of God.

Because these prophecies interpreted in their normal and natural way would unmistakably affirm the premillennial interpretation of prophecy, amillenarians deny these conclusions and usually hold that the new covenant as given to Israel is being fulfilled by the church today. Though this is quite foreign to the Old Testament presentation, they claim that the New Testament authorizes this transfer of promises from the nation to the church and that particulars such as the coming time of tribulation, regathering of Israel, their re-establishment in the land, their being ruled by one king, and being united as one nation must be interpreted spiritually as being fulfilled in the gathering out of the church from all nations into the one body of Christ. Before turning to other New Testament evidence confirming the continuance of Israel as a nation, attention must be directed to this amillennial interpretation of the new covenant.

There are five references in the best texts of the New Testament in which the term *new covenant (kaine diatheke)* is found (Luke 22:20; I Corinthians 11:25; II Corinthians 3:6; Hebrews 8:8; 9:15). In addition there are several other references which are properly within the sphere of this study as referring to the new covenant without the precise words being used (Matthew 26:28; Mark 14:24; Romans 11:27; Hebrews 8:10, 13; 10:16; 12:24). It is, of course, hardly possible to treat the subject adequately without a more prolonged discussion than can be undertaken here. A more complete presentation is afforded in *The Millennial Kingdom,* chapter 18, by the writer, and in Dr. J. Dwight Pentecost's *Things to Come,* chapter 8.

In regard to Israel's continuance as it relates to the new covenant, it is significant that only one passage specifically identifies the new covenant with that spoken of by Jeremiah. This is found in Hebrews 8. It is not too much to say that amillenarians who are careful scholars consider this passage one of the most important in their argument identifying the church with Israel.

The argument of Hebrews at this point is that Jesus Christ as our High Priest has a more excellent ministry and is the Mediator of a better covenant providing better promises than that of the Aaronic priesthood built on the Mosaic covenant. This is stated in Hebrews 8:6: "But now hath he obtained a ministry the more excellent, by so much as he is also the mediator of a better covenant, which hath been enacted upon better promises." The writer of Hebrews then proceeds to prove this by quoting the new covenant of

Jeremiah as demonstrating that the Mosaic covenant was faulty and needed to be replaced. He states in verse 7: "For if that first covenant had been faultless, then would no place have been sought for a second." He continues by quoting Jeremiah's new covenant with the words: "For finding fault with them, he saith, Behold, the days come, saith the Lord, that I will make a new covenant with the house of Israel and the house of Judah." Verses 9 through 12 are a quotation from the provisions of the new covenant given in Jeremiah 31. The writer of Hebrews then concludes in verse 13: "In that he saith, A new covenant, he hath made the first old. But that which is becoming old and waxeth aged is nigh unto vanishing away."

The interpretation of this quotation as it relates to the new covenant is complicated by the fact that conservative scholars have no less than five differing points of view, one of which is the amillennial interpretation. Briefly stated, these five positions are these: (1) The postmillennial interpretation that the promise of future blessing for the Jews will be fulfilled in the people of Israel in the latter days of the period of the church on earth when the Jews are converted and accept Christ as Saviour. This was typical of the conservative postmillennialism of the nineteenth century. (2) That the new covenant in both the Old and New Testaments concerns Israel and Israel alone and has no relationship specifically to Gentiles or the church. This was the viewpoint of Darby and is one of several premillennial approaches. (3) That the new covenant has a twofold application to the church in the present age and to Israel in the future millennial age. This view was popularized by the *Scofield Reference Bible*. (4) That there are in fact two new covenants, one for Israel to be fulfilled in the future, one for the church to be fulfilled in the present age, both founded upon the grace of God and the sacrifice of Christ. This view was supported by Lewis Sperry Chafer in his *Systematic Theology* and by Charles Ryrie in his book, *The Basis of the Premillennial Faith*. (5) The amillennial position that the church is true Israel and that the prophecies given to Jeremiah and other prophets are being fulfilled in the church age in a spiritualized way.

The postmillennial point of view has been largely discarded with a defunct postmillennialism and does not figure prominently in current eschatological discussions. Interpreters usually choose either between the amillennial point of view or one of the three premillennial interpretations. Darby's teaching that the new covenant both in the New and Old Testaments concerns Israel alone is not usually accepted by premillenarians, though it has many attractive arguments. The principal difficulty is that the Lord's Supper seems to relate a new covenant to the church which makes it difficult to confine the term to Israel's future. Usually the choice is between Scofield's position or that of Chafer in premillennial circles. For the purpose of our present discussion relative to the perpetuity of the nation Israel, it will suffice to show that the amillennial point of view is not that which is taught in Hebrews, though there are problems that remain in the premillennial understanding of this passage.

Oswald Allis defines the amillennial interpretation in these words: "For the gospel age in which we are living is that day foretold by the prophets when the law of God shall be written in the hearts of men (Jeremiah 31:33) and when the Spirit of God abiding in their hearts will enable them to keep it (Ezekiel 11:19, 36:26f)" (*Prophecy and the Church*, p. 42). He argues that the quotation before us in Hebrews 8 is a clear and unmistakable statement to this effect. Allis writes: "The passage speaks of the new covenant. It declares that this new covenant has already been introduced and that by virtue of the fact that it is called 'new' it has made the one which it is replacing 'old,' and that the old is about to vanish away. It would be hard to find a clearer reference to the gospel age in the Old Testament than in these verses in Jeremiah" (*ibid.*, p. 154). An examination of the passage in Hebrews, however, does not support what Allis claims. Though the writer quotes the entire new covenant as given by Jeremiah, in his exegesis he uses only one word, namely, the word *new*. His argument in brief is based on the fact that Jeremiah predicted a new covenant in the Old Testament. This prediction proved that the Mosaic covenant was not intended to be an everlasting covenant and would in fact be done away. He does not say that Jeremiah's covenant is in effect now. While the New Testament in other passages alludes to the covenant of Jeremiah as in the quotation in Hebrews 10:16 and states that Jesus is the Mediator of a new covenant in Hebrews 12:24, nowhere in the New Testament is the church specifically put under the detailed provisions of the covenant of Jeremiah. The normal premillennial interpretation therefore considers these references (1) as an application of the general truth of the grace of God illustrated in the new covenant with Israel but also of the church, or (2) as two new covenants, one for Israel and one for the church. The problem yields to the patient exegesis of all passages relating to this subject in the New Testament, but even the New Testament, as in Romans 11:27, refers the detailed fulfillment of the covenant of Jeremiah to the second coming of Christ and the deliverance of Israel, a passage which amillenarians characteristically avoid as the plague. The amillennial point of view is the most extreme of the five possible viewpoints and is not supported by a careful study of the new covenant in the New Testament.

A study of further particulars in the New Testament related to the question of Israel's continuity serves to confirm that the word *Israel* is used in the New Testament in the same sense as in the Old and that promises to Israel continue to be inviolate, including their future restoration.

Amillenarians, while denying any future to Israel as a nation, are, however, divided as to whether Israel continues as a race. Allis follows the traditional amillennial approach in making Israel and the church one and the same as far as New Testament teaching is concerned. More recently amillenarians of both conservative and liberal backgrounds have tended to regard Israel as something distinct from the church. William Hendriksen, for instance, a well-known amillenarian, takes the position that Israel means Israel in the New Testament, not the church. In a similar way Charles Hodge, the postmillenarian of the last generation, held that the term *Israel* is never used in the New Testament except for those who were physical descendants of Jacob. It would seem in view of the fact that some amillenarians and postmillenarians concede that Israel means Israel in the New Testament it would be unnecessary to debate this point. However, in view of the evidence that many amillenarians consider it, as Allis does, "an almost unprecedented extreme" to insist that Israel actually means Israel (*Prophecy and the Church*, p. 218), it is necessary to dispose of this point first.

NEW TESTAMENT EVIDENCE

A study of the New Testament demonstrates beyond question that there is a continued contrast between Israel and Gentiles as such throughout the New Testament. Israel as a nation is addressed again and again after the beginning of the New Testament church in such passages as Acts 3:12; 4:8, 10; 5:21, 31, 35; 21:28, etc. A most significant illustration is Paul's prayer for Israel that they might be saved found in Romans 10:1 which is a clear reference to the use of the term *Israel* as a nation outside the church. The term *Jews*, derived from the tribe of Judah, is also used in I Corinthians 10:32. The argument of Paul in Romans 9 is certainly built on the idea of Israel as a separate nation. He surveys their peculiar promises and privileges in Romans 9:4, 5 and expresses the wish that he himself might be cursed if by this means his brethren, i.e., Israel, could be saved (Romans 9:3, 4).

Not only is Israel regarded as a separate nation, but Gentiles as such are expressly excluded. In Ephesians 2:12: "Ye [Gentiles] were at that time separate from Christ, alienated from the commonwealth of Israel, and strangers from the covenant of promise, having no hope and without God in the world." In the discussion which follows it is important to note that Paul does not indicate that Gentiles come into these promises given to Israel, but rather pictures both Jew and Gentile as being joined in an entirely new entity, namely, the body of Christ. The fact, therefore, that in the New Testament Israel and Gentiles are contrasted to each other is strong evidence that the term *Israel* continues to mean what it meant in the Old Testament, namely, the descendants of Jacob.

Perhaps more to the point in this discussion is the New Testament contrast between natural Israel and the church. As has been previously pointed out, there is a tendency on the part of some amillenarians to regard the church as the New Testament Israel. The New Testament in continuing the contrast between Israel and the church first of all notes that natural Israel — that is, unsaved Israelites — are not in the church. There is then no teaching that the nation of Israel as such becomes the church as such. Instead the nation Israel is promised a future, and, though this future is largely fulfilled by spiritual Israel, the existence of these promises as distinct from God's program for the church maintains the difference between the two terms.

A central passage in the New Testament on this point is found in Romans 11 where Paul raises the question that is before us: "I say then, Did God cast off his people?" (Romans 11:1). In his argument which follows he, first of all, answers this question in an absolute negative by asserting that there always has been a remnant of Israel and that there will be a remnant in the future. He notes the fact that the great majority in the nation Israel are spiritually blinded and that their hardness of heart has occasioned God's turning to the Gentiles in the present age. He anticipates, however, that this is a temporary situation which will be followed by a future blessing of the nation Israel. He states in Romans 11:15: "For if the casting away of them is the reconciling of the world, what shall the receiving of them be, but life from the dead?" He acknowledges that Israel at the present time is broken off from the

olive tree or the place of divine blessing, but he predicts
a future ingrafting of Israel into "their own olive tree"
(Romans 11:24). This is to take place when Israel's blindness is lifted (Romans 11:25), which will be followed
by the fulfillment of Israel's covenants and their restoration
as a nation as indicated in Romans 11:26-32. This extended
passage then expressly denies the contention that Israel
has no future or continuance as a nation. The hope that is
set before is not the hope given to the church which already
is in the place of blessing in this present age and has no
title to the promises given to Israel of possession of the land
and other portions of their predicted future.

Not only is the nation Israel contrasted to the church,
but spiritual Israel is contrasted to Gentile Christians who
are in the body of Christ. This perhaps is the crux of the
entire question, namely, are Gentile Christians ever designated Israelites? The argument of Romans 9:11 where
this problem is expressly discussed makes clear that spiritual
Israel and Gentile Christians continue to be contrasted.
Spiritual Israelites never become Gentiles, and Gentile Christians never become Israelites. The statement of Romans 9:6,
"For they are not all Israel, that are of Israel," does not deny
this, but rather indicates that all who are physical descendants of Abraham do not necessarily inherit the spiritual promises. The contrast is between Israel according to the flesh and
Israel which is spiritual, rather than a reference to Gentile
believers. As has been previously pointed out, Gentile believers are the spiritual seed of Abraham who received
the promise of blessing to all nations which was to come
through Abraham. This does not mean, however, that they
received the promises that came through Jacob to the nation of Israel.

Probably the most important text used by those who
attempt to prove that Israel and the church are one is that
found in Galatians 6:15, 16, which reads as follows: "For
neither is circumcision anything, nor uncircumcision, but
a new creature. And as many as shall walk by this rule,
peace be upon them, and mercy, and upon the Israel of

God." It has been argued that the expression "Israel of God" is used here of the church as a whole.

It may be observed first that if this passage does use the term "Israel of God" for the church, it is the only passage in the entire New Testament where there is any evidence in the text for such a conclusion. Seen in the setting of its context, it is by no means the clear assertion that the church is the Israel of God as is sometimes claimed by its proponents. Paul is stating in these closing verses of the epistle to the Galatians the pre-eminence of the cross of Christ before which neither circumcision nor uncircumcision availed. The important fact is that those who trust in Christ who died for them become a new creature quite apart from any rite of circumcision or its lack. Upon those who have thus apprehended the grace of God and have been delivered from the law and its religious regulations, Paul breathes a benediction of peace and mercy. Then he adds, "And upon the Israel of God." The most natural explanation of this is that Paul is stating that anyone, whether Jew or Gentile, who walks by this rule is worthy of his benediction, but especially is this so for the Israel of God, i.e., Israelites who are the godly remnant of this age, that is, believers in the Lord Jesus Christ. The use of the Greek *kai* is best translated by the word *and* and only rarely is used in the sense of *even* as would be required if the term Israel of God is entirely equivalent to the expression "as many as walk by this rule." The passage does not state that the Israel of God and the church, i.e., the new creation, are coextensive. At the most, such identification is possible, but not probable. Paul's statement is simply a recognition of his particular interest in Israelites who have come to know Christ and expresses the hope that they would enter into the freedom of grace of which he is such an able exponent in the epistle to the Galatians.

One of the familiar arguments against the continuance of Israel as a nation is the idea that when Israel rejected Christ they failed to meet the necessary conditions for the fulfillment of their promises and are in fact disinherited

as far as national promises are concerned. According to
this point of view, an Israelite today has only the possibility of entering spiritually into the promises given to the
church, not the promises given to Israel as a nation.

This question is largely answered by the materials already presented. The fact of continued recognition of Israel
as a nation and the presentation of their future hope in
Romans 11 would seem to be a sufficient answer. Two additional passages, however, may be considered.

In Matthew 21:43 Christ said in connection with the
parable of the householder: "Therefore say I unto you,
The kingdom of God shall be taken away from you, and
shall be given to a nation bringing forth the fruits thereof."
A casual examination of this text would seem to indicate
the taking away of the kingdom of God from Israel. Even
amillenarians, however, have seldom claimed this text, as
a careful examination of it indicates quite another conclusion. First, those to whom He was addressing this verse
were by no means the total of Israel. He could hardly say
to the religious leaders of His day or to those within the
hearing of His voice that their unbelief was sufficient to
take away Israel's future hope from the nation as a whole.
Second, the question can be raised — To what nation is the
kingdom of God going to be given? Certainly no other people or race are any more qualified to receive the kingdom
of God than the nation of Israel. Third, what did He mean
by the kingdom of God?

This declaration of Christ is understood when it is interpreted as a statement that the scribes and Pharisees who
rejected Christ, illustrated in the rejection of the son of the
householder in the preceding parable, would never enter into
the blessings of the kingdom of God. The term *nation*
here should be understood as a people, i.e., anyone who
would bring forth the fruits of faith. Some have interpreted the word *nation* here as referring to Israel, but to
another generation of Israel, namely, the godly remnant of

the future. Still others refer it to the church. It is probably better to leave it undefined as referring to any people who meet the conditions. In any case, the passage is not a proper basis for Israel's disinheritance. The Kingdom, as the sphere of divine blessing, is for all true believers.

A second major text in the New Testament has already been mentioned, namely, the question raised by Paul in Romans 11:1: "Did God cast off his people?" To this Paul gives a categorical negative in the words, "God forbid." He not only expressly denies that God has cast off Israel, but he argues that this has never been God's method with His people when they have sinned. While the unbelieving in Israel bore their judgment, as is true even in the present age, there was a continuing program for the godly remnant in Israel as illustrated in the present age as well as in the Old Testament. The argument of Romans 11, which has already been reviewed, comes to a climax in the expression "All Israel shall be saved" (Romans 11:26). This certainly does not mean all the church shall be saved, nor is it simply a reference to all the elect in Israel. It is rather, as many scholars have pointed out, the concept of Israel's national deliverance at the time of the second coming of Christ at which time they are saved from their persecutors and delivered from physical destruction. The contrast is between the individual salvation of Israel in the present age through faith in Christ and the collective deliverance of Israel at the end of the age.

SUMMARY

In this discussion three points of view concerning Israel's continuance as a nation have been considered: (1) The view that denies that Israel exists today, and therefore has no future. (2) The concept that Israel continues as a race, but not as a nation. (3) The premillennial interpretation that Israel has not only continuity as a race, but a future as a nation in the premillennial kingdom. It was shown that Israel's continuance as a nation depended first of all upon the nature of her promises as contained, for instance, in Genesis 17 where the Abrahamic covenant is declared to be everlasting and the land is promised to Israel as an everlasting possession. This was confirmed by the new covenant revealed by Jeremiah in which Israel was promised that it would continue as long as the moon endured. The New Testament interpretation of the new covenant was shown not to shake or alter this clear revelation in the Old Testament. New Testament evidence was cited to prove that Israel as a nation continues throughout the period of New Testament revelation. Israel continues to be addressed as a nation and is distinguished both from Gentiles and the church. Both the nation Israel is contrasted to the church as a whole and spiritual Israel is contrasted to Gentile Christians in the body of Christ. Miscellaneous texts and arguments such as Galatians 6:15, 16, Matthew 21:43, and Romans 11, when properly interpreted, would seem to confirm the conclusion that Israel is promised continuance as a nation throughout human history. The faithfulness of God to Israel is a convincing proof that God keeps His word whether to Israel or to the church, and in this we can rest our faith.

CHAPTER IV

THE PROMISE OF THE LAND TO ISRAEL

In the broad program of prophecy relating to Israel, few factors are more important than the promise to Abraham of the perpetual possession of the land. It is not only constantly reiterated in prophecies relating to the hope of Israel, but it is an integral part of the call to Abraham which begins the program. According to Genesis 12:1 God had said to Abraham: "Get thee out of thy country, and from thy kindred, and from thy father's house, unto the land that I will show thee." It is almost impossible to avoid the plain ·implication that the term *the land* was a geographic designation and that Abraham understood it in this way.

Practically all conservative expositors agree that Abraham was instructed in his original call to leave his native country, Ur of the Chaldees, and proceed to the land of Canaan. The historical record of his journey is recorded in Genesis 11:31: "And Terah took Abram his son, and Lot the son of Haran, his son's son, and Sarai his daughter-in-law, his son Abram's wife; and they went forth with them from Ur of the Chaldees, to go into the land of Canaan; and they came unto Haran, and dwelt there." After delay in Haran, still outside the land of Canaan, they finally entered the land itself after the death of Terah as recorded in Genesis 12:5: "And Abram took Sarai his wife, and Lot his brother's son, and all their substance that they had gathered, and the souls that they had gotten in Haran; and they went forth to go into the land of Canaan; and into the land of Canaan they came." The original call to Abraham, therefore, involved a geographic understanding and that to

Abraham the expression *the land* meant the land of Canaan promised to him and his seed.

It would seem redundant to cite these proofs if it were not for the fact that the term *the land* and its related promises are frequently spiritualized as if they had no geographic implications whatever. As has been pointed out in previous discussion, amillenarians usually follow one of two routes in evading the premillennial interpretations of this passage, namely, (1) that the promises of the land are to be spiritualized and relate to heaven; or (2) that the promises are to be interpreted literally but are conditional and will never be fulfilled. In order to consider the amillennial argument, it is necessary to examine first the promise of the land to the seed of Abraham as unfolded in the Old Testament; second, to study the dispossessions of the land involved in the three dispersions of Israel; third, to ascertain whether these promises have in some sense already been fulfilled or whether they are subject to future fulfillment; and, fourth, whether taking the evidence as a whole there is good ground for belief in the future fulfillment of these promises. Certain conclusions may then be drawn concerning Israel's prophetic hope.

THE PROMISE OF THE LAND TO ABRAHAM'S SEED

In examining the promise of the land, it may be observed first that Abraham understood the promises of God as relating to the literal land of Canaan. This is demonstrated by his movement from Ur to Canaan as has already been pointed out. It is further confirmed by the promise in Genesis 12:7 given after his entrance into the land: "Unto thy seed will I give this land." Certainly Abraham understood it to refer to the physical land of Canaan. This is reinforced by his experience in Genesis 13 where after being separated from Lot he is urged to look northward, southward, eastward, and westward (Genesis 13:14). At that time God assured him: "For all the land which thou seest, to thee will I give it, and to thy seed for ever" (Genesis 13:15). Further, he is instructed: "Arise, walk through the land in the length of it and in the breadth of it: for unto thee will I give it" (Genesis 13:17). It is practically impossible to evade understanding these verses as referring to the literal land.

In Genesis 15:18-21 the exact dimensions of the land are given and the territory is described as running from the river of Egypt, which was the borderline between Egypt and Canaan, and the great river, the river Euphrates, hundreds of miles to the east. It becomes clear from the description which follows which itemizes the heathen tribes occupying this territory that God had in mind more than just the small area occupied by the Canaanite himself, but rather the entire area between these two boundaries. Here again it is obvious Abraham understood that a large geographic area was involved.

The New Testament comments on this expectation of Abraham in Hebrews 11:8, 9 where it is written: "By faith Abraham, when he was called, obeyed to go out unto a place which he was to receive for an inheritance; and he went out, not knowing whither he went. By faith he became a sojourner in the land of promise, as in a land not his own, dwelling in tents, with Isaac and Jacob, the heirs with him of the same promise." So far, all must agree that a literal land is in view. Amillenarians are quick to point out, however, that verse 10 goes on to say: "For he looked for the city which hath the foundations, whose builder and maker is God." Also, in Hebrews 11:16 it adds: "But now they desire a better country, that is, a heavenly: wherefore God is not ashamed of them, to be called their God; for he hath prepared for them a city."

Do these allusions to a heavenly city nullify the idea of a literal land? A careful study of this passage will demonstrate that the subject is Abraham's faith. His faith first of all was in regard to the land, and his faith was indicated by his obedience and his sojourning in the land in tents. The same faith which he manifested in God's promise concerning the land is also manifested in Abraham's faith concerning the heavenly city. The land represented God's promise in relation to time, more specifically, the future kingdom of Christ on earth, while the heavenly city has to do with eternity, the New Jerusalem and the new earth. In the case of both, Abraham never possessed in life the fulfillment of the promises and like others he died in faith before the promises were fulfilled. The fact that Abraham believed both the temporal promises of God and the eternal promises of God does not lead to the conclusion that the earthly promise and the heavenly promise are one and the same. It is rather that they require the same attitude of faith. The major emphasis of Scripture, however, is on Abraham's belief in the temporal promises of God and to this the Scriptures constantly refer. The allusions to the eternal state and Abraham's expectation and faith are in fact rare, while the promises relating to possession of the land are one of the major themes of the Old Testament.

In presenting the Messianic hope, Isaiah, in the major passage of Isaiah 11:1-12, after describing the justice which will characterize the land when the Messiah reigns, prophesies the regathering of the children of Israel "from Assyria, and from Egypt, and from Pathros, and from Cush, and from Elam, and from Shinar, and from Hamath, and from the islands of the sea." He goes on to state that He is going to "gather together the dispersion of Judah from the four corners of the earth." The whole context makes clear that they are being brought back to the land.

Similar passages abound in Isaiah. For instance, in Isaiah 14:1 it is declared: "For Jehovah will have compassion on Jacob, and will yet choose Israel, and set them in their own land." According to Isaiah 27:13 the children of Israel are going to be gathered from Assyria and Egypt and "they shall worship Jehovah in the holy mountain at Jerusalem." This of course involves a return to the land.

In Isaiah 43:5-7 the regathering of Israel to the land is described: "Fear not; for I am with thee: I will bring thy seed from the east, and gather thee from the west; I will say to the north, Give up; and to the south, Keep not back; bring my sons from far, and my daughters from the end of the earth; every one that is called by my name, and whom I have created for my glory, whom I have formed, yea, whom I have made." It is stated categorically in Isaiah 60:21: "Thy people also shall be all righteous; they shall inherit the land for ever."

The book of Isaiah concludes with a great prophecy concerning the regathering of Israel as it will be consummated when they are brought from the ends of the earth to the Promised Land in the beginning of the millennium. According to Isaiah 66:20: "And they shall bring all your brethren out of all the nations for an oblation unto heaven, upon horses, and in chariots, and in litters, and upon mules, and upon dromedaries, to my holy mountain Jerusalem, saith Jehovah, as the children of Israel bring their oblation in a clean vessel into the house of Jehovah."

This theme of Israel is continued in Jeremiah 16:14-16: "Therefore, behold, the days come, saith Jehovah, that it shall no more be said, As Jehovah liveth, that brought up the children of Israel out of the land of Egypt; but, As Jehovah liveth, that brought up the children of Israel from the land of the north, and from all the countries whither he had driven them. And I will bring them again into their land that I gave unto their fathers. Behold, I will send for many fishers, saith Jehovah, and they shall fish them up; and afterward I will send for many hunters, and they shall hunt them from every mountain, and from every hill, and out of the clefts of the rocks." It should be noted that the regathering of Israel to their ancient land is here described as being a regathering to the last man, something that was not remotely approached in any previous return.

In describing the time of the great tribulation in Jeremiah 30:1-7, it is declared in verse 3: "For, lo, the days come, saith Jehovah, that I will turn again the captivity of my people Israel and Judah, saith Jehovah; and I will cause them to return to the land that I gave to their fathers, and they shall possess it." It is further stated in Jeremiah 30:10, 11: "Therefore fear thou not, O Jacob my servant, saith Jehovah; neither be dismayed, O Israel: for, lo, I will save thee from afar, and thy seed from the land of their captivity; and Jacob shall return, and shall be quiet and at ease, and none shall make him afraid. For I am with thee, saith Jehovah, to save thee: for I will make a full end of all the nations whither I have scattered thee, but I will not make a full end of thee; but I will correct thee in measure, and will in no wise leave thee unpunished." In Jeremiah 31 the return of Israel to the land is predicted in verse 5: "Again shalt thou plant vineyards upon the mountains of Samaria; the planters shall plant, and shall enjoy the fruit thereof." The regathering is described in Jeremiah 31:8: "Behold, I will bring them from the north country, and gather them from the uttermost parts of the earth, and with them the blind and the lame, the woman with child and her that travaileth with child together: a great company shall they return hither."

In the description of the new covenant in Jeremiah 31:31-40 it is predicted that Israel will return to the land and that Jerusalem will be built in a certain area which had formerly never been used for building purposes. It is remarkable that this precise area has been built into a portion of the modern city of Jerusalem in fulfillment of this prophecy.

Another clear reference to the regathering of Israel and their being planted in their land is found in Jeremiah 32:37-44. In verse 37 it is stated: "Behold, I will gather them out of all the countries, whither I have driven them in mine anger, and in my wrath, and in great indignation; and I will bring them again unto this place, and I will cause them to dwell safely." Again, in verse 41 it is declared: "Yea, I will rejoice over them to do them good, and I will plant them in this land assuredly with my whole heart and with my whole soul." Jeremiah promises that they will again possess the fields in and about Jerusalem and that God will cause their captivity to return. In Jeremiah 33, God solemnly swears that He will cause their captivity to return, that justice and righteousness will be executed in the land, and that the seed of David will reign on the throne. Such passages could be multiplied, such as Ezekiel 11:14-21 where in verse 17 God says plainly: "I will give you the land of Israel."

Ezekiel 20:33-38 describes the judgment upon Israel at the beginning of the millennial kingdom, when the rebels are prohibited from entering the land in contrast to the righteous who do. In Ezekiel 20:42 it is written: "And ye shall know that I am Jehovah, when I shall bring you into the land of Israel, into the country which I sware to give unto your fathers." Again in Ezekiel 34:13 God promises: "And I will bring them out from the peoples, and gather them from the countries, and will bring them into their own land; and I will feed them upon the mountains of Israel, by the watercourses, and in all the inhabited places of the country."

In the great prophecy concerning the valley of dry bones in Ezekiel 37 the significant statement is given in verses 21, 22: "And say unto them, Thus saith the Lord Jehovah: Behold, I will take the children of Israel from among the nations, whither they are gone, and will gather them on every side, and bring them in to their own land: and I will make them one nation in the land, upon the mountains of Israel; and one king shall be king to them all; and they shall be no more two nations, neither shall they be divided into two kingdoms any more at all." Ezekiel adds in verses 24, 25 that David is going to reign over them. In verse 25 he writes: "And they shall dwell in the land that I have given unto Jacob my servant, wherein your fathers dwelt; and they shall dwell therein, they, and their children, and their children's children, for ever: and David my servant shall be their prince for ever."

The process of the regathering of Israel is declared in Ezekiel 39:25-29 to extend to the whole house of Israel and indicates that they will be brought back into their land to the last man, as stated in verse 28: "And they shall know that I am Jehovah their God, in that I caused them to go into captivity among the nations, and have gathered them unto their own land; and I will leave none of them any more there." The meaning of this passage is that they will be gathered to their land and that God will not allow a single Israelite to remain in dispersion. This has never been fulfilled by any previous regathering.

Most of the minor prophets continue this prophetic strain, so prominent in Isaiah, Jeremiah, and Ezekiel. The undying love of God for Israel is declared in Hosea, and, though according to 3:4 the children of Israel will be without a king and a priesthood, they are assured in verse 5: "Afterward shall the children of Israel return, and seek Jehovah their God, and David their king, and shall come with fear unto Jehovah and to his goodness in the latter days." The Prophet Joel, after declaring the judgment of God upon Israel, closes his book by declaring: "But Judah shall abide for ever, and Jerusalem from generation to generation" (3:20).

The Prophet Amos, after an almost unrelieved indictment on Israel for their sin, closes his book with five verses in chapter 9 beginning in verse 11, where it is affirmed that the tent of David which is fallen will be raised up again. The abundance of crops is described and Amos declares God's intention in verses 14 and 15: "And I will bring back the captivity of my people Israel, and they shall build the waste cities, and inhabit them; and they shall plant vineyards, and drink the wine thereof; they shall also make gardens, and eat the fruit of them. And I will plant them upon their land, and they shall no more be plucked up out of their land which I have given them, saith Jehovah thy God." This major passage on the regathering of Israel is significant because it pictures the revival of Israel after divine judgment upon them, the abundant crops that will characterize Israel in those days, and closes with the assurance that they will no more be scattered once they are brought back to the land. Here again is a prophecy which was not fulfilled in previous regatherings and demands a future regathering in which this prophecy will be completely fulfilled. It is to this prophecy that James alludes in Acts 15:15-18 when he declared at the council of Jerusalem that it was the divine order that there should be blessing on the Gentiles first and that this was to be followed by the restoration of Israel and the rebuilding of the tent of David.

Obadiah continues this strain on the regathering of Israel when he writes in verse 17: "But in mount Zion there shall be those that escape, and it shall be holy; and the house of Jacob shall possess their possessions." In that day according to verse 21: "the kingdom shall be Jehovah's."

Micah gives a comprehensive picture of the future Messianic kingdom in 4:1-8. Israel is pictured in their ancient land in peace and security, regathered from their former scattered position and sitting under their vines and fig trees in safety. The book concludes with these words: "Thou wilt perform the truth to Jacob, and the lovingkindness to Abraham, which thou hast sworn unto our fathers from the days of old" (7:20).

The remaining minor prophets continue this theme. Zephaniah closes chapter 3 with the picture of Israel regathered and rejoicing in the Lord in their ancient land. Zechariah speaks at length on the future blessings of Israel, describing the streets full of happy children in Zechariah 8:5 and Israel is being regathered from the east and from the west in chapter 8:7, 8. Jerusalem is pictured as the capitol of the earth in 8:22. The regathering of Israel is mentioned specifically in Zechariah 10:10 where Israel is described as gathered out of Assyria and Egypt. The concluding chapter of Zechariah, beginning as it does with the second coming of Christ, pictures the changes in the land in the millennial kingdom and the wealth and prosperity and spiritual blessing of Israel. All of these prophecies imply that the promises of the land are going to be fulfilled and Israel will once again be established in the area promised to the seed of Abraham.

The careful analysis of these many promises relative to Israel's possession of the land and their regathering from the ends of the earth makes clear certain important principles. First, as intimated in previous discussion, the land, though subject to delay and Israel's temporary dispossession, is promised unconditionally to the seed of Abraham. Its ultimate possession is therefore based on the grace principle rather than the law principle. Second, it should be evident that the promise of the land is not given to Gentiles, but to the physical seed of Abraham; to be sure, not all the seed, but nevertheless to be fulfilled literally by the future generation of Israelites on earth at the time of the second coming of Christ. Third, the title of the land is declared to be unending in its character. By this we should understand that the land belongs to Israel as long as the present earth endures. Fourth, not only is the title to be given forever, but the land is actually to be possessed as long as the earth endures, once it is given to Israel at the beginning of the millennial kingdom. Fifth, it is clear that the promises are geographic and that the boundaries announced in Genesis 15 will have specific application when Israel is finally installed in their land in the millennial period. Only by indiscriminate spiritualization of all the terms and promises relating to the land can these prophecies be nullified. The fact that they are stated and restated so many times in so many different periods of Israel's history, even in times of apostasy and departure from God as in the days of Jeremiah and Ezekiel, and by so many of the minor prophets makes clear that God intended them to be taken at their face value.

THE DISPOSSESSIONS OF THE LAND

Though only premillenarians insist that Israel is eventually to possess the Promised Land and fulfill literally the promises pertaining thereto, it is agreed by all that Israel in the course of its past history has suffered three major dispossessions. Jacob and his family voluntarily went to Egypt at Joseph's invitation to avoid the famine and thereby left the land promised to Abraham's seed. In Egypt they sojourned for many generations until the time of the Exodus. After the return to the land under Moses and Joshua, the children of Israel lived for hundreds of years within the general area promised to Abraham, but never possessing it in its entirety even in the most extended period of the kingdom under Solomon. The moral disintegration which followed Solomon and the division of the kingdom of Israel into two kingdoms ultimately resulted in the second dispersion, first, in the captivity of Assyria beginning in 721 B.C. and then in the later captivity of the two remaining tribes following the invasion by Babylon beginning in 606 B.C. The second dispersion is the subject of prophecy by Moses in Deuteronomy 28:62-65 and is mentioned in Deuteronomy 30:1-3. At the same time there were frequent promises of restoration from this dispersion as indicated in the prophecies already cited in Jeremiah. The return after the second dispersion is indicated specifically by Jeremiah in chapter 29:10, 11 where the prediction is given that after seventy years they would be able to return to Jerusalem.

The third and final dispersion began in A.D. 70, with the destruction of Jerusalem and the desecration of the entire land which followed in the next century. From this dispersion, Israel has begun to return in the twentieth century as witnessed in the establishment of the nation Israel. Two million of these people are now established in their ancient land. The present regathering being witnessed by our generation is the largest movement of the people of Israel since the days of Moses, and may be understood to be the beginning of that which will be completed subsequent to the second coming of Christ and the establishment of His kingdom on earth.

The principles involved in the dispersion and regathering of Israel are sometimes called the Palestinian covenant. This is outlined in particular in the final message of Moses in Deuteronomy, chapters 28, 29, and 30. According to Deuteronomy 28:63-68, Israel was warned that they would be scattered over the face of the earth if they departed from God. Along with this, however, it was anticipated that there would be a future return in which a godly remnant of Israel would repent. This is stated explicitly in Deuteronomy 30:1-3: "And it shall come to pass, when all these things are come upon thee, the blessing and the curse, which I have set before thee, and thou shalt call them to

mind among all the nations, whither Jehovah thy God hath
driven thee, and shalt return unto Jehovah thy God, and
shalt obey his voice according to all that I command thee
this day, thou and thy children, with all thy heart, and with
all thy soul; that then Jehovah thy God will turn thy captivity, and have compassion upon thee, and will return and
gather thee from all the peoples whither Jehovah thy God
hath scattered thee."

This regathering is connected with the return of Christ
mentioned in Deuteronomy 30:3 and involves the restoration
and regathering of all the children of Israel scattered over
the face of the earth including righteous Israelites who have
died and gone to heaven. As stated in Deuteronomy 30:4:
"If any of thine outcasts be in the uttermost parts of heaven,
from thence will Jehovah thy God gather thee, and from
thence will he fetch thee." According to Deuteronomy 30:
5-9, they are promised that they will be regathered to their
land, restored spiritually, delivered from their enemies,
and abundantly blessed. Though the prophecy is given
in a context which conditions fulfillment on the future repentance of Israel, both this Scripture and many others relating to the regathering of Israel predict that Israel will
repent and will therefore be restored and regathered.

The dispossessions of the land, therefore, are temporary
judgments upon the generations of Israel who turned from
God. While they lost possession of the land in the captivities and suffered as the Scriptures prophesied, at the same
time God abundantly declares in His Word that their dispersion was temporary and their regathering is the ultimate purpose of God. Confirming this judgment is the
dramatic fact of Israel's return to the land in our day after
many centuries of dispersion, persecution, and affliction.

HAS THE PROMISE OF THE LAND ALREADY BEEN FULFILLED?

Generally speaking, amillenarians who deny that Israel
will possess the Promised Land in the future tend to ignore the promises to the contrary in the Major and Minor
Prophets and in many cases do not even attempt to offer

evidence that these promises are conditional or are to be interpreted in a nonliteral way. Occasionally, however, some arguments are offered in the attempt to sustain the thesis that the promises have already been fulfilled in historic possessions of the land. George L. Murray for instance, in his book *Millennial Studies,* page 27, offers I Kings 4: 21-24 as evidence. It is stated in verse 21: "And Solomon ruled over all of the kingdoms from the River unto the land of the Philistines, and unto the border of Egypt: they brought tribute, and served Solomon all the days of his life." In I Kings 4:24 this same thought is continued: "For he had dominion over all the region on this side the River, from Tiphsah even to Gaza, over all the kings on this side the River: and he had peace on all sides round about him."

A careful study of this passage in the light of its context, however, will demonstrate that, while Solomon ruled over all this area, he did not possess it, inasmuch as the kings are indicated as continuing their rule even though they paid tribute and served Solomon. The area was therefore not incorporated in the kingdom of Solomon, but rather came under his sway in the sense that the nations paid tribute and were at peace with Solomon. If this portion had been incorporated into the kingdom of Solomon, it would not have involved the kings' remaining on their thrones and paying tribute to him.

A similar argument is offered by Murray in reference to Joshua 21:43-45 where it is stated: "So Jehovah gave unto Israel all the land which he sware to give unto their fathers; and they possessed it, and dwelt therein." On the face of it this would seem to be a plain declaration that they did possess all the land. This promise, however, has to be limited by subsequent Scriptures. According to Judges 1:21 the Benjamites did not conquer the Jebusites. According to Judges 1:27, the children of Manasseh did not conquer all of their territory, and in verse 28 it is stated: "And it came to pass when Israel was waxed strong, that they put the Canaanites to taskwork, and did not utterly drive them out." In the verses which follow are itemized the areas which

Ephraim, Zebulun, Asher, and Naphtali did not possess. In other words, the statement of Joshua 21:43-45 must be understood as teaching that God on His part was faithful, but that the children of Israel did not enter into their possession.

Much later in Israel's history Murray notes that Nehemiah refers to the promise given to Abraham relative to the land and states, "Thou . . . hast performed thy words; for thou art righteous" (9:8). This must be understood in the same sense as Joshua in that indeed God did "give them the land," but they never possessed it historically in the Old Testament period.

The passages already cited relative to Israel's regathering and possession of the land are in themselves a complete refutation of this idea that Israel has already possessed the land in the past in its entirety. If the promise of the land was fulfilled in Joshua's time or in Solomon's, why do the many Scriptures later appeal to a future possession? Even though it may be conceded that the reference in Nehemiah is late in Israel's history, it by no means proves that the promises pertaining to the last regathering and establishment of Israel in the land have been fulfilled. In fact, it is quite to the contrary as we examine the context of Nehemiah.

There are three essentials to the fulfillment of the original promises given to Abraham regarding the possession of the land. First, the land must be actually possessed, that is, occupied, not simply controlled. Second, the possession must continue as long as the earth lasts, i.e., forever. Third, the land during this period of possession must be under the rule of the Messiah in a time of peace, tranquillity, and blessing. Nothing in history fulfills the many promises given to the prophets and, if it be judged that these promises must be fulfilled literally and surely, there remains only one possible conclusion — that is, that Israel in some future time will possess their promised land, including the entire area described in Genesis 15.

ARGUMENTS FOR FUTURE FULFILLMENT OF THE PROMISE

In reviewing the material already presented relative to Israel's future possession of the land, it may be seen that this is integral in the whole prophetic scheme involving the millennial kingdom, the return of Christ, and the consummation of the ages. The ground for fulfillment lies first in the nature of the promises themselves rooted as they are in the original proposition made to Abraham to leave his father's land and to go to a land that God would show him. The promises originally given to Abraham are reiterated again and again and form the backbone of Old Testament prophetic revelation. The promise of the land sustained Abraham, Isaac, and Jacob as they contemplated the future of their seed. The promise of the land was that which dominated Moses and Joshua as they brought the children of Israel from Egypt to the land. The hope of regathering was that which sustained Jeremiah and Ezekiel at the time of the captivities and Israel's moral apostasy. It formed the basis of their hope in future restoration both spiritually and politically. It has been further noticed that the very statement of the promises, though linked with a future repentance of Israel, is stated as certain and sure. It is linked with the perpetuity of the seed of Abraham which is promised continuance as long as the sun and moon endure.

The strongest kind of promises are related to the possession of the land in that not only the nation Israel is promised eternal continuity, but the land is promised as an everlasting possession. The emphatic description of the land given in Genesis 15:18-21 almost defies spiritualization, including as it does the heathen tribes which possessed it at the time the promise was given. The fact that Israel has been dispossessed of the land in three periods of its history is by no means an argument against ultimate possession, for imbedded in the very promises of dispossession are the promises that Israel will return and repossess the land. It has been demonstrated that these promises were not fulfilled in the past. Though Solomon temporarily controlled the area described by Abraham, he did not possess it and he did not occupy it. The prophets following Solomon certainly did not understand that Solomon had fulfilled the promise of the land and therefore promised future fulfillment. While God had been faithful, as witnessed by Nehemiah, it should be obvious to all that in Nehemiah's day the promises of possession of all the land were not fulfilled.

On every hand, therefore, an examination of the promises of the land of Israel supports the eschatology of Israel as a whole and the premillennial interpretation of the Scriptures. By so much also any spiritualization of Israel which would require fulfillment to the church in the present age or which would look to fulfillment in the eternal state would undermine not only the eschatology of Israel, but the program of eschatology as a whole. It is therefore not too much to say that the subject of the eschatology of Israel is a determinative one in the theology of future things, and as one decides these important questions he therefore decides the validity of eschatology in its broader scope. Inasmuch as the promises relating to Israel pervade the entire Scriptures, by so much a disclaiming of the promises given to Israel affects one's theology as a whole. It is for this reason that this subject is important, not only in the study of Israel itself, but in the establishment of premillennial theology.

SUMMARY

The theological implications of the promise of the land to Israel have been shown to be central in God's eschatological purpose for His ancient people. The promise of the land was integral in the original covenant with Abraham and was understood by him in a literal way. This is demonstrated in the constant reiteration of the promise in which literal possession of the land is implied or stated. The countless promises of the Old Testament which relate to the promise of the land were considered seriatim in a representative way. Such major passages as Isaiah 11, 14, 43, 60, 66, Jeremiah 16, 30, 31, 32, 33, Ezekiel 11, 20, 34, 37, 39, Hosea 3, Joel 3, Amos 9, Obadiah, Micah 4, Zechariah 8,

and 10 were cited. Certainly this is an overwhelming proof
that the entire Old Testament lends its confirmation to a
promise of future possession of the land to Israel. These
promises, though subject to delay and temporary dispossession, were never transferred to Gentiles but were declared
to be unending in character, its title given forever with
specific boundaries announced in Genesis 15 to Abraham
himself.

The dispersions predicted when Israel was out of the
land were prophesied, but it was demonstrated that not
only were the dispersions fulfilled, but also the regathering.
Evidence was adduced that the final regathering will include every Israelite to the last man, a promise which today
has never been fulfilled.

The amillennial argument that the promise of the land
was fulfilled in Solomon's day was refuted by the fact that
Solomon never fulfilled the promise in any proper sense,
and that subsequent Scriptures regarded the promise as
subject to future fulfillment. Assertions of Joshua and Nehemiah to the fact that God had fulfilled all His promises to
Israel were found to be limited by the context to the thought
that God had kept His Word though Israel had failed to
possess the land. The arguments for future fulfillment of
the promise hang therefore on the certainty of the Word of
God. Just as the prophecy concerning Israel has always
had its fulfillment in the past, so it will also in the future.
Israel's promise of the land is just as sure as the Christian's
promise of heaven.

CHAPTER V

THE KINGDOM PROMISED TO DAVID

In the study of the prophecy relating to Israel, one of the major themes is the kingdom promised to David. In this aspect of prophecy converge the other principal elements of Israel's predicted future. The promise to Abraham concerning his seed and the land, and the frequent prophecy of Israel's ultimate regathering are part of a larger pattern which promises a future kingdom to Israel.

First intimations of a future kingdom are found in the promises given to Abraham in Genesis 17:6 where it is recorded: "And I will make thee exceeding fruitful, and I will make nations of thee, and kings shall come out of thee." This is restated in verse 16 of the same chapter in relation to the promise of the son of Sarah: "And I will bless her, and moreover I will give thee a son of her: yea, I will bless her, and she shall be a mother of nations; kings of peoples shall be of her." The promise of a kingdom given to Abraham's seed is subsequently narrowed to Isaac and Jacob, and in Genesis 49:10 is further limited to the tribe of Judah. Jacob in his prophetic summary of the future of Israel prophesied concerning Judah: "The sceptre shall not depart from Judah, nor the ruler's staff from between his feet, until Shiloh come; and unto him shall the obedience of the peoples be." Though the full significance of this passage has been debated by some scholars, it can hardly be disputed that it limits the throne to Judah and his descendants. It may be concluded therefore that early in Israel's history the concept of a future kingdom constituted the matrix for Israel's eschatology.

The subject of the kingdom as it relates to Israel is so large that it will be possible to survey only some of its principal characteristics. Four areas will be considered: first, the covenant with David; second, Old Testament confirmation; third, New Testament confirmation; fourth, prophetic fulfillment.

THE COVENANT WITH DAVID

In understanding the promises of a future kingdom given to Israel, one of the major Scriptures is that containing the Davidic covenant recorded in II Samuel 7 and I Chronicles 17. In this covenant the promise of a king and a kingdom is narrowed to David's seed.

According to the context, David had been concerned that the worship of the Lord had centered in the tabernacle, a tent-like structure, which had been originally built by Moses. David himself had built permanent houses for his family, and he felt it was unfitting for the worship of God to center in such a temporary structure. Accordingly, he called in Nathan the prophet and said to him: "See now, I dwell in a house of cedar, but the ark of God dwelleth within curtains." Nathan responded as recorded in II Samuel 7:3: "Go, do all that is in thy heart, for Jehovah is with thee." That night the Lord corrected Nathan the prophet in reminding him that God had never commanded them to build Him a house of cedar. Nathan was instructed to deliver a message to David, the substance of which was that God would build a house to David in the sense of a posterity and that his son, yet to be born, would build a temple for the Lord.

The provisions of the covenant are given in II Samuel 7 beginning in verse 11: "Moreover Jehovah telleth thee that Jehovah will make thee a house. When thy days are fulfilled, and thou shalt sleep with thy fathers, I will set up thy seed after thee, that shall proceed out of thy bowels, and I will establish his kingdom. He shall build a house for my name, and I will establish the throne of his kingdom for ever. I will be his father, and he shall be my son: if he commit iniquity, I will chasten him with the rod of men, and with the stripes of the children of men: but my lovingkindness shall not depart from him, as I took it from Saul, whom I put away before thee. And thy house and thy kingdom shall be made sure for ever before thee: thy throne shall be established for ever."

The promise given to David includes the following provisions: (1) David is promised a child who would succeed him on the throne. (2) The temple which David desired to build would be constructed by this son. (3) The throne of his kingdom would be continued forever and would not be taken away from David's son even if he committed iniquity. (4) In summary, the prophet declared that David's house, kingdom, and throne would be established forever. Part of these promises were fulfilled in Solomon in that Solomon was later born and ultimately built the temple. The promise goes far beyond Solomon, however, in that the kingdom, throne, and David's house itself were established forever. There seems to be little disposition to question that Solomon is the son mentioned in the covenant and that he built a literal temple as a house for the Lord. The difficulties in interpretation come in examining the exact meaning of the term *house* as it pertains to David's posterity and the words *throne* and *kingdom*.

By way of preliminary definition, it would seem only natural to assume that by the term *throne* was meant the political rule of David over Israel. It was assured that a future king over Israel would come from David's line. This is the meaning of the promise that David's house would continue forever. The term *kingdom* is probably the most difficult term to define, but it would seem quite clear to David that God was referring to his own rule over Israel in a political sense. This is confirmed by David's own remarks in connection with the giving of the covenant. He understood the promise meant that his house would continue forever. David addresses Jehovah in II Samuel 7: 18, 19: "Who am I, O Lord Jehovah, and what is my house, that thou hast brought me thus far? And this was yet a small thing in thine eyes, O Lord Jehovah; but thou hast spoken also of thy servant's house for a great while to come; and this too after the manner of men, O Lord Jehovah!" David after recounting Israel's history adds this word in verse 25: "And now, O Jehovah God, the word that thou hast spoken concerning thy servant, and concerning his house, confirm thou it for ever, and do as thou hast spoken." In similar vein he concludes in verse 29: "Now therefore let it please thee to bless the house of thy servant, that it may continue for ever before thee; for thou, O Lord Jehovah, hast spoken it: and with thy blessing let the house of thy servant be blessed for ever."

OLD TESTAMENT CONFIRMATION OF THE COVENANT

It is probable that there would be little question about the meaning of this covenant, if it did not involve eschatology as a whole. It would seem that the promises are simple and direct that David's posterity should continue forever and that his political kingdom would not end. However, even such a simple interpretation presents some immediate problems, as David himself seems to anticipate when he notes that the prophecy concerns a long time to come.

The principal difficulty, however, seems to be that the connotation of the Davidic covenant supports the premillennial interpretation of the Bible involving a future reign of Christ on earth as David's greater Son. This point of view is quite unacceptable to the amillenarian and therefore for them some interpretation of the Davidic covenant must be found other than that of a literal fulfillment. Generally speaking, amillenarians deny that this covenant has any decisive force on the millennial question and find its terms fulfilled in the present day with God's dealings with the church. Quite often the attempt is made to deny that anything in the Old Testament construes a premillennial eschatology and statements are made such as that of Louis Berkhof: "The only Scriptural basis for this theory [i.e., premillennialism] is Revelation 20:1-6, after an Old Testament content has been poured into it" (*Systematic Theology,* p. 715).

In brief, the amillennial point of view is that the Davidic

kingdom promised to David's posterity is not a rule over the house of Israel, but a spiritual rule over the saints fulfilled in Christ's present session at the right hand of God. Such an idea of course is not contained in the Davidic covenant as it is recorded in II Samuel 7, but it is asserted that later Scriptures give this interpretation. For this reason the implications of the provisions of the Davidic covenant can be determined only after ascertaining the interpretation placed upon this covenant by other Old Testament Scriptures. Then a further step must be taken of examining the New Testament treatment of the same subject. Though this can be done only briefly within the limits of our present discussion, some important facts can be cited which decisively determine the ultimate interpretation of the Davidic covenant.

The covenant with David is not only given twice in its major content — namely, II Samuel 7 and I Chronicles 17 — but it is also confirmed in Psalm 89. In this and other Old Testament references there is no allusion anywhere to the idea that these promises are to be understood in a spiritualized sense as referring to the church or to a reign of God in heaven. Rather, it is linked to the earth and to the seed of Israel, and to the land. According to Psalm 89:3, 4 Jehovah declares: "I have made a covenant with my chosen, I have sworn unto David my servant: Thy seed will I establish for ever, and build up thy throne to all generations." This concept is declared again later in the same psalm beginning in verse 29 where it is promised that the seed will endure forever in spite of the specific problem of Israel's sins and departure from God. It is affirmed unalterably that God is going to fulfill His Word to David regardless of what his seed does: "His seed also will I make to endure for ever, and his throne as the days of heaven. If his children forsake my law, and walk not in mine ordinances; if they break my statutes, and keep not my commandments; then will I visit their transgression with the rod, and their iniquity with stripes. But my lovingkindness will I not utterly take from him, nor suffer my faithfulness to fail. My covenant will I not break, nor alter the thing that is gone out of my lips. Once have I sworn by my holiness: I will not lie unto David: his seed shall endure for ever, and his throne as the sun before me. It shall be established for ever as the moon, and as the faithful witness in the sky" (Psalm 89:29-37). According to this psalm the covenant concerns David, his physical seed, and the relationship of his rule to the children of Israel. There is no indication that this kingdom extended to a spiritual entity such as the church nor that the throne in view is the throne of God in heaven rather than the throne of David on earth.

In the well-known prophecy concerning the birth of Christ given in Isaiah 9:6, 7 it is stated again that the throne of David is in view: "For unto us a child is born, unto us a son is given; and the government shall be upon his shoulder: and his name shall be called Wonderful, Counsellor, Mighty God, Everlasting Father, Prince of Peace. Of the increase of his government and of peace there shall be no end, upon the throne of David, and upon his kingdom, to establish it, and to uphold it with justice and with righteousness from henceforth even for ever. The zeal of Jehovah of hosts will perform this." Again the throne of David is mentioned specifically and the promise indicates that the fulfillment will go on forever.

In Jeremiah 23:5, 6 the reign of the king who is the son of David is described as coming to pass in a day when Judah and Israel shall be saved and dwell safely. Jeremiah writes: "Behold, the days come, saith Jehovah, that I will raise unto David a righteous Branch, and he shall reign as king and deal wisely, and shall execute justice and righteousness in the land. In his days Judah shall be saved, and Israel shall dwell safely; and this is his name whereby he shall be called: Jehovah our righteousness." In the verses immediately following, this reign is linked with the regathering of the children of Israel and their occupation of their ancient lands. Jeremiah writes in Jeremiah 23:7, 8: "Therefore, behold, the days come, saith Jehovah, that they shall no more say, As Jehovah liveth, who brought up the children of Israel out of the land of Egypt; but, As Jehovah liveth, who brought up and who led the seed of the house of Israel out of the north country, and from all the countries whither I have driven them. And they shall dwell in their own land."

It is certainly extreme spiritualization to take the regathering of Israel as an equivalent of the outcalling of the church and the execution of "justice and righteousness in the land" as being a reference to the rule of Christ in heaven, as amillenarians would need to interpret the passage. This is another strong confirmation that the literal interpretation of the Davidic covenant was intended.

In Jeremiah 30:8, 9 another reference is found to the reign of the seed of David and again it is in a context of Israel's future regathering which will be consummated following the great tribulation. According to Jeremiah 30:9, 10 it is predicted that Israel will be free from Gentile oppression and will serve the Lord and David their king. Jeremiah writes: "But they shall serve Jehovah their God, and David their king, whom I will raise up unto them. Therefore fear thou not, O Jacob my servant, saith Jehovah; neither be dismayed, O Israel: for, lo, I will save thee from afar, and thy seed from the land of their captivity; and Jacob shall return, and shall be quiet and at ease, and none shall make him afraid." As in other passages, the fulfillment of the Davidic covenant is linked with the return of Israel to the land following their time of Jacob's trouble, as indicated in the preceding context. Here it is stated that they will serve Jehovah and David their king. There is no good reason for not taking this exactly as it is written, namely, that David will be raised from the dead and will with Christ reign over the people of Israel in the millennium. Even if David is understood to refer to Christ as David's greater Son, it is still a clear reference to a future millennium rather than to a situation that exists today.

A similar confirmation is found in Jeremiah 33:14-17 where the same particulars are spelled out in detail. Jeremiah writes: "Behold, the days come, saith Jehovah, that I will perform that good word which I have spoken concerning the house of Israel and concerning the house of Judah. In those days, and at that time, will I cause a Branch of righteousness to grow up unto David; and he shall execute justice and righteousness in the land. In those days shall Judah be saved, and Jerusalem shall dwell safely; and this is the name whereby she shall be called: Jehovah our righteousness. For thus saith Jehovah: David shall never want a man to sit upon the throne of the house of Israel." The context concerns itself with Israel's restoration and specifically speaks of the house of Israel and the house of Judah. Mention again is made that righteousness and justice will exist in the land and that Judah will be in the land and Jerusalem will be in safety. Such a situation does not prevail in this present age and is not related here or elsewhere to the reign of Christ from the throne of His Father in heaven.

It would seem hardly necessary to cite all the additional passages that might be available, but, inasmuch as this subject has been controverted, the mass of Old Testament prophecies that deal with the subject certainly give added stature to the literal interpretation of the Davidic covenant. Ezekiel 37:22-25 indicates that Israel in that future day will have one king over them and will be a people of God. In verses 24 and 25 Ezekiel writes: "And my servant David shall be king over them; and they all shall have one shepherd: they shall also walk in mine ordinances, and observe my statutes, and do them. And they shall dwell in the land that I have given unto Jacob my servant, wherein your father dwelt; and they shall dwell therein, they, and their children, and their children's children, for ever: and David my servant shall be their prince for ever." It should be obvious that in Ezekiel's days David had been dead over four hundred years and that this is a prophecy that David will be raised from the dead prior to the millennial reign of Christ and share with Christ the rule of the people of Israel. Such a situation is quite foreign to the present age.

One of the problems which is often raised concerning

the fulfillment of the Davidic covenant is the fact that for many years the throne was unoccupied. From the time of the Babylonian captivity on there was no literal earthly kingdom. This, however, is taken into full consideration in the Word of God. According to Hosea 3:4, 5, written long before the Babylonian captivity, it was predicted: "For the children of Israel shall abide many days without king, and without prince, and without sacrifice, and without pillar, and without ephod or teraphim: afterward shall the children of Israel return, and seek Jehovah their God, and David their king, and shall come with fear unto Jehovah and to his goodness in the latter days." According to this passage, therefore, it can be assumed that God, while permitting the throne to be empty, nevertheless assured it to David and his seed prophesying Israel would return to the Lord, i.e., in the future millennial kingdom and resurrected David would be their king.

It is also promised in Amos 9:11 that the tabernacle of David would be restored in the latter days, apparently another reference to the revival of the political kingdom of Israel over which David was king. Further light will be cast upon this passage in the study of the New Testament confirmation. A concluding word is found in Zechariah 14 where it is predicted that after the second coming of Christ when His feet will touch the Mount of Olives (Zechariah 14:4), and "Jehovah shall be king over all the earth" (Zechariah 14:9). This of course is not a contradiction of the fulfillment of the Davidic covenant, but is a part of the same picture.

As far as the Old Testament narrative is concerned, the prophets are clear in these multiplied passages that God anticipated a literal fulfillment of His promise to David. It would seem evident, therefore, that the people of Israel were acting in good faith when they expected God to revive their kingdom, deliver them from their enemies, and restore them to their ancient land. Such as was their expectation when Christ came the first time, and such can be their expectation at His second coming.

NEW TESTAMENT CONFIRMATION

It has been demonstrated that the Old Testament clearly predicts a future kingdom in which David and his posterity would rule over the children of Israel regathered and dwelling in their ancient land. Amillenarians, however, have countered this evidence by their assertion that the New Testament interprets these predictions as being fulfilled in the present age. Before turning, therefore, to some of the theological arguments in support of an eschatology for Israel, some of the New Testament evidence should be examined.

One of the first texts dealing with this subject is found in the announcements of the angel to Mary that she is to be the mother of Christ. In this connection she is told that Christ will reign on the throne of His father David over the house of Jacob. According to Luke 1:30-33 the angel said: "Fear not, Mary: for thou hast found favor with God. And behold, thou shalt conceive in thy womb, and bring forth a son, and shalt call his name JESUS. He shall be great, and shall be called the Son of the Most High: and the Lord God shall give unto him the throne of his father David: and he shall reign over the house of Jacob for ever; and of his kingdom there shall be no end." In the light of the prominence given this same subject in the Old Testament, the question may be fairly raised: What would such a prophecy mean to Mary? For any Jewish maiden who accepted the Old Testament prophecy concerning the future of Israel and entertained the hope of a coming Messiah, would hardly question that the prophecy given by the angel would be interpreted literally, that is, she would understand by the throne of David an earthly throne such as David enjoyed in his lifetime.

Further, it is declared that Mary's Son would reign over the house of Jacob forever. Mary certainly would not understand by the phrase "the house of Jacob" a reference to saints in general regardless of racial background. To her it could mean only one thing and that is the descendants of Jacob, namely, the twelve tribes of Israel. Inasmuch as this would be the normal and natural understanding on the part of Mary in such a prophecy, it is almost unthinkable that God would have used this terminology if as a matter of fact the hope of Israel was a mistake and the prophecies given in the Old Testament were not intended to be understood literally.

It seems quite clear that the disciples anticipated much the same kind of a literal fulfillment. According to Matthew 20:20-23, the mother of James and John came to Christ with a request concerning them: "Command that these my two sons may sit, one on thy right hand, and one on thy left, in thy kingdom." She certainly was not asking that these disciples would share the Father's throne in glory, but it is obvious that what she anticipated was that they would share the earthly rule of Christ in the kingdom promised to Israel. Though Christ refused the request on the ground that only the Father had the right to bestow such an honor, He did not deny that such an honor might be afforded someone, which would hardly have been the case if the throne of God itself had been in view. In any case, Christ did not tell her that her request was out of bounds because there was to be no earthly rule. It was rather that it was improper to obtain such an honor as a requested privilege.

It is entirely possible that the request originated in the incident recorded in Matthew 19 where Christ had promised them in verse 28: "Verily, I say unto you, that ye who have followed me, in the regeneration when the Son of man shall sit on the throne of his glory, ye also shall sit upon twelve thrones, judging the twelve tribes of Israel." Here Christ is specifically confirming the concept of a future kingdom in which Israel would be the subjects and in which the disciples would have part in the government. If indeed the Old Testament prophecies were not intended to teach a rule of God from heaven over saints on earth, the language of this prediction would be misleading.

As late as Luke 22 on the night before His crucifixion, Christ said to His disciples in verses 29, 30: "I appoint unto you a kingdom, even as my Father appointed unto me, that ye may eat and drink at my table in my kingdom; and ye shall sit on thrones judging the twelve tribes of Israel." Thus, late in His life after He had already been rejected by the people of Israel Christ repeats the same promises which had characterized the Old Testament, the announcement to Mary, and His conversation with His disciples on previous occasions. There was going to be a kingdom over Israel and the disciples would sit on thrones participating in the government.

A final confirming word is given by Christ in connection with His ascension in Acts 1. Here it is recorded that the disciples came to Christ and asked the question according to Acts 1:6: "Lord, dost thou at this time restore the kingdom to Israel?" From the question itself it becomes apparent that the disciples were still anticipating an earthly kingdom and hoped for its immediate realization. In reply to them, Christ did not say that their hope was vain, that there was not going to be a literal fulfillment. Rather He replied: "It is not for you to know the times or seasons, which the Father hath set within his own authority." By so much, He was affirming that the kingdom would be fulfilled, but that the time was not for them to know. In the verses which follow He directs their attention to the task that was immediately before them, and to the power of the Spirit which would aid them in the world-wide proclamation of the gospel. He said in effect that before the kingdom could come there had to be a fulfillment of God's purpose in the church. The consummation of the prophecies regarding the kingdom therefore was postponed, but not cancelled. The kingdom on earth is consistently interpreted in a literal way and is not spiritualized in the narratives dealing with the subject in the gospels and Acts.

One of the important passages in the New Testament bearing on this subject is found in Acts 15:14-18. Here in the council in Jerusalem the question had been raised concerning the status of the Gentiles in the present age. It was difficult for the Jews to understand that for the time being the Gentiles should have a place of equality with Israel, in view of the many prophecies in the Old Testament which anticipated Israel's pre-eminence and glory. In the settlement of this problem it is recorded that James made the following address: "Brethren, hearken unto me: Symeon hath rehearsed how first God visited the Gentiles, to take out of them a people for his name. And to this agree the words of the prophets; as it is written, After these things I will return, and I will build again the tabernacle of David, which is fallen; and I will build again the ruins thereof, and I will set it up: that the residue of men may seek after the Lord, and all the Gentiles, upon whom my name is called, saith the Lord, who maketh these things known from of old." The passage concludes with the suggestion that Gentiles be not obligated to keep Jewish customs except in cases where this might hinder fellowship with the Jews, and winning them to Christ.

Of major importance is the main thesis of his remarks which is based on a reference and partial quotation of Amos 9:11, 12. Scholars have not agreed on the precise interpretation of this passage and amillenarians in particular have labored to make this a contradiction of the premillennial point of view. However, it seems that "after these things I will return" refers to the return of Christ after the period of Gentile prominence which began in 606 B.C. and is destined to continue until the second coming. It is after these things — i.e., judgment on Israel, their scattering, and discipline — that Christ will return and build again the tabernacle or tent of David. The reference to the tent of David, of course, does not concern itself with any building as such but rather with the political power and sway which David enjoyed.

That the rebuilding of the tabernacle of David is the restoration of the kingdom to Israel and not the construction of the church in the present age is borne out by the prophecies that are related to it in Amos, which have already been noted in a previous discussion. Amos 9:14 reads as follows: "And I will bring back the captivity of my people Israel, and they shall build the waste cities, and inhabit them; and they shall plant vineyards, and drink the wine thereof; they shall also make gardens, and eat the fruit of them." In other words, the kingdom concerns itself with the rule over the people of Israel in their ancient land which will be characterized by revival and restoration, exactly what we would expect by the reference to rebuilding the tent of David. This is further confirmed by the final verse of Amos 9: "And I will plant them upon their land, and they shall no more be plucked up out of their land which I have given them, saith Jehovah thy God." In other words, the kingdom is related to the time when Israel will be regathered and be established in their ancient land. The normal and natural exegesis of these passages therefore requires a future restoration to Israel and a future fulfillment of the kingdom promises. The divine order therefore is judgment on Israel and blessing upon Gentile first, to be followed by judgment on Gentile and blessing on Israel. This is not only the order of the Old Testament, but it is the order of this portion in Acts and is further confirmed by the order indicated in Romans chapter 11 where Israel is to be grafted back into the place of blessing which Gentiles now enjoy.

The consummating Scripture of course in the New Testament which puts the capstone on all these indications is found in Revelation 20 where it is stated plainly that Christ will rule for 1000 years. His rule is marked off by certain events which occur before and certain events which follow His millennial reign. The claim of the amillenarian that Revelation 20 is the only passage in the Bible which teaches an eschatology for Israel is certainly not sustained by the abundant evidence which has been cited from both the Old and New Testaments.

Is the Covenant to Be Interpreted Literally?

With the Scripture testimony before us, it is now possible for us to consider some of the problems which exist in this interpretation. It has already been pointed out that postponement and delay of the kingdom is by no means an argument against it, for Hosea 3:4, 5 anticipates precisely such a situation. Further, the long years in which no one was on the throne of David did not hinder the angel from assuring Mary that her Son would sit on the throne. As in other promises of God, delay and postponement does not affect the certainty of the ultimate fulfillment.

Probably the leading question in the entire argument is whether a literal fulfillment of these promises is to be expected. This of course faces frontally the whole premillennial-amillennial argument which can only be resolved on the relative cogency of the results of the methods. Amillenarians, generally speaking, tend to spiritualize promises which would teach a future millennium, though they interpret literally prophecies which do not interfere with their system. Premillenarians, on the other hand, believe that prophecy is not a special case requiring spiritualization any more than any other area of divine revelation and they believe also that prophecy should be interpreted normally — that is, in an ordinary, grammatical and literal sense unless the context or theology as a whole plainly indicates to the contrary. Premillenarians do not find the amillennial charge — that the premillennial position is untenable, self-contradictory, and hopelessly confused — is sustained. While obviously the premillennial system of interpretation has much more detail than the amillennial denial, and even though there are countless minor problems, the major elements of the premillennial system have seemed quite cogent to thousands of careful Bible students and scholars. The question of literal interpretation therefore cannot be brushed aside *a priori* as if the literal interpretation of prophecy is impossible. Rather, there are sound and good arguments to the contrary.

George N. H. Peters in his *Theocratic Kingdom* provides a masterly summary of the arguments in favor of literal interpretation. In his proposition 52, he lists 21 arguments in favor of literal interpretation and includes other collateral material. These can be summarized under ten arguments for literal interpretation: "(1) The solemn char-

acter of the covenant which was confirmed by an oath.
(2) A spiritual fulfillment would not be becoming to a
solemn covenant. (3) Both David and Solomon apparently
understood it to be literal (II Samuel 7:18-29; II Chronicles
6:14-16). (4) The language used, which is also used by the
prophets, denotes a literal throne and kingdom. (5) The
Jews plainly expected a literal fulfillment. (6) The throne
and kingdom as a promise and inheritance belong to the humanity of Christ as the seed of David rather than belong to
His deity. (7) There is no ground for identifying David's
throne and the Father's throne. (8) A symbolical interpretation of the covenant leaves its interpretation to man.
(9) The literal fulfillment is requisite to the display of God's
government in the earth, necessary to the restoration and
exaltation of the Jewish nation and deliverance of the earth
from the curse. (10) Literal fulfillment is necessary to
preserve the Divine unity of purpose" (cf., *Millennial Kingdom*, by the writer, p. 199). These arguments, usually ignored by amillenarians, have great weight and seem to
provide a reasonable approach to the Davidic covenant
and the promise of the kingdom.

The matter of literal fulfillment of the promises is confirmed also by the fact that certain portions of it have been
literally fulfilled. One of these is in the birth of Christ
Himself who literally fulfilled many promises pertaining to
David's seed. Here the meticulous accuracy of the promises
given to David and Solomon is illustrated. In the covenant as originally given there is a careful distinction between the seed of David, the seed of Solomon, and their
respective thrones. In the covenant David is assured that
his seed will reign forever, while Solomon is only promised
that his throne will continue forever. In this fine point
is an illustration not only of the literalness of the prophecy,
but of God's intention to cut off Solomon's line at the time
of the captivity of Judah embodied in the declarations in
Jeremiah 22:20 and 36:30. In the New Testament in the
lineage of Christ as recorded in Matthew 1 and Luke 3, it
seems to be made evident that Joseph descended from

Solomon, which line was cut off, while Mary descended from Nathan, another son of David, rather than from Solomon. This point of view not only confirms the necessity of the virgin birth, that is, that Joseph could not be the father of Christ, but also supports the idea that God intended the prophecy embodied in the covenant with David to be taken literally even to such a fine distinction.

This literal interpretation and expected fulfillment of the Davidic covenant is of course in keeping with the other covenants previously studied. Certainly it fits in beautifully with the idea that the Abrahamic covenant anticipates Israel continuing eternally as a nation and possessing the land forever. The possession of the land is limited by the continuance of the earth itself and terminates with the destruction of the heavens and the earth at the end of the millennium. The force of the Hebrew, however, is that Israel will continue to possess the land perpetually, that is, until eternity begins.

The assertion of amillenarians that the Davidic throne is simply a reference to God's throne in heaven is not supported by either the Old or the New Testament prophecies relating to the future of Israel. Of the 59 references to David in the New Testament, there is not one connecting the Davidic throne with the present session of Christ. Such an inference could be established only by spiritualizing many prophecies both in the Old and New Testaments.

Samuel H. Wilkinson, in his book, *The Israel Promises and Their Fulfillment*, pp. 56, 57, has given a forceful summary of this point. "Nevertheless, facts are stubborn things. It is a fact that God has declared that Israel is not to cease from being a nation before Him for ever. It is a fact that the Jewish nation, still in unbelief, survivor of all others, alone retains its national identity. . . . It is a fact that the promise of a land (the territorial limits of which were defined) to the posterity of Abraham, as also the promise of a son of David's own line to occupy David's throne for ever, were *unconditional* promises, ratified by covenant and oath. It is a fact that the posterity of Abraham has never yet fully possessed and enjoyed the whole of the land so granted and that no son of David occupies David's throne. . . . The O. T. promises are all as certain of fulfillment in their O. T. sense and meaning and purpose to Israel, as are the N. T. promises certain of fulfillment to the Church." A study of the Old and New Testament therefore seems to confirm a genuine eschatology for Israel involving their continuity as a nation, their regathering and restoration to their ancient land, and their enjoyment of a kingdom in which Christ will reign over them. David resurrected from the dead will share this position of authority as a prince under Christ. Such an interpretation not only provides a literal fulfillment of many prophecies pertaining to it, but is fully honoring to the Word of God as that which is inspired infallibly by the Holy Spirit.

THE FUTURE PROGRAM OF ISRAEL IN RELATION TO THE KINGDOM

On the basis of prophecy which has already been fulfilled and prophecies which can be expected to be fulfilled in the future, a broad future program for Israel can be established in the Bible. This anticipates that the regathering of Israel, begun in the twentieth century, will be continued. If the rapture of the church may be assumed to be pretribulational, Israel's program will unfold immediately after the church is translated. With the realignment of nations, Israel will enter into a covenant with the Gentile rulers of the Middle East, as anticipated in Daniel 9:26, 27. A covenant will be signed for a period of seven years, which will be the last seven years of Daniel's 490 years allotted to Israel. During the first half of this seven years Israel will enjoy prosperity. Orthodox Jews will apparently revive their ancient sacrifices and a temple will be provided. After three and one-half years of the covenant have run their course, it will be abruptly broken, in keeping with the predictions of both the Old and New Testaments and especially the words of Christ in Matthew 24:15-22. A period of great trouble which Jeremiah refers to as "the time of Jacob's trouble" will follow. Israel will be persecuted, and their only hope will be to escape their enemies by hiding. The period of great tribulation will feature not only a time of trouble for Israel, but will be a period in which divine wrath is expressed on the earth. Great judgments will take place including warfare, earthquakes, famines, and stars falling from heaven. According to the book of Revelation, the majority of the earth's population will be destroyed in these catastrophes. A major world war brings the period to a close. As Christ returns from heaven, He descends to the Mount of Olives and delivers His persecuted people. The precise situation is described in Zechariah 14 and Revelation 19 and is confirmed in Romans 11:26, 27.

With the destruction of the enemies of Christ and the establishment of the millennial kingdom, the process of Israel's regathering and restoration will be completed. According to Ezekiel 20:34-38, regathered Israel will be judged and rebels or unbelievers will be purged out. Only those who pass the searching judgment of Christ are allowed to enter into the millennial period. These are brought back to their ancient land and possess the area from the River of Egypt to the river Euphrates. Over this land Christ will rule as He rules over the entire world. David who is raised from the dead along with Old Testament saints has a part in the government of the people of Israel. This will also be shared by the twelve apostles, whom Christ assured participation in His government of Israel in the millennial state.

During the thousand-year reign of Christ, the remnant nation Israel, surviving the great tribulation, will greatly increase as will the Gentile nations, and repopulate the earth and rebuild their cities. At the end of the millennial reign of Christ, Satan is loosed and divine judgment overtakes any born in the millennium who rebels against Christ, who are Jewish and Gentile unbelievers. Though all the details are not supplied, it seems clear that the saints living on earth at the end of the millennium will be translated into their eternal state. The new heaven and the new earth will be created. The heavenly city, the New Jerusalem, will descend and rest upon the new earth. The description of the new earth given in Revelation 21:22 seems clearly to include Israel as well as Gentile saints of all ages. It is interesting to note, however, that the people of Israel retain their identity as Israelites even as the Gentiles retain their identity as Gentiles in the eternal state. Though there are distinctions depending on their backgrounds, all alike enjoy the presence of the King of kings and the countless blessings that belong to the eternal state.

The future of Israel is the fulfillment of a divine purpose sovereignly conceived in which the children of Israel constitute one of the major vehicles of divine revelation. Through them God gave the Scriptures and through them God has illustrated many of His attributes, especially those of His faithfulness, love, and righteousness. Inasmuch as Israel has not only a prominent place in the plan of God for the past, but also in the future, a proper understanding of the eschatology of Israel does much to open up a proper understanding of God's purpose as a whole and is seemingly indispensable to any detailed exegesis of the eschatology unfolded in the Old and New Testaments.

SUMMARY

The provisions of the covenant of David therefore form a broad platform for the eschatology of Israel embodied in the Davidic kingdom. It would seem that this covenant assured to David that his political rule as well as his physical posterity would continue forever even though it might be interrupted, just as the possession of the land was temporarily interrupted. The covenant with David is confirmed not only by its dual revelation in II Samuel 7 and I Chronicles 17, but by the major confirmation of Psalm 89 and by many additional prophecies in the Old Testament such as Isaiah 9:6, 7; Jeremiah 23:5-8; 30:8-10; 33:14-17; Ezekiel 37: 22-25; Hosea 3:4, 5; Amos 9:11, 15, and similar Old Testament passages. New Testament confirmation was found in such major passages as Luke 1:30-33; Matthew 19:28; 20:20-

23; Luke 22:29, 30; Acts 1:6; 15:14-18; and the climactic prophecy of Revelation 20. The massive arguments for literal interpretation of these promises were presented as a proper basis for the fulfillment of this covenant in the future. On the expectation involved in the fulfillment of the Davidic covenant, a future program of Israel can be outlined, including God's dealing with Israel in the time of tribulation, to be followed by their blessing in the millennial reign of Christ and ultimate enjoyment of the eternal state in the New Jerusalem. The eschatology of Israel in a word depends on the authority and accuracy of Biblical prophecy and the legitimacy of its normal and literal interpretation.

Chapter VI

THE SUFFERING OF ISRAEL

The predicted suffering of Israel is one of the major aspects of Biblical prophecy concerning the future of this people. It is paradoxical that the nation chosen for exaltation and selected to be a special means of divine revelation should also be destined for suffering which would exceed that of any other nation of the world.

Causes of Israel's Suffering

The trials of Israel stem from the basic conflict between divine purpose and satanic opposition. The very fact that God selected Israel as a special means of divine revelation makes the nation the object of special satanic attack. Satanic hatred of the seed of Abraham is manifested from the beginning of God's dealings with Abraham and continues through the entire course of human history culminating in the rebellion at the end of the millennium.

Spiritual warfare in relation to Israel is in evidence from the beginning. The fulfillment of God's purpose of bringing Abraham from Ur of Chaldees to the Promised Land was delayed and thwarted by Abraham's incomplete obedience in bringing his father and nephew Lot with him. Entrance to the land was delayed until his father died, and Lot continued to be a hindrance to him until he and Abraham separated. Satanic opposition to fulfillment of God's purpose in Abraham is also revealed in the delayed birth of Isaac, and only the miraculous intervention of God made it possible for Him to fulfill His prophecy of a seed to Abraham through whom He would bless the nations. In the case of Isaac, a similar situation is evident in the fact that only after years of supplication was a seed granted to Isaac and Rebekah. When Jacob and Esau were born, it was expressly an answer to prayer. The corrupting influence of Satan is manifest in both the lives of Esau and Jacob, and only by the grace of God was Jacob rescued from his compromising position. Jacob's life ended in Egypt, to which he had fled to avoid the famine, with none of his family remaining in the Promised Land. The subsequent experience of Israel in Egypt, where for a time they enjoyed prosperity but eventually were threatened with extermination, is well known to every student of the Bible. Only by divine intervention was Israel brought from Egypt to the Promised Land, and then only after years of failure and wandering in the wilderness.

The incomplete possession of the land, the spiritual degeneracy which characterized the time of the judges, and the apostasy that followed the days of Solomon are given large place in the Old Testament. In every particular Satan sought to spoil, to hinder, and to mar the purpose of God in the elect nation. The scattering of Israel in the captivities, the attempt recorded in the book of Esther to exterminate the Jew, and the ultimate capstone of satanic opposition to Israel's place of spiritual leadership was recorded in the gospels. In the New Testament, Israel's rejection of her Messiah is related, with Israel's resulting dispersion following the Roman persecution A.D. 70-135. Undoubtedly one of the principal causes for Israel's suffering has been the unending opposition of Satan to the fulfillment of God's purpose in the nation.

Coupled with Israel's failures as recorded in the Scriptures is the fact of divine discipline exercised on the nation. Israel was not only to be the channel of divine revelation of God, but also the example of God's faithfulness to a sinning people who are the objects of His love and grace. Accordingly, many pages of the Old Testament are dedicated to giving the sacred records of God's dealings with His wandering people. The studies of Israel's sufferings will illustrate this basic reason for the sufferings inflicted on the nation.

The sufferings of Israel, while revealing God's discipline and righteousness, are also demonstrations of His love. Joined to every righteous judgment upon Israel are many manifestations of divine grace in preserving a godly remnant, in giving them that which is far greater than they deserved and fulfilling His divine purpose in and through them in spite of their own failure and Satan's efforts to hinder the purpose of God. There is a majestic drama in the whole sequence of events that relate to Israel's history, and they epitomize to some extent the conflict between good and evil which is the basic Christian philosophy of history. The sufferings of Israel, therefore, should be seen in the context of satanic persecution, of divine discipline for sin, and of divine faithfulness to His chosen people.

THE SUFFERING OF ISRAEL IN FULFILLED PROPHECY

Early in the recorded history of Israel intimations are given of the fact that Israel would suffer. Moses solemnly warned the children of Israel in Deuteronomy 4:25-28 that God would bring them into suffering for their sins: "When thou shalt beget children, and children's children, and ye shall have been long in the land, and shall corrupt yourselves, and make a graven image in the form of anything, and shall do that which is evil in the sight of Jehovah thy God, to provoke him to anger; I call heaven and earth to witness against you this day, that ye shall soon utterly perish from off the land whereunto ye go over the Jordan to possess it; ye shall not prolong your days upon it, but shall utterly be destroyed. And Jehovah will scatter you among the peoples, and ye shall be left few in number among the nations, whither Jehovah shall lead you away. And there ye shall serve gods, the work of men's hands, wood and stone, which neither see, nor hear, nor eat, nor smell."

In the verses which immediately follow, however, hope is held out to Israel that if they will seek the face of God they will find forgiveness and restoration. In Deuteronomy

4:29, 30 Moses assured them: "But from thence ye shall seek Jehovah thy God, and thou shalt find him, when thou searchest after him with all thy heart and with all thy soul. When thou art in tribulation, and all these things are come upon thee, in the latter days thou shalt return to Jehovah thy God, and hearken unto his voice."

Important in this promise of restoration is the first reference to a time of special tribulation in the latter days which will be related to their return to their ancient land. This seems to be a reference to events which are yet future, connected with God's dealings with Israel in the time of trouble preceding the millennial kingdom.

One of the major sections in the Bible on Israel's sufferings is found in the closing chapters of Deuteronomy. After outlining the basis for blessing while they were in the land (Deuteronomy 28:1-14), Moses turns to the subject of God's chastening discipline upon them if they depart from His law. He points out that God will curse them and He will smite them with all types of afflictions and that ultimately they will be scattered over the face of the earth.

The closing verses of Deuteronomy 28, beginning with verse 62, are a graphic description of God's future discipline of the nation. Moses writes: "And ye shall be left few in number, whereas ye were as the stars of heaven for multitude; because thou didst not hearken unto the voice of Jehovah thy God. And it shall come to pass, that, as Jehovah rejoiced over you to do you good, and to multiply you, so Jehovah will rejoice over you to cause you to perish, and to destroy you; and ye shall be plucked from off the land whither thou goest in to possess it. And Jehovah will scatter thee among all peoples, from the one end of the earth even unto the other end of the earth; and there thou shalt serve other gods, which thou hast not known, thou nor thy fathers, even wood and stone. And among these nations shalt thou find no ease, and there shall be no rest for the sole of thy foot: but Jehovah will give thee there a trembling heart, and failing of eyes, and pining of soul;

and thy life shall hang in doubt before thee; and thou shalt fear night and day, and shalt have no assurance of thy life. In the morning thou shalt say, Would it were even! and at even thou shalt say, Would it were morning: for the fear of thy heart which thou shalt fear, and for the sight of thine eyes which thou shalt see" (Deuteronomy 28:62-67).

In this massive prediction of Israel's future sufferings, God makes plain that Israel will be left few in number, they will be scattered among all the nations of the earth, and they will have no rest of mind or heart, their very lives being in danger from morning until evening. The fearful consequences of neglecting the law have been only too graphically fulfilled in the history of the nation.

Recorded in the Old Testament itself are the captivities which were a major form of suffering for Israel. The ten tribes were carried off by the Assyrians in the eighth century B.C. This was followed by the captivity of Babylon in the seventh and sixth centuries B.C. Once again the land lay desolate, the beautiful city of Jerusalem was in ruins, and the evidences of God's loving favor were in a large measure erased. The divine judgment came only after centuries of warning not only in the written Word, but the oral ministry of prophets who plainly told the children of Israel of that which would beset them if they did not return to the Lord. The Old Testament, however, closes with Israel back in the land, re-established in their ancient cities, and once again worshiping at the temple of God.

In the New Testament after the four hundred years which separate the Old and New Testaments, the strain of prophecy concerning Israel's future sufferings is continued. With the gathering opposition of the religious leaders of the Jews as well as widespread defection among those who had originally followed Christ, the closing messages of Christ were messages of judgment. In the twenty-third chapter of Matthew, Christ solemnly pronounces divine judgment upon the scribes and the Pharisees: "Woe unto you, scribes and Pharisees, hypocrites! for ye build the sep-

ulchres of the prophets, and garnish the tombs of the righteous, and say, If we had been in the days of our fathers, we
should not have been partakers with them in the blood
of the prophets. Wherefore ye witness to yourselves, that
ye are the sons of them that slew the prophets. Fill ye
up then the measure of your fathers. Ye serpents, ye offspring of vipers, how shall ye escape the judgment of hell?
Therefore, behold, I send unto you prophets, and wise men,
and scribes: some of them shall ye kill and crucify; and some
of them shall ye scourge in your synagogues, and persecute from city to city: that upon you may come all the
righteous blood shed on the earth, from the blood of Abel
the righteous unto the blood of Zachariah son of Barachiah,
whom ye slew between the sanctuary and the altar. Verily
I say unto you, All these things shall come upon this generation. O Jerusalem, Jerusalem, that killeth the prophets,
and stoneth them that are sent unto her! how often would
I have gathered thy children together, even as a hen gather-
eth her chickens under her wings, and ye would not! Behold, your house is left unto you desolate. For I say unto
you, Ye shall not see me henceforth, till ye shall say, Blessed
is he that cometh in the name of the Lord" (Matthew 23:
29-39).

In pronouncing judgment upon His generation, Christ
was in effect predicting the final dispersion and their ultimate regathering when the godly remnant of Israel in
repentance would say: "Blessed is he that cometh in the
name of the Lord." In the early portion of the twenty-fourth
chapter of Matthew the postscript to this prediction is
given. When the disciples came to show Christ the splendor
of the buildings of the temple, Christ answered: "See ye
not all these things? verily I say unto you, There shall not
be left here one stone upon another, that shall not be thrown
down" (Matthew 24:2). In reply to further questions from
His disciples, He predicted the course of the present age
including the dramatic prediction of Matthew 24:9: "Then
shall they deliver you up unto tribulation, and shall kill
you: and ye shall be hated of all the nations for my name's

sake." Like Moses of old, He solemnly warned the children of Israel. Christ, the prophet of whom Moses spoke, delivered a similar message to His generation much of which has already been fulfilled in the centuries since Christ. In A.D. 70 Jerusalem was destroyed and with it the magnificent temple. In the years that followed, Israel was the object of fearful persecution, culminating with the complete desecration of the land of Israel in A.D. 135 by the Roman soldiers. The sad condition of being scattered to the ends of the earth has persisted until the twentieth century, and with it has come untold sufferings to the people of Israel climaxing in the terrible scourge of Hitler who murdered some six million of the people of Israel. But, according to the prophets, the end is not yet and ahead of Israel is a terrible time of suffering before the day of restoration.

THE FUTURE TIME OF JACOB'S TROUBLE

The predictions of Israel's suffering as given in the Old and New Testaments, while fulfilled in part to the present hour, are yet to have their climax. As intimated as early as Deuteronomy 4, Israel is destined to have a particular time of suffering which will eclipse anything that it has known in the past. The Prophet Jeremiah gave an extensive revelation on this subject in the thirtieth chapter of his prophecy in connection with his prediction of the ultimate restoration of the people of Israel. A tragic picture of that future hour is given in Jeremiah 30:5-7: "For thus saith Jehovah: We have heard a voice of trembling, of fear, and not of peace. Ask ye now, and see whether a man doth travail with child: wherefore do I see every man with his hands on his loins, as a woman in travail, and all faces are turned into paleness? Alas! for that day is great, so that none is like it: it is even the time of Jacob's trouble; but he shall be saved out of it."

In Jeremiah's prophecy the main elements of Israel's future time of tribulation are unfolded. It is declared to be a time of great trouble which will be greater than any time of suffering in Israel's past. It will be peculiarly "the time of Jacob's trouble" in that Israel will be singled out for suffering in that day. Yet coupled with the prediction of unprecedented tribulation is the prediction that "he shall be saved out of it." The time of trouble is going to be climaxed by a time of deliverance when the prophecy given in Jeremiah 30:3 is fulfilled: "For, lo, the days come, saith Jehovah, that I will turn again the captivity of my people Israel and Judah, saith Jehovah; and I will cause them to return to the land that I gave to their fathers, and they shall possess it."

The Prophet Daniel in a similar way refers to Israel's time of trouble. After predicting the warfare which will characterize the Middle East at the time of the end, Daniel goes on to prophesy: "And at that time shall Michael stand up, the great prince who standeth for the children of thy people; and there shall be a time of trouble such as never was since there was a nation even to that same time: and at that time thy people shall be delivered, every one that shall be found written in the book" (Daniel 12:1). Like the prophecy of Jeremiah, Daniel predicted that the future time of Israel's tribulation would surpass anything they had ever known and that it would be climaxed by their deliverance.

The purge of Israel in their time of trouble is described by Zechariah in these words: "And it shall come to pass, that in all the land, saith Jehovah, two parts therein shall be cut off and die; but the third shall be left therein. And I will bring the third part into the fire, and will refine them as silver is refined, and will try them as gold is tried" (Zechariah 13:8, 9). According to Zechariah's prophecy, two thirds of the children of Israel in the land will perish, but the one third that are left will be refined and be awaiting the deliverance of God at the second coming of Christ which is described in the next chapter of Zechariah.

On this same subject of Israel's coming time of suffering, Christ Himself delivered a dramatic prediction. In the course of His prophetic message in Matthew 24, He instructed the disciples: "When therefore ye see the abomination of desolation, which was spoken of through Daniel the prophet, standing in the holy place (let him that readeth understand), then let them that are in Judaea flee unto the mountains: let him that is on the housetop not go down to take out the things that are in his house: and let him that is in the field not return back to take his cloak. But woe unto them that are with child and to them that give suck in those days! And pray ye that your flight be not in the winter, neither on a sabbath: for then shall be a great tribulation, such as hath not been from the beginning of the world until now, no, nor ever shall be. And except those days had been shortened, no flesh would have been saved, but for the elect's sake those days shall be shortened" (Matthew 24: 15-22).

In this passage Christ introduces the fact that the time of the great tribulation is going to be that of which Daniel the Prophet spoke in connection with his reference to the abomination of desolation. It seems clear that Christ had in mind the prediction of the climax of Israel's seventieth week or seventy sevens of years mentioned in Daniel 9:27. Here many expositors understand the passage to teach that the prince that shall come, the future Roman dictator mentioned in Daniel 9:26, will make a covenant with Israel for a period of seven years. This covenant, after running half its course, is broken in the middle of the seven years and Israel, instead of being a protected nation, becomes the object of fearful persecution.

We read of this in Daniel 9:27 in these words: "And he shall make a firm covenant with many for one week: and in the midst of the week he shall cause the sacrifice and the oblation to cease; and upon the wing of abominations shall come one that maketh desolate; and even unto the full end, and that determined, shall wrath be poured out upon the desolate." Further light on this abomination of desolation is given in Daniel 12:11 where it is predicted: "And from the time that the continual burnt-offering shall be taken away, and the abomination that maketh desolate set up, there shall be a thousand two hundred and ninety days." This apparently is a reference to the breaking of the covenant, the stopping of Jewish sacrifices, and the erection of an idol representing the prince that shall come who will become a world ruler.

In commenting on Daniel's prophecy, Christ exhorts those who are living in the day of its fulfillment in Judea to flee to the mountains, not bothering to get their ordinary possessions. It will be a time of special trial to those with small children and their flight will be made doubly difficult if it occurs in the winter, or in inclement weather, or on the Sabbath day when journeys are usually avoided and would therefore be conspicuous. Christ sums it up in Matthew 24:21, 22, in words that are reminiscent of Jeremiah and Daniel. He predicts that this period will be a time of great tribulation without parallel since the beginning of the world and will never be followed by a period of equal severity. He goes beyond the prophecies of Daniel and Jeremiah in His statement in verse 22: "And except those days had been shortened, no flesh would have been saved." In other words, the trials and difficulties of that day would be so severe that it would exterminate the entire human race if it were not for the fact that they are cut short by the return of Jesus Christ in power and glory to establish His kingdom. This future time of great tribulation is to be climactic in Israel's experience of suffering and is to be the final purging before God Himself interposes the judgments which begin the millennial kingdom.

The significance of Christ's statement that all flesh would perish unless the period were cut short is borne out by a study of this same period afforded in the book of the Revelation. Even a casual study of the description of the time of trouble which will characterize the end of the age will reveal a time of unprecedented difficulty.

As held by many expositors, the chronological structure of the book of Revelation is supplied by the sequence of seven seals affixed to the scroll in the possession of the Lamb. As each seal is broken, it unfolds a new period in the order of end-time events. The seventh seal is a comprehensive one, apparently including in its scope the details provided in the seven trumpets which subsequently sound and including the events described as the outpouring of seven bowls of the wrath of God which is related to the seventh trumpet.

The scene of devastation of divine judgment and human iniquity which is unfolded in these events is without parallel in the history of the world. According to Revelation 6:7, the judgments attending the opening of the fourth seal involve the death with sword, famine, and wild beasts of one fourth of the earth's population. If this were applied to the present world population now approaching three billion, it would mean that 750,000,000 people would perish, more than the total population of North America, Central America, and South America combined. It seems clear that this is only one of a series of gigantic catastrophes. In the judgments described as following the trumpets of the angels, a third part of the remaining population of the world is described as destroyed in Revelation 9:15. The concluding judgment proceeding from the seventh bowl of the wrath of God poured out on the earth in Revelation 16:17-21 is even more devastating than anything that had occurred previously. The stark reality of the words of Christ that the entire race would be blotted out if that period were not terminated by His return seems to be supported by these details.

Though the judgments will obviously fall on all races and people, it seems that Israel is to be the special object of satanic hatred. This is borne out in the prophecy concerning the woman with child in Revelation 12. The best explanation of this symbolic presentation is that the woman is Israel and the child is the Lord Jesus Christ. The dragon, representing Satan, is portrayed as being cast down to the earth in Revelation 12:13 and, realizing that his time is short, according to the Scripture, "he persecuted the woman that brought forth the man child" (Revelation 12:13). The Scriptures which follow indicate the unrelenting warfare against the woman and her seed and only by divine intervention is partial protection afforded her.

Out of the total number of Israel, a representative group of 144,000 are sealed and thereby protected from destruction in this period. In Revelation 7, they are enumerated with their respective tribes. In Revelation 14, they are depicted on Mount Zion with the Lamb at the close of the tribulation, still intact and singing praises to the Lord. They form therefore the core of the godly remnant which will be awaiting Christ when He returns to set up His millennial kingdom.

ISRAEL'S DELIVERANCE FROM SUFFERING

Just as the Scriptures faithfully portray the fact of Israel's suffering climaxing in the great tribulation, the Word of God also promises deliverance at its close. This was noted in all the great passages dealing with the subject, as in Deuteronomy 4, Jeremiah 30, Daniel 12, and Matthew 24. Of special importance is the prediction given by the Apostle Paul in Romans 11:25-27: "For I would not, brethren, have you ignorant of this mystery, lest ye be wise in your own conceits, that a hardening in part hath befallen Israel, until the fulness of the Gentiles be come in; and so all Israel shall be saved: even as it is written, There shall come out of Zion the Deliverer; he shall turn away ungodliness from Jacob: and this is my covenant unto them, when I shall take away their sins." In this passage it is predicted that the present age of fullness of blessings for the Gentiles will pass and be succeeded by a restoration to Israel. At that time Israel will be delivered, as indicated in the words: "And so all Israel shall be saved."

Though the meaning of this passage has been debated, probably the best interpretation is to regard it as a national promise, namely, that at the time of the end when her period of suffering has been fulfilled, Israel as a nation or Israel as a whole shall be delivered from her enemies. The salvation in view is not that of freedom from the guilt of sin, but deliverance from persecution and trial. This will be accomplished when the Deliverer comes out of Zion, an unmistakable reference to Jesus Christ. When He returns, He will come to the Mount of Olives. As depicted in Zechariah 14:4, He will establish His government in Jerusalem and from Zion will go forth the law. According to Isaiah 2:3: "And many peoples shall go and say, Come ye, and let us go up to the mountain of Jehovah, to the house of the God of Jacob; and he will teach us of his ways, and we will walk in his paths: for out of Zion shall go forth the law, and the word of Jehovah from Jerusalem." At that time God's covenant of blessing upon Israel will be fulfilled as embodied in the new covenant of Jeremiah 31 and mercy will be shown the people of Israel instead of the searching judgments of the tribulation period which have preceded.

In contemplating this tremendous revelation of God's divine purpose and plan for Israel, the Apostle Paul breaks forth in a doxology: "O the depth of the riches both of the wisdom and the knowledge of God! how unsearchable are his judgments and his ways past tracing out! For who hath known the mind of the Lord? or who hath been his counsellor? or who hath first given to him, and it shall be recompensed unto him again? For of him, and through him, and unto him, are all things. To him be the glory for ever. Amen" (Romans 11:33-36).

SUMMARY

The important world events which are taking place today may be regarded as a prelude to the consummation which will include Israel's time of suffering. Heart-rending as it may be to contemplate, the people of Israel who are returning to their ancient land are placing themselves within the vortex of this future whirlwind which will destroy the majority of those living in the land of Palestine. The searching and refining fire of divine judgment will produce in Israel that which is not there now, an attitude of true repentance and eager anticipation of the coming of their

Messiah. The tribulation period will then be followed by Israel's day of glory.

For the Christian these events are of utmost significance, for many Scriptures seem to teach that Christ will come for the church, the body of saints, in this present age of grace, before these end-time events take place. Israel's day of suffering will be preceded by the translation of the church and the resurrection of the dead in Christ. The swiftly moving events of our generation are not a basis for despair, but another reminder that God majestically fulfills His will. Every prophecy will find its counterpart in complete fulfillment, and the wisdom and mercy and sovereignty of God will be vindicated before all His creatures. Christ is not only the hope of Israel, but also the hope of all those who are trusting Him.

Chapter VII

THE GLORIOUS RESTORATION OF ISRAEL

The partial restoration of the nation Israel to their ancient land in the middle of the twentieth century should be recognized by all careful students of the Bible as a most remarkable event. It seems to be a token that God is about to fulfill His Word concerning the glorious future of His chosen people. As has been pointed out in previous discussion, the return of Israel to their ancient land and the establishment of the state of Israel is the first step in a sequence of events which will culminate in Christ's millennial kingdom on earth. The present return of Israel is the prelude and will be followed by the dark hour of their suffering in the great tribulation. This will in turn be succeeded by the return of Christ, the establishment of Christ's kingdom on earth, and the exaltation of the people of Israel to a place of prominence and blessing. Scriptures already discussed have brought out these major aspects of Israel's future program. This concluding study will concern itself with the fulfillment of countless prophecies relating to them in relationship to the millennial reign of Christ.

The Final Judgment of Israel

At the time of the second coming of Christ to establish His kingdom, two major aspects of Israel's judgment may be observed. First, the righteous dead of Israel will be raised and will be judged relative to rewards. Second, those in Israel who have survived the great tribulation will be judged, and the righteous in Israel will enter into the Promised Land and enjoy the blessings of the millennial kingdom.

The resurrection of the righteous of Israel is indicated in Daniel 12:2, 3 in these words: "And many of them that sleep in the dust of the earth shall awake, some to everlasting life, and some to shame and everlasting contempt. And they that are wise shall shine as the brightness of the firmament; and they that turn many to righteousness as the stars for ever and ever." Scholars have not all agreed on the details indicated by this prophecy. It has been characteristic of some branches of premillenarians to include the resurrection of Israel with the resurrection of the church at the time of the rapture. Those who have followed this interpretation have been somewhat embarrassed by the fact that Daniel 12:1, 2 seems to place the resurrection of Israel after the tribulation instead of before it. This would indicate either that the rapture is postribulational in that the resurrection follows the tribulation, or that they were wrong in their preliminary judgment that the resurrection of Israel occurred at the time of a pretribulational rapture.

Though disagreement on the interpretation of this passage continues, many careful students of premillennial truth have come to the conclusion that the opinion that Israel's resurrection occurred at the time of the rapture was a hasty one and without proper Scriptural foundation. It seems far more preferable to regard the resurrection of Daniel 12:2 as a literal one following the tribulation, but not to be identified with the pretribulational rapture of the church. If this interpretation be allowed, then the expression "many of them that sleep in the dust of the earth shall awake" can be regarded as a literal and bodily resurrection of righteous Israel from the grave in order that they might participate in the millennial reign of Christ as resurrected beings along with the resurrected and translated church of the New Testament.

A further difficulty is found in the fact that Daniel 12:2 states that some awake to everlasting life and "some to shame and everlasting contempt." Premillenarians are agreed that the resurrection of the wicked does not occur until after the thousand-year reign of Christ. The declaration of the resurrection of the righteous in almost the same breath as the resurrection of the wicked, separated as they are by the thousand-year reign of Christ, is a difficulty for some premillenarians.

A careful study of the passage, however, reveals that most of the difficulty is in the English translation. The Hebrew seems to make quite a sharp contrast between those who are raised to everlasting life and those who are raised to shame and everlasting contempt. A paraphrase would render the passage this way: "Many of them that sleep in the dust of the earth shall awake, these to everlasting life, and those to shame and everlasting contempt." The passage then becomes a statement that subsequent to the tribulation all the dead will be raised, but in two groups, one group to everlasting life and the other group to everlasting contempt. The fact that these are separated in time is clearly spelled out in Revelation 20, and the fact that this detail is not given here should not be considered a major problem.

It is evident from Daniel 12:3 that the main purpose of this revelation is to deal with the resurrection of the wise. These are declared to "shine as the brightness of the firmament; and they that turn many to righteousness as the stars for ever and ever." In this statement it is evident that the resurrected saints of the Old Testament, which is primarily the resurrection of Israel but will undoubtedly include the righteous of the Gentiles as well, will be an occasion for recognition of their good works. Rewards will be distributed to them much in the way that rewards were given to the church, that is, those who are righteous will be given places of prominence and privilege in the millennial kingdom of Christ and their righteousness will be displayed for all to see.

A parallel passage to this resurrection of Israel from the dead is found in Isaiah 26:14, 19. Verse 14 says: "They are dead, they shall not live; they are deceased, they shall not rise: therefore hast thou visited and destroyed them, and made all remembrance of them to perish." In contrast to the wicked whose end is here described as not being included in the resurrection of the righteous, the prospect of Israel is declared in verse 19: "Thy dead shall live; my dead bodies shall arise. Awake and sing, ye that dwell in the dust; for thy dew is as the dew of herbs, and the earth shall cast forth the dead." Though perhaps less clear than the Daniel 12 reference, Isaiah 26 confirms the idea of the resurrection of the righteous dead in Israel. It may be concluded that at the beginning of the millennium all of the righteous dead have been raised. The church will be raised at the time of the rapture before the tribulation, and Old Testament saints, including Israel, at the beginning of the millennial reign of Christ. Only the wicked dead remain in the graves awaiting their resurrection at the end of the millennial kingdom.

Those in Israel who survive the tribulation and who are on earth at the time of Christ's second coming are declared to be judged in Ezekiel 20:34-38. Ezekiel states: "And I will bring you out from the peoples, and will gather you out of the countries wherein ye are scattered, with a mighty hand, and with an outstretched arm, and with wrath poured out; and I will bring you into the wilderness of the peoples, and there will I enter into judgment with you face to face. Like as I entered into judgment with your fathers in the wilderness of the land of Egypt, so will I enter into judgment with you, saith the Lord Jehovah. And I will cause you to pass under the rod, and I will bring you into the bond of the covenant; and I will purge out from among you the rebels, and them that transgress against me; I will bring them forth out of the land where they sojourn, but they shall not enter into the land of Israel: and ye shall know that I am Jehovah."

As in previous declarations concerning God's work of restoring Israel at the beginning of the millennial kingdom, the judgment of Israel is preceded by their regathering from all the peoples of the earth. They are assembled in the place described as "the wilderness of the peoples" and there God declares that He will enter into judgment upon them. It will be like the judgment of their forefathers at the time of the Exodus when the adult population perished in the forty years of wandering, but the younger generation was permitted to enter into the land. In this judgment of living Israel at the beginning of the millennial kingdom, God says that He will have them pass under the rod and that He will purge out the unrighteous described as "the rebels" and as "them that transgress against me." Though included in the work of regathering, they will not enter into the Promised Land and apparently perish like their gainsaying forefathers in the wilderness.

The clearcut division in Israel of those who are righteous and those who are unrighteous arises from the fact that some are saved by faith in Christ, but others rejected Him and were worshipers of the beast, the world ruler of the great tribulation. According to Revelation 13:8 all those on earth during the great tribulation will worship the world ruler except for those whose names are written in the book of life. It is stated in Revelation 14:9 that those who are worshipers of the beast come under the fearful wrath of God and are cast into everlasting torment forever and ever. A similar conclusion is derived from the parable of the wheat and the tares in Matthew 13 where all the tares are burned up and the wheat is gathered into the barn. Israel's purging judgment at the end of the age will therefore not only include the trials of the great tribulation in which two thirds of the nation will perish, but will culminate in the judgment of God following their regathering in which all unbelievers who remain will be purged out. The millennial kingdom, therefore, will begin with the godly remnant of Israel who have put their trust in the Lord and who will desire to follow the leadership of their Messiah and King.

THE RULE OF CHRIST OVER ISRAEL

According to the second Psalm, it is the divine purpose of God that His Son will reign over the earth. In spite of the raging of the nations and their rebellion against God, the sovereign purpose of God that His Son will rule is plainly stated in these words: "Yet I have set my king upon my holy hill of Zion. I will tell of the decree: Jehovah said unto me, Thou art my son; this day have I begotten thee. Ask of me, and I will give thee the nations for thine inheritance, and the uttermost parts of the earth for thy possession. Thou shalt break them with a rod of iron; thou shalt dash them in pieces like a potter's vessel" (Psalm 2:6-9). In this declaration God not only affirms that Christ will reign from Mount Zion, but that all the nations of the world will come under His reign. It will be an absolute government as shown in the expression: "Thou shalt break them with a rod of iron; thou shalt dash them in pieces like a potter's vessel."

The rule of the Son of God is described in a similar way in many other passages. In Daniel 7:13, 14 it is written: "I saw in the night-visions, and, behold, there came with the clouds of heaven one like unto a son of man, and he came even to the ancient of days, and they brought him near before him. And there was given him dominion, and glory, and a kingdom, that all the peoples, nations, and languages should serve him: his dominion is an everlasting dominion, which shall not pass away, and his kingdom that which shall not be destroyed." Here the kingdom is described, not simply in its millennial context, but as that which continues after the millennium in the eternal state.

According to Isaiah 2:1-4, Jerusalem will be the center of the millennial government. Beginning in verse 2 Isaiah writes: "And it shall come to pass in the latter days, that the mountain of Jehovah's house shall be established on the top of the mountains, and shall be exalted above the hills; and all nations shall flow unto it. And many peoples shall go and say, Come ye, and let us go up to the mountain of Jehovah, to the house of the God of Jacob; and he will teach us of his ways, and we will walk in his paths: for out of Zion shall go forth the law, and the word of Jehovah from Jerusalem. And he will judge between the nations,

and will decide concerning many peoples; and they shall
beat their swords into plowshares, and their spears into
pruning-hooks; nation shall not lift up sword against nation,
neither shall they learn war any more" (Isaiah 2:2-4).
From this passage it is evident that Jerusalem is to be the
capitol of the world, that from Zion the law will go forth,
and all nations will be under the sway of this righteous
government. The result will be that "they shall beat their
swords into plowshares, and their spears into pruning-hooks;
nation shall not lift up sword against nation, neither shall
they learn war any more" (Isaiah 2:4).

One of the interesting aspects of the millennial government is the fact that resurrected David will apparently
be a prince under Christ in administering the millennial
kingdom in so far as it relates to Israel. According to Ezekiel,
David will act as a shepherd over the people of Israel:
"And I will set up one shepherd over them, and he shall
feed them, even my servant David; he shall feed them,
and he shall be their shepherd. And I, Jehovah, will be
their God, and my servant David prince among them; I,
Jehovah, have spoken it" (Ezekiel 34:23, 24). Some have
interpreted this mention of David as a reference to Christ.
However, there is no good reason for not taking it in its
ordinary literal sense inasmuch as David will certainly be
raised from the dead and will be on the scene. What would
be more natural than to assign him a responsible place in
the government of Christ in relation to the people of Israel?
The concept that David will rule under Christ is found
not only here, but also in Jeremiah 30:9; 33:15-17; Ezekiel
37:24, 25; Hosea 3:5; and oblique references in Isaiah 55:
3, 4 and Amos 9:11.

The government of Christ will obviously be one of
righteousness and justice. In the comprehensive view of
the kingdom afforded in the prophecy of Isaiah 11:1-10,
the character of Christ's rule is revealed. In verses 3 to 5
the following description is given: "And his delight shall be
in the fear of Jehovah; and he shall not judge after the sight
of his eyes, neither decide after the hearing of his ears; but

with righteousness shall he judge the poor, and decide
with equity for the meek of the earth; and he shall smite the
earth with the rod of his mouth; and with the breath of his
lips shall he slay the wicked. And righteousness shall be the
girdle of his waist, and faithfulness the girdle of his loins."
The millennial kingdom will therefore be a time of justice
for all, and any who dare to rebel against the king will be
subject to immediate divine judgment. For the first time
since Adam the entire earth will be under the immediate
control and direction of God with resulting blessing in every
aspect of human life.

GENERAL CHARACTERISTICS OF THE MILLENNIAL KINGDOM

Students of prophecies relating to the millennial kingdom are embarrassed by the wealth of materials which is
afforded. Passage after passage describes in glowing character the righteousness of the kingdom, the universal peace
which will characterize the world, and the fact that there
will be universal knowledge of the Lord. Peacefulness
will not only extend to relationships of men, but even the
natural world will be affected. Beasts that are naturally
ferocious and enemies of other beasts will live together
harmoniously. As depicted in Isaiah 11:6-9, it will be a
time of universal knowledge of the Lord. According to
Isaiah 11:9; "The earth shall be full of the knowledge of
Jehovah, as the waters cover the sea." According to the
provisions of the new covenant outlined by Jeremiah 31:
33, 34, God will write the law in the hearts of Israel and all
will know the Lord. Jeremiah expresses this in these words:
"But this is the covenant that I will make with the house
of Israel after those days, saith Jehovah: I will put my law
in their inward parts, and in their heart will I write it; and
I will be their God, and they shall be my people. And
they shall teach no more every man his brother saying,
Know Jehovah; for they shall all know me, from the least
of them unto the greatest of them, saith Jehovah: for I
will forgive their iniquity, and their sin will I remember
no more." It should be quite obvious that this is not a situ-

ation which exists today and in no literal sense are these millennial prophecies being fulfilled now. This could only be possible under the peculiar circumstances of the universal reign of Christ, the purging out of unbelievers at the beginning of the millennium, and the constant proclamation of the truth regarding Christ.

Many other passages confirm these conclusions. Isaiah 9:6, 7 affirms that Christ is the Prince of Peace who will reign on the throne of David and establish justice and righteousness. Isaiah 16:5 reveals that Christ will sit in the tent of David ministering perfect justice. Isaiah 24:23 states that Jehovah of hosts will reign in Mount Zion. Isaiah 32:1 predicts that a king will administer absolute righteousness. Isaiah 40:1-11 is a classic passage predicting the coming of the King, climaxing its revelation in verses 10 and 11: "Behold, the Lord Jehovah will come as a mighty one, and his arm will rule for him: behold, his reward is with him, and his recompense before him. He will feed his flock like a shepherd, he will gather the lambs in his arm, and carry them in his bosom, and will gently lead those that have their young."

The ministry of Christ as King will not only be one of absolute justice, but one of great beneficence, as is brought out in Isaiah 42:3, 4. According to Isaiah 52:7-15, the introduction to the great Messianic chapter, Isaiah 53, the King will come to Zion. The kingdom which shall never be destroyed will be set up by God, according to Daniel 2:44, and Christ's kingdom is declared to be everlasting in Daniel 7:27. The prophecy of Micah 4:1-8 is similar to that found in Isaiah 2. Micah 5:2-5 predicts the birth of Christ in Bethlehem as One who is to be ruler in Israel and who shall "be great unto the ends of the earth." The familiar prophecy of Zechariah 9:9, quoted as fulfilled in Matthew 21:5, pictures the King in His first coming, but anticipates that "his dominion shall be from sea to sea, and from the River to the ends of the earth" (Zechariah 9:10).

The concluding prediction of Zechariah 14:16, 17 gives us an insight into the character of the millennial reign of

Christ. Zechariah writes: "And it shall come to pass, that every one that is left of all the nations that came against Jerusalem shall go up from year to year to worship the King, Jehovah of hosts, and to keep the feast of tabernacles. And it shall be, that whoso of all the families of the earth goeth not up unto Jerusalem to worship the King, Jehovah of hosts, upon them there shall be no rain." It is evident from this Scripture that Christ actively rules, requires the nations of the world to conform to His rule, and observe the religious rites which characterize the millennial kingdom. Taking the whole picture as provided by the prophets, the millennial kingdom depicts a world situation of righteousness, peace, and knowledge of the Lord which is quite foreign to the present age, but which will be subject to literal fulfillment when Christ actually reigns on earth.

Israel's Spiritual Life in the Millennium

The very fact that Christ will be bodily and gloriously present in the earth during the millennial kingdom and that Satan will be bound and inactive (Revelation 20:1-3) provides a context of spiritual life on the part of Israel which is most favorable. As has been previously pointed out, everyone will have the basic facts about the Lord (Isaiah 11:9; Jeremiah 31:33, 34). The millennial government will assure that there will be peace among nations and righteousness in the administration of justice in relation to the individual (Isaiah 2:4; 11:3-5). The resulting world situation will be a joyous one in sharp contrast to the dark hour of Israel's suffering in the tribulation and her bitter experiences of centuries of wandering. Isaiah speaks of the joy of the Lord in that day in these words: "And in that day thou shalt say, I will give thanks unto thee, O Jehovah; for though thou wast angry with me, thine anger is turned away, and thou comfortest me. Behold, God is my salvation; I will trust, and will not be afraid: for Jehovah, even Jehovah, is my strength and song; and he is become my salvation. Therefore with joy shall ye draw water out of the wells of salvation" (Isaiah 12:1-3). Joy and gladness will be as common as sighings and sadness were in Israel's earlier experience.

The millennial period for both Israel and the Gentiles will also be a time of special ministry of the Holy Spirit. In this period, according to Isaiah 32:15, the Spirit will be poured out from on high. A similar prophecy is found in Isaiah 44:3: "For I will pour water upon him that is thirsty, and streams upon the dry ground; I will pour my Spirit upon thy seed, and my blessing upon thine offspring." Ezekiel predicts: "And I will put my Spirit within you, and cause you to walk in my statutes, and ye shall keep mine ordinances, and do them" (Ezekiel 36:27). In Ezekiel 39:29 a further similar statement is found: "Neither will I hide my face any more from them; for I have poured out my Spirit upon the house of Israel, saith the Lord Jehovah." The presence of Christ, the evident power of the Holy Spirit, and the context of the knowledge of the Lord and peace, righteousness, and joy will provide a basis for spiritual life in the millennium far more favorable than any preceding dispensation.

A number of Scriptures also describe the temple worship which will characterize the millennial kingdom. According to Ezekiel, a magnificent temple will be built, and a system of priesthood and memorial sacrifices will be set up. Scholars have not all agreed as to the interpretation of this difficult portion of Ezekiel. Some have felt it impossible to have a system of animal sacrifices subsequent to the one sacrifice of Christ on the cross in the light of New Testament passages stating that the sacrifice of Christ makes other sacrifices unnecessary. Though varied explanations have been given for Ezekiel 40-48 which unfolds these details, no satisfactory explanation has been made other than that it is a description of millennial worship. In any case, it is clear that the sacrifices are not expiatory, but merely memorials of the one complete sacrifice of Christ. If in the wisdom and sovereign pleasure of God the detailed system of sacrifices in the Old Testament were a suitable foreshadowing of that which would be accomplished by the death of His Son, and if a memorial of Christ's death is to be enacted, it would seem not unfitting that some sort of a sacrificial system would be used. While problems remain, it seems clear that Israel will have an ordered worship with Jerusalem once again the center of their religious as well as political life. A new order of priesthood would be required somewhat different than the Aaronic order, and rituals will be observed similar to the Mosaic order but differing in many aspects. In any case, a spiritual life of wonderful depth and reality far beyond anything Israel had known in her entire history will characterize her experience in the millennial kingdom. There will be complete fulfillment of Joel 2:28, 29 and blessings unmeasured will extend throughout the entire kingdom period.

SOCIAL, ECONOMIC, AND PHYSICAL ASPECTS OF ISRAEL IN THE KINGDOM

The combination of righteous government and abundant spiritual life will issue in many practical results in the millennial kingdom, and Israel will enjoy a period of physical as well as spiritual prosperity. Universal justice and peace will provide a proper basis for economic development without the curse of military expenditures, injustice, or inequities. Evidence seems to point to the fact that at the beginning of the millennium all adults who are permitted to enter the kingdom will be saved. The probability is that as children grow to maturity and a new generation is born a majority of those on the earth will experience real salvation, a situation far different than any previous period since the early days of man on earth. The curse inflicted upon the earth as a result of Adam's sin seems to be lifted, at least in part, during the millennial kingdom. Isaiah records the happy situation in Isaiah 35:1, 2: "The wilderness and the dry land shall be glad; and the desert shall rejoice, and blossom as the rose. It shall blossom abundantly, and rejoice even with joy and singing; the glory of Lebanon shall be given unto it, the excellency of Carmel and Sharon: they shall see the glory of Jehovah, the excellency of our God." As a result, the earth will bring forth in abundance and desert places formerly unproductive will have rich vegetation. There will be rainfall in areas where before there was drought (Isaiah 30:23; 35:7). Not only crops but cattle will prosper (Isaiah 30:23, 24).

There will be general prosperity in all aspects of economic development. Jeremiah speaks of this in Jeremiah 31:12: "And they shall come and sing in the height of Zion, and shall flow unto the goodness of Jehovah, to the grain, and to the new wine, and to the oil, and to the young of the flock and of the herd: and their soul shall be as a watered garden; and they shall not sorrow any more at all." Ezekiel speaks of causing evil beasts to depart out of the land, permitting them to sleep safely in the woods at night (Ezekiel 34:25). Increased rainfall is mentioned and abundant yielding of fruit trees (Ezekiel 34:26, 27). A similar picture is given in the prophecies of Joel 2:21-27. Joel writes of rich pastures, trees bearing fruit, and the vine yielding its strength, of rain coming down in abundance, of floors being full of wheat, of vats overflowing with wine, and Israel enjoying plenty of all the good things of the land. Amos gives a similar picture in the closing two verses of his book: "And I will bring back the captivity of my people Israel, and they shall build the waste cities, and inhabit them; and they shall plant vineyards, and drink the wine thereof; they shall also make gardens, and eat the fruit of them. And I will plant them upon their land, and they shall no more be plucked up out of their land which I have given them, saith Jehovah thy God" (Amos 9:14, 15).

Israel's experience in the millennium will also be one of physical health and freedom from disease. Isaiah 35:5, 6 seems to speak of this: "Then the eyes of the blind shall be opened, and the ears of the deaf shall be unstopped. Then shall the lame man leap as a hart, and the tongue of the dumb shall sing; for in the wilderness shall waters break out, and streams in the desert." In Isaiah 33:24 it is predicted: "And the inhabitant shall not say, I am sick: the people that dwell therein shall be forgiven their iniquity." A similar description of healing is given in Isaiah 29:18.

It would seem clear from prophecy that most of the earth's population will perish in the great tribulation and subsequent judgments and that the millennial kingdom begins with a comparatively small number of people. According to Jeremiah 30:19, 20, however, the earth's population will mushroom during the millennium and from those who have survived the tribulation who are still in their natural bodies, a multiplied offspring will come. According to Jeremiah 30:19, 20 God declares: "And I will multiply them, and they shall not be few; I will also glorify them, and they shall not be small. Their children also shall be as aforetime, and their congregation shall be established before me; and I will punish all that oppress them."

THE CONCLUSION OF THE MILLENNIAL KINGDOM

This selective study of the many Scriptures bearing upon the future restoration of Israel in the millennial kingdom of Christ constitutes a convincing demonstration of the glories of this period. Nothing comparable to this has ever been experienced in the history of man. It would seem that in the closing dispensation prior to the eternal state God is erecting the most favorable possible circumstances to which man could be subjected. When Satan is loosed again according to Revelation 20:7-9, how sad is the record that many born in the ideal circumstances of the millennium are revealed to have only outward profession and not real faith and submission to Christ. Once again judgment must fall upon those who have spurned every possible help in bringing them into proper relationship to their Lord and Saviour. The glorious millennial reign will be the capstone of Israel's history. Though the evidence seems to indicate that Israel will continue as a people into eternity, the millennium will be the final chapter of their history in the present earth. To this consummation the world is rapidly moving and the predicted sequence of events will unfold in proper succession once the present age has come to its close with the rapture of the church.

ISRAEL'S RESTORATION IN RELATION TO THE HOPE OF THE CHURCH

In the present world scene there are many indications pointing to the conclusion that the end of the age may soon be upon us. These prophecies relating to Israel's coming day of suffering and ultimate restoration may be destined for fulfillment in the present generation. Never before in the history of the world has there been a confluence of major evidences of preparation for the end.

Today, to the north of the nation Israel is the armed might of Russia. Never before has it seemed more likely that the prediction will be fulfilled given by Ezekiel (chapters 38 and 39) of an invasion from the north. To the east is the rising might of Red China, with the growing force of nationalism in India as well as the revival of Japan. Never before has it seemed more likely that there should be a tremendous military host coming from Asia, crossing the Euphrates river, and moving down on the scene of battle in the Middle East as predicted in Revelation 9:16.

The formation of the United Nations and the universal recognition of some form of world government as an alternative to war seem to be paving the way for the acceptance of the world ruler of Revelation 13 which will characterize the great tribulation. Never before have more people been persuaded that a world government is the only way to world peace.

The rising might of communism, embracing as it has a large portion of the world, and its spectacular rise which is without parallel in the history of the world, also has its prophetic portent. Though communism as such does not seem to enter into the prophetic picture of the end, its basic philosophy of materialistic atheism seems to be precisely the character of the false religion of the great tribulation (Daniel 11:36-38). Millions of youths in communistic lands are being systematically taught to trust only military might and to give blind allegiance to a human leader in place of worship of and service to the omnipotent

God. Just such a point of view and just such blind devotion will be required by the world ruler who will honor only the god of military might and disregard all other deities.

The modern movement toward a world church embodied in the ecumenical program seems also a preparation for acceptance by the world of a world church in the earlier phases of the tribulation period. The wicked woman of Revelation 17, the epitome of apostate ecclesiasticism, seems to be the representation of this ultimate ecclesiastical organization after every true Christian is removed by the rapture. The apostasy and unbelief which exists in our day seems to be the forerunner of the utter blasphemy which will characterize the worship of the beast in Revelation 13.

One of the most dramatic evidences that the end of the age is approaching is the fact that Israel has re-established her position as a nation in her ancient land. Israel today is in the proper place to enter into the covenant anticipated in Daniel 9:27 which will begin the last seven-year period leading up to the second coming of Christ. Even the modern city of Jerusalem built by Israel is occupying the precise area predicted in Jeremiah 31:38-40 and constitutes a fulfillment of this prophecy given twenty-five hundred years ago and never before fulfilled. Jeremiah states that when Jerusalem is built in the area described, as it has been in our generation, it will be a sign of the final chapter in the history of Jerusalem, in preparation for the millennial kingdom of our Lord.

The study of the history and prophecy of Israel is not a mere academic exercise on the part of the theologian or Bible student, but provides an unparalleled perspective of the majestic dealings of God with this prophetic nation. In it is revealed the faithfulness of God to the people whom He sovereignly chose, the effective outworking of God's wise purpose for them in spite of failure, delay, and indifference to God's will. The fact that in our day there is again movement and development in relation to this ancient nation is a sign that the stage is being set for the final world drama. Certainly as Israel's promises are being fulfilled before our eyes other aspects of prophecy such as the resurrection of the dead in Christ and the translation of living saints become a real and an imminent possibility. The hope of Israel is also the hope of the church. With John the Apostle all faithful students of the prophetic Word can say: "Amen: come, Lord Jesus."

SELECTED BIBLIOGRAPHY

Allis, Oswald T., *Prophecy and the Church*. Philadelphia: The Presbyterian and Reformed Publishing Company, 1945.

Baron, David. *The History of Israel*. London: Morgan and Scott, Ltd., [n.d.].

Berkhof, Louis, *Systematic Theology*. Grand Rapids: Wm. B. Eerdmans Publishing Company, 1941.

Chafer, Lewis Sperry. *The Kingdom in History and Prophecy*. Findlay, Ohio: Dunham Publishing Company, 1919.

———. *Systematic Theology*, 8 vols. Dallas: Dallas Seminary Press, 1947.

DeHaan, M. R. *The Jew and Palestine in Prophecy*. Grand Rapids: Zondervan Publishing House, 1950.

Evans, Robert L. *The Jew and the Plan of God*. New York: Loizeaux Brothers, Inc., 1950.

Feinberg, Charles L. *Israel in the Spotlight*. Chicago: Scripture Press, 1956.

———. *Israel in the Last Days*. Altadena, California: Emeth Publications, 1953.

———. *Premillennialism or Amillennialism?* Fourth Edition. Wheaton: Van Kampen Press, 1954.

Hendriksen, William, *And So All Israel Shall Be Saved*. Grand Rapids: Baker Book Store, 1945.

Henry, Carl F. H. "The Christian Witness in Israel," *Christianity Today*, 5:22:22-23, August 14, 1961, 5:23:17-21, August 28, 1961.

———. "Israel: Marvel Among the Nations," *Christianity Today*, 5:24:13-16, September 11, 1961, 5:25:15-18, September 25, 1961.

———. "The Messianic Concept in Israel," *Christianity Today*, 6:1:7-12, October 13, 1961, 6:2:11-14, October 27, 1961.

Hodge, Charles, *Systematic Theology*. 3 vols. New York: Charles Scribner's Sons, 1887.

Kac, Arthur W. *The Rebirth of the State of Israel*. London: Marshall, Morgan, and Scott, Ltd., 1958.

Kligerman, Aaron J. *Messianic Prophecy in the Old Testament*. Grand Rapids: Zondervan Publishing House, 1957.

132

McClain, Alva J. *The Greatness of the Kingdom*. Grand Rapids: Zondervan Publishing House, 1959.

Murray, George L., *Millennial Studies*. Grand Rapids: Baker Book House, 1948.

Pentecost, J. Dwight. *Things to Come*. Findlay, Ohio: Dunham Publishing Company, 1958.

Peters, George N. H., *The Theocratic Kingdom*. 3 vols. Grand Rapids: Kregel Publications, 1952.

Pieters, Albertus. *The Seed of Abraham*. Grand Rapids: Wm. B. Eerdmans Publishing Company, 1950.

Pocket Guide to Middle East Questions. New York: The American Jewish Committee.

Ryrie, Charles C., *The Basis of the Premillennial Faith*. New York: Loizeaux Brothers, 1953.

Sale-Harrison, L. *The Remarkable Jew*. New York: Sale-Harrison Publications, 1934.

Saphir, Adolph. *Christ and Israel*. London: Morgan and Scott, Ltd., [n.d.].

Smith, Wilbur. *World Crisis in the Light of Prophetic Scriptures*. Chicago: Moody Press, 1951.

Thorbecke, Ellen. *Promised Land*. New York: Harper and Brothers, 1947.

Urquhart, John. *The Wonders of Prophecy*. Harrisburg, Pennsylvania: Christian Publications, Inc., [n.d.].

Vilnay, Z. *Israel Guide*. Jerusalem: Ahieber, 1961.

Walvoord, John F. *The Millennial Kingdom*. Findlay, Ohio: Dunham Publishing Company, 1959.

Wilkinson, John. *God's Plan for the Jew*. London: Mildnay Mission to the Jew, 1944.

————. *Israel, My Glory*. London: Mildnay Mission to the Jew Bookstore, 1894.

Wilkinson, Samuel H. *The Israel Promises and Their Fulfillment*. London: John Bale, Sons and Danielsson, Ltd., 1936.

TOPICAL INDEX

Abraham, continuance of his seed, 47, 48; eternal faith of, 40; failure to possess the land, 15; liberal denial of his historicity, 47; migration to the land, 15.

Abrahamic covenant, 27-45; amillennial exegesis of, 38-42; as conditional in amillennial theology, 40-43; as everlasting, 48; as unconditional, 40-44; Gentile blessing, 36-38; interpreted literally, 34-40; requirement of circumcision, 43; summary, 33, 34, 44, 45.

Agriculture, of Israel, 21, 22.

Alexander the Great, conquest of Palestine, 17.

Allis, Oswald, on Israel in New Testament, 56; view of Abrahamic covenant, 41-43; view of new covenant, 54, 55.

Angels, eschatology of, 28.

Apostasy, 130.

Army, of Israel, 20, 21.

Asia, in prophecy, 129.

Captivities, of Israel, 16.

Chafer, L. S., interpretation of new covenant, 53, 54.

Christ, government in the millennium, 119-22; rule over Gentiles, 119-20; rule over Israel, 119-22.

Church, eschatology of, 28.

Circumcision, in relation to the Abrahamic covenant, 43.

Cities, of Israel, 23.

Communism, 129.

Constitution, of Israel, 20.

Covenant theology, 29, 30.

David, prince of the millennial kingdom, 121; promise of the kingdom to, 80-100.

Davidic covenant, 80-100 (see Kingdom, Davidic).

Dispersion of Israel, by Romans, 17; followed by regatherings, 72-74.

Ecumenical movement, 130.

Educational system, of Israel, 23, 24.

End of the age impending, 129-131.

Eschatology, definition of, 27; four major divisions, 28; modern concept, 27; principle of organization, 28; program for angels, 28; program for Gentiles, 28; program for Israel, 28; program for the church, 28.

Eternal state, in Abraham's faith, 40.

Exodus, from Egypt to the Promised Land, 15, 16.

Gentiles, as Seed of Abraham, 36-38; eschatology of, 28.

Government, of Israel, 20; world, 129.

Hebrew, revival of, 23, 24.

Hendriksen, William, on Israel in the New Testament, 56; on Israel's future, 46.

Herzl, Theodor, 15.

History, of Israel in the Old Testament, 15; proof of continuance, 47, 48.

Hodge, Charles, on Israel in New Testament, 56; on Israel's future, 46.

Industry, of Israel, 23.

Interpretation, Augustinian principle of, 30, 31; principles of Biblical, 30, 31.

Israel, as seed of Abraham, 36-38; contrasted to church, 55-59; contrasted to church by recent amillenarians, 55, 56; contrasted to Gentiles, 56; deliverance from future sufferings, 112, 113; denial of future, 46; eschatology in its covenants, 28; final judgment, 115-19; fulfillment of prophecy of suffering, 103-7; future as a nation, summary, 61, 62; future of, 46-62; 101-31; future restoration, 115-31; future suffering, predicted by Christ, 105-7; future time of suffering, 101-14; future time of suffering, causes, 101-3; God's faithfulness to, 102, 103; in eternity, 128; in great tribulation, 106, 107; in millennium, 98, 99; in relation to Davidic kingdom, 97, 98; in tribulation, 97, 98; postmillennial concept of future, 46; regathering of, 66-71; restoration to land, 130; resurrection, 116-18; resurrection before tribulation, 116-18; rule of Christ over, 119-22; satanic opposition, 101-3; suffering, in the book of Revelation, 108-12; sufferings, summary, 113, 114; war with Arabs, 19.

Jerusalem, capitol of millennial kingdom, 120, 121; modern city of, 130.

Judgment, of Israel, 115-19.

Kingdom, Davidic, amillennial interpretation, 96; argument of Peters,

134

INDEX TO SCRIPTURES

The
CHURCH in
PROPHECY

CHAPTER I

THE CHURCH IN THE OLD TESTAMENT

THE PROMISE OF A SEED

When Adam buried Abel after he was murdered by his brother Cain, it must have seemed that all hope was dead. Adam and Eve had enjoyed the marvelous experience of a life in perfect fellowship with God unmarred by sin. Then had come temptation, the act of disobedience, and the experience of evil. In the wreckage of what they once had been, as created by God, Adam and Eve heard the solemn words of divine judgment. They were now under a severe curse. Sorrow, pain, and struggle were to be their portion, and ultimately the dust of the earth was to reclaim their bodies. But there had been one ray of light. God had predicted that the woman would have a son, and that from his descendants One would come who would bruise the head of the serpent (Genesis 3:15). In anticipation of this, "Adam called his wife's name Eve; because she was the mother of all living" (Genesis 3:20).

In keeping with this promise, Cain and then Abel were born in due time, and the prospect of ultimate redemption from sin seemed to rest in one of these two young and active boys. As they grew up, it became evident that God's blessing was in a special way upon Abel. But now Abel was dead, and how could God use Cain, the murderer, to fulfill His purpose of redemption?

It was in this context of sin and divine judgment that another son was born whose name was Seth. The Hebrew name means "appointed," and Adam and Eve accepted the little child in place of Abel. As he grew up, it became more evident that God's purpose for fulfillment of the

13

promise was to rest in Seth and his posterity, and a postscript appended to the record of the birth of a son to
Seth revealed that "then began men to call upon the name
of the LORD" (Genesis 4:26).

The purpose of God not only to provide a Redeemer
but also a testimony to His name through a godly seed
gradually unfolds in the Old Testament. It soon became
evident that the great mass of humanity would not honor
God. In the words of Genesis 6:5, "God saw that the wickedness of man was great in the earth, and that every imagination of the thoughts of his heart was only evil continually."
As a result, God announced His purpose to destroy the race
by a great flood and instructed Noah to prepare for it by
building an ark for himself and his family. Once again,
God was starting over with a godly seed.

The new beginning, however, did not result in any
better situation than that of the civilization prior to the
flood. The eleventh chapter of Genesis records the rebellion
of men as they attempted to build a tower into the heavens.
The divine history of the Old Testament now reveals a new
divine purpose. In His selection of Abraham and his seed,
God undertook to fulfill the promise of a Redeemer as well
as to provide a continuing channel of testimony to the world
in a nation to come from Abraham's descendants.

THE PROMISE OF A NATION

In the covenant given to Abraham in Genesis 12:1-3,
God not only promised to make Abraham great and to provide through him the Messiah who was to be a blessing to
all nations of the earth, but He made the pronouncement,
"And I will make of thee a great nation." To this nation
God promised perpetuity in an everlasting covenant (Genesis 17:7), and gave the perpetual title to the land of Canaan
defined in Genesis 15:18 as extending from the River of
Egypt unto the River Euphrates. This was to be an everlasting covenant as indicated in the words: "And I will give
unto thee, and to thy seed after thee, the land wherein thou

art a stranger, all the land of Canaan, for an everlasting possession; and I will be their God" (Genesis 17:8).

The promise of a great nation was ultimately fulfilled in the birth of Isaac, Jacob, the twelve patriarchs, and their posterity. The blessing pronounced upon Rebekah and the prayer that she should be the mother "of thousands of millions" perhaps not yet been literally fulfilled (Genesis 24:60), but the children of Israel have indeed become beyond enumeration as the dust of the earth and the stars of the heavens. In spite of many attempts to exterminate them and blot them from the face of the earth as recorded in Scripture as well as in the history of our modern era, the children of Israel have continued to this hour with more than two million of them now established in their new state of Israel.

The purpose of God in Israel is evident from the Scriptures themselves. Through Israel God was to have a testimony to the world concerning His sovereignty, His righteousness, His faithfulness, and His love. Israel was the object lesson both of the grace of God and His righteous judgment. Through the prophets of Israel came the voice of God to a people who needed to know Him. From the pens of Israelites flowed the Holy Scriptures. The moral law contained in the law of Moses as well as the religious system which it set up instituted a revelation of divine truth which has rewarded richly all who have studied it.

THE PROMISE OF THE KINGDOM

Among the wonderful prophecies unfolding God's purpose were the promises of God to the nation Israel containing predictions of a future kingdom. This is anticipated in the promise to Abraham that "kings should come out of thee" (Genesis 17:6). The line of the promised king is narrowed to the tribe of Judah in Genesis 49:10, and subsequently is outlined in detail to David in God's covenant with him (II Samuel 7:12-16). David is promised that his physical posterity would continue forever and that one of his seed would sit on the Davidic throne forever (II Samuel 7:16). Conservative scholarship agrees that this promise is fulfilled in Christ. Premillenarians generally accept the interpretation that this will be fulfilled in Christ's millennial reign on earth in keeping with the concept that it is a Davidic throne rather than a heavenly throne that is in view.

The promise given to David is subsequently enlarged in many other portions of Scripture (I Chronicles 17:4-27; Psalm 89:20-37) and becomes an important part of the future of Israel as a nation when they are regathered from the ends of the earth and brought back to their ancient land. At that time they will be ruled by a king described as fulfilling the promise: "Behold, the day is come, saith the LORD, that I will raise unto David a righteous Branch, and a King shall reign and prosper, and shall execute judgment and justice in the earth. In his days Judah will be saved, and Israel shall dwell safely: and this is his name whereby he shall be called, THE LORD OUR RIGHTEOUSNESS" (Jeremiah 23:5, 6).

The Old Testament as a whole is not only a remarkable record of prophecy itself but also contains the literal fulfillment of many of these promises. God's promises to Adam and Eve and their posterity were largely fulfilled in the subsequent history of the race. The promise to Abraham was realized through the nation Israel, though the ultimate possession of the land and the restoration of Israel are unfulfilled as the Old Testament closes. The prediction of an everlasting kingdom to David, though not fulfilled in the Old Testament, is confirmed by the birth of Christ and the announcement to Mary that her Son would reign over the house of Israel (Luke 1:31-33). If interpreted literally, the promises of the Old Testament assure a future restoration of Israel and a future kingdom of David in the millennial period.

A point of view typical of amillenarianism is to regard these prophecies in a nonliteral sense. By some, the nation Israel is considered to be an early stage of the church and organically one with the church of the New Testament. Likewise, the promises addressed to David concerning his future are spiritualized to represent divine government over the earth such as is true in the present age. This point of view has also supported the concepts that the church in the Old Testament is essentially one with the church of the New Testament. Premillenarians who interpret prophecy literally, rather than figuratively, tend to distinguish believers in Christ in the present age from the saints of Old Testament. It is important in attempting to understand these various points of view to recognize both points of agreement and points of disagreement.

All agree that the Old Testament records promises to Israel, some of which are fulfilled in the Old Testament. Some disagreement exists concerning how these prophecies are to be fulfilled in the future. All agree that there are saints in the Old Testament, that is, a body of believers whose sins are forgiven and who will have a blessed eternity in the presence of God. Disagreement exists as to whether the term church is properly applied to these saints of the Old Testament. Many times it is taken for granted that if there are saints in the Old Testament they belong to the universal church.

A careful study of both the Old and New Testament, however, seems to justify the conclusion that something new began on the Day of Pentecost, namely, a body of believers distinct in divine purpose and situation from saints who preceded them in the Old Testament. The New Testament word for *church, ekklesia,* is a common Greek word which has a long history. It was originally used to describe the assembly of Greek citizens. The word comes from the verb *ekkaleo* meaning "to call out," but its usage seems to emphasize the resultant meaning of being called out, namely, an assembly or gathering of a people for some purpose. It is in this sense that it is used many times in the New Testament.

The Greek word *ekklesia* was used in a Greek translation of the Old Testament known as the Septuagint, which was in common use during the first century A.D. Though many different Hebrew words have the idea of assembly or congregation, only one of them, the Hebrew word *qahal*, was translated *ekklesia*. The use of *ekklesia* in seventy-seven passages in the Old Testament has been cited by some as proof sufficient that the church in a religious sense is found in the Old Testament.

An examination of these passages demonstrates, however, that *qahal*, when translated *ekklesia*, is always used in reference to an assembly or meeting of some description in one locality, i.e., a physical assembly, and the word is never used to represent the idea of a mystic company of saints joined in a spiritual way, though scattered geographically. The idea of the church as an *ekklesia* composed of individual saints widely scattered geographically is never found in the Old Testament. Though Israel was in some sense a spiritual community, its character was principally racial and political rather than a spiritual entity. While the term, "the seed of Abraham," is used in Galatians 3:6-9 to represent anyone, either Jew or Gentile, who follows Abram's example of faith in God, the term, *Israel*, or *Jew* or *seed of Israel*, is never used to include Gentile believers. These terms, therefore, are not equivalent to the idea of the church. Though the concept of a church in the Old Testament in the sense of a spiritual community is a common idea in theology, it has no support in the terminology used in the Old Testament itself. The use of *ekklesia* as a term describing the body of Christ, i.e., all believers in the present age both in earth and heaven, is peculiar to the New Testament and signified a new undertaking of God divorced from His program for Israel and for Gentiles which was revealed in the Old Testament history and prophecy.

The fact that there were saints in the Old Testament demonstrates the underlying redemptive purpose of God spanning the whole of human history and constitutes a unifying factor in the revelation of divine love and redemptive purpose. But the concept of the church as it is unfolded in the New Testament is dramatically different and is an important division of the over-all work of God in salvation.

The divine purpose of God for salvation as revealed in the Old Testament is therefore not synonymous with God's purpose for the seed of Abraham, the nation of Israel, nor the Davidic kingdom. These divine purposes will have their ultimate fulfillment which will involve saints. But these programs are not God's redemptive purpose specifically. Prophecy as it relates to the church is, therefore, a different subject having a different program and having factors which are foreign to God's program for either Jews or Gentiles as contained in Old Testament revelation.

The Old Testament forms an important background and setting for the incarnation, and Christ came to earth to fulfill the promise of the coming seed of the woman which would bruise the head of the serpent. Christ was indeed the Son of Abraham who would bring blessing to all nations. Christ came also as the Son of David who was qualified to sit upon the Davidic throne. Christ came in His first advent to provide salvation through His death and resurrection for all who believe in Him. In His second and yet future coming, He will fulfill His role as the Son of David and deliverer of the nation Israel. Between the first and second coming of Christ, the pronouncement He made, "I will build my church" (Matthew 16:18), will be fulfilled. Prophecy, as it relates to the church, is therefore concerned with the fulfillment of this prediction rather than those relating to the nation Israel or to the kingdom promised to David.

CHAPTER II

THE CHURCH AS THE NEW TESTAMENT ASSEMBLY

MAJOR CONCEPTS OF THE CHURCH

The Old Testament ended with the major prophecies relating to Israel and the world as a whole unfulfilled. The most important factor was lacking, namely, the fulfillment of the prophecies concerning the coming Messiah. With the coming of Christ as recorded in the New Testament, a new order is introduced, recognized by the very title, "The New Testament." Though in a large measure it constituted a fulfillment of that which was anticipated in the Old Testament, it soon became evident that much was now to be revealed which formerly was hidden.

The Gospel of Matthew especially traces this important transition. Christ, who is introduced as the King of Israel, of the line of David, and of the seed of Abraham, is rejected by His own people. The ethical principles of His kingdom outlined in Matthew 5-7 do not capture the interest or faith of the majority of the nation and especially its leaders. The miracles which Christ performed, which were the prophesied credentials of the Messiah, are rejected, and Christ is accused of performing His miracles by the power of the devil (Matthew 12:24).

In the face of such rejection, Christ pronounces a solemn judgment upon His generation, and His message turns from that of presentation of Himself as the Messiah of Israel to one of invitation to personal discipleship as illustrated in Matthew 11:28-30. In Matthew 13, the rejection of Christ is anticipated and the period between

His first and second advent is made the subject of prophecy. After further evidence of rejection on the part of His people, a dynamic new proclamation is revealed in connection with Peter's confession of faith, recorded in Matthew 16:16, "Thou art the Christ, the Son of the living God." In reply, Christ says: "Blessed art thou, Simon Bar-jona: for flesh and blood hath not revealed it unto thee, but my Father which is in heaven. And I say also unto thee, That thou art Peter, and upon this rock I will build my church; and the gates of hell shall not prevail against it" (Matthew 16: 17, 18).

Of major significance is the declaration, "I will build my church." What is here contemplated is obviously not a continuation of that which had begun in the Old Testament. Christ did not say, "I will redeem Israel," or, "I will proclaim my salvation to the Gentiles." Rather, in the face of national rejection on the part of Israel, He proclaims a new divine purpose, namely the formation of a new assembly to be delineated on spiritual rather than racial lines and without territorial or political characteristics. It was to be composed of those who, like Peter, had confessed Jesus Christ as the Son of God.

A wide variety of opinion has arisen concerning the exact meaning of this dramatic pronouncement. All agree that the church is part of the plan of God for salvation of the elect. Some hold that the church is only a continued development of the plan of God for Israel in the New Testament and try to identify the church with Israel. Others consider it a phase of fulfillment of God's covenant purpose relating to salvation. Still others regard it as an aspect of the over-all kingdom of God of which the church is a segment. There are also those who combine various aspects of these ideas.

Much of the confusion that exists in the doctrine of the church has resulted from contrasting too sharply the various viewpoints. There are elements of truth in each approach. What is adopted for this discussion is the view that the

church which Christ stated He would build is indeed an
aspect of God's general program of salvation, but that this
program in many respects is distinct from the Old Testament revelation and is not a fulfillment of God's plan and
purpose for the nation of Israel. Further, the ·purpose of
Christ for the church is not a realization of the kingdom
promises of the Old Testament which will be fulfilled in
the future millennium following Christ's advent. The support for this point of view is found in the details revealed
in the New Testament concerning the church as the body
of Christ. These will be unfolded ·in later discussion.

THE DAY OF PENTECOST

Most expositors agree that the New Testament church in
some sense began on the Day of Pentecost. Though Christ
anticipated a new fellowship and a new selective testimony
for God, He did not bring into being a genuine fulfillment
of the prophecy that He would build His church. The
church could not be properly begun until after His death and
resurrection and the coming of the Spirit.

On the Day of Pentecost, the prophecy of Christ that
they would be baptized by the Spirit "not many days hence"
(Acts 1:5) was fulfilled and with this the New Testament
church formally began. The Apostle Peter later referred
to this as "at the beginning" (Acts 11:15), when the Lord's
prophecy of the baptism of the Spirit was fulfilled (Acts
11:16). Not only were they baptized with the Spirit, but
as Acts 2:4 testified, "They were all filled with the Holy
Ghost." With the advent of the Spirit, three thousand souls
were added (Acts 2:41), and the body of believers from
then on was characterized as the church. There now was
a genuine New Testament assembly, as most Christian
scholars recognize in some form.

The apostolic church could be distinguished as having
two major aspects: (1) its outer testimony as a body of
professed followers of the Lord Jesus Christ, and (2) the
spiritual church composed of all true believers and referred

to as "the body of Christ" (I Corinthians 12:13, 27). The distinction is one of a sphere of profession in contrast to a sphere of reality, the outward in contrast to the inward, the geographic or local in contrast to the universal. Though there has been confusion and disagreement on this distinction, it seems to be a justifiable concept, and is recognized to some extent by all branches of Christendom. From the standpoint of prophecy, it is important that the two entities be distinguished.

The New Testament has much teaching concerning the church as a local assembly. The body of believers originally formed in Jerusalem was soon duplicated in smaller measure elsewhere. Reference is made in Scripture to "the church which was at Jerusalem" (Acts 1:8); "the church which is at Cenchrea" (Romans 16:1); "the church of God which is at Corinth" (I Corinthians 1:2); and the New Testament contains many similar references. Sometimes the word church is used as a plural, a clear reference to a local assembly as in Acts 15:41 and Romans 16:16. It sometimes had a geographic designation as a reference to "the churches of Galatia" (Galatians 1:2), i.e., the churches located in the area of Galatia. The concept of local churches as in contrast to the church of the body of Christ, which is always in the singular, is consistently observed in the New Testament.

In some instances, however, the professing church seems to be referred to in the Bible without reference to locality, as illustrated in Romans 16:16, "the churches of Christ" (cp. I Corinthians 15:9; Philippians 3:6). These could, however, be interpreted as references either to local assemblies when in the plural or to the body of Christ when in the singular. The mention of the church in Galatia (Galatians 1:13; cp. Philippians 3:6) may well be taken as referring to the professing church in general. The many instances where the church is mentioned in its outer geographic character justifies the concept of the gradual formation of the New Testament assembly composed of local congregations which included not only true Christians but those who professed to follow Christ. That these local congregations cannot be equated with the body of Christ is evident from such passages as Revelation 3:14-19 where the church of Laodicea obviously includes those who are not regenerated. Thus in apostolic days arose the early organized church which later developed into the far-flung body of professed believers which constitutes Christendom in its largest dimension.

One of the important themes of prophecy in the New Testament is that pertaining to the course of the present age. Many of these prophecies relate to the organized church, in contrast to prophecies that relate to the body of Christ. The course of the age in general is developed under the prophetic theme of the kingdom of heaven revealed in Matthew 13 with other Scriptures, such as Matthew 24, I Timothy 4, II Timothy 2, 3, and Revelation 17, describing the trend toward apostasy which will have its climax in the future great tribulation. The course of the professing church extends from the first coming of Christ to His second coming to the earth and is a broader revelation than that relating to the body of Christ which properly began on the Day of Pentecost and culminates in the translation of the true church before the professing church comes to its end.

THE COURSE OF THE CHURCH IN THE PRESENT AGE

The relationship of the kingdom of heaven to the church is one of the difficult areas of Biblical interpretation. Some have equated the kingdom idea with the church for all practical purposes, and others have attempted sharp distinction. Generally speaking, however, a distinction may be observed between God's general government over the world and God's particular rule over the saints. In contrast to both of these ideas is the prophesied kingdom of the Old Testament in which Christ will rule on earth and bring in a kingdom of perfect righteousness, justice, and peace. It is this earthly, Messianic kingdom which is given

prominence in the Old Testament and which will find fulfillment after the second coming of Christ according to Revelation 20. The kingdom on earth, while obviously having
spiritual characteristics and constituting a major aspect of
the delivering and saving work of God, is essentially political and theocratic. It was this Messianic kingdom which
was announced at hand in connection with the coming of
Christ, and it was this kingdom that was rejected when
Christ was rejected.

A basic cleavage in the interpretation of prophecy over
the doctrine of the kingdom is found in comparing the
amillennial and premillennial interpretations. Amillenarians generally hold that the kingdom of the Old Testament
is realized in the church in the present age, whereas premillenarians view the kingdom as future and following the
second coming of Christ. If the premillennial interpretation be adopted, it still leaves some important decisions
for the interpreter of Scripture, and one of these areas is
in relation to the kingdom of heaven in Matthew 13.

In Matthew, chapter 13, a series of parables is used
by our Lord to unfold the mysteries of the kingdom of
heaven. The expression, "kingdom of heaven," which is
peculiar to the Gospel of Matthew has been usually considered identical to a similar expression in the other gospels, "the kingdom of God." In many respects, the two expressions seem to be the same, as the term *heaven* is a
Hebraism for God.

In some instances, however, there seems to be a contrast
between the kingdom of heaven as it is portrayed in Matthew's Gospel and the kingdom of God as it is unfolded
in the other Gospels and the rest of the New Testament.
This distinction in its simplest form is a contrast between
the kingdom of God, viewed as containing all saints and
excluding those not regenerated, and the kingdom of heaven
as a sphere of profession, which includes those who are
outwardly related to Christ but not actually to be numbered
with the saints. If the kingdom of God be viewed as God's

universal government, it of course would include all these, but when it is used in the sense of containing only the saved and as requiring new birth to enter (John 3:5), then the kingdom of heaven is the broader term and is so used in Matthew 13. This distinction, though helpful, is largely an exegetical one which does not affect either the doctrine of the church or prophecy as a whole. A further distinction, however, can be observed between the kingdom in its present form, whether the kingdom of God or the kingdom of heaven, and the kingdom in its future or millennial form. It is this latter distinction between the present and future forms of the kingdom in which prophecy comes to the fore.

It is a major error to make the word *kingdom*, which is a common term, always mean the same in all its uses. Rather, it must be interpreted by its context. Outside the Gospel of Matthew, however, the kingdom of God is used in the New Testament only to refer to God's spiritual kingdom or His governmental kingdom. Only in Matthew and in the terminology of "the kingdom of heaven" is the concept of a sphere of a profession presented. It is for this reason that Matthew 13 assumes major proportions in an attempt to understand God's prophetic program for the professing church.

The term, "kingdom of God," is never in Scripture made a synonym of the church either as the body of Christ or as a sphere of profession. Because it refers to the same time period, i.e., the interadvent period, and because it relates to the same spiritual and moral problems, however, it does reveal spiritual truth which characterizes the present age. Hence, the parables of Matthew 13, though related to the mysteries of the kingdom of heaven, also constitute a revelation of the progress of the professing church in the period between the first and second advent.

In understanding the mysteries of the kingdom of heaven, it is most significant that they are introduced as "mysteries." This term is properly used throughout the New

Testament to describe truth revealed in the New Testament which was hidden from view as far as Old Testament revelation is concerned. It is specifically New Testament truth. The truths contained in the mysteries of the kingdom, therefore, are not an exposition of the Old Testament doctrine of the kingdom as it will be fulfilled in the millennium, but rather a presentation of truth as it relates to the kingdom in the present age. In contrast to the millennial period, when the kingdom will be visible and the King will be on earth, the present age features the King's absence and the rule of His subjects by invisible and spiritual means only.

In attempting to understand the seven parables of Matthew 13 as they constitute prophecy of the church in the present age, it is most important to observe that the first two parables are interpreted by Christ Himself. By using this key, the other parables also can be understood.

The seven parables were expounded by Christ as He sat in the ship just off the shore of the Sea of Galilee with a multitude on the bank to hear His proclamation. The first parable was suited for such a situation, relating the parable of the sower casting seed on various kinds of soil. As interpreted by Christ, the good news of the kingdom is received in various ways. Some seed falls on the hard-beaten wayside which is totally unreceptive and is carried away by the fowls without bearing fruit. Other seed falls upon places where the soil is shallow and where its lack of depth does not provide room for the seed to root. This is related to those who eagerly hear the Word, but soon give it up when trial comes.

Two classes of believers are said to receive the Word with some effectiveness. One of these is characterized as having heard the Word, but the Word is described as becoming unfruitful because of the "cares of this world, and the deceitfulness of riches" (Matthew 13:22). The one who receives the seed in good soil and properly hears the Word brings forth fruit, "some an hundredfold, some sixty, some thirty" (Matthew 13:23). This parable, which relates to reception of the proclaimed Word, makes clear that the present age cannot be equated with the millennium when all will be forced to obey Christ and make at least an outward profession of faith in Him. Here a picture of the present age is given. Just as the word of the kingdom in Christ's day was rarely received by more than a few, so the word of truth in the present age will seldom fall on good ground and only occasionally will come into soil where it will bring forth its hundredfold fruit. In the present age, only a fraction of those who hear the Gospel will come to Christ.

The second parable concerning the wheat and the tares brings out the same idea, but in a different figure. Here the seed sown represented in the wheat is the believer himself. Along with believers, however, described as children of the kingdom (Matthew 13:38), "tares" are sown, representing imitation wheat which grows with the good wheat until the harvest time. When the harvest occurs, the tares are gathered first and burned, but the wheat is gathered into the barn (Matthew 13:30). The truth presented in this parable is that when Christ comes to establish His kingdom on earth false profession will be judged and unbelievers destroyed. Only those who are true believers will be gathered into the kingdom. This judgment occurs when Christ comes to the earth after the great tribulation rather than at the rapture of the church when the tares are left undisturbed, according to the pretribulational interpretation.

The other parables, though left uninterpreted, contribute further elements to our understanding of the progress of the present age. The parable of the mustard seed (Matthew 13:31, 32) indicates the tremendous growth of the professing church from a small beginning, symbolized by the mustard seed, to its present tremendous proportions. History has certainly confirmed this interpretation as well as the details which are added, namely, that the birds of the air, representing Satan and those that he controls, will come and lodge in its branches.

The fourth parable recorded in Matthew 13:33-35 states, "The kingdom of heaven is like unto leaven, which a woman took, and hid in three measures of meal, till the whole was leavened." This illustration taken from common life refers to the practice of taking leaven or fermented dough and adding it to new dough in order to extend the leavening process. There has been some disagreement as to what the leaven signifies. In the postmillennial interpretation, the leaven has been likened to the Gospel which permeates the whole lump, referring to the whole world. While it is true that Christianity has had its effect upon the world as a whole, this interpretation seems to violate the usual use of leaven to represent that which is evil. In the Passover, unleavened bread had to be used because of this significance.

In the New Testament, leaven seems to symbolize externalism, worldliness, hypocrisy, and bad doctrine. It is unfortunately true that the professing church has all of these elements and if leaven was intended to signify evil, it has already been fulfilled. The same is the case even with the true church which has fallen far short of what it ought to have been. The optimism of the postmillennial view has largely been discarded today, and with the new realization of the power of evil, the interpretation of this parable should be brought into proper focus. Nowhere does the Bible picture the present age as one of gradual improvement. It is rather, as will be seen in the study of the doctrine of apostasy in the church, that evil represented in this parable as leaven will increase and the professing church eventually will be engulfed by it.

The fifth parable is presented in Matthew 13:44: "Again, the kingdom of heaven is like unto treasure hid in a field; the which when a man hath found, he hideth, and for joy thereof goeth and selleth all that he hath, and buyeth that field." This has often been taken as a parallel to the sixth parable of Matthew 13:45, 46 referring to the pearl:

"Again, the kingdom of heaven is like unto a merchant man, seeking goodly pearls: who, when he had found one pearl of great price, went and sold all that he had, and bought it."

What is the meaning of the treasure described as hidden in the field and the pearl described as of great price? A common interpretation has been that the treasure in the field and the pearl of great price are none other than Christ and that the man who finds the treasure and the merchant man who buys the pearl are a picture of the believer. This interpretation, however, disregards the theological context of our salvation, for a believer has nothing with which to buy Christ and, as a matter of fact, Christ is not for sale. Salvation rather originates in God and is God's free gift bestowed without regard to merit on the part of the recipient.

A better interpretation is that in these two parables is revealed the twofold aspect of the death of Christ, on the one hand redeeming Israel, signified by the treasure hid in the field, and on the other hand the redemptive purpose of ·Christ for the church, signified by the pearl of great price. Israel in spiritual significance is largely hidden in the world and yet is a treasure in the eyes of God (Exodus 19:5; Psalm 135:4). Christ in His death actually bought the whole world represented by "that field" but in the process redeemed Israel, the treasure hidden in the field. In like manner, the merchantman who buys the pearl of great price symbolizes Christ in His redemptive act on the cross. Just as a pearl is an outgrowth of an irritation in the side of the oyster, so the church in a symbolic sense is begotten in the wounds of Christ and is a precious jewel for which Christ gave all that He had. The two parables taken together, therefore, seem to reflect Christ's love for Israel and for His church. Both of these are, of course, illustrated in the present age as well as in the future purpose of God.

The concluding parable, that of the dragnet, is presented in Matthew 13:47-50, "Again, the kingdom of heaven is like unto a net, that was cast into the sea, and gathered of every kind: which, when it was full, they drew to shore, and sat down, and gathered the good into vessels, but cast the bad away. So shall it be at the end of the world: the angels shall come forth, and sever the wicked from among the just, and shall cast them into the furnace of fire: there shall be wailing and gnashing of teeth." Here again is dramatic proof that the present age is quite different from the millennium for the net gathers of every kind, both good and bad fish. The kingdom of heaven in this passage also stands in contrast to the kingdom of God in the other Gospels where the kingdom of God seems to be restricted to those who are born again. Here the kingdom of heaven includes the bad fish in the net as well as the good, and the Scriptures say specifically that the net "gathered of every kind" (Matthew 13:47).

The Scriptures make clear that this judgment will occur at the second coming of Christ "at the end of the world," or better translated, "at the end of the age." Just as the good and bad fish are separated, so here in Mathew 13:49, 50 the angel is seen putting the good into vessels, but casting the bad away, symbolic of the future judgment at the second coming of Christ when the righteous will go into the millennial kingdom and the wicked will be cast into the furnace of fire (cp. Matthew 25:41). The time when this will occur is at the end of the tribulation and at the beginning of the millennial kingdom when the sphere of profession is brought to a close in its present form.

As in the parable of the wheat and the tares, there is emphasis here on the dual line of development within the sphere of profession, namely, those that are true believers symbolized by the wheat and the good fish as contrasted to those who are merely professing believers who, though intermingled with the true believers now, will be separated from them at the end of the age. In contrast to the millennium when judgments will be inflicted immediately upon those that rebel against Christ, this is descriptive of the present age when God is withholding judgment and reserving it for the consummation.

The seven parables taken together therefore reveal that the general characteristics of the present age include the elements of a proclaimed message which will be only partially received. The parables show the intermingling of the saved with those who merely profess salvation, the rapid growth of the professing church to a great world-wide organization symbolized by the mustard seed, the permeation within the professing church as well as the true church symbolized by the leaven, the demonstration of the love of Christ both for Israel and the church symbolized in the purchase of the field with its treasure and the purchase of the pearl of great price, and finally the fact that the present age is subject to divine judgment when the saved will be separated from the unsaved as illustrated in the parable of the dragnet. Matthew 13, therefore, consti-tutes a comprehensive picture of the general features of the present age as distinguished from the Old Testament period in which Israel was in prominence and also in contrast to the millennial kingdom in which Christ will rule with a rod of iron.

THE PREDICTED TREND TOWARD APOSTASY

No notion was ever imposed upon the evangelical church with less justification than the postmillennial idea of gradual progress and ultimate spiritual triumph of the church. The idea that the Gospel would gradually subdue the people of the world and eventually bring them to the feet of Christ is contradicted alike both by the Scriptures and by history, and the result has been the rapid decline in the twentieth century of optimism in relation to the triumph of the church in the present age.

A survey of Scriptural prophecy as it relates to the spiritual trends of the present age should have made clear to any inquirer that the present age will end in apostasy and divine judgment rather than victory for the cause of Christ through the triumph of the church. Major passages of Scripture deal with this subject and the expositor is embarrassed by the wealth of material which plainly teaches that the end of the age will be characterized by apostasy (Matthew 24:4-26; II Thessalonians 2:1-12; I Timothy 4: 1-3; II Timothy 3:1-9; 4:3, 4; II Peter 2:1 — 3:18; Jude 3-19; Revelation 3:14-16; 6:1 — 19:21). An examination of these major passages on apostasy in the New Testament will reveal that the development of apostasy will be in three stages: (1) the doctrinal and moral departure in the church prior to the rapture, i.e., during the last days of the true church on earth; (2) the apostasy in the professing church after the true church is raptured, i.e., in the period immediately following the rapture: (3) the final apostasy in which the professing church as such will be destroyed and the worship of the beast, the world ruler, as the human representative of Satan will be inaugurated (Matthew 24: 15; II Thessalonians 2:3-12; Revelation 13:4-8; 17:16-18). Of major importance is the fulfillment of the prophecy relating to apostasy in the church being fulfilled in the contemporary situation, a subject to which the Scriptures give considerable space. Attention will be directed to prophecies related to the end of the age in later discussion.

CHAPTER III

THE CHURCH AS THE BODY OF CHRIST

THE ANNOUNCEMENT OF THE DIVINE PURPOSE

In the first mention of the church in the New Testament, a pronouncement was made by Christ Himself which is fundamental to the unfolding doctrine of the church as the body of Christ. In Matthew 16:15, Christ has asked His disciples, "But whom say ye that I am?" Simon Peter in response to this question answered, "Thou art the Christ, the Son of the living God" (Matthew 16:16). In commenting on this confession of faith in which Peter spoke representing the disciples, Jesus replied: "Blessed art thou, Simon Bar-jona: for flesh and blood hath not revealed it unto thee, but my Father which is in heaven. And I say also unto thee, That thou art Peter, and upon this rock I will build my church; and the gates of hell shall not prevail against it" (Matthew 16:17, 18).

The enigmatic statement of Christ in verse 18 has been the subject of much discussion. The Roman Church has taken the position that Christ was affirming that the church would be built upon Peter as the first pope. Protestants generally have rejected this interpretation, some holding that Christ meant that the church would be built upon the confession of faith of Christ as made by Peter, and others that the reference to "this rock" was a reference to Christ Himself. There is evidently a play on words in verse 18 as the reference to Peter in the Greek is *petros* which, while referring to Peter, has also the meaning of a "little rock." The reference to "this rock" uses a similar word, *petra*. Translated literally it would be, "Thou art Little Rock, and upon this rock I will build my church." The resultant meaning is that Peter as a believer in Christ is a little rock, but that the church as a whole must be built upon Christ, the rock, as Peter himself is most careful to point out (I Peter 2:4-8).

From the standpoint of the doctrine of the church itself, the importance of this statement is in its sharp contrast with the divine purpose in the Old Testament as related to Israel and the nations, and God's present purpose here announced by Christ Himself in the statement, "I will build my church." Each word of this pronouncement is freighted with meaning.

Christ, first of all, makes clear that the church to which He is referring is something which is built by God rather than by man. It is a sovereign undertaking by divine omnipotence, not a building to be erected by human hands. The tense of the verb is future and the statement, therefore, constitutes a prophecy of things to come. Christ did not say, "I am building my church," which would imply that He had already begun the church, which, perhaps, would justify the idea that the church is a continuation of what God was doing in the Old Testament. The future tense clearly shows that something new is about to be done.

The word *build* has the thought of building a house and implies a gradual process, not an immediate act of God. The concept of the church as a building is common in Scripture (cf. I Corinthians 3:11-15; Ephesians 2:10-22; I Peter 2:4-8).

What Christ proposes to build is described as "my church." That which is to be constructed is the peculiar possession of Christ as purchased by His blood and formed by the Holy Spirit whom He sends. The use of the word *church* (Gr. *ekklesia*) is the first instance of this word in the New Testament, and in the light of subsequent revelation this seems clearly to refer to the body of Christ or the assembly of true believers rather than to a local church or a group of local churches or Christendom as a whole.

The vast superstructure of ecclesiasticism which characterizes the modern church can hardly be attributed to the work of Christ. The concept that the true church is in view here is supported by His final statement, "The gates of hell shall not prevail against it." This implies that even death cannot thwart the purpose of Christ in building the church. Ultimately it will stand complete through resurrection and translation into the presence of God.

The announcement thus made by Christ, detached as it was from His previous messages concerning the kingdom which had been largely rejected by the Jewish people, reflects the new divine purpose which would grow out of His death and resurrection, namely, that which would be formed by the Spirit of God whom Christ would send. The exposition of His program for the church does not seem to be found in any passage in the Synoptic Gospels. The program for the church was unfolded in principle on the last night Christ spent with His disciples prior to His crucifixion and is contained in the Upper Room Discourse (John 13-17). Here is the great Magna Charta of the church and the declaration of the essential principles which would govern its character and life.

THE TEACHING OF CHRIST CONCERNING THE CHURCH AS HIS BODY

While it undoubtedly is true that the Apostle Paul was especially chosen of God to unfold the fact of the church as the body of Christ, it is often overlooked that a comprehensive revelation is also given by Christ Himself long before Paul was ever called to the ministry. The truth of the church as the body of Christ is, therefore, not an exclusive Pauline revelation, but was given by Christ to the faithful eleven who gathered with Him in the Upper Room. Delivered as it was on the night before His crucifixion, it anticipates His rejection, resurrection, and ascension, and deals specifically with the period between the two advents

in which God would fulfill His purpose, declared by Christ
in Matthew 16:18, to build His church.

Prominent in the revelation given by Christ to His dis·
ciples is the promise of the gift of the Holy Spirit fulfilled
on the Day of Pentecost and in the subsequent experience
of the church. Christ ·announced this in John 14:16, 17,
"And I will pray the Father, and he shall give you another
Comforter, that he may abide with you for ever; even the
Spirit of truth; whom the world cannot receive, because it
seeth him not, neither knoweth him: but ye know him; for
he dwelleth with you, and shall be in you." In these verses
Christ anticipated that the Spirit of God would come after
His ascension to heaven and would take up the task
of building a church or a body of true believers composed
of both Jews and Gentiles. The coming of the Spirit is in
response to the prayer of Christ and to His Father, and the
Spirit thus given is promised to abide with believers in this
present age forever, in contrast to the ministry of the Spirit
in the Old Testament in which He would come only in a
temporary way as in the case of King Saul.

The Holy Spirit is described as "the Spirit of truth"
who will be unknown and not received by the world. His
relationship to believers will be a most intimate one. Christ
contrasts what was true before and after Pentecost in the
expression, "for he dwelleth with you, and shall be in you."
Here is the theological distinction between the work of the
Spirit before Pentecost and after Pentecost. That there
was a ministry of the Spirit to saints prior to Pentecost is
evident from Scripture, but it is described as the ministry of
one who dwells *with* the saints. After Pentecost, a new relationship is described as the Holy Spirit being *in you*
(John 14:17). This is intended to represent a more intimate
identification with the Spirit and a more effective fellowship and program of divine enablement for the child of
God. The Holy Spirit thus indwelling believers was not
only to be the divine presence of God, but was to be "an-

other Comforter," that is, one who will be their constant companion and helper.

One area in which the Holy Spirit will be especially active is that of teaching divine truth. Christ told His disciples in John 14:26, "But the Comforter, which is the Holy Ghost, whom the Father will send in my name, he shall teach you all things, and bring all things to your remembrance whatsoever I have said unto you." The promise that the Holy Spirit will reveal to them the things of God is confirmed again in John 16:12-14, "I have yet many things to say unto you, but ye cannot bear them now. Howbeit when he, the Spirit of truth, is come, he will guide you into all truth: for he shall not speak of himself; but whatsoever he shall hear, that shall he speak: and he will shew you things to come." Though the disciples had enjoyed the blessings of the teachings of Christ throughout His earthly life, there were many things that they were not yet prepared to receive, including a full exposition of the purpose of His death and resurrection and the divine purpose of calling out Jews and Gentiles to form the body of Christ. As Christ Himself said, "Ye cannot bear them now." He promises, however, that the Spirit of God will guide them and will carry to them the message which is on Christ's heart for them. Of special emphasis in the prophecy of Christ is the declaration that the Spirit of God would show them "things to come," i.e., God's prophetic program. The Spirit of God would also glorify Christ or manifest His perfection. The church was to enjoy a fullness of spiritual revelation and intimacy in the knowledge of the Word and will of God which far exceeds that which was experienced by saints in the Old Testament.

In addition to the promise of Christ of sending the Spirit, He promises also to come Himself. In John 14:18 Christ said, "I will not leave you comfortless: I will come to you." Though Christ was to be bodily in heaven, He was to be spiritually present in the church, not simply representatively in the Holy Spirit as the Third Person, but in

His own character as the Second Person. This must not be confused with His promise of coming again in John 14:3, where it is a reference to His bodily return to receive His church. Here the spiritual presence of Christ in the church is meant, in keeping with His omnipresence. He therefore declares in John 14:18, "I will not leave you comfortless: I will come to you," which more literally translated is, "I will not leave you orphans: I am coming to you." Though they would not see Him with their physical eyes as He indicates in John 14:19, He affirms His spiritual presence with them. Later in this same chapter in verse 23, He promises that God the Father would also come and dwell with the believer. Thus the Scriptures teach that the believer is indwelt by the Triune God, God the Father, God the Son, and God the Holy Spirit, but that the primary ministry to the believer will be through the Third Person, the Holy Spirit.

In John 14:20, an additional fact is mentioned very briefly and without comment which is of great significance in view of the subsequent unfolding of the doctrine of the body of Christ. Christ not only declares that He would be with the believers, but that this would be part of the intimate relationship described simply in the words, "ye in me, and I in you." The expression, "I in you," refers to His indwelling presence, but the statement, "ye in me," affirms a new position to be given the church, the body of Christ, far more intimate and blessed in its relationship than anything ever offered to the nation Israel in the Old Testament.

The expression, "ye in me," is a specific indication that truth concerning the church as the body of Christ was revealed to His disciples even before the Day of Pentecost. Though they probably did not comprehend it at the time, it nevertheless anticipated the new relationship. Instead of being related to God as Israel was by covenant relationship and by being members of a chosen physical race, the church was to have a spiritual unity with Christ in which they would be identified with Christ, the Head of the church, would be members of His body, and would constitute together an organism with a living union rather than an association based essentially either on race or covenant. In the new relationship, racial background was to lose its significance and geographic connotation would be ignored. The important fact was their personal union with Jesus Christ and to all fellow believers. The subsequent truth of the body of Christ as enlarged in the Pauline letters gives substance to this preliminary declaration.

The Upper Room Discourse is replete with spiritual and moral truths relating to the church, including the central concept that disciples of Christ should be made known by their love for one another (John 13:34, 35). The intimacy of the new relationship is unfolded in the figure of the vine and the branches in John 15. Here the doctrine of the church as the body of Christ is given a natural illustration, Christ Himself being the vine and the individual members being the branches. The figure is designed to show living union and at the same time to illustrate the principles of bearing fruit for God in the new relationship. The disciples are instructed in John 15:7, "If ye abide in me, and my words abide in you, ye shall ask what ye will, and it shall be done unto you." It was necessary not only to have position in Christ which would be true of all believers, but it was also necessary for them to abide in that relationship, that is, to enter experientially into the dependence and yieldedness which is essential to a true member of Christ.

As they sought to bear fruit for God, they needed to have the guidance of God's revelation implied in "my word." Their program must. be God's program as revealed for His church. When their program had this character, Christ told them, "Ye shall ask what ye will, and it shall be done unto you." The marvelous power of prayer depends in the present age not only upon our position in Christ, but upon our right to pray in His name, and thereby accomplish the will of God. Those who thus enter into the precious provision of God for His own are assured that they will bring forth much fruit.

In the concluding portion of the Upper Room Discourse containing the high priestly prayer of Christ (John 17), a series of petitions are recorded which constitute the major chart of the divine purpose for the present age. These include the following elements: (1) that Christ should be glorified (v. 1; cp. Philippians 2:9-11; (2) the security and safety of saints in the present age from the world (v. 11) and Satan (v. 15); (3) the sanctification of believers (v. 17); (4) that believers in the present age should be one as the Father and the Son are one (vv. 21, 22, 23); (5) that a testimony may be given before the world bringing some to faith in Christ (vv. 20, 21, 23); (6) that believers may be with Christ in glory (v. 24); (7) that the love of Christ might be in the believers (v. 26). In connection with these truths, the Lord refers to eternal life which is possessed by believers in the church (17:2, 3), and to His work of intercession for them (vv. 9, 15, 20, 24). Taken as a whole, the high-priestly prayer of Christ in John 17 is a panoramic view of God's divine purpose in this present age, and is in sharp distinction to His purpose for Israel in many respects, since it is a revelation of God's divine purpose for the church composed of both Jews and Gentiles.

THE FORMATION OF THE CHURCH AT PENTECOST

The Day of Pentecost records the coming of the Spirit to the world in obvious parallelism to the coming of Christ as a babe to Bethlehem. Instead of being incarnate in human flesh, the Holy Spirit was to be clothed with the church which is Christ's body.

The Day of Pentecost is anticipated not only in the pronouncement of Christ in the Upper Room relative to the coming of the Spirit, but in the specific promise given on the day of ascension as recorded in Acts 1:5, "For John truly baptized with water; but ye shall be baptized with

the Holy Ghost not many days hence." He further promises
in Acts 1:8: "But ye shall receive power, after that the
Holy Ghost is come upon you: and ye shall be witnesses
unto me both in Jerusalem, and in all Judea, and in Samaria, and unto the uttermost part of the earth."

In keeping with these promises, in the second chapter
of Acts as the disciples were gathered in a public meeting
on the Day of Pentecost the experience of the coming of the
Spirit was realized by the church. It was accompanied with
the outer phenomena of "a sound from heaven as of a rushing mighty wind" and the appearance of "cloven tongues
like as of fire" which appeared on each one of them. The
immediate result was, "They were all filled with the Holy
Ghost, and began to speak with other tongues as the Spirit
gave them utterance" (Acts 2:4). As the multitude gathered
when the report reached them of these unusual happen-
ings, they heard Peter's sermon which ended in public
confession of faith on the part of three thousand who were
baptized in public demonstration of their faith in Christ.

The significance of the Day of Pentecost is clearly one
of a new milestone in the undertaking of God. It set apart
the period prior to Pentecost as belonging to the old order
and signified that the period following Pentecost would
be a fulfillment of a dispensation in which the Holy Spirit
would have prominence. The subsequent theological interpretation of the Day of Pentecost is found first in Peter's
experience in Acts 10 and 11 and in Paul's declaration concerning the baptism of the Spirit in I Corinthians 12:13.

In Peter's experience, he was instructed to partake of
unclean things by his vision from heaven (Acts 10:9-16).
Peter was commanded by the Spirit of God to accompany
the Gentiles who came for him to bring him to Cornelius
the centurion (Acts 10:17-20). When Peter preached his
sermon as recorded in Acts 10:34-43 relating that Jesus
Christ was indeed the Saviour through His death and resurrection and that remission of sins is promised those who
believe in Him, there was the immediate response of faith

on the part of his hearers. The Scriptures record the aston-ishment of Peter as he sees poured out upon these Gentiles the same gift of the Holy Spirit which had characterized the church on the Day of Pentecost.

In the subsequent explanation of Peter to those who had criticized him for eating with Gentiles, he explained in Acts 11:15-17: "And as I began to speak, the Holy Ghost fell on them, as on us at the beginning. Then remembered I the Word of the Lord, how that he said, John indeed baptized with water; but ye shall be baptized with the Holy Ghost. Forasmuch then as God gave them the like gift as he did unto us, who believed on the Lord Jesus Christ; what was I, that I could withstand God?"

In his explanation, the Apostle Peter clearly identified the experience of Cornelius and his friends as being the same as that which occurred on the Day of Pentecost, namely, that they had been baptized with the Holy Ghost. He also referred to the Day of Pentecost as "the begin-ning." This is a plain indication that something new be-gan on the Day of Pentecost, namely, the body of Christ formed by the baptism of the Spirit.

In I Corinthians 12:13 in connection with the discus-sion of the church as the body of Christ, the Apostle Paul declared: "For by one Spirit are we all baptized into one body, whether we be Jews or Gentiles, whether we be bond or free; and have been all made to drink into one Spirit." Here is revealed that the baptism of the Spirit is the universal work of the Spirit which places every true believer in Christ into the body of Christ, the church. This is accomplished for them regardless of whether they are Jews or Gentiles, whether they are bond or free, and is the basis by which they participate in all the ministries of the Spirit described as drinking into one Spirit in this text. In con-trast to the filling of the Spirit which is experienced only by some Christians, the baptism of the Spirit forming the body of Christ is the structural work of the Spirit by which the body is formed and properly related to Christ, its Head.

The Day of Pentecost, therefore, is the fulfillment of the original pronouncement of Christ in Matthew 16:18.

THE PAULINE DOCTRINE OF THE ONE BODY

At least seven figures are used in the New Testament to describe the relationship between Christ and the church: (1) Christ as the Shepherd and the church as the sheep (John 10:1-16); (2) the vine and the branches (John 15:1-11); (3) the last Adam and the new creation (I Corinthians 15:45; II Corinthians 5:17); (4) Christ as the head and the church as the body (Ephesians 1:20-23; 3:6; 4:11-16); (5) Christ as the foundation and the church as the building (Ephesians 2:19-22; I Corinthians 3:11-15); (6) Christ as the high priest and the church as a royal priesthood (I Peter 2:9; Revelation 1:6; cp. Hebrews 8:1-6); (7) Christ as the bridegroom and the church as the bride (Matthew 22:2; 25:1-13; II Corinthians 11:2; Revelation 19:7-9).

Each of the seven figures relating Christ to the church has its own body of truth, but central in the theological concept of the church is the revelation concerning the church as the one body. This truth is introduced in Ephesians 1: 20-22 where it is related to the resurrected Christ and His exaltation in glory resulting in all authority being put under Him, including the church, His body. As expressed by Paul, the power of God "hath put all things under his feet, and gave him to be head over all things to the church, which is his body, the fulness of him that filleth all in all." The true church composed of all true believers is here described under the symbolism of the human body being subject to its head and accordingly united to the head in a living union.

In the second chapter of Ephesians, this truth is expanded in the declaration that the church is a new creation "created in Christ Jesus unto good works" (Ephesians 2:10). In the discussion which follows, Paul contrasts the situation of the Ephesian Christians in the past, before their salvation, as being uncircumcised Gentiles, and states, "that at that time ye were without Christ, being aliens from the commonwealth of Israel, and strangers from the covenants of promise, having no hope, and without God in the world." The desperate spiritual state of all Gentiles is thus graphically described and forms a stark background for their new position in Christ.

Beginning in Ephesians 2:13, Paul lists the tremendous factors which have been changed now that they are Christians: "But now in Christ Jesus ye who were sometimes far off are made nigh by the blood of Christ."

Having been redeemed, he states that Christ "is our peace, who hath made both one, and hath broken down the middle wall of partition between us" (Ephesians 2:14). The reference is to the contrast between Jew and Gentile which in Christ is eliminated in that both have been made one in the body of Christ. This is enforced by the verses which follow in which the apostle states that the enmity which separated Jew and Gentile is now abolished and in grace Christ has made "in himself of twain one new man, so making peace" (Ephesians 2:15). The new man is another reference to the unity of the body of Christ. This is made plain in the verse in Ephesians 2:16 which follows, "And that he might reconcile both unto God in one body by the cross, having slain the enmity thereby." The figure of the one body is supported by the concept of the church as the household of God built upon Christ the chief cornerstone and fitted together as a holy temple unto the Lord constituting a habitation of the Spirit (Ephesians 2:19-22).

With this general introduction to the subject of the church as the body of Christ, the apostle unfolds its character as a mystery in the third chapter of Ephesians. Paul reveals that the doctrine of the church as the body of Christ was a subject of special revelation to him (Ephesians 3:1-3). He states further that the truth of the church as the body of Christ, "in other ages was not made unto the sons of men, as it is now revealed unto his holy apostles and prophets by the Spirit; that the Gentiles should be fellowheirs, and of the same body, and partakers of his promise in Christ by the gospel." In an effort to evade what seems to be the plain teaching of this passage of Scripture that the church is something new and the subject of new revelation, these verses have been interpreted by some as merely indicating additional truth rather than a new revelation. Seizing upon the word *as*, the thought is advanced that the truth concerning the church was revealed in the Old Testament but not in the same way as it is revealed now.

The uniform use of the word *mystery* in the New Testament, however, is that it refers to truth which was "not made known unto the sons of men" in the Old Testament. A normative instance is found in Colossians 1:26 where the statement is made, "Even the mystery which hath been hid from ages and generations, but now is made manifest to his saints." In Ephesians 3:5, the same meaning is intended. The contrast is not between degrees of revelation, but between that which was not revealed in the Old Testament but is now revealed unto the apostles and prophets of the New Testament. That this absolute character of contrast between what is hidden and what is revealed is intended is brought out plainly in verse 6 where the contents of the mystery is said to be the revelation "that the Gentiles shall be fellowheirs, and of the same body, and partakers of his promise in Christ by the gospel." In the Old Testament, Gentiles and Jews are distinguished beginning in Genesis 12 and continuing until the Day of Pentecost. Jews and Gentiles are never equated in the Old Testament, as the Jews are the chosen people in contrast to the Gentiles who are outside the covenant. This is brought out even in the context of Ephesians as, for instance, in 2:12 where the lot of the Jew and the Gentile is sharply contrasted.

The idea that Gentiles should be on exactly the same plane as Israelites and, furthermore, in the intimate relationship as being members of the same body, is absolutely foreign to the Old Testament. According to Isaiah 61:5, 6, the Gentiles are pictured as being the servants and Israel as the priests of God. While it is true that the Gentiles were promised blessings in the future millennial kingdom, they are never given equality with the Jews in the Old Testament. What was new and unpredicted as far as the Old Testament is concerned, here forms the content of the special revelation given Paul concerning the church, the body of Christ. A Jew or a Gentile who through faith in Christ becomes a member of the body of Christ, by so much is detached from his former situation, and his prophetic program then becomes that of the church rather than that of Jews or Gentiles as such. It is only as the prophetic program of the church as the body of Christ is distinguished from that of Israel or that of the Gentiles that confusion can be avoided in the interpretation of unfulfilled prophecy.

The subject of the church as the one body is given further revelation in Ephesians 4 where it is declared that in keeping with the figure of a body, each individual member in the church has his particular gift, and "the whole body fitly joined together and compacted by that which every joint supplieth, according to the effectual working in the measure of every part, maketh increase of the body unto edifying of itself in love" (Ephesians 4:16). The same truth is unfolded in Romans 12:3-8 where individuals are likened to the members of the body having different gifts and different capacities, but all essential to the perfection of the body.

Taken as a whole, the doctrine of the body of Christ is a marvelous vehicle for divine revelation, demonstrating the supreme benefits given to believers in this present age under God's divine program of grace, disregarding racial and cultural backgrounds such as are prominent in the Old Testament. In the church, all believers are on an equal plane. Though distinguished by their spiritual gifts sovereignly bestowed, they have a common destiny and program in God's unfolding of His will for the church. Central in this purpose is that declared in Ephesians 2:7, "That in the ages to come he might shew the exceeding riches of his grace and his kindness toward us through Christ Jesus." Though the grace of God is manifested in all dispensations from the salvation of Adam and Eve to the last soul that is added, the church is selected to be the supreme revelation of that grace and will constitute a display of the grace of God not only in time but in eternity to come. In a similar way, Israel was selected of God to demonstrate His faithfulness and His righteousness and through eternity will display supremely these blessed aspects.

The contrast of the church as the body of Christ to the professing church or Christendom as a whole is essential to a proper understanding of God's prophetic program. While the church as the body of Christ will have its climax in the translation of the church and its rapture into heaven with subsequent events that pertain only to those who are saved, Christendom as a whole as an ecclesiastical organization will move on into the tribulation time and fulfill the prophecies that relate to it as it ends in complete apostasy. This dual development is paralleled to some extent by prophecy relating to the godly remnant of Israel throughout history as contrasted to the nation as a whole, but the church never becomes Israel, and Israel never becomes the church.

Chapter IV

THE CHURCH IN THE END OF THE AGE

Are There Signs of the Rapture of the Church?

One of the neglected areas of prophetic study is that pertaining to the end of the church age. The assertion is often confidently made that there are no signs of the rapture of the church, as it is presented everywhere in Scripture as an imminent event. Therefore, it is argued, we should be looking for the coming of the Lord, rather than for signs that precede, as the rapture of the church is before the time of tribulation predicted in Scripture.

Most of the prophetic word relating to the end time has to do with the second coming of Christ to establish His kingdom in the earth. Prophecy is devoted to the events which precede the second coming rather than a series of events preceding the rapture itself. In the Gospel of Matthew, for instance, the general and specific signs leading up to the second coming of Christ are clearly outlined and the great tribulation is presented as the great, unmistakable sign of the second coming of Christ to the earth. In a similar way in the book of Revelation, an extended revelation is given beginning in chapter 6 of the events which will mark the end of the age preceding Christ's return to the earth. If these events follow rather than precede the rapture of the church, they cannot be taken as signs of the rapture itself.

There are, however, two bona fide areas of study relating to anticipation of the rapture itself. One of these has to do with preparation for events which will follow the rapture. There are extensive preparations in the present

world scene which seem to be a foreshadowing and preparation for events which will follow the rapture. If so, these
would constitute evidence that the rapture itself may be
near. These signs will be presented in a later discussion.

Another important area, however, is the Scriptural
description of the church at the end of the age. According
to Scripture, there will be a progression of fulfilled prophecy
in the church age itself which will be observable before
the rapture even though its final form will not come into
existence until after the true church has been caught up
to be with the Lord. In a word, the Scriptures predict that
there will be a growing apostasy or departure from the Lord
as the church age progresses, and its increase can be understood as a general indication that the rapture itself is
near. The Scriptures dealing with this subject are those
which describe the church in the end of the age. These
are in contrast to events of the tribulation itself which come
to pass subsequent to the rapture.

THE HISTORY OF APOSTASY

The concept of apostasy or departure from the faith
is by no means a new idea, but can be traced throughout
Scripture beginning in the Garden of Eden. There the
taunting question expressed by the serpent to the woman,
"Yea, hath God said?" (Genesis 3:1), introduced unbelief
to the human race which has borne its sad fruit through the
centuries since Adam. Basically, apostasy has always been
a departure from faith in God's revealed Word, whether
oral or written. It was that unbelief which inspired the
first sin and in subsequent generations made necessary the
terrible judgments of God upon human sin. In the Old
Testament, it took the form of questioning God's revelation concerning sacrifices as revealed in Cain's rejection of
blood sacrifices as a way of approach to God which ended
in the murder of his brother, Abel. It was this same attitude
of unbelief which rejected the preaching of righteousness
through Noah even as he was building the ark which ended

in the terrible judgment of the flood. It was the departure from the revealed worship and will of God which led to the construction of the Tower of Babel and the introduction of God's plan for Abram and his seed. It was lack of apprehension of the plan of God for Abram's posterity that caused Jacob to leave the land and ultimately to find his way down into Egypt to escape the famine. It was through unbelief that Israel failed to conquer the land under Joshua and to ignore in subsequent generations the solemn warning of Moses. It was unbelief that produced the awful immorality of the period of the Judges. It was unbelief that led Israel into idolatry which ended in the captivities of Assyria and Babylon. Finally, it was unbelief which blinded the eyes of Israel in rejecting the credentials of their Messiah and Saviour.

The history of the church subsequent to the close of the canon is also a sad record of departure from God. The church, kept pure through persecution in the early centuries, soon began to depart from the faith contained in the Scriptures once the church became a popular organization under Constantine. The first casualty was a departure from chiliasm, or the doctrine of the premillennial coming of Christ and the establishment of His millennial kingdom. Though the early church as well as the church of the Middle Ages seems to have clung resolutely to the idea of a bodily second coming as indicated by their creeds, the precious truths of the imminent coming of the Lord for His church and the establishment of Christ's righteous reign on earth soon lost its prominence. The teaching arose that Christ could not come back until a thousand years after the time of the apostles. This was based on the erroneous idea that the church was already in the millennium and that the millennium had to run its course before Christ could return.

The next important casualty in Scriptural doctrine was the departure from grace beginning with Augustine and his theology. While holding resolutely to the doctrine of human depravity with its corresponding need of divine grace,

Augustine and subsequent theologians in the Roman Catholic Church maintained that grace was channeled through the church and the sacraments and, apart from this medium, there could be no true salvation or bestowal of grace. As a result, the great doctrine of justification by faith, the truth of the fullness and power of the Holy Spirit, and the truth that believers had immediate access to the throne of grace without an earthly priest as mediator became dim. Soon the authority of the Scriptures as the Word of God became subordinate to the authority of the church, and the interpretation of the church took precedence over the teaching ministry and illumination of the Holy Spirit. The Word of God, thus shackled and to a large extent kept from the people, cast its restricted light on the darkness of the Middle Ages.

The Protestant Reformation, of course, brought a fresh study of great essentials of Christian truth. Once again the Word of God was made its own authority. The great doctrine of justification by faith was proclaimed. The Roman priesthood was thrust aside in favor of the clear teaching that every Christian is a priest once he has put his faith in Christ and can have immediate access to the throne of God in the name of his Saviour. Likewise the grace of God came as an immediate bestowal of the Holy Spirit. Though Protestantism did not completely shake loose the sacramental idea of the Romanish system, it was a new state of freedom. Every man now could interpret the Bible guided by the Holy Spirit as his teacher and could revel in the abundance of God's sanctifying truth.

The Protestant Reformation, however, had barely begun before the sad evidence of further departure began. In the centuries that followed, the enlightenment freed men's minds and wills to believe and do as they pleased. No longer shackled by the dogma of the church, men could achieve new understanding of the physical and philosophic realm. Soon higher criticism began to rear its ugly head, and rationalism demanded that Christian doctrines be sub-

mitted to the bar of reason. Mystics arose who made experience the criteria of theological judgment. Critics began
to divide the Bible and challenge traditional views of au-
thorship and historical backgrounds. Apostasy invaded Protestantism with the same devastating effect it had had on
the Roman Church.

The departure from the doctrine of infallible inspiration of the original writings in the nineteenth century in
Europe soon found its way to the Western Hemisphere
and precipitated the modernist-fundamentalist controversies
of the first quarter of the twentieth century. With the departure from the doctrine of inspiration, there came ultimately a like departure from the doctrine of Christ. The
virgin birth began to be questioned and declared unimportant. The deity of Christ was reduced to a divine quality
rather than to a state of divine being. The bodily resurrection of Christ was made a spiritual resurrection instead
of a literal raising of His body from the grave. Open skep-
ticism arose within the church concerning doctrines of
final judgment and of heaven and hell. The love of God was
regarded as making impossible a God of righteous judgment.

The twentieth century marked not only the departure
from Biblical Christianity to an extent never before witnessed in the history of the church, but also signaled the
rise of new and confusing heresies. Multiplied cults and
new forms of religion arose with varied degrees of allegiance to Christianity, a new combination of old errors came
into being, of which the most powerful and important is
neo-orthodoxy. The growth and character of apostasy in
the world today, when viewed in the light of predictions
in the Scripture concerning the last days of the church,
seem to be a clear parallel to what one might have a right
to expect in the days immediately preceding the rapture.

THE GENERAL CHARACTER OF HERESY
IN THE LAST DAYS

One of the major revelations concerning apostasy in the
last days is that contained in I Timothy 4:1-3: "Now the

Spirit speaketh expressly, that in the latter times some shall depart from the faith, giving heed to seducing spirits, and doctrines of devils; speaking lies in hypocrisy; having their conscience seared with a hot iron; forbidding to marry, and commanding to abstain from meats, which God hath created to be received with thanksgiving of them which believe and know the truth."

This revelation given by Paul to Timothy according to the passage itself has to do with the "latter times." The character of departure from the faith is specified as containing the following items: (1) giving heed to seducing spirits, and doctrines of devils; (2) speaking lies in hypocrisy; (3) having a conscience which is insensible; (4) forbidding to marry; (5) and commanding to abstain from certain food. While these factors can be seen to some extent throughout the history of the church, they are increasingly evident in modern Christianity. The satanic character of departure from the faith is evident in the confusion existing in the church regarding its proper theology. That which is contrary to the Scriptures is offered as the truth of God. Much that is traveling in the guise of religion is to spiritually minded Christians nothing other than an evidence of the power of Satan with all its deceptiveness. False doctrines are advanced without any attempt to relate them to the Word of God. In the name of religion much is promoted that demonstrates an insensitivity to the morality and holiness commanded of true Christians.

Of special interest is the prophecy that in the end of the age there will be prohibition of marriage and requirement to abstain from certain foods. It is evident in the Roman Church today that priests are forbidden to marry on the ground that the single estate is more holy than the married estate, something which is not taught in the Word of God. It should be clear to any reader of Scripture that the creation of Eve was God's plan, not Adam's, and that the command to populate the earth by bearing children preceded rather than followed the fall. Though in individual cases it may not be God's will for some to marry, as illustrated in the case of Paul, others were in the will of God in the married estate as in the case of the Apostle Peter. The prohibition regarding marriage originates in the commands of men, not in the Word of God, and is a sign of the encroaching false religion which characterizes the end of the age in contrast to the true faith contained in the Scriptures.

Another obvious factor is the religious custom to abstain from meats on Friday and to refrain from certain foods during Lent. This again is a man-made invention and certainly not taught in the Word of God. As the apostle indicates, if the food is that which God has created to be received with thanksgiving, then it can be eaten without violation of the moral will of God. The encroaching ritualism represented in these two items of I Timothy 4:3 is typical of religion as it attempts to curtail freedom which belongs to the child of God under grace. The fact that these three verses provide such an accurate picture of the contemporary scene leads to the conclusion that that which Paul described as coming to pass in the latter time is already being fulfilled in the professing church today.

THE DENIAL OF THE PERSON AND WORK OF CHRIST

One of the major sections on apostasy in the last days is that provided in II Peter 2-3. In these two chapters a comprehensive picture of the false teachers of the last days is given. In II Peter 2:1, 2, the major features of apostasy are predicted: "But there were false prophets also among the people, even as there shall be false teachers among you, who privily shall bring in damnable heresies, even denying the Lord that bought them, and bring upon themselves swift destruction. And many shall follow their pernicious ways; by reason of whom the way of truth shall be evil spoken of."

According to Peter, there would arise in the church period false teachers corresponding to the false prophets which Israel endured. These false teachers would by stealth bring in that which he described as "damnable heresies" or "destructive heresies." It is clear here that the apostle is not dealing with minor variations within the Christian faith such as often characterized difference of opinion within the orthodox church. It is rather that he predicts departures of such character that they are destructive completely to the Christian faith, that is, make impossible the salvation of those who adhere to them. He states that these heresies can be described as "denying the Lord that bought them" with the result that they will bring upon themselves swift destruction.

It would be almost impossible to state more succinctly the fundamental denial of the Christian faith which characterizes our day, for modern Christianity has indeed denied the Lord that bought them. This is actually a twofold error which is having a devastating effect upon the church. It is, first of all, the denial of the person of Christ and, second, a denial of His work.

It is characteristic of modern liberalism to teach that Jesus Christ was not born of a virgin, but actually was the natural child of Joseph and Mary. In attempting to explain the unusual influence of Christ upon His generation, and to account for the formation of the Christian church, it is often admitted that Christ was an unusual person even if He were only an ordinary man.

Modern liberals often explain that Jesus as a lad was an unusual person. He had an unusual consciousness of God and an unusual devotion to the will of God. Liberals explain that this was so noticeable in His character that people began to identify Him with God and called Him the Son of God. Accordingly, they point to Christ as the great example. They say that just as Christ became the Son of God by yielding to the will of God, by thinking God's thoughts, by worshiping God, and by doing God's will so others also can follow in His example and also become the sons of God.

From the standpoint of orthodox Christianity, of course, this is indeed a damnable heresy. It is affirming that Christ was an ordinary man who became divine in His experience but not in His person. It by-passes the whole matter of Christ's substitutionary atonement, the natural depravity of men, and the need for supernatural grace. Though often taught cleverly and covered up with evangelical terminology, it is all the more a deceptive device to take people from the truth as it is in Christ Jesus.

Modern neo-orthodoxy, while not straying as far as many liberals have gone, nevertheless tends to ignore the question whether Christ existed from all eternity past as the Second Person. They tend to by-pass the problem of whether there was indeed a genuine incarnation of the infinite God and man and whether Christ as a man was indeed all that He was before as the infinite God. Though the expression "Son of God" and the adjective "divine" are often attributed to Christ, it is not at all clear whether they mean by this something distinctive and unique. There is far more denial of the person of Christ in modern Christianity than is immediately apparent. It is probable that never before in the history of the church has there been more subversion of the true doctrine of Christology than there is in the contemporary theology of the church.

If denial of the person of Christ is common, even more so is there denial of the concept that Christ bought us. The idea that Christ is a substitute for sinners, that He died as a Lamb upon the cross, that He bore our sins as the Scriptures indicate, and by the shedding of His blood effected a judicial basis for our salvation, is all most offensive to the modern mind. To modern men the death of Christ is at best a noble example of sincerity of purpose or a demonstration of the wickedness of man, in that man would crucify such a noble character. To the liberal, the love of God is redemptive itself apart from the sacrifice of Christ and in effect liberals do exactly what Peter predicts, they deny that the Lord bought us with His shed blood. While there may be differences of opinion on the interpretation of prophecy within the body of Christ, which do not affect the eternal salvation of those who hold these opinions, it should be obvious to every careful student of the Word of God that a denial of the person of Christ and a denial of the sacrifice of Christ strikes a blow at indispensable Christian truths and, as Peter predicts, those who deny this will bring upon themselves the righteous judgment of God.

Peter goes on to prophesy that many will follow their pernicious ways. It is sadly true that the way of truth is in a minority in the modern day. While churches beautiful in architecture and rich in appointment are evident in every city, their existence and their popularity is not in itself an evidence that the truth is being preached. Instead, Bible-believing Christians are sometimes viewed as cultic, as abnormal, as reactionary, as anti-intellectual, and as those who do not keep abreast of the times. Not many churches today welcome either to the pulpit or to the pew those who expound apostolic doctrine which is normally considered orthodox in the history of the church. Instead, those who have platitudes of good works, who preach interesting but unchallenging sermons and who leave their congregation undisturbed seem to be in the ascendancy.

The Apostle Peter spares no words in describing these false teachers. He accused them of "covetousness," of "feigned words," of making "merchandise of you," as being subject to God's "judgment," and "damnation" (II Peter 2:3). He accuses them of walking "after the flesh in the lust of uncleanness," of being such as "despise government," who are "presumptuous," "self-willed," who "speak evil of dignities" (II Peter 2:10). He declares that they are "as natural brute beasts, made to be taken and destroyed," who "speak evil of things that they understand not" and who "shall utterly perish in their own corruption" (II Peter 2:12). He declares that they "shall receive the reward of unrighteousness, as they that count it pleasure to riot in the daytime" (II Peter 2:13). Even in the observance of the Lord's Supper, they are "spots" and "blemishes" (II Peter 2:13). Their immorality is revealed in that they have "eyes full of adultery," and "cannot cease from sin; beguiling unstable souls" (II Peter 2:14). They are "covetous," "cursed children"; "they have forsaken the right way, and are gone astray, following the way of Balaam the son of Bosor, who loved the wages of unrighteousness" (II Peter 2:14, 15). They "are wells without water, clouds that are carried with a tempest; to whom the mist of darkness is reserved for ever" (II Peter 2:17). They "speak great swelling words of vanity, they allure through the lusts of the flesh" (II Peter 2:18). They promise "liberty" though "they themselves are the servants of corruption" (II Peter 2:19). They are said to fulfill "the true proverb, The dog is turned to his own vomit again; and the sow that was washed to her wallowing in the mire" (II Peter 2:22).

In the Epistle of Jude, a similar indictment is leveled against those who are apostates. They are said to be "ungodly men, turning the grace of our God into lasciviousness, and denying the only Lord God, and our Lord Jesus Christ" (v. 4). Jude does not spare denunciation of apostate teachers, comparing them to the apostates in Sodom and Gomorrah, both in their rebellion against God and against Christian moral standards. In most details, Jude parallels II Peter.

From these extended references to the moral character of apostasy, it is clear that God takes a far more serious view both of the theology and morality of false religion than is common among Christians today. The Word of God strips the apostates of any veneer of respectability, sincerity of motives, or worthy purpose, and reveals them for what they are, tools of Satan and the enemies of Christ and of all who love Him.

This shocking portrayal of the character of false teachers and their doctrines is too little realized by the church of Jesus Christ today. Misguided by religious phrases and the pomp and ceremony of modern Christianity, with its appearance of scholarship and its supposed progress in theology, many today are not willing to face the stark reality of heresy within the church and the widespread departure from Biblical faith. Here in the words of Peter and forming this portion of the inspired Word of God, heresy is unmasked and the contemporary church is seen from God's viewpoint. The hypocrisy, immorality, vanity, and emptiness of modern liberalism has its culmination in denying the Lord who died for a lost humanity.

DENIAL OF THE SECOND COMING OF CHRIST

In the form of a postscript to the Apostle Peter's general description of apostates in the last days, the prediction is added that there would also be departure from the truth of the second coming of Christ. Peter writes: "Knowing this first, that there shall come in the last days scoffers, walking after their own lusts, and saying, Where is the promise of his coming: for since the fathers fell asleep, all things continue as they were from the beginning of the creation" (II Peter 3:3, 4). In this passage false teachers are described as "scoffers, walking after their own lusts." On the one hand they are unbelievers, that is, those who will not accept the Word of God concerning the coming of the Lord, and, second, they are motivated by their own lusts and immorality.

It is an obvious fact that modern liberals scoff at the second coming of Christ, motivated primarily by their desire to avoid the doctrine of divine judgment upon sin which is commonly associated with it in Scripture. The widespread denial of a bodily return of Christ is prompted by a desire to avoid the teaching of Scripture concerning the revelation of righteousness which will accompany fulfillment of prophecy relating to the second coming. These false teachers approach the doctrine of the second coming with a question born of unbelief as they ask, "Where is the promise of his second coming?" They attempt to support their unbelief by the statement, "Since the fathers fell asleep, all things continue as they were from the beginning of the creation."

Both the questions raised and the supporting evidence is, of course, contradicted by the facts of history. There is no logical support of the idea that a delay in the second coming of Christ is a valid argument against its ultimate fulfillment. Many prophecies in the Scriptures were fulfilled thousands of years after their deliverance, and there is no reason to believe that the passage of time alters the sure Word of God. The argument that all things have continued undisturbed since creation is contradicted by many Scriptures.

Peter points out that their assumption that all things have continued without interruption from beginning of creation is an absolute untruth. The entire Word of God bears its testimony to the fact that God does intervene in human events, that He does guide human history, that both naturally and supernaturally the providential government of God is manifest in the history of the world. An illustration is afforded first of all in the doctrine of creation itself in that God by His own command caused the earth to stand out of the water and in the water and created the starry heavens above. In verse 6 he refers to the earth as being destroyed by being overflowed with water. This is usually considered a reference to the flood of Noah. Peter says that just as God once destroyed the earth with water, so it is predicted He will in the future destroy the earth by fire.

Though not mentioned by Peter, it is obvious that the history of Scripture contains many other interventions of God into the natural situation. Many of His chastisements of Israel are illustrations of the fact that all things have not continued as they were from the beginning of creation. The greatest intervention of all was in the first coming of Christ when God invaded the human sphere in the form of the incarnation. The literal fulfillment of promises pertaining to the first coming is a foreshadowing of the literal fulfillment of promises pertaining to the second coming. For liberals, of course, who deny a genuine incarnation and

who do not accept the testimony of Scripture, probably
the appeal to nature used by Peter is the most valid and
telling argument.

The promise of a future destruction by fire is joined
to an explanation as to why the second coming has not already been fulfilled. As Peter explains it, in the first place,
"one day is with the Lord as a thousand years, and a thousand years as one day" (II Peter 3:8). By this he means
that time is not a factor with God in the same sense as it
is with man, in that a thousand years pass as quickly for
God as one day does with man. On the other hand, he
means that there is the same planning in one day of human
experience as there is in a thousand years of human history.
God views the world in its history both from the micro-
scopic and telescopic viewpoint. For this reason, the passage of several thousand years since the first coming of
Christ is no argument at all that the second coming will
not be fulfilled in God's time.

In contemporary theology, however, even liberals have
been forced to give renewed attention to the doctrine of
the second coming. Liberals have been jarred from their
complacency by the events of the first half of the twentieth
century including World War II. They have had to face
the fact that the world could come to a sudden and dramatic end and that such an end is not beyond reason and
certainly not beyond the Scriptural revelation. As the second
half of the twentieth century began, however, it soon became clear that this renewed attention to the doctrine of
the second coming of Christ was not a return to the Biblical truth, but rather an attempt to evade its plain teaching.
The second coming of Christ is thus regarded as a spiritual
experience, as a divine intervention into human consciousness or possibly as fulfilled in the death of the believer.
The dramatic events related in Scripture as preceding and
following the second coming of Christ are usually ignored.

Further light is given on the real cause for delay in
Christ's return to the earth in II Peter 3:9: "The Lord is
not slack concerning his promise, as some men count slack-

ness; but is longsuffering to us-ward, not willing that any should perish, but that all should come to repentance." The reason for the seeming delay in the coming of the Lord is not due to slackness or inability to fulfill His promise, but is inspired instead by the longsuffering of God who wishes to extend mercy to the ultimate limit, permitting all who will come and escape the divine judgment which attends the second coming. God is "not willing that any should perish, but that all should come to repentance." This is His desire and though the Scriptures clearly reveal that God's heart will not be completely satisfied in this respect in that many will perish, it is the will of God that opportunity should be afforded as long as possible.

In due time, however, the Day of the Lord will come. Peter describes this in verse 10 as a time "in which the heavens shall pass away with a great noise, and the elements shall melt with fervent heat, the earth also and the works that are therein shall be burned up" (II Peter 3:10). From Revelation 20:11; 21:1, we learn that this will take place at the end of the Day of the Lord rather than at its beginning, that is, the Day of the Lord is viewed as the extended period of time between the rapture of the church and the end of the millennium, and will be climaxed by destruction of the present heaven and earth and the creation of a new heaven and earth.

It is stated plainly that the earth and the works in it are going to be burned up. According to II Peter 3:11: "All these things shall be dissolved." This could not be at the beginning of the millennium, for life continues including identifiable geographic locations such as the Mount of Olives, the city of Jerusalem, and the nations which surround Israel. Peter states clearly that God's ultimate purpose is something more than simply Christ coming back to earth. It is the fulfillment of God's plan to bring in the eternal state where righteousness will reign and where the saints will enjoy the blessings of the grace of God throughout eternity. Those who scoff at the second coming of Christ are thereby denying the total of God's program prophetically for the world and will participate in what Peter refers to in II Peter 3:7 as "the day of judgment and perdition of ungodly men."

The prediction that there will be scoffing concerning the second coming of Christ is sadly fulfilled in the twentieth century. Few pulpits today proclaim a bodily second coming of Christ to the earth. In the minds of many professing Christians, truths concerning the second coming are considered as proper items of faith only for cults and those outside the main body of Christendom. Countless thousands of professing Christians are totally ignorant concerning the facts of Scripture which describe the second coming of Christ.

Though modern liberals have written in recent days numerous works dealing with the second coming of Christ, an examination of their contributions revealed that they are not talking about the second coming of Christ as presented in the Bible, but are using the terminology to refer to crisis in Christian experience or to the death of the believer. Actually, though using the terminology, they do not believe in a bodily second coming of Christ and thereby contribute to the confusion and unbelief that is characteristic of modern Christendom in relation to these great truths. Never before in the history of the church has the truth of the second coming of Christ been so vaguely held so far as the church at large is concerned as in our day. Actually the modern church denies the very idea of the prophetic and declares that it is impossible for anyone to predict the future whether it be the second coming of Christ or any other event in prophecy. Thus, unbelief is on the throne and faith and hope are shoved aside.

COLDNESS AND INDIFFERENCE IN THE CHURCH

In the letter to the church at Laodicea, the last of the seven churches of Asia, the charge was made that they were lukewarm: "I know thy works, that thou art neither cold nor hot: I would thou wert cold or hot. So then be cause thou art lukewarm, and neither cold nor hot, I will spue thee out of my mouth" (Revelation 3:15, 16). Whether or not the seven churches of Asia are prophetic of the entire age as many have held, the charge against the church at Laodicea is remarkably accurate for the church today. In contrast to the church of the Middle Ages which was dead, the modern church fulfills the description of being neither hot nor cold, quite self-content with its supposed riches and attainment. It is characteristic of much of the modern church to say complimentary words about Christ, but to avoid any clear testimony concerning His unique deity and His eternity. There is constant reference to "Jesus of Nazareth" but less clear is the question as to whether He was what He claimed to be, one with the Father in being as well as in fellowship.

The church today is too evidently overtaken by its worldliness. The lives of its people are often indistinguishable from those outside the church. Its prayer meetings are the poorest attended meetings of the week. Its congregations build great cathedrals to house their own worship, but often have little concern for the dying millions who have never heard of Christ. In some of our major denominations, it takes over forty congregations to support one full-time missionary on a foreign field. Rejection of such a pseudo-Christianity is evident in the striking statement, "I will spue thee out of my mouth" (Revelation 3:16). If the Laodicean church is characteristic of the church of the last days, it does not foreshadow any glorious triumph such as is prophesied in postmillennialism.

In II Timothy 3:1-5, there is a graphic picture of apostasy in the last days. Paul described it as a time of peril (II Timothy 3:1), a time when "men shall be lovers of their own selves, covetous, boasters, proud, blasphemers, disobedient to parents, unthankful, unholy, without natural affection, trucebreakers, false accusers, incontinent, fierce, despisers of those that are good, traitors, heady, highminded, lovers of pleasures more than lovers of God; having a form of godliness, but denying the power thereof: from such turn away" (II Timothy 3:2-5). His summary of the situation at the end time in II Timothy 3:13 makes it clear that the end of the age will be one of apostasy, "But evil men and seducers shall wax worse and worse, deceiving, and being deceived."

The increment of evil, the growth of hypocrisy, selfishness, and unbelief within the bounds of professing Christendom are according to Scriptures the signs of the approaching end of the age. Though there are thousands of faithful congregations and many pious souls still bearing a faithful testimony to Christ in our modern day, it is hardly true that the majority of Christendom is bearing a true testimony. It is the exception rather than the rule for the great fundamentals of the church to ring from the pulpit and for the pew to manifest the transforming grace of God in life and sacrificial devotion. In a word, the last days of the church on earth are days of apostasy, theologically and morally, days of unbelief, and days that will culminate in divine judgment.

THE RELATION OF THE RAPTURE TO THE APOSTASY

In the church at Thessalonica, a misunderstanding concerning prophecy is corrected in II Thessalonians 2. Apparently through a false letter or report, they had been led to believe that the Day of the Lord had already come, and they were now in the predicted time of trouble from which they had been assured they would be delivered in I Thessalonians 5. In correcting this misunderstanding, the apostle definitely states that the Day of the Lord cannot come until apostasy of a special character takes place as defined in II Thessalonians 2:3, 4: "Let no man deceive you by any means: for that day shall not come, except there come a falling away first, and that man of sin be revealed, the son of perdition; who opposeth and exalteth himself above all that is called God, or that is worshipped; so that he as God sitteth in the temple of God, shewing himself that he is God."

According to this revelation, the Day of the Lord which apparently follows the rapture of the church cannot come, that is, cannot fulfill its predicted character until there be "a falling away first" or, as it may be literally translated, "a departure first." It has been debated whether this departure refers to the departure of the church as indicated in the rapture or whether the traditional interpretation that it refers to a departure from the faith should be in view. If it refers to the rapture, it is an explicit statement that the rapture must occur before the Day of the Lord and it constitutes a support of the pretribulational position. If it refers to the departure from faith, i.e., apostasy, it teaches that the Day of the Lord cannot come until the man of sin be revealed, a person described as "the son of perdition; who opposeth and exalteth himself above all that is called God, or that is worshipped; so that he as God sitteth in the temple of God, shewing himself that he is God" (II Thessalonians 2:3, 4). Most expositors refer this description to the first beast of Revelation 13, the one described as the coming world ruler who will be worshiped by all men. Some refer it to the second beast of Revelation 13, that is, the false prophet who will be the religious head of the world in that day. In either case the reference is to a period between the rapture of the church and the second coming of Christ to the earth, a period described by our Lord as a time of great tribulation.

The apostasy here described, while a ·culmination of the apostasy which characterizes the end of the church age, has the peculiar character of centering in a man who claims that he is God and demands that the entire world worship him. The description corresponds to that found in Revelation 13 where the world ruler is described as one who blasphemes God, who has power for forty-two months, the exact length of the great tribulation, who makes war with the saints, who has power over all kindred, tongues, and nations, and whom all that dwell upon the earth shall worship (Revelation 13:5-8).

When the rapture of the church takes place, every true Christian will be caught up out of the world. Those who are within the professing church who are left behind are unsaved and without real redemption in Christ. There is little to hinder their progression into the utter apostasy described for this period which is completely devoid of Biblical truth. The false religion of that day will be inspired of Satan, and culminates in the worship of a man who blasphemes God and all that is called Christian. The character of apostasy before and after the rapture therefore stands in sharp contrast, though in some sense the apostasy following the rapture builds upon that which has preceded it.

As will be brought out in later discussion, apostasy in this period takes two forms. First, that which has the semblance of Christianity and is the culmination of the movement toward a world church, as will be characteristic of the first part of the period between the rapture and the second coming. Second, the final stage of apostasy will follow, which will be that predicted in II Thessalonians 2 and Revelation 13, namely, the worship of Satan's man who will be both the political dictator of the world and the object of its worship as God. The superchurch foreshadowed in Revelation 13 is seen also in Revelation 17 in the symbolism of the harlot sitting upon the beast. The final state is that of the worship of the world ruler who has destroyed the superchurch in favor of the worship of himself (Revelation 17:16).

PROPHECIES OF THE END OF THE CHURCH AGE FULFILLED

The important conclusion which may be reached upon a careful study of prophecies dealing with the end of the church age is that all that is necessary before the rapture has been fulfilled, and that we can confidently await the coming of the Lord for His church as the next step in the fulfillment of prophecy relating to the church. There is a sense in which this has always been true inasmuch as these prophecies were to some extent fulfilled even in the first century. With the passing of the years, however, the trend has been irresistibly in the direction foreshadowed by these prophecies and today the situation is clearly parallel to that which is anticipated in the great prophecies of Paul, Peter and John.

In the Middle Ages, the ignorance and unbelief of the masses as well as the blindness of the church could be traced in part to a lack of dissemination of ideas. In a modern world, however, where communications have reached a new peak with multiplied thousands of books and other publications supplemented by radio and television, there is less excuse today than ever before in the history of the world for unbelief. To a large portion of the world, at least, the facts are available for those who wish to investigate. In the face of such modern conveniences and opportunity, unbelief is all the more startling because, humanly speaking, God has no other device than that of proclamation of the truth.

The world today is responsible not because the truth is inaccessible but because they have turned away from it deliberately. There is no recourse in such a situation but divine judgment. The best efforts of the evangelical church are falling far short in keeping up with the increasing birth rate, much less countering the avalanche of unbelief and ridicule which expresses the world's attitude toward divine revelation. The stage is therefore set for a demonstration of the power of God, first in the period of judgment preceding the second coming, and then climaxing in the second coming of Christ and the gathering of the nations before the bar of divine justice.

For the true church, it means that the days of its pilgrimage may be coming fast to a close. On the one hand, this calls for expenditure of every effort to snatch as brands from the burning those who have not yet come to Christ. On the other hand, the hope of His soon return should constitute both a comfort and a challenge to be "always abounding in the work of the Lord" (I Corinthians 15:58) and to purity of life and motive (I John 3:3).

CHAPTER V

THE RESURRECTION OF THE CHURCH

The doctrine of the resurrection of the dead in Christ and the translation of the living church is one of the prominent aspects of the earlier epistles of Paul. In I and II Thessalonians, which are probably the first two books of the Bible to come from the pen of Paul, the coming of the Lord is mentioned in every chapter. In addition to the classic revelation of the resurrection and translation of the church in I Thessalonians 4:13 — 5:11, the subject is mentioned in I Thessalonians 1:10; 2:19; 3:13; 5:23; II Thessalonians 2:1-12; 3:5. In addition there seems to be a clear reference to Christ coming to establish His kingdom in II Thessalonians 1:7-10.

The ministry of the Apostle Paul to the Thessalonians is remarkable in many particulars. According to Acts 17: 1-10, Paul accompanied by Silas and Timothy had ministered in Thessalonica "three sabbath days" involving at the least fifteen days and at the most twenty-seven days. In this comparatively brief period of time, their ministry had been so effective that a small group of believers was formed. Paul had instructed them in the rudiments of the Christian faith, including the doctrine of the first coming of Christ with its gospel message and the doctrine of the second coming of Christ attended by the resurrection of the dead and the rapture of the living. In addition, he had also taught them concerning election (I Thessalonians 1:4), the Holy Spirit (1:5, 6; 4:8; 5:19), the doctrine of the assurance of salvation (1:5), the doctrine of the Trinity, Father, Son, and Holy Spirit (1:1, 5, 6, etc.), the doctrine

of conversion and Christian walk (1:9; 2:12; 4:1), sanctification (4:3; 5:23), the coming Day of the Lord (5:1-9),
and the nature of man (5:23). Though all of these doctrines may not have been explained fully or technically, it
is apparent that the Thessalonians knew something about
them, for Paul seems to appeal to previous knowledge as
he expounds these subjects in I Thessalonians.

The coming of the Lord is one of the central themes
of the Thessalonian epistles. In I Thessalonians 1:10 they
were exhorted "to wait for his Son from heaven, whom he
raised from the dead, even Jesus, which delivered us from
the wrath to come." In I Thessalonians 2:19, exulting over
the wonderful spiritual progress made by the Thessalonians
and their testimony before the world, Paul asked the question, "For what is our hope, or joy, or crown of rejoicing?"
He answered, "Are not even ye in the presence of our
Lord Jesus Christ at his coming? For ye are our glory
and joy" (I Thessalonians 2:10, 20).

In I Thessalonians 3:13, after exhorting them "to increase and abound in love one toward another and toward
all men" (I Thessalonians 3:12), he held before them the
goal of holiness at the coming of the Lord. "To the end he
may stablish your hearts unblameable in holiness before
God, even our Father, at the coming of our Lord Jesus
Christ with all his saints" (I Thessalonians 3:13). In a similar way he challenged them to realize the fullness of spiritual attainment in the Christian life and expressed the prayer
that "the very God of peace sanctify you holy; and I pray
God your whole spirit and soul and body be preserved
blameless unto the coming of our Lord Jesus Christ." It
is obvious from these references that the Thessalonians
had not only been taught the coming of the Lord, but it
was a prominent factor in Paul's exhortations to them for
holy living and faithful witness. Here as throughout the
Pauline epistles, the rapture and translation of the church
is viewed as an imminent event and one for which Christians should be constantly ready.

After Paul had left Thessalonica, being forced to flee because of the persecution which threatened his life, he sent Timothy back to Thessalonica. This is indicated in I Thessalonians 3:2, where he declared his purpose for Timothy "to establish you and to comfort you concerning your faith." Timothy after ministering to them was instructed to bring back tidings to Paul. Upon rejoining Paul, Timothy informed him of the steadfast faith of the Thessalonian Christians. They had stood fast in the midst of affliction and persecution in unwavering joy of the Spirit with the result that their testimony had reached not only to all Macedonia and Achaia, but even to more distant points, as Paul indicates in I Thessalonians 1:6-8. With the good tidings Timothy brought back to Paul were several questions the Thessalonian Christians had asked which were beyond Timothy's understanding. These are answered by the apostle in this epistle.

One of the important questions concerned the relationship of the translation of the living church to the resurrection of Christians who had died. It seems apparent that this issue had not been raised while Paul was with them at Thessalonica as they had not faced the possibility that some of their number would die before the Lord came. In the short time since Paul's departure, however, some of the Thessalonians had gone to be with the Lord, possibly as a result of persecution. Their question was whether these dead in Christ would be raised at the same time the living church was raptured, or whether this resurrection would take place at some later time.

It may be presuming too much to assume that the Thessalonians understood clearly the sequence of end-time events including the order of the rapture, followed by the time of tribulation, and climaxing in the second coming of Christ to establish His kingdom. The question, however, fits naturally into this context, inasmuch as they did not question the fact of the resurrection of the dead in Christ, but only the time when this would take place. It would seem from this that they did not have in mind, what the post-tribulationist takes for granted, that the rapture and the resurrection both occur in connection with Christ's coming to establish His kingdom.

Their understanding of prophecy presumed a series of events preceding Christ's coming to establish His kingdom. They probably would not have asked the question if they had not had in mind something equivalent to the present position of pretribulationists who hold that the rapture precedes the tribulation. Specifically, they may have wondered whether the resurrection of the church would take place in connection with Christ's establishment of His kingdom, even though the translation of living saints preceded the tribulation. In answer to this question, the classic passage beginning in I Thessalonians 4:13 constitutes the divine exposition of this important aspect of the Christian hope relating to the Lord's return.

THE COMFORT OF THE LORD'S RETURN
I Thessalonians 4:13, 14

In the introduction to the revelation concerning the rapture, the apostle begins by stating, "But I would not have you to be ignorant, brethren, concerning them which are asleep, that ye sorrow not, even as others which have no hope." In twentieth-century Christianity, it has become fashionable in some quarters to downgrade prophecy as an unimportant aspect of Biblical revelation. The plea is often made that because of the controversial character of eschatology and the fact that there is widespread difference of opinion on some important facts relating to the future, the best policy for the church would be to emphasize other aspects of Christian doctrine and to be relatively silent in the area of prophecy.

The Apostle Paul and the early church did not share this point of view, for the hope of the church and especially the hope of the Lord's return were large factors in their faith. Here the apostle rather bluntly states that he does not want the Thessalonian Christians to be ignorant concerning the facts which he is now going to expound. Instead, they should have a real hope, and he is zealous that they know the details which pertain to it.

His reason for instructing them is a practical one, namely, "that ye sorrow not, even as others which have no hope." The hopelessness of the unbeliever embodied in the expression, "no hope," is in dramatic contrast to the bright expectation of the Christian looking for the Lord. It is important to note that the unbeliever has no hope at all, that there is no second chance, no probation in the eternal state, no purgatory from which he will finally emerge acceptable to God. The future of the unbeliever is one of stark despair. The Christian, however, has a wonderful hope which Paul proceeds to unfold. This hope relates not only to the believer's personal destiny but also involves His loved ones in Christ who are described as "asleep," a softened expression for death, having implicit in it the idea that a Christian will awake at the time of the resurrection.

Not only is the Christian hope a wonderful comfort in the time of bereavement, but it is also a fundamental aspect of Christian faith. In I Thessalonians 4:14, Paul states, "If we believe that Jesus died and rose again, even so them also which sleep in Jesus will God bring with him." Here the truth of the Lord's return is tied in with the indispensable essentials of the faith, namely, that Jesus died and rose again. It should be clear to all students of Scripture that, while Christians may differ in their understanding of certain aspects of prophecy as well as in other areas of doctrine, there is an irreducible minimum to a true Christian theology apart from which Christianity loses its meanings and significance. The deity of Christ and His work on the cross in that He both died for our sins and rose again is such a central doctrine. Faith in Christ becomes meaningless unless it includes this aspect of confidence in His person and His work. This, according to I Corin-

thians 15:3, 4, is the Gospel of salvation and the faith of
every true believer, as indicated in the words of Romans
10:9, "If thou shalt confess with thy mouth the Lord Jesus,
and shalt believe in thine heart that God hath raised Him
from the dead, thou shalt be saved."

The clause, "if we believe," does not introduce an element of uncertainty but refers to the fact of faith, namely,
that which is absolutely true. The thought is, "because we
believe that Jesus died and rose again," we can have certain
hope. Just as surely as one accepts the death of Christ for
one's sin and His bodily resurrection from the grave, so
also one can accept with equal assurance the wonderful
truth of the coming of the Lord and the resurrection of
those who have died in Christ. Christian hope is an outgrowth of the historic faith of the church in what has already been accomplished in the death and resurrection of
Christ.

The expression, "them also which sleep in Jesus will
God bring with him," refers to the fact that when Christ
returns from heaven, He will be accompanied by the dead
in Christ. When Christians experience physical death on
earth, their bodies are laid in the grave, but their souls and
spirits go to be with the Lord. As Paul wrote later to the
Corinthians, "to be absent from the body" is "to be present
with the Lord" (II Corinthians 5:8). On the occasion of
His return to the earth and in anticipation of the resurrection of the bodies of the saints, the Lord brings with Him
the souls and the spirits of these who have died in Christ.
The thought is that in the resurrection their souls and
spirits will re-enter their bodies which will be restored
and transformed.

RESURRECTION BEFORE TRANSLATION
I Thessalonians 4:15, 16

The apostle now proceeds to answer their question as
to whether the translation of the living church will precede
that of the resurrection of the dead in Christ. He states

plainly that the translation of the living will not precede the resurrection of the dead: "For this we say unto you by the word of the Lord, that we which are alive and remain unto the coming of the Lord shall not prevent them which are asleep" (I Thessalonians 4:15). The revelation is introduced by the unusual phrase, "by the word of the Lord." By this should be understood that Paul had a special revelation from God on this point which preceded the writing of this Scripture. In some cases, inspiration coincides with the revelation of the truth in that the truth is contained in what is being written even though it was not previously completely understood. In this case, however, the apostle had a special revelation from God which he is now recording for the benefit of the Thessalonian church. The revelation of the order of events as given to the apostle is that the resurrection of the saints, who have died in Christ, shall occur first, and that the translation of the living saints should occur next. This is explained in the verses which follow.

Paul, in revealing the order of events, declares, "For the Lord himself shall descend from heaven with a shout, with the voice of the archangel, and with the trump of God: and the dead in Christ shall rise first" (I Thessalonians 4:16). A threefold event takes place in connection with the resurrection of the dead in Christ. First, the Lord Himself shall descend from heaven with a shout. This involves the descent of the Lord from the third heaven or the immediate presence of God in the atmospheric heaven. Upon His arrival in the earthly scene, the Lord gives "a shout." The particular Greek word used by Paul for "shout" has the meaning of a military command. No explanation is given as to the exact character of this command, but it undoubtedly refers to the resurrection of the dead and possibly includes the translation of the living saints.

At the tomb of Lazarus in John 11, it is recorded that Christ going to the tomb had cried with a loud voice, "Lazarus, come forth" (John 11:43). At the command of

Christ, Lazarus came forth still bound in grave clothes and his face covered with a napkin. To the astounded witnesses, Christ issued the order, "Loose him, and let him go" (John 11:44). This incident is in keeping with the declaration of Christ in John 5 that the dead shall be raised at His command.

In John 5:25, Christ predicted, "The hour is coming, and now is, when the dead shall hear the voice of the Son of God: and they that hear shall live." This apparently refers to those who are spiritually dead but still alive physically who shall hear the voice of the Son of God and receive eternal life. In commenting on this, He goes on to add in John 5:28, 29, "Marvel not at this: for the hour is coming, in the which all that are in the grave shall hear his voice, and shall go forth; they that have done good, unto the resurrection of life; and they that have done evil, unto the resurrection of damnation." In I Thessalonians 4, there is a partial fulfillment of this resurrection of life.

It should be clear from many other Scriptures that all the dead are not raised at the time of the resurrection of the dead in Christ. This is a resurrection of life in contrast to the resurrection of damnation which occurs over a thousand years later, as indicated in Revelation 20. At the voice of the Lord, however, the dead in Christ hear His voice and rise. This selective resurrection is described in Philippians 3:11 as "the resurrection out from among the dead" (literally translated). Just as the resurrection of Lazarus was selective in that Lazarus' name was called and only he was restored to life, so in this resurrection only the dead in Christ hear the voice and rise in answer to the summons. Christ has authority to raise all the dead and ultimately will use this authority, but here the command is addressed only to those who qualify for this particular resurrection.

Accompanying the shout of command which the Lord Himself issued is the voice of the archangel, who is called Michael five times in the Scripture (Daniel 10:13, 21; 12:1;

Jude 9; Revelation 12:7). Only here in the Bible is he referred to as the archangel without the name, and only in Jude 9 is both the name and his title of archangel mentioned. Michael has the honor of being head of the holy angels, the leader of the forces of righteousness against the forces of Satan. Some intimation of the angelic struggle with the forces of darkness is indicated in other passages of Scripture such as Daniel 10, Ephesians 6:11-18, and Revelation 12:7. Michael was not only the leader of the angelic throng, but also the special champion of Israel as shown in his relationship to Daniel in Daniel 10 and the express statement of Daniel 12:1 that he was "the great prince which standeth with the children of thy people." The introduction of the voice of the archangel at this point has suggested to some that not only the dead in Christ, that is, the saints of the present age since Pentecost, but also Israel and all the saints of the Old Testament will be included in the rapture.

A careful examination of the references pertaining to the resurrection of Israel, however, seem to point to the conclusion that Israel will be raised at the end of the tribulation rather than at its beginning. This has led some to accept the post-tribulation interpretation of the rapture on the basis that if Israel and the church are raised at the same time, and Israel is not raised until after the tribulation, the church also must endure the tribulation before experiencing resurrection and translation.

There is no reason, however, to confuse the resurrection of the church with the resurrection of Israel as these seem to be two separate events. According to Daniel 12:1, apparently at the time of the end of the great tribulation described in Daniel 11:36-45, Michael shall stand up and there shall be a "time of trouble, such as never was since there was a nation even to that same time." The deliverance of the people of Israel will then take place as indicated in the phrase, "at that time my people shall be delivered, everyone that shall be found written in the book." The deliverance obviously has to do with Israelites still living on the earth at the end of the tribulation. Immediately following this revelation, however, in Daniel 12:2, mention is made of the resurrection of Israel, "and many of them that sleep in the dust of the earth shall awake, some to everlasting life, and some to shame and everlasting contempt." Like the passage in John 5:28, 29, the resurrection of all men is included here as a fact even though that resurrection, according to other Scriptures, will take place in stages. The important point, however, in Daniel's revelation is that resurrection of Israel is associated with the deliverance of Israelites living on the earth at the end of the tribulation. Apparently the deliverance of living Israelites is going to coincide in time with the resurrection of Israelites who have died but who are worthy of everlasting life.

In view of the fact that the Scriptures clearly indicate that there will be a resurrection of the tribulation saints at the end of the tribulation period (Revelation 20:4-6), it is probable that the resurrection of Old Testament saints including the resurrection of righteous Israel will take place at the same time in preparation for the reign of Christ on earth in which some of the resurrected Israelites such as David will be prominent. The resurrection of the "dead in Christ" is a different event including only those baptized into the body of Christ, i.e., the saints of the present age.

The voice of the archangel in I Thessalonians 4:16 may be best interpreted as a shout of triumph. It is understandable that Michael, as a leader of the forces of righteousness through many millenniums, should rejoice in this great demonstration of the power and the grace of God. In spite of all that Satan had been able to do in thwarting the work and testimony of God through the centuries as witnessed in the failure of the professing church, here at long last is the church perfect and complete, a testimony to the certainty of God's divine purposes and a witness to His grace for all eternity to come. The voice of the command of the Lord is therefore accompanied by the archangel's voice of triumph.

The third stage of the events described in I Thessalonians 4:16 is that of the sounding of the trump of God. According to the context, this trump has to do with the resurrection of the dead in Christ and the translation of the living and therefore should not be confused with other trumps in Scripture. In the Old Testament, trumpets were used on a great variety of occasions and signaled various things in connection with the Word of God. In the first century the trump also was a familiar sound. It was used by the Roman soldiers for many different purposes. They were aroused in the morning by trumpets, were assembled for the march of that day by another trumpet, and the forward march was signaled by still another trumpet.

The expression here, "the trump of God," must therefore be considered a parallel to the last trump of I Corinthians 15:52, but should not be confused with other trumpets in the New Testament. In contrast to the seven trumps of angels in Revelation 8:2-9, 21; 11:15-18, this is a trump of God, a trump of grace, a trump of triumph, and a trump pertaining to the righteous dead and living saints. The trumpets of Revelation by contrast are trumps sounded by angels related to judgment poured out upon a Christ-rejecting world and signaling various catastrophes which were a form of the divine chastisement of the world in future time of tribulation. Other than the word *trump*, there is no relationship between these two events as they announce an entirely different aspect of the divine program.

The trump of God here should also not be confused with the trumpet mentioned in Matthew 24:31, though there are some similarities. The trumpet of Matthew has to do with the gathering of the elect from one end of heaven to another. Mark's Gospel adds that it also includes the uttermost part of the earth. Some have taken the elect in view in Matthew as the elect nation Israel, while others refer it to the elect of all ages, but no resurrection or translation is in view in either case. It is simply that the elect are gathered from all areas and brought together. Such a gathering will take place at the time of the second coming of Christ to establish His earthly kingdom; but those gathered include not only the resurrected and translated church, the resurrected saints of the Old Testament, and the resurrected saints of the tribulation, but extends to those who are living on earth at that time. In a word, it is all the elect in Matthew 24, whereas in I Thessalonians 4, it seems to refer only to the dead in Christ and those who are living at that time.

The expression, "the dead in Christ," is most distinctive because the phrase, "in Christ," is used in the Bible only to refer to saints who lived in the period beginning at Pentecost. The term is never used of Israel or of Gentile believers in the Old Testament, nor is it ever used of saints in the tribulation time, though Christ representatively died on the cross for all men with a special view to the salvation of the elect. The church enjoys a special relationship embodied in the phrase, "in Christ," which is a result of the baptism of the Holy Spirit (I Corinthians 12:13). It is this relationship which makes the church a distinct body of saints and marks the limits of the inclusion of the resurrection that is in view in I Thessalonians 4:16.

At the threefold event of the shout of the Lord, the voice of the archangel, and the trump of God, Paul reveals that the dead in Christ shall rise first. In other words, the first response to this great event is that the dead in Christ shall be raised. As will be considered later in the discussion of I Corinthians 15:51, 52, they will receive a resurrection body comparable to that of Christ Himself (I John 3:2), a body which will be holy, immortal, and incorruptible, suited for the presence of the holy, infinite God.

THE TRANSLATION OF THE LIVING CHURCH
I Thessalonians 4:17

Immediately following the resurrection of the dead in Christ, the living saints are declared in I Thessalonians 4:17 to be caught up to meet the Lord with the resurrected saints, "Then we which are alive and remain shall be caught up together with them in the clouds, to meet the Lord in the air: and so shall we ever be with the Lord." It is obvious from this description that the time gap between the resurrection of the dead and the translation of the living is momentary. They are "caught up together." The answer to the question which had originally been proposed by the Thessalonians is, therefore, clear. Living Christians will not have to wait for the resurrection of their loved ones for, as a matter of fact, they will precede them momentarily and having been raised from the dead will be joined by the living church which is also caught up to be with the Lord.

The expression, "caught up together," is the Biblical source of the word *rapture*. The Latin translation of "caught up" is *rapturo*, from which the English word *rapture* is derived. Though often the word *rapture* means to be carried away with joy, here it refers to a bodily "snatching up," that is, the bodily removal of the living church from the earth and meeting the Lord in the air.

It is clear from this passage that the living church at the time will never experience death. Such a possibility of passing into heaven without dying is anticipated in the translation of Enoch and Elijah in the Old Testament, the only exception to the normal rule that resurrection is preceded by death. Even Christ died on the cross and followed the order of death first, and a later resurrection. Here a whole generation of saints will pass into the immediate presence of the Lord without experiencing physical death.

The expression, "in the clouds," is without the article in the Greek, and some have interpreted this as referring not to atmospheric clouds but to the living saints appearing in great numbers as a cloud. In a similar way, there is reference in Hebrews 12:1 to "so great a cloud of witnesses." It is probable, however, that just as atmospheric clouds received the Lord when He ascended into heaven (Acts 1:9) and as He will come in "the clouds of heaven" at His return to the earth, so here also at the rapture the church will be enveloped by the atmospheric heavens and thus be taken out of sight of men on earth. There is no indication, however, that residents of earth will be able to see the church thus raptured.

The place of meeting of the church with the Lord is specified as "in the air." This makes plain that this passage does not refer to physical death as some have attempted to interpret it. The passage itself contains a sharp contrast between the dead in Christ who are resurrected and living saints who are caught up to meet the Lord. In the case of the death of Christians, their souls and spirits go to the third heaven. There is no evidence whatever that they are met by angels or by the Lord or by anyone else. Here, however, the entire company caught up at one moment is to be assembled to meet the Lord in the air.

Some have attempted to explain this expression, "in the air," as referring to the state of the church throughout the tribulation, namely, that the church is in the air, rather than on earth, but not in the third heaven. Such does not seem to be the case. According to John 14:1-3, when the Lord comes for His own, He comes to take them to the place prepared in heaven, i.e., the third heaven or the immediate presence of God. The Father's house is where God characteristically resides and this apparently is the destination of the church after meeting the Lord in the air. When the Lord returns to earth later to establish His millennial kingdom, He comes from the third heaven (Revelation 19:11). In any case, the comforting assurance is given, "so shall we ever be with the Lord." From this time on, where the Lord is, so will be the church. There will be no separation either physically or spiritually but perfect fellowship and perfect harmony. Though the apostle does not state it in so many words, it is also implicit in the passage that we will also be with our loved ones in Christ forever and that our separation from them also will cease on the occasion of the rapture of the church. This blessed prospect is the hope of the church and the reason why

Paul exhorts them to "sorrow not even as others which have no hope."

THE COMMAND TO COMFORT
I Thessalonians 4:18

The tremendous revelation concerning the coming of Christ both for the dead in Christ and living saints culminates in the exhortation, "Wherefore comfort one another with these words." Here again the apostle firmly takes the position that prophecy is a practical truth concerning which Christians should not be ignorant, and which should inspire hope and assurance, as well as comfort for those in bereavement. The word translated "comfort" implies, however, much more than simply help in times of bereavement. It has the idea of help in general, of exhortation, of urging on in the task, and of encouragement. The subject of the rapture should be included not only in the teaching and the preaching ministry of the church, but also in the conversation of Christians. They were to comfort one another with these words in times of special stress and strain when the cares of earth and its trials seemingly become burdensome. In such an hour, the comfort of the Lord's return is indescribably wonderful.

The fact that this truth is extended here to those who have lost loved ones is another indication that the Thessalonian Christians were expecting the Lord's return any day. There does not seem to be any indication in this passage that they were extended this hope only as something which could be realized after passing through the indescribable persecution of the great tribulation. Such a comfort would be tenuous at best, as the Scriptures seem to indicate the great majority of those saved in the great tribulation will perish before the second coming. If the hope of the Thessalonian Christians was endurance through this period with the possibility of survival and rapture at its end, it would not have been the comfort and hope which Paul was now expressing. In contrast to this, there is not any indication in this passage that their hope was anything other than an imminent hope. They are not warned that they must go through this period first. Instead, they have extended to them the wonderful hope that any day the Lord may come and that they may be caught up in His presence with their loved ones raised from the dead. Not only is the matter of tribulation never interposed in a rapture passage, such as this is, but in the revelation following in chapter 5 they are assured that the troubles predicted of the end times are not part of their schedule in God's program.

THE DAY OF THE LORD IMMINENT
I Thessalonians 5:1-3

Immediately following this great passage on the rapture of the church is a further discussion obviously arising from the rapture doctrine, namely, the question of the times and seasons when end-time events will have their fulfillment. In the opening verses of chapter 5, the apostle reveals that the Day of the Lord will come as a thief in the night i.e., unexpectedly and without warning: "But of the times and the season, brethren, ye have no need that I write unto you. For yourselves know perfectly that the day of the Lord so cometh as a thief in the night. For when they shall say, Peace and safety; then sudden destruction cometh upon them, as travail upon a woman with child; and they shall not escape."

In his discussion of the doctrine of the rapture, he states that he does not need to write to them concerning the times, that is, the general times, or the seasons, that is, the particular times which relate to the coming of the Lord. This is in contrast to I Thessalonians 4:13 where he states that he does not want them to be ignorant concerning the details of the prophecy concerning the rapture. Here he tells them that they already know the facts concerning the times and seasons, namely, that the coming of the Day of the Lord is imminent.

The expression, "The Day of the Lord," is a common one in both the Old and New Testament and seems to refer to that extended period of time in which the Lord will deal directly with human sin in various forms of divine judgment. The Old Testament commonly speaks of the Day of the Lord as a period characterized as "a day of darkness and gloominess, a day of clouds and of thick darkness" (Joel 2:2), "when all the inhabitants of the land tremble" (Joel 2:1), when there will be warfare and destruction of the land (Joel 2:3-9), and when "the earth shall quake. . . ; the heavens shall tremble: the sun and the moon shall be dark, and the stars shall withdraw their shining" (Joel 2:10). As Joel explains, "The day of the LORD is great and very terrible; and who can abide it?" It is, therefore, the period of divine judgment preceding the return of Christ to the earth. According to Zephaniah, however, it will also include, following the period of the "day of wrath" (Zephaniah 1:14-18), a time of rejoicing which will follow the day of judgment (Zephaniah 3:14-20). From these various passages, it has been concluded that the Day of the Lord includes not only the time of tribulation subsequent to the rapture but also the entire thousand-year reign of Christ on earth.

In the perspective of the Thessalonian church, they were living in the day of grace, the present dispensation in which God is gathering out both Jew and Gentile to form one body of the church. When the rapture occurs, this work of God will be brought to its close and the Day of the Lord will begin. Though some of its major events would not take place immediately, the period in general would extend from the rapture until the end of the millennium. This in turn would be followed by the Day of God according to II Peter 3:12, 13 beginning with the destruction of the heaven and the earth with fire and the creation of a new heaven and a new earth. The destruction, therefore, predicted by Peter in II Peter 3:10 as occurring in the Day of the Lord actually is the boundary between the Day of the Lord and the Day of God. Putting these facts together, the prophetic perspective therefore is for three general periods, the first the day of grace or the present age, next the Day of the Lord or the Day of Jehovah from the rapture to the end of the millennium, and then the Day of God or the eternal day. The coming of the Day of the Lord, therefore, is coincident with the rapture itself and for this reason the apostle discusses its arrival as if it were one and the same as the rapture of the church itself. Just as the Day of the Lord would come as a thief, so also the rapture. Though expected by those who believe in the doctrine of the rapture, it would come upon the earth in their state of total unpreparedness.

The time of the coming of the Day of the Lord is described in verse 3 as a period when the world is going to be saying, "Peace and safety." The world at that time will be considering ways and means of achieving world peace and safety apart from Christ and His kingdom of peace and righteousness. There is some indication that in the period immediately following the rapture, there will be concerted effort on the part of the world to solve the problems created by an atomic age and to do what is humanly possible — to achieve a world peace. It is in the midst of this that sudden destruction will come upon them.

This sudden destruction will be preceded by the rapture and the beginning of the period in which the sudden destruction will take place. It does not mean that the world will be destroyed immediately after the rapture of the church or at the beginning of the Day of the Lord, but the rapture of the church having already occurred, they are now plunged into the maelstrom of the judgments of God to be inflicted at the end of the age. Their situation is described as similar to that of travail coming upon a woman with child. Though the birth of a child can in general be predicted and anticipated, the exact hour is unknown. Their time of trouble, however, is just as inevitable as the ultimate birth of a child. The sad pronouncement is made, "They shall not escape." In contrast to the church which will escape, because they will be caught up to be with the Lord before this time of trouble begins, those who are left behind are inevitably doomed to pass through this time of unprecedented trouble.

THE CHURCH NOT IN DARKNESS
I Thessalonians 5:4, 5

The statement, "But ye, brethren, are not in darkness, that that day should overtake you as a thief," contrasts the position of a Christian to that of one who is an unbeliever in that day. The world at the present time is in spiritual darkness which will be followed by the Day of the Lord when the rapture occurs. By contrast, the Christian is living today in the knowledge of divine revelation. Though the church also does not know the precise date of the rapture, it is not unexpected as in the case of the unbeliever. Because of the peculiar fact that the church is going to be caught up to be with the Lord at the time the Day of the Lord begins, the Day of the Lord will not overtake the church as a thief at all and the church will lose nothing when the Day of the Lord comes.

In verse 5, the contrast between the Christian and the unbeliever is continued, "Ye are all the children of light, and the children of the day: we are not of the night, nor of darkness." The apostle reassured the Thessalonians that they are all the children of light, meaning by that all who were in the Thessalonian church. Knowing them personally, as he does, he is assured of their individual salvation as he had previously indicated in I Thessalonians 1:4-10. Christians are described as living in the light of divine revelation and the grace of God. In the latter part of the verse the apostle includes himself when he states, "we are not of the night, nor of darkness." They have the wonderful position of living in the daylight rather than in the night of unbelief and ignorance. The spiritual darkness which characterizes the unbelieving world is going to extend into the Day of the Lord even as the spiritual light which is presently possessed by the church is going to merge into the eternal light of being in the presence of the Lord. The absolute contrast between the believer and the unbeliever, established not only by the fact of their difference in relation to light but also their destiny relative to the Day of the Lord, reassured the Thessalonians that they do not need to fear this future time of trouble. It is most important to note that the apostle does not in any wise indicate that they will enter the day of the Lord and the judgments which it will bring upon the world. Rather, they have nothing to fear for the Lord is coming for them.

EXHORTATION TO WATCH AND BE SOBER
I Thessalonians 5:6-8

The fact that the Thessalonians and all other true believers are children of the light involves not only a wonderful hope but a present responsibility. Here, as throughout the Word of God, prophecy is not viewed simply as something to be admired and looked forward to but a revelation from God which emphasizes present duty and responsibility. In view of the fact that they are children of the light, he exhorts them in verse 6, "Therefore let us not sleep, as do others; but let us watch and be sober." It is characteristic for the world to sleep at night and unbelievers are spiritually asleep even in the present day of grace. By contrast, however, the Christian living in the atmosphere of spiritual light should be alert and should be watching for the coming of the Lord in contrast to drunkenness which often characterizes the world as they celebrate in the night. The Christians should watch and be sober. Concerning unbelievers, in verse 7 he states, "For they that sleep sleep in the night; and they that be drunken are drunken in the night." The world, characteristically, is either asleep or drunken in the night. In relation to their spiritual situation, they are stupefied either by sleep or by drunkenness and are unaware of their terrible danger. In exhorting the Christian to watch, it is noteworthy that Paul does not hold before them signs such as would normally be included in a revelation concerning Christ's coming to establish His kingdom as illustrated in the Olivet discourse, Matthew 24-25. Here they are exhorted to watch for the coming of the Lord itself and not for preceding signs. The idea is that the coming of the Lord is imminent and an event that they could expect at any time.

Again applying the truth that they are in the day and should be sober, he elaborates on what ought to characterize their life and testimony. They should "be sober, putting on the breastplate of faith, hope, and love" in order of experience. The Christian life begins with faith which opens the windows of the mind and heart and lets the light of the Word of God shine in. Faith is not only the means by which God pours the blessings of grace upon the believers, but it also is the breastplate, that which protects from Satan and the evil world. Through faith also comes love, both the love of God and love for fellow Christians which is a fruit of the Holy Spirit. In view of the fact that Christians will spend eternity in fellowship one with the other as well as in the presence of God, they are exhorted to begin that love relationship which is the unmistakable mark of a disciple of Jesus Christ. As Christ said in the upper room, "By this shall all men know that ye are my disciples, if ye have love one for another" (John 13:35).

The final piece of armor to protect the Christian is the helmet which is symbolically the hope of salvation. The Christian not only has salvation in the present tense in that he knows that he belongs to the Lord and is experiencing the Lord's delivering power, but the Christian also has the expectation of future deliverance such as will be his at the rapture of the church. The figure of a helmet as a type of salvation is also mentioned in the later epistle of Paul to the Ephesians (6:17) where the spiritual realities which are the possession of the Christian are described also in terms of armor. The Christian is to enter fully into what God has provided for his present pilgrim walk as well as to look for that ultimate deliverance which will bring him into the presence of the Lord.

OUR APPOINTMENT TO SALVATION, NOT TO WRATH
I Thessalonians 5:9-11

By way of summary of what the apostle has been discussing in the preceding verses of this chapter, he concludes in verse 9, "For God hath not appointed us to wrath, but to obtain salvation by our Lord Jesus Christ." This is a categorical denial that the church will go through the tribulation which is described as a day of wrath (Revelation 6:17). The whole argument of this section is that the Christian will not enter the Day of the Lord, that he belongs to a different day, that he is looking for the coming of the Lord and not for the Day of the Lord. The idea sometimes advanced that the Christian will be preserved through the tribulation and in this sense will be kept from the wrath of God is beside the point. It is not that the Christian will be kept from wrath which, of course, is always true under all circumstances even if a Christian is martyred; but it is rather that this is not our appointment. The characteristics of the day of wrath, unfolded in the book of Revelation and anticipated in prophecies concerning the Day of the Lord in the Old Testament, reveal forms of divine judgment which inevitably will afflict the entire human race. War, pestilence, famine, earthquakes, and stars falling from heaven are not by their nature selective but are almost universal in their application. This is not the Christian's appointment who is looking for the coming of the Lord at the rapture. It is rather that our expectation is one of obtaining salvation by our Lord Jesus Christ. The salvation that is here viewed as in verse 8, where it is called the "hope of salvation," is salvation in its total aspect, not simply salvation from the guilt of sin or deliverance from the present evil world, but that salvation which will be made complete when we stand in the presence of the Lord.

The deliverance which is thus provided does not stem from human attainment and righteousness but is based upon the work of Christ on the cross. This the apostle points out clearly in I Thessalonians 5:10 when in reference to the Lord Jesus Christ he states, "Who died for us, that, whether we wake or sleep, we should live together with him." He is referring in this verse to the contrast between those who have died in Christ and those who will be living at the time

Christ comes. Those who wake are those who are still alive, who have not died and who are waiting the Lord at His coming. Those who sleep are those who have fallen asleep in Jesus. Both classifications are going to live together with Christ forever once the rapture of the church has taken place.

As in the close of chapter 4, so here after the discussion of the Day of the Lord and the Christian's deliverance from it, he closes with the exhortation in I Thessalonians 5:11, "Wherefore comfort yourselves together, and edify one another, even as also ye do." They are to comfort or exhort one another on the basis of this truth and also to edify or build up one another in the Christian faith. After a further series of exhortations in I Thessalonians 5:12-22, Paul concludes with the final appeal again stemming from the hope of the Lord's return: "And the very God of peace sanctify you wholly; and I pray God your whole spirit and soul and body be preserved blameless unto the coming of our Lord Jesus Christ." They are, therefore, exhorted, to be living not as those who anticipate a time of dark tribulation such as the great tribulation, nor the Day of the Lord with its hour of the wrath of God poured out upon the earth, but they should be rather looking forward in anticipation and joyous expectation to the coming of the Lord in seeking to live day by day by the power of the Spirit in such a way that they will be preserved blameless in body, soul, and spirit at that future wonderful event. In closing the first epistle, he assures them in I Thessalonians 5:24, "Faithful is he that calleth you, who also will do it."

The glad day when these events will be fulfilled for the Christian may soon be upon us, for if the coming of the Lord was imminent in the first century, it is even more so in this present hour. The promises of God stand undimmed from the erosion of time, and in God's appointed hour He will come for His own even as the infallible Word of God promises.

CHAPTER VI

THE TRANSLATION OF THE CHURCH

Though the translation of the living church is expressly taught in I Thessalonians 4:17 and implied in numerous other passages including John 14:3, its formal exposition was undertaken later by the Apostle Paul in I Corinthians 15:51-58. This passage and I Thessalonians 4:13 — 5:11 are the two classic passages on the rapture of the church and constitute its major exposition.

THE CONTEXT OF THE TRANSLATION IN I CORINTHIANS

The revelation concerning the translation of the living church in I Corinthians 15:51-58 comes as the climax to the divine instruction as found in the preceding chapters. The Corinthian church had the unenvied distinction of portraying in its experience most of the frailties of the church throughout its history. After only a brief introduction in the first chapter, the apostle plunged immediately into a long series of admonitions and rebukes. The Corinthian church was divided into four parties, those following Paul, Apollos, Cephas, and Christ. Their differences had arisen from their adoption of human leaders and those following Christ were perhaps the most hypocritical. The Corinthians had also imbibed some of the Greek pride in their heritage, and their love of worldly wisdom had led them to regard the preaching of the cross as rather naive. Paul had to defend the Gospel as the wisdom of God. The apostle also rebuked them for being carnal and unable to receive the deeper things of divine revelation. He had to chide them for building their lives of wood, hay, and stubble, when they should have been erecting edifices of gold, silver, and precious stone, upon the foundation which is Jesus Christ.

In the church at Corinth, there was a notorious case of incest which they had not judged or regarded seriously. In their midst also were those who were going to courts of law to settle their disputes. Some of their number had apparently stumbled at the sanctity of the human body and were at least tempted to return to the gross immorality which characterized the pagan religions of that day. The apostle had to enlarge upon the sanctity of marriage and the responsibility it represents to Christians.

The matter of Christian liberty was also a serious problem in the Corinthian church. Some of their number tended to continue their fellowship with pagans who worshiped idols, and the Corinthians had to be reminded that they would only hurt their testimony by association in the pagan feasts. The church at Corinth had been guilty also of disorders at the Lord's table, observing it in an irreverent and thoughtless manner and without proper spiritual preparation.

Three long chapters had to be devoted to their foolish exaltation of the gift of tongues and the gift of healing, to the neglect of important gifts of proclaiming the Word of God and teaching it faithfully. In the process of all these difficulties, the Corinthian church had lost sight of the fact that service without love is empty. The exhortation of the apostle as contained in I Corinthians 13 is a classic in Biblical exhortation. It was only after this debris had been cleared away that Paul was able to get to the subject that was most on his heart, namely, the great fundamentals of the faith including the precious truths of the Lord's return for His own.

THE DOCTRINE OF RESURRECTION

In the opening verses of the fifteenth chapter of I Corinthians, Paul reminded them of the Gospel that he preached which had resulted in their salvation. He defined this Gospel as the fact that Christ died and rose again, "For I delivered unto you first of all that which I also received, how that Christ died for our sins according to the scriptures" (I Corinthians 15:3, 4). In affirming the fact that Christ died for our sins according to the Scriptures, the apostle is reminding them that this is a fulfillment of the plan of God foretold early in the Old Testament and now fulfilled in the work of Christ on Calvary. The fact that Christ is buried indicates the certainty of His death lest any should foolishly believe that He merely had swooned and had not really died.

They are again reminded that Christ rose from the dead on the third day, according to the Scriptures, alluding to the prophecies of Psalm 16:10, which Peter had also cited in his Pentecostal sermon in Acts 2:22-31. In the verses which follow, Paul presents the proofs which demonstrate the certainty of His bodily resurrection, namely that He was seen of Cephas, then of the Twelve, and on one occasion by more than five hundred people at once. As far as the apostle himself was concerned, the final proof was the appearance of Christ to him on the way to Damascus.

Having established the certainty of the resurrection of Christ, the argument then proceeds to the theology which results from this event. Some in the Corinthian church, as he indicates in I Corinthians 15:12, had denied bodily resurrection of the dead. The apostle demonstrates that if Christ is not risen, then there is no Christian faith. The Gospel also becomes meaningless and Paul's preaching becomes empty. As a matter of fact, the apostle says that those who preach the Gospel would be "false witnesses of God" when they preached His death for our sins and His bodily resurrection if actually there were no bodily resurrection. He concludes in I Corinthians 15:19, "If in this life only we have hope in Christ, we are of all men most miserable."

Having demonstrated the theological necessity of the resurrection of Christ for the total Christian faith, Paul builds the whole future program of God upon the fact of Christ's resurrection, including not only the resurrection of men but the ultimate victory of Christ over the world

"when he shall have put down all rule and all authority
and all power" (I Corinthians 15:24). A long discussion
follows, showing the necessity of death and resurrection.
The present body of sinful men is not suited for the presence of God due to the fact that it is mortal or subject to
death. The human body is natural and belongs to this
world and is corruptible or subject to decay and age. What
man needs is a spiritual body suited for the presence of
God, a body which will not grow old and which will not
be subject to death. The normal means for obtaining this
body is for the old body to die and to be buried, and the
new body must be formed in the act of resurrection as in
the case of Jesus Christ. This is God's appointed method
of solving the problem stated in I Corinthians 15:50, "that
flesh and blood cannot inherit the kingdom of God; neither
doth corruption inherit incorruption." It is with this comprehensive introduction that the apostle moves now in the
latter part of this chapter into the great truth of the translation of the church.

THE MYSTERY OF THE TRANSLATION OF THE CHURCH

In I Corinthians 15:51-53, the wonderful truth is announced that the bodies of living saints at the time of the
coming of the Lord will be instantly transformed from mortal bodies to immortal and from corruptible bodies to incorruptible: "Behold, I shew you a mystery; We shall not all
sleep, but we shall all be changed, in a moment, in the
twinkling of an eye, at the last trump: for the trumpet
shall sound, and the dead shall be raised incorruptible, and
we shall be changed. For this corruptible must put on
incorruption, and this mortal must put on immortality."

It is most significant that this truth is introduced as
"a mystery." The word *mystery* is found twenty-seven times
in the New Testament and is used to describe a divine
secret not revealed in the Old Testament but revealed at
least to some extent in the New. The descriptive definition
given in Colossians 1:26 brings this out: "Even the mystery

which hath been hid from ages and from generations, but now is made manifest to his saints." The truth of the translation of the church is therefore described as New Testament truth.

The Old Testament records the notable illustration of translation in the cases of Enoch and of Elijah who went to heaven without dying. There is no intimation in the Old Testament of the idea of a whole generation of saints being translated in this way. By contrast, the Old Testament in its prophecies of the second coming of Christ shows life as continuing on earth and the saints surviving the great tribulation are seen entering the millennial earth and continuing in their natural state. It is for this reason that the apostle declares that the truth of the translation of the church is a mystery.

It was, of course, no secret that when Christ would come back to earth to establish His kingdom there would be living people on earth at that time who would be numbered among the saints. This, of course, was anticipated in Old Testament prophecies concerning His second coming, but no rapture is ever indicated in these prophecies. The new truth which is here being revealed relates to an earlier coming of Christ, preceding the tribulation. Saints living on earth at the time of the rapture will never die physically, but instead will experience an instantaneous change from their present bodies to bodies that are suited for the presence of God. This transformation is the translation of the church and parallels the resurrection of the dead in Christ. According to verse 52 it will occur in a moment and in the twinkling of an eye. In other words, it will take place instantaneously at the sounding of the last trump. This trump is to be identified with the trump of God in I Thessalonians 4:16 and is not to be confused with other trumps that deal with other issues such as the trumps of the angels in the book of Revelation or the trump gathering all the elect in Matthew 24:31. The context relates this trump to the resurrection of the dead in Christ and the translation of living saints. It does not have any effect upon the population of the world as a whole and is not related to any judgment such as will be inflicted upon the earth in the end times.

Just as the dead in Christ receive a new body by resurrection, so living saints will be given a new body by translation. Instantaneously, they will exchange the bodies which they have in this present life for new bodies described in this revelation as incorruptible and immortal. They are incorruptible in the sense that they will be ageless and not subject to the normal progression of decay which is so manifest in natural life. They will also be immortal or deathless. Apparently their bodies thus transformed will endure forever. Though the apostle does not state it in so many words, it is obvious also that their bodies will be holy, patterned after the resurrection body of Christ. According to I John 3:2, "When he shall appear, we shall be like him; for we shall see him as he is." Christians living today, therefore, have the prospect of this instantaneous change at the time that the Lord comes back to raise the dead in Christ and to translate the living church.

Aside from the revelation given in I Corinthians 15, there is no other extended passage dealing with the resurrection body and its characteristics. The apostle's description makes clear that the resurrection body will be incorruptible (I Corinthians 15:42), a body of glory (cf. Philippians 3:21), and power (v. 43), a spiritual rather than a natural body (v. 44), a heavenly body (vv. 48, 49), and an immortal body (v. 53).

Much light is cast on the truth of our resurrection body by examining the description of the body of Christ following His resurrection. Prior to the resurrection of Christ, there were numerous cases of people raised from the dead and restored to life. In all these instances, such as that of Lazarus in John 11, the resurrection is in the form of restoration, that is, those restored to life receive the same body which they had when they died. It is assumed that all of these characters in Scripture died subsequently and their bodies were buried. Actually, their resurrection was a restoration, not a transformation such as is expected in the resurrection of Christ. When Christ rose from the dead, He began the order of the first resurrection, mentioned in Revelation 20:5, 6, as including the resurrection of all the saints regardless of time.

At the time of the resurrection of Christ, according to Matthew 27:52, 53, following the earthquake and the rending of the temple, "the graves were opened; and many bodies of the saints which slept arose, and came out of the grave after his resurrection, and went into the holy city, and appeared unto many." This mysterious event attending the resurrection of Christ is nowhere explained in the Bible. A careful reading of the passage will indicate that the resurrection here mentioned took place not at the time of the death of Christ, but after His resurrection as stated in Matthew 27:53. It would hardly seem possible for them to have been raised from the dead and remain in the grave in that state for three days. Therefore, the statement that they came out of the grave after His resurrection also seems to date the time of the resurrection. Though some believe that these were only restored to life, the preferable view is that they actually were raised and given resurrection bodies. There is no evidence that this resurrection included all the saints of the Old Testament, but rather only a few. The passage does not say that all the saints arose but only that "many bodies" were involved.

It is probable that the reason for this strange event stems from the ceremony of the feast of the first fruits which was part of Israel's religious program for each year. In the feast of first fruits as described in Leviticus 23:9-14, the children of Israel were instructed at the time when the harvest began to bring a sheaf of the grain unto the priest. The priest would wave this before the Lord, offering a male lamb as a sacrifice along with a meal offering and a drink offering. The significance of the sheaf of grain was that it was not only one stalk but a handful. The handful was a token of the coming complete harvest. This accordingly was fulfilled at the time of the resurrection of Christ. The great fact was not only that Christ Himself was raised from the dead but that this was the token of the harvest to come. The saints, therefore, who were raised after Christ's resurrection were the divine pledge of God's intent to raise all the saints in their order and according to the divine program.

Of great significance, however, is the series of appearances of Christ following His resurrection. According to John 20, the first appearance was to Mary Magdalene. She had come early in the morning and found the tomb empty and had rushed back to tell the disciples that someone had taken the body of her precious Lord. After delivering her message, she had come back to the garden and there was weeping not knowing what else to do about the situation. As she looked into the sepulchre, she saw two angels, according to John 20:12, who said to her, "Woman, why weepest thou?" (John 20:13). She replied, "Because they have taken away my Lord, and I know not where they have laid Him" (John 20:13). Turning around, she saw Jesus standing but did not recognize Him. Jesus addressed her, "Woman, why weepest thou? whom seekest thou?" (John 20:15). Mary did not immediately recognize the Lord possibly because she was weeping and took Him to be the gardener. In addressing Him accordingly, she said, "Sir, if thou have borne him hence, tell me where thou hast laid him, and I will take him away" (John 20:15). At this query, Jesus replied simply, "Mary."

Recognizing His voice, Mary said, "Rabboni" (John 20:16), or "Master." Jesus then said to her, "Touch me not, for I am not yet ascended to my father: but go to my brethren, and say unto them, I ascend unto my Father, and your Father; and to my God, and your God" (John 20:17). From the fact that Jesus told her "Touch me not," literally, "Stop clinging to me," it seemed that Mary in her ecstasy had embraced her Lord bodily. Christ gently reproved her by reminding her that He had not yet ascended to His Father and instructed her to tell the brethren of His resurrection.

In the details of Mary's encounter with Christ, two important facts stand out. First, Mary recognized Christ's voice. From this preliminary statement, it can be seen that the resurrection body is to be identified with the body of this life in various ways including that of voice. Our loved ones in heaven will not be strangers to us and regardless of what language may be used in heaven, we will be able to recognize their voices as the voices of those whom we loved and held in earth. Second, it is obvious that in embracing the Lord there is a testimony to the reality of the resurrection body. Mary did not grasp thin air. This was not simply a mirage or a spirit. Christ had a real body. This, of course, is a natural deduction from the fact that His body in which He had died on the cross had departed from the tomb. The old body was gone. The new body, though it had differing characteristics, was nevertheless a real body.

Later, when the other women went to meet the Lord according to Matthew 28:9, they were greeted by Christ, "All hail." The passage goes on to say, "And they came and held him by the feet, and worshipped him." Here again it is evident that Christ had a real body and that when they held Him by the feet they found there was real substance to them. In fact, as we learn later, the nailprints were still in the feet from His crucifixion. Still later, on the resurrection day, the Scriptures record that Christ met Peter. There was a wonderful restoration of the one who had denied his Lord thrice (Luke 24:34; I Corinthians 15:5).

The next appearance was to the disciples on the road to Emmaus, recorded in Luke 24:13-32. In this extended passage in which Christ discusses His own death and resurrection with Cleopas and His unnamed companion, He was not immediately known to these disciples. This is explained in Luke 24:16 by the fact that "their eyes were holden that they should not know him." In other words, if there had not been a supernatural blindness imposed upon them, they would have immediately recognized the Lord. Considering the natural unbelief and incredulity attending the recognition of one who has died and has been raised from the dead, it is most significant that in the resurrection appearances the identity of the Lord is unquestioned, and any delay in His recognition is always carefully explained in the Scriptures. In this instance, Christ in order to minister to these disciples withheld His identification until he had unfolded the wonderful truth of the Messianic prophecies of the Old Testament. How marvelous it would have been if we could have had this discussion recorded for us today.

It was not until they came to Emmaus at the eventide and Christ "took bread, and blessed it, and brake, and gave to them," that "their eyes were open, and they knew him" (Luke 24:30, 31). However, as soon as they recognized Him, He vanished from their sight. Then they became aware of the fact that there had been a strange excitement in their hearts as they had talked with Him concerning the Old Testament Scriptures. Luke 24:32 says, "And they said one to another, Did not our heart burn within us, while he talked with us by the way, and while he opened to us the scriptures?" Luke records that they then returned to Jerusalem and found the eleven faithful disciples. From them, the two disciples learned that Christ had indeed been raised from the dead and had appeared to Simon Peter who was there. Then they also gave their report how Christ had appeared to them in the way and how He was revealed to them when He broke the bread.

Having already thus appeared four times on the resurrection day, the fifth appearance is now recorded in Luke 24:36. Apparently without any opening of the door, Christ is revealed to have suddenly appeared in the room. Luke 24:36 states, "And as they thus spake, Jesus himself stood in the midst of them, and saith unto them, Peace be unto you." Such a dramatic appearance, of course, terrified them as recorded in Luke 24:37. They thought they were seeing a spirit. In reply, however, Christ said unto them, "Why are ye troubled? and why do thoughts arise in your hearts? Behold my hands and my feet, that it is I myself: handle me, and see; for a spirit hath not flesh and bones, as ye see me have" (Luke 24:38, 39). From this pronouncement of Christ, a number of things become immediately apparent.

First of all, the disciples had no reason for fear. The fact of the resurrection should be a tremendous comfort and blessing to believers, and Christ wanted His disciples to enter into this glorious truth. In order to dissipate their fear that He was an apparition, He invited them to inspect His hands and His feet. It is evident from John 20:27, in a later appearance, that the nailprints were still in His hands and the wounds still in His side, and it may be presumed that the nailprints were still also in His feet. Here was unmistakable evidence that this was indeed Christ and not someone else. His was a real body to be identified with the one that died on the cross even though marvelously transformed and changed into a resurrection body. He invites them to handle Him, indicating that His body was a body of tangible form.

Further He declares that He has both flesh and bones. From this can be learned that the resurrection body is not a body which deceived the senses and gave the impression of being a physical body without the corresponding reality. Christ says that His body had both flesh and bones. The resurrection body, therefore, will correspond to our present physical bodies in outward characteristics and will have both flesh and bone, though the actual physical substance may differ. It is most significant, however, that no mention is made of blood. In I Corinthians 15:50, Paul had concluded: "Now this I say, brethren, that flesh and blood cannot inherit the kingdom of God; neither doth corruption inherit incorruption." By this, Paul meant the type of flesh that we have now with its blood virculation which sustains the body is not a suitable type of body for heaven. Our resurrection body will have a new flesh which will be sinless and not subject to the restoration principles involved in our present body.

As the disciples pondered these proofs of the resurrection of Christ, for joy they could hardly bring themselves to believe the evidence which was before them (Luke 24:41). Christ asked them for food (Luke 24:42, 43), and taking the broiled fish and honey, He ate it before them. It was another form of demonstration that He had a real body and was not merely a spirit. It also introduced the interesting conclusion that in their resurrection bodies, the saints will be able to eat food, though apparently it will not be necessary for sustaining life or strength.

Though Luke 24:33 indicates that the disciples returning from Emmaus had gone to the "eleven gathered together," it is evident from John 20:24 that Thomas was not there and only ten of the eleven disciples were actually in the upper room. It was not until a week later that Thomas had the joy of meeting his Lord. The subsequent experience, however, confirms the evidence previously presented. Thomas, according to John 20:25, found it impossible to believe that Jesus was actually raised from the dead and had said to the disciples: "Except I shall see in his hands the print of the nails, put my finger into the print of the nails, and thrust my hand into his side, I will not believe."

A week later, as Thomas and the other disciples were in a room with the door shut, Jesus again appeared to them and, as in His former appearance, said, "Peace be unto you" (John 20:26). Then addressing Himself to Thomas, our Lord said, "Reach hither thy finger, and behold my hands; and reach hither thy hand, and thrust it into my side: and be not faithless, but believing" (John 20:27). In reply, Thomas, forgetting his unbelief and his dogmatic demands for factual evidence replied, "My Lord and my God" (John 20:28). Thomas needed no proof. The evidence was all too clear that this was indeed the Lord and Saviour.

The fact, however, that Christ invited him to inspect His body to see the evidences of His crucifixion proves that it was the same body which died on the cross. In commenting on Thomas' unbelief changed into faith, Christ said, "Thomas, because thou hast seen me, thou hast believed: blessed are they that have not seen, and yet have believed" (John 20:29).

Subsequent appearances of Christ confirm this evidence. The body of Christ was identified with the body He had prior to His death. It was a body of flesh and bone which had real substance. His voice as well as His general appearance could be identified as belonging to the same person who was with the disciples through their years of fellowship with Him prior to Calvary. It was a body, therefore, which could be seen and felt, a body which could consume food, a body which in many respects corresponds in appearance to our present earthly bodies, and yet marvelously delivered from limitations which hinder here. There is no evidence, for instance, that Christ walked back from Emmaus to Jerusalem. Apparently transportation takes on a new character for a resurrection body. It was also true that He could enter rooms with the doors being shut, indicating that physical confinement is not possible for a resurrection body. In all of these things, the testimony is that the resurrection body of believers, patterned after the resurrection body of Christ, will be wonderfully delivered from the limitations of this life and will be gloriously suited for the immediate presence of the Lord.

A most significant fact is often overlooked in I Corinthians 15:51-53 in that the passage states plainly, "We shall all be changed." In the consideration of the problem of the time of the rapture, many have followed the conclusion that the translation of the church is somehow to be identified as a part of Christ's coming to establish His kingdom on the earth. This is known as the post-tribulation rapture view as opposed to the pretribulation rapture teaching which holds that the translation takes place some years before Christ returns to establish His kingdom. In the simple expression, "We shall all be changed," there seems to be decisive evidence that the rapture must be distinguished from the second coming of Christ to the earth. In fact, it demands that there be a considerable time period between these two events.

If an attempt is made to reconstruct the usual post-tribulational concept, it is evident that in order to accommodate I Thessalonians 4:17 the rapture must take place in the process of Christ's procession from heaven to the earth at that moment when He enters the atmospheric heaven. In other words, the rapture in the post-tribulation theory must occur before Christ ever actually comes to the earth itself and His feet touch the Mount of Olives (Zechariah 14:4). It should be further evident that, if the rapture takes place at this time, all the saints will be with the Lord in the air and all the remaining people on the earth are those who are not saved.

The Scriptures seem to indicate plainly that at the second coming of Christ all unbelievers are purged out. This is the teaching of the parable of the wheat and the tares, and it is plainly indicated in such passages as Revelation 14:9-12 which reveals that all worshipers of the beast will be put to death. According to Revelation 13:8, everyone on earth will worship the beast except true believers. According to Matthew 25:31-46, the goats representing the unsaved among Gentiles will also be purged out as will the rebels of Israel representing unbelief in Israel according to Ezekiel 20:38.

Those who hold the premillennial interpretation of Scripture are, therefore, faced with an insuperable problem if they attempt to accommodate this with the post-tribulational idea. If all the wicked are put to death and if all the saints are translated, it leaves no one in their natural bodies to populate the millennial earth. Hence, the simple fact that everyone will be transformed who believes in Christ on the occasion of the rapture of the church makes it necessary to move this event forward and leave a sufficient time period between the rapture and Christ's coming

to establish His kingdom to raise up a whole new generation of saints from both Jews and Gentiles to populate the
millennial earth. Thus, the godly remnant of Israel will
come into being after the rapture and during the time of
trouble preceding the second coming of Christ. Likewise
among the Gentiles there will be raised up a host of believers, some of whom will survive the martyrdom, which
many will suffer, and will be on earth waiting for the coming of the Lord. These will be the sheep of Matthew 25.
There seems to be built into the revelation concerning
the rapture of the church that this is an event distinct from
the second coming and one which could not be fulfilled si-
multaneously with it.

The expression, "We shall all be changed," is also significant as making impossible the contention of those who
hold to a partial rapture, namely, that at the coming of
Christ for His church only those especially spiritual or un-
usually well prepared who are looking for His coming will
be raptured. It is rather that "all" will be involved. This
means all Christians in Christ, whether they are what they
ought to be or not, are raised from the dead, if in the grave,
or translated, if living in the earth. The issue will not be
spirituality but whether they have been born again and
have been baptized into the body of Christ by the Spirit
of God.

A careful study of the major rapture narratives found in
I Corinthians 15 and I Thessalonians 4 would do much to
correct the confusion that exists in the modern church
concerning the time and character of the rapture itself.
Too often theories are advanced with little reference to
the details of these specific revelations, and with an impa-
tience to account for the specifics which are enfolded in
the Word of God.

As previously indicated, "the last trump" is to be
identified with the trump of I Thessalonians 4:16 where it
is called "the trump of God." The question, however, has
been raised why the words, "the last," should be used. It
seems apparent from Matthew 24:31 that this is not the last

trumpet in the sequence of events. The answer seems to be simply that this is the final call for the church. Whether or not there are any previous trumpets to be sounded in the history of the church, this is the last one. As pointed out earlier, it may be that Paul is using a familiar pattern established in his day by the Roman soldiers. As was commonly known, a series of trumpets marked the beginning of their day; the first, raising them from sleep, the second, calling them to form the march of the day, and the third or last in the series, signaling the beginning of the march. The last trump then is for the church a "forward march" or actually a command to rise to meet the Lord in the air. The church previously had heard the call of the Gospel through the convicting power of the Spirit. They had listened to the exhortation of the Word of God as applied by the Spirit to their life and witness. Now the time had come to begin the majestic march to glory and the last trump sounded. If normal rules of exegesis be applied to this, the passage loses much of its problem. The context plainly indicates that this trump has to do with resurrection and translation whereas other trumps of the New Testament have an entirely different context and in none of them is either resurrection or translation involved.

THE HOPE OF VICTORY OVER DEATH

In I Corinthians 15:54-57, the apostle sounds a note of praise for the victory over death which Christians translated at the rapture will experience. This will be shared by those who have died and are raised from the dead at this time. He writes the Corinthians, "So when this corruptible shall have put on incorruption, and this mortal shall have put on immortality, then shall be brought to pass the saying that is written, Death is swallowed up in victory. O death, where is thy sting? O grave, where is thy victory? The sting of death is sin; and the strength of sin is the law. But thanks be to God, which giveth us the victory through our Lord Jesus Christ" (I Corinthians 15: 54-57).

The ultimate victory for all Christians will be achieved on that glad day when corruption and mortality will be replaced by incorruption and immortality. Paul says that then will be fulfilled the prediction of Isaiah 25:8 embodied in the expression, "Death is swallowed up in victory." It should be obvious that the translation and resurrection of the church is only a partial fulfillment of the Isaiah passage, as Isaiah contemplates this as it embraces all humanity including Israel. The final victory over death does not come until after the millennium. At present, Christians do not have victory over death, but when this event takes place their victory will be complete and no longer will they be subject to death and decay.

As the apostle exults in the coming victory over death, he raises the question, "O death, where is thy sting? O grave, where is thy victory?" (I Corinthians 15:55). He gives the answer in verse 56, "The sting of death is sin, and the strength of sin is the law." Physical death afflicts the Christian because of the inexorable law of judgment pronounced upon Adam that his body should return to the dust. Though Christians are relieved from the guilt of sins, somehow the principle of death continues for those who have died preceding the rapture of the church. That the law is reversed for those translated at the rapture proceeds from the pure grace of God which has satisfied the law and in this case finds it unnecessary to exact this form of divine judgment upon sin. As the apostle states in I Corinthians 15:57, "But thanks be to God, which giveth us the victory through our Lord Jesus Christ." The translation of living saints as well as the resurrection of the dead in Christ is a part of God's program of salvation for those who have put their faith in Christ. It is the ultimate form of salvation which was begun at the moment of faith in Christ and completes the plan of God that every true believer should be presented faultless in His presence. By faith, the Christian even in the midst of earth's trials can contemplate this future victory which will be true of every Christian, made possible entirely by the finished work of

Christ on the cross and His own triumph over death in bodily resurrection.

As in other prophetic portions of the New Testament, the truth of the rapture leads naturally to a stirring exhortation with which chapter fifteen of I Corinthians concludes, "Therefore, my beloved brethren, be ye stedfast, unmoveable, always abounding in the work of the Lord, forasmuch as ye know that your labour is not in vain in the Lord." Here is the watchword for those who are looking for the coming of the Lord. They should first of all be steadfast, a word meaning to become seated or to put your full weight upon. God wants us to rest upon these promises and depend upon the certain fulfillment of the promises of resurrection and translation. In facing the storms of life, the Christian should also be unmoveable. This solid situation can only be possible as the Christian rests upon Christ the Rock who cannot be moved. The exhortation, however, does not contemplate simply standing or holding our ground, but the idea is presented that if we believe in the coming of the Lord, we should be "always abounding in the work of the Lord." This superabundant expression indicates that Christians should be busy about our Lord's work at all times and to the greatest possible extent. The teaching of the rapture does not properly lead to an attitude of the folded hands. There is much to be done and the time is short. One who believes the rapture will instead be ceaselessly active in the work while there is yet time.

The apostle concludes the exhortation by the reminder, "Forasmuch as ye know that your labour is not in vain in the Lord." Following the rapture of the church will come the judgment seat of Christ when the church in heaven receives her rewards. Christians are reminded that there is a day of reckoning coming when they as stewards must give an account. It will be a glad day for those who have been faithful in their service for the Lord as they receive their just due.

Chapter VII

THE IMPORTANCE OF THE RAPTURE

The doctrine of the coming of the Lord for His own with its promise of the resurrection of the dead in Christ and the translation of the living church was a prominent feature in the church of the first century. Most scholars agree that the early church believed in the imminent return of the Lord and considered it a possibility that the Lord could come at any time. Such a hope seemed to have permeated apostolic thinking. In I and II Thessalonians, for instance, it is mentioned in every chapter. Most of the epistles make some mention of the coming of the Lord and anticipate the end of the age.

In spite of the apostolic emphasis on the doctrine, there is a studied avoidance of the subject in much of the theological literature of the past and present. Many systematic theologies barely mention the subject of the rapture, and, if mentioned at all, it is included as a minor phase of end-time events. In modern liberalism and neo-orthodoxy, no attention whatever is paid to the subject of the rapture. Even in conservative theological discussion, the tendency is to play down the importance of this theme of Scripture.

This neglect of the doctrine of the rapture is all the more remarkable because the place given to the rapture in any system of theology is a significant commentary upon its theological premises, its hermeneutical principles, and its prophetic program as a whole. An analysis of the doctrine of the rapture in relationship to theology as a whole will demonstrate that the doctrine has significance far beyond its own particulars, and that, therefore, conclusions reached concerning the rapture reveal a system of thought. The con-

tention of some contemporary scholars that eschatology is
unimportant and that the rapture doctrine in particular is
a matter of little interest to theology as a whole is an error
of considerable proportion.

THEOLOGICAL PREMISES OF THE RAPTURE

In the study of the truth concerning the rapture of the
church, it soon becomes apparent that one of the major issues is the inspiration of the Scriptures. Modern liberals
who deny that the Bible is the infallible Word of God have
in general taken the position that prophecy is an impossibility. Passages in the New Testament, therefore, which
speak of the rapture they consider a record of the hope
of the early church or in some cases a statement of divine
purpose. They do not believe that prophecy should be accepted at face value as a bona fide prediction of a future
event. Liberals, when pressed, will acknowledge that human life cannot go on forever and that there must be some
end to human existence in this present state. Nevertheless, they deny that the Bible outlines in any specific way
a future program which will be literally fulfilled. The dis-
interest of the church at large in the doctrine of the rapture
may be traced in part to this attitude of unbelief in prophecy
as a whole and questions concerning the authority, integrity,
and accuracy of Scripture. Accordingly, writers who do not
accept the infallibility of the Scriptures seldom add anything to the doctrine of the rapture, and for the most part
avoid or ignore the subject completely.

Only theological conservatives can engage in any vital
discussion concerning the rapture. Normally, they hold to
the concept that the Bible can predict the future. Regardless of their particular point of view, they usually agree
that the Bible predicts the end of the age and a personal,
bodily return of the Lord. For such, the question is how
the passages dealing with the translation of the living
church and the resurrection of the dead in Christ relate to
end-time events. Their judgments in these areas are largely

determined by their broader eschatological conviction, namely, whether they are premillennial, postmillennial, or amillennial.

Generally speaking, amillenarians, such as have followed the traditional view of Augustine, have combined the doctrine of the rapture with the second coming of Christ to the earth at the end of the age. They seldom, therefore, give separate consideration to this truth and regard it merely as an incident in the total program which brings human history to a close. One, therefore, can hardly expect an amillenarian to deal adequately with this doctrine. Usually their writings tend to refute pretribulationism or premillennialism, as the case might be, rather than to set up their own doctrine of the rapture.

Practically the same point of view is adopted by the postmillennialist of the conservative type. They, too, tend to combine all end-time events as having their culmination in the second coming of Christ, and the rapture becomes a phase of this program. In their writings likewise the rapture is given scant attention. It is only in premillennial discussion that the rapture doctrine has assumed any large proportion. For all practical purposes, a formal consideration of the rapture of the church, including the debate as to when it will occur in relationship to other events, is a problem within premillennialism.

If the view of the partial rapture concept be excluded, there are three major viewpoints advocated today, namely, pretribulationism, midtribulationism, and post-tribulationism. Of primary interest and contrast is the post-tribulational view as compared to the pretribulational view. Post-tribulationism views the rapture as occurring in the sequence of events described as the second coming of Christ. They believe the church will be raptured at the time Christ is descending from heaven to the earth. The church will be translated, according to I Thessalonians 4, meet the Lord in the air, and then continue with the heavenly throng to the earth to accompany Christ in His establishment of the millennial kingdom. The post-tribulational view, as held by some premillenarians, is often quite similar to that advocated by the amillenarian, differing from it principally in its concept of the millennial reign of Christ following the rapture. For the amillenarian the eternal age begins immediately.

The post-tribulationism of our day in some respects corresponds to the view of the early church fathers and in other aspects is decidedly different and recent. In the church of the second and third century, it was commonly believed that the church was already in the great tribulation predicted by Christ. For this reason, they believed in the imminency of Christ's return as an event which could happen any day. Their view of the Lord's return was that it was both post-tribulational and imminent.

Most conservative scholarship agrees that the early church fathers were in error in their conclusion that they were already in the great tribulation. The passing of the centuries makes it clear that their persecutions were those which could be normally expected throughout the age rather than the particular trials which could be expected in the great tribulation. Modern post-tribulationists, however, believe that the early church fathers were right in their conclusion concerning post-tribulationism even if they were wrong in believing they were already in the great tribulation. In contrast to the early fathers, however, modern post-tribulationists do not believe in imminency in the same sense as did the early church, but rather hold that certain events must take place first, namely, the events outlined in the Scriptures as preceding the second coming of Christ to the earth. Modern post-tribulationists, therefore, while affirming post-tribulationism as such, deny imminency in the sense of an any-moment return, and hold a decidedly different point of view from the early church fathers.

In contrast to post-tribulationism, the pretribulational position holds that the rapture of the church is an event separated from the second coming of Christ to the earth by a period of time usually considered to be at least seven years on the basis of Daniel's prophecies in Daniel 9:27. Pretribulationists therefore generally accept the doctrine of imminency, that is, that Christ could come at any moment. They deny post-tribulationism, and hold that there must be a period of time between the rapture and the second coming itself during which certain events of the end time must be fulfilled. Since these events are viewed as following rather than preceding the rapture, there is nothing hindering the rapture occurring any day.

A third view largely promoted in our present generation is the so-called midtribulational view which places the rapture three and one-half years before Christ's second coming to establish His kingdom. There is comparatively no literature on the subject and few scholars have been willing to advocate openly this point of view. Some have adopted it, apparently motivated primarily by the desire to mediate the pretribulational and post-tribulational view and accept some tenets from both views. Though this interpretation has proved attractive to some, it has not as yet assumed any large proportion in the scholarship and writings related to the rapture doctrine. While it has certain advantages over both pretribulationism and post-tribulationism, it creates problems which are far greater than the benefits derived. While the midtribulational view would lend itself to some extent to a considerable treatment of the doctrine of the rapture as a separate aspect of the Christian hope, from a practical standpoint it has not done so and writers who have contributed in this area have done little to enhance the doctrine of the rapture as a whole.

In comparing the theological premises of the various views of the rapture, it soon becomes apparent that those who observe some dispensational distinction tend to the pretribulational rapture position whereas those who hold to covenant theology or kingdom theology tend toward the midtribulational or post-tribulational position. It is not too much to say that the theological presuppositions which enter into the study of the rapture are usually largely determinative in its outcome. Those who distinguish the program of Israel from the program of the church tend to pretribulationism whereas those who merge the two consider them phases of the soteriological program of God and tend toward midtribulationism or post-tribulationism. One's view on the rapture therefore, becomes indicative of one's theology as a whole, which lends support to the contention that the rapture doctrine is, after all, important theologically

HERMENEUTICAL PRINCIPLES OF THE RAPTURE

It is gradually being recognized in contemporary theology that hermeneutical principles have much to do with the total problem of establishing eschatology. Amillenarians and premillenarians agree that their respective points of view stem from their principles of interpretation. Augustine, who advanced the dual hermeneutics, has largely set the pattern for amillennial eschatology. He held that while the Scriptures as a whole should be interpreted normally, historically, and grammatically, prophecy was a special case which required spiritualization or allegorical interpretation, and therefore a nonliteral interpretation of prophecy. By contrast, premillenarians generally have adopted a single hermeneutic, namely, that prophecy should be interpreted by the same principles by which any other type of Scripture is interpreted. While some premillenarians, especially those who are not dispensational, have used to some extent the dual hermeneutics of Augustine, the principle still holds that the hermeneutic rather than the individual argument determines the outcome of the discussion.

What is true of premillennialism in contrast to amillennialism is also true of the pretribulational view in contrast to midtribulationism and post-tribulationism. It is impossible to hold the modern point of view of post-tribulationism or midtribulationism without introducing to a considerable degree the principles of spiritualization of prophecy. The specifics of the great tribulation are often ignored. Even within premillennialism, Israel and the church are not kept distinct as to their divine programs. Though a widespread variation exists in the interpretation of end-time events, the tendency has been for post-tribulationism to spiritualize the tribulation whereas pretribulationism tends to take it more literally. A conclusion, therefore, can be fairly reached that in so far as one's hermeneutics follows the pattern of amillennialism, one tends to be post-tribulational and, to the extent that he follows dispensational or literal interpretation, he tends to the pretribulational position. The doctrine of the rapture, therefore, becomes indicative not only of theology as a whole but of the hermeneutics by which its doctrine is established.

Prophetic Program

Not only is the doctrine of the rapture related to the theological premises and hermeneutical principles of a given theology, but a direct relationship can be established between the doctrine of the rapture and the prominence given prophecy as a whole. Generally speaking, amillenarians and postmillenarians do not provide a large place in their systems for prophecy. One never hears of a prophecy conference sponsored by amillenarians or postmillenarians. Such an emphasis on prophecy is almost limited to the premillenarian group. Further, the same distinction can be observed between those who are post-tribulational and midtribulational, as opposed to the pretribulational position. Rarely, if ever, are prophecy conferences conducted by post-tribulationists or midtribulationists even if they are premillennial. It is almost a foregone conclusion that if a church or an institution of learning sponsors a special series of studies in prophecy it is motivated primarily by its pretribulational convictions. The prominence given to prophecy as a whole, therefore, is linked to the prominence given the doctrine of the rapture and vice versa.

Not only is there a link between emphasis on the rapture and emphasis on prophecy as a whole, but the same principle can also be observed in the practical application of prophecy to the Christian life. While all conservative points of view share to some extent the blessings of Christian hope such as our ultimate resurrection from the dead and the blessings which will be experienced by the saints in heaven, the practical application of prophecy to the daily life is given additional incentive under the pretribulational position. This is an obvious deduction from its intrinsic character.

The fact that Christ could come any day is certainly more arresting and dramatic than the possibility of His coming some years hence. The doctrine of imminency is inevitably related to the pointed application of certain prophecies. While even a post-tribulationist can claim that the hope of the coming of the Lord is a purifying hope, a blessed hope, and a comforting hope, it is nevertheless true that in proportion as the realization of the hope is imminent so there is increased pertinence to the application. Hence, in John 14 where Christ tells His disciples, "Let not your heart be troubled," one of the reasons which He gives is, "I will come again and receive you unto myself." In a similar way in the Thessalonian church after outlining to them the fact that the dead in Christ will be raised just a moment before the living church is translated, Paul concludes, "Wherefore comfort one another with these words." The comfort of the possibility of reunion with their loved ones any day is certainly more pointed and more helpful than the ultimate possibility of such an event in the distant future.

Of particular relevance is the purifying effect of the doctrine of the rapture. As mentioned in I John 3:3 and in the preceding verse, Christians are assured, "When he shall appear, we shall be like him; for we shall see him as he is." Then the application is made, "And every man that hath this hope in him purifieth himself, even as he is pure." While the hope of being like the Saviour is an incentive to purity of life regardless of when it occurs, if the event of the Lord's return could happen at any moment, in any day, there is an urgency about the whole matter of sanctification in that one wants his life to be in order at the time that the Lord comes. Any housewife can testify to the difference in preparation for an expected guest depending on the expected time of arrival. If she receives a letter stating that some friend plans to visit several years hence, such a letter produces no change in the schedule of the household. If, however, a letter should come saying a guest may be expected any day, this requires an entirely different form of preparation. Ordinary schedules are cancelled in favor of a program of immediate preparedness.

It may be concluded, therefore, that from a practical standpoint, the concept of the rapture held in any system of theology has an important bearing upon its theology as a whole, not so much from the standpoint of being causal, but from the standpoint of being indicative of the theological premises and principles of interpretation of which the doctrine of the rapture is an eloquent expression.

THE RAPTURE IN RELATION TO ORTHODOXY

One of the side effects of a proper emphasis on the doctrine of the rapture is that it seems to have the curious result of promoting orthodoxy in theology as a whole. It is, of course, true that systems of theology which are basically conservative and support the great fundamentals of the faith do not necessarily emphasize the doctrine of the rapture. Failure to agree on the doctrine of the rapture is not per se a token of unorthodoxy in major doctrine.

It is, however, strangely true that in the mainstream of evangelicalism, those who emphasize the imminency of the Lord's return are almost invariably orthodox in the major tenets of their theology. They almost always hold to the verbal and plenary inspiration of the Bible. They inevitably accept the deity of Jesus Christ and the sufficiency of His sacrifice. They have few problems in accepting the miraculous and the accuracy of Scripture as a whole. There is no tendency toward a superficial intellectualism or a philosophical approach to the Bible which robs it of its content and spiritual vigor. While much of modern scholarship writes off any emphasis on the doctrine of the rapture as somewhat naive, it is also significant that such modern scholarship as a whole has not been able to maintain its own orthodoxy. The freshness of the hope of the Lord's return and the day-by-day expectation of the fulfillment of the precious promises relating to the hope of the Christian are a wonderful means of strength for Christians who are tested in their faith. In too many cases where the precious hope of the rapture has become dim, it is the prelude for departure from the faith in the fundamentals, as neglect or unbelief in one area of theology often spreads to another.

Those who adhere strictly to the pretribulational view of the Lord's return should exercise, on the one hand, caution lest they label those who differ from them as heterodox because of failure to agree on this aspect of God's prophetic program. On the other hand, they should not be discouraged by the fact that they are a minority in the total professing church of our day and should stand resolutely for their convictions even if subjected to ridicule and misrepresentation. The precious hope of the Lord's return is far more rewarding than any of its substitutes and though it may not appeal to the intellectuals of our day and may be lacking in sophistication and philosophic ramification and terminology, it nevertheless is deeply satisfying to the devout soul who is looking for the return of His precious Lord any day.

CHAPTER VIII

THE CHURCH AND THE TRIBULATION

One of the important problems in prophecy concerning the church is the relationship of the church to the time of tribulation preceding the second coming of Christ to the earth. Those who approach the subject of prophecy from the viewpoint of the amillennial or postmillennial theology, generally speaking, consider the church as going through this time of trouble with the hope of being translated at the close of the tribulation when Christ comes to earth. Both the resurrection of the dead in Christ and the translation of the living church, therefore, become events immediately preceding the inauguration of the final judgments and the eternal state. Both the postmillennial and amillennial views regard the millennium as already past.

It is only within the premillennial interpretation of prophecy that much attention has been paid to the rapture. A few have followed the partial rapture concept, holding that a portion of the church will be raptured before the tribulation with the rest of the church awaiting rapture at the close of the tribulation. This view, however, has not gained much acceptance and is for practical purposes an oddity rather than a principal consideration in the study of prophecy.

Another view which has attracted a few adherents is the midtribulational view which considers the rapture as taking place three and one-half years before the second coming of Christ to the earth and therefore before what Christ calls "the great tribulation" (Matthew 24:21). They place the rapture at the end of the first half of Daniel's seventieth week (Daniel 9:27). Relatively few have adopted this hypothesis. The great majority of premillenarians are divided between the post-tribulational concept of the rapture and the pretribulational concept. Most contemporary premillenarians follow the pretribulational view that Christ's coming for His church precedes the fulfillment of Daniel's seventieth week, and is therefore before the end-time period of trouble.

The argument for and against these various viewpoints are detailed in the writer's previously published work *The Rapture Question* and his *The Millennial Kingdom* as well as in a host of other publications by many authors. The more important considerations and a review of the principal arguments for and against the pretribulational rapture can be restated here. For the purpose of this discussion, the midtribulational theory and the partial rapture view, held only by a small minority, will be disregarded in favor of a comparison of the post-tribulational and pretribulational points of view.

POST-TRIBULATIONAL INTERPRETATION OF THE RAPTURE

As in the case of other problems of interpretation in the realm of prophecy, post-tribulationism is determined largely by the premises which it assumes. Among these premises is the spiritualization of some of the prophecies pertaining to the tribulation. Just as the amillenarians and postmillenarians spiritualize the doctrine of the millennium, so post-tribulationists tend to spiritualize the details of the tribulation. A great variety of opinion, however, exists within the post-tribulational view. Some contend that the tribulation itself is not a specific period of time and that it is proper to consider the church as always being in tribulation. Some begin the time of tribulation with Adam. Some begin it with Christ. This post-tribulational explanation regards as obvious that the church will go through the tribulation because they hold the church is already in the tribulation.

This type of post-tribulationism, of course, disregards the specific details given in the Word of God concerning the tribulation such as are found in Jeremiah 30:3-11, Matthew 24:15-30, and extended portions of the book of Revelation. These passages make clear that the great tribulation can only take place after a large portion of Israel has been re-gathered, something that did not occur until the twentieth century. More particularly, it follows the breaking of the covenant made with Israel (Daniel 9:27) when their holy place will be desecrated (Matthew 24:15). No literal ful-fillment of this has occurred. If the great tribulation be interpreted literally, it is a three and one-half year period culminating in Christ's second coming to the earth and preceded by a period of three and one-half years during which the covenant made with Israel is observed. Post-tribulationists, therefore, who spiritualize the tribulation by finding supposed fulfillment in the past are following the same principles of interpretation found in amillennialism. It is quite inconsistent to follow an amillennial interpreta-tion of the tribulation and join this to a premillennial in-terpretation of a millennium.

Other post-tribulationists, however, regard the seven-tieth week of Daniel as yet future much as do the pretribu-lationists, but expect the church to be safely conducted through it. This view, while granting to the tribulation a future status, usually involves a severe toning down of the specifics of the judgments poured out on the earth in the tribulation. It is rare to find a post-tribulationist who takes at face value the tremendous judgments portrayed in the book of Revelation. Almost invariably, however, post-tribulationists spiritualize other aspects of prophecy. In particular, they usually consider the church of the present dispensation and the nation Israel as the same body, that is, they regard the church as the true Israel. This is a common teaching of covenant theology and is quite a normal feature of amillennialism. Premillenarians who follow covenant theology usually are post-tribulationists.

Still another approach to the problem is taken by some post-tribulationists who attempt to steer a middle course between spiritualization of the tribulation itself and spiritualization of Israel. Such scholars usually find their unifying principle in the concept of the kingdom and view Israel, the church, and the saints of all ages, as embodied in the kingdom of God. Under this point of view, the church loses its distinctive New Testament character and for all practical purposes is one and the same as the saints of the tribulation time. Such writers find evidence of the church in the tribulation simply from the fact that there are saints in this period. A survey of post-tribulationism therefore demonstrates that it always involves a spiritualization of some entities which pretribulationists consider in a more literal way. Post-tribulationists spiritualize either the tribulation itself, the church and Israel, or follow a soteriological approach to the divine purpose which merges the saints of all ages into one entity.

Post-tribulationism, building upon these premises, attempts to prove that the church is or will be in the tribulation period, and therefore must pass through this time of trial before the rapture itself can occur. A detailed study of post-tribulationism is provided by the writer's discussion in *The Rapture Question*, pp. 127-70.

Most important, however, to the solution of this problem is the fact that post-tribulationists have never proved that the church, the body of Christ, is in the tribulation. On this point, the Scriptures are silent. While post-tribulationists characteristically throw the burden of proof on the pretribulationists and often challenge them to prove that the church is not in the tribulation, it would seem, however, a reasonable point of view to require the post-tribulationists to offer proof. None of the terms relating to the church as the body of Christ in this present age are ever used in relation to tribulation saints. In fact, they are uniformly referred to as either belonging to Israel or to the Gentiles, never as forming the one body described as the church. As the arguments of post-tribulationists are largely of a negative character, namely, an argument against the pretribulational position, the approach which brings the points of issue immediately to the front are the arguments for pretribulationism.

INTERPRETATIVE PRINCIPLES OF PRETRIBULATIONISM

Just as a principle of spiritualization of important concepts in relation to the tribulation is the interpretative approach of post-tribulationism, so the interpretation of prophecy in its normal and literal sense is the key to pretribulationism. Augustine, the father of orthodox amillennialism, adopted a dual hermeneutics which provided for the spiritualization of prophecy though he considered it proper for the rest of Scripture to be interpreted normally and literally. This principle led to the abandonment of premillennialism by the Roman Church. The same principle in smaller dimensions is found in the arguments relating to pretribulationism and post-tribulationism, with the post-tribulationist following a dual hermeneutics like that of Augustine and pretribulationists following a single hermeneutic such as is characteristic of premillennialism.

The literal interpretation of prophecy leads to the conclusion that there is a future time of trouble which will be a major feature of the end time. Daniel's prophecy of a period of seven years culminating Israel's history (Daniel 9:27) is regarded as future and providing the major structure of the period between the rapture and the second coming of Christ. Likewise, the literal interpretation of prophecy maintains a contrast between Israel and the church. The church is a separate body of believers, distinct in the divine purpose of God's plan from the nation Israel and more particularly to be contrasted to His plan for the saved or elect in Israel. The teaching contrasting Israel and the church is sometimes referred to as the dispensational interpretation. Actually, however, the distinction between Israel and the church does not stem from dispensationalism itself, but from the single hermeneutic or the literal interpretation of prophecy. Dispensationalism is the result not the cause of this doctrine.

Pretribulationism also considers the tribulation itself with a large degree of literalness and views the judgments poured out upon the earth revealed in the book of Revelation as subject to literal fulfillment. While recognizing that some of these prophecies are given in symbolic form, the stark awfulness of the future period of tribulation nevertheless emerges from any reasonably literal interpretation of prophecies having to do with the great tribulation. Christ Himself declared that there would be no other time in all of human history equal to that of the great tribulation in severity (Matthew 24:21) and with this agree the prophecies of Jeremiah 30:7, "That none is like it: it is even the time of Jacob's trouble," and the prophecy of Daniel 12:1, "There shall be a time of trouble, such as never was since there was a nation." Undoubtedly the application of literal interpretation to prophecy leads to the pretribulational view whereas the spiritualization of prophecy leads to the post-tribulational view. It is not too much to say that this really determines the issue and that subsequent arguments merely confirm the reasonableness of their respective points of view.

THE HISTORY OF THE PRETRIBULATIONAL INTERPRETATION

Undoubtedly, one of the most impressive arguments used by post-tribulationists is the contention that they represent the view of the early church in contrast to pretribulationism which is new and novel and therefore wrong. The fact is, however, that neither post-tribulationism nor pretribulationism as it is held today corresponds to the viewpoint of the early church fathers. In the early church, the Lord's coming was viewed as imminent, that is, an event which could occur any day. Coupled with the doctrine of imminency, however, was the view that the church was already in the great tribulation and that therefore Christ would come at the close of the time of trouble. The early church did not, therefore, distinguish the rapture from the second coming. It is obvious that this to some extent corresponds to post-tribulationism. However, modern post-tribulationism does not accept the doctrine of imminency, that is, that Christ could come at any moment, and usually regards the future as involving a number of prophecies being fulfilled first, such as that of the great tribulation before Christ could come. Modern post-tribulationism, therefore, generally denies imminency but affirms post-tribulationism in contrast to pretribulationism which denies a post-tribulational rapture but like the early fathers affirms the imminency of the Lord's return.

The truth is that in the study of eschatology there has been considerable progress. Probably more refinement and study has been given to the subject of the future of the church in the last century than for many centuries preceding. There is some evidence that the church has been progressing throughout the centuries of its history through the major areas of doctrine beginning with bibliology and theology proper as in the early centuries of the church, advancing to such subjects as anthropology and hamartiology in the fourth and succeeding centuries, and dealing with soteriology and ecclesiology in the Protestant Reformation. It has been mostly in the last century that eschatology has really come to the fore as an area for scholarly study and debate. It is only natural that there should be refinement and improvement in this area just as there have been in other areas throughout the history of the church.

The fact, therefore, that ideas relating to prophecy are new or sharper in their distinctions than in previous generations is not an argument in itself that the truth thus presented is actually an error. It is evident from the study of such works as Ladd's *The Blessed Hope* and Alexander Reese's *The Approaching Advent* of Christ that the deciding point in their systems was not their exegesis of the Scriptures, but the fact that the early church fathers did not teach pretribulationism as it is now held by its adherents.

The truth is, however, that the early fathers did not hold to
post-tribulationism as taught by Ladd and Reese either.
The history of the doctrine of the rapture does not really
support either post-tribulationism or pretribulationism as it
is now held. The ultimate question, after all, is not what
the fathers taught but what the Bible teaches. In their understanding of prophecy as in many other areas, the early
church fathers were immature and perhaps have been given
a halo of orthodoxy which they only partially deserved.
Pretribulationists can point to the early church fathers as
being chiliastic or premillennial and as believers in the imminent return of Christ. They cannot, however, claim that
the specifics of their view were held by the early church
any more than most post-tribulationists can do so with
complete accuracy.

THE PRETRIBULATIONAL CONCEPT OF THE TRIBULATION

Though some variation exists in pretribulational teaching about the tribulation, in general pretribulationists hold
that there will be a period of at least seven years between
the rapture of the church and Christ's coming to establish
His kingdom in the earth. Many pretribulationists believe
that immediately after the rapture there will be a short
period of preparation. During this period the revived Roman
Empire will come into being, formed of ten nations as predicted in Daniel 7 and Revelation 13. The one who becomes
the head of this ten-nation confederacy is identified as
"the prince that shall come" of Daniel 9:26 who according
to Daniel 9:27 makes a covenant of seven years duration
with the people of Israel. When this covenant is signed,
it sets up the absolute chronology of the period between
the signing of the covenant and the second coming of Christ
as a period of seven years, quite in contrast to the inde-
terminancy of the length of the present age which will culminate in the rapture. Those living at that time, if they
know the date when the covenant is signed, will be able to

foretell the approximate time of the return of the Lord though still not able to fix the day or the hour.

Pretribulationists regard this seven-year period as being divided into two parts. In the first half, there is a period of protection, one of comparative rest and tranquility for Israel. They are protected from their enemies and granted religious freedom. With the beginning of the second half of the seven years, a period of persecution begins when the covenant is broken. Israel is plunged into the time of Jacob's trouble and the great tribulation of which the Scriptures speak (Jeremiah 30:7; Daniel 12:1; Matthew 24:21; Revelation 6:17).

Pretribulationists view the end of the great tribulation as culminating in the second coming of Christ, the deliverance of Israel, and the establishment of Christ's millennial kingdom on earth. The great tribulation which precedes the second coming of Christ is not only a time of persecution of Israel and of those who turn to Christ in that day from both Jews and Gentiles, but it is a time of unprecedented divine judgments upon the earth which decimate the human population of the earth and leave its physical monuments and great cities in ruins. Interpreted literally, the tribulation clearly eclipses anything that the world has ever known by way of destruction of human life, great earthquakes, pestilence, war, famine, and stars falling from heaven. It is a time of trouble which leaves the earth in shambles. It is indeed the day of God's wrath and righteous judgment upon a wicked earth. There will be multiplied thousands of martyrs, both of Jews and Gentiles, who refuse to worship the beast and therefore suffer a martyr's death.

The nature of the tribulation, if Scriptures relating to it are interpreted normally and literally, gives no basis for the idea that the church, the body of Christ, the saints of this present age, will be forced to remain on earth through it. According to the Scriptures, it is specifically the time of Jacob's trouble (Jeremiah 30:7) and coincides with the

last seven years of Israel's program as outlined in Daniel
9:24-27. It is God's program for Israel, therefore, rather
than God's program for the church that is primarily in view.
It is also specifically the consummation of the times of the
Gentiles foreshadowed in Daniel's visions in Daniel 2 and
7, the progress of which was interrupted by the interposi-
tion of the present purpose of God in the church. The dual
purpose of God to fulfill Israel's program and the times of
the Gentiles culminating in the second coming of Christ are
quite different than His purpose for the church in this
present age. The church is composed of Jews and Gentiles
without distinction as to their racial origin and quite independent of God's program for either the Gentiles or
Israel as a nation. The fact is most significant that the
terms normally used of the church and which set it apart
as distinct from saints of previous ages are never found in
any tribulation passage. Though the argument from silence
is quite eloquent, in view of this complete absence of reference to the church as such, the burden of proof shifts to the
post-tribulationist to prove that the church is in this period.
That there is reference to Israel, to saints, to saved Israelites,
and to saved Gentiles does not prove that the church is in
this period as these terms are general terms, not specific.
Likewise, the term "elect" is not limited in any sense to
the church of this present age and, therefore, is not an
equivalent term.

Not only is the church not mentioned as being in the
tribulation time, but specific promises seem to be given to
the church that they will not enter this time of trouble. A
principal passage is found in I Thessalonians 5:9, previously discussed, where it is specifically said, "For God hath
not appointed us to wrath, but to obtain salvation by our
Lord Jesus Christ." The tribulation is definitely a time of
wrath (Revelation 6:17) and this appointment does not
belong to the church.

Confirming evidence is found in the promise given to
the church at Philadelphia in Revelation 3:10, "Because

thou hast kept the word of my patience, I will also keep thee
from the hour of temptation, which will come upon all the
world, to try them that dwell upon the earth." Whether or
not the church at Philadelphia is properly considered as
a type of the church as the body of Christ existing on earth
at the time of the rapture, it is evident that this promise
could not have been given to the church at Philadelphia
properly if, as a matter of fact, the church was destined to
go through the tribulation. The church at Philadelphia is
definitely promised that they will be kept out of "the hour
of temptation, which shall come upon all the earth" (Revelation 3:10). It is not as some have alleged that the church
will be kept through the tribulation, in other words, protected in this period. To the contrary, the Scriptures relating to the tribulation indicate that probably the majority
of saints in that period will not be protected, that is, they
will be martyred. Only a few, both Jews and Gentiles, will
escape the awful hatred of Satan and the world ruler. If
these passages pertaining to the tribulation are taken literally, the possibility of one who is identified as a believer in
Christ at its beginning, surviving to its end is indeed quite
remote. Probably the majority of those who survive the
period will be recent converts who come to Christ in the
awful time of great tribulation through the personal witness
of those who in many cases seal their testimony with their
own blood.

THE PRETRIBULATIONAL DOCTRINE OF IMMINENCY

One of the important arguments in favor of the pretribulational position is the fact that the rapture as presented in the Bible is constantly viewed as an imminent
event. In none of the major passages which predict the
translation of the living saints and the resurrection of the
dead in Christ are any events interposed as signs or indications of the approaching rapture. In such major passages
as John 14:1-3; I Thessalonians 4:13-18; and I Corinthians
15:51-58, the rapture is viewed as the immediate expecta-

tion of those who put their hope and trust in Christ. This is
in sharp contrast to passages that deal with the second coming of Christ to the earth, such as Matthew 24-25, which
outline a series of events that must necessarily precede His
return and give special attention to the fact that the great
tribulation must run its course first. The same view is outlined in great detail in the book of Revelation where the
events portrayed from chapter 6 through chapter 18 must
precede the coming of Christ pictured in Revelation chapter 19. It is impossible according to the pretribulationist
to harmonize two such drastically different events as the
coming of Christ for His church and His second coming to
the earth attended as it is by all these important events preceding and following.

In like manner, the rapture doctrine is related to exhortations which lose much of their force if they are connected with the second coming of Christ following a great
tribulation. In John 14:1 the introduction of the rapture
truths in the upper room is prefaced by the exhortation,
"Let not your heart be troubled" (John 14:1). In I Thessalonians 4:18 the rapture teaching is summarized in the
exhortation, "Wherefore comfort one another with these
words." Likewise in I Corinthians 15:51-58 the revelation
concerning the translation of the living church is concluded
with an exhortation to faithfulness and steadfastness in
view of the fact that their labor is not in vain. In none of
these passages are Christians warned that they must go
through the great tribulation before they can see Christ
coming for His own; and if such a contingency were in
force, it certainly would remove much of the significance
of these exhortations. The exhortation in I John 3:2, 3, is
of similar character where the hope of the Lord's return
is declared to be a purifying hope. Though a distant return of the Lord would also have some effect, it is clear that
imminency makes much more urgent the need for present
sanctification and purity of life.

Post-tribulationists often counter these arguments by

noting exhortations to "watch" and to be ready related to the second coming of Christ as for instance in Matthew 24-25. Here, however, the exhortation is clearly addressed to those who will be living in the period when the signs have already appeared. It is noteworthy that the exhortations are not given until the great tribulation is unfolded. It is therefore implicit in the passage that the exhortations do not apply specifically to those who are living in preceding generations, but rather have their immediate point in the lives and expectancy of those who go through the period of the signs related to the Lord's return. While they have general application to the entire interadvent age, their particular application is to those living at the time of the end.

THE HOLY SPIRIT IN RELATION TO THE TRIBULATION

In the discussion of the coming man of sin in II Thessalonians 2:1-12, a chronology seems to be set up which tends to confirm the pretribulational viewpoint. The Thessalonians, apparently misguided by a false letter, had thought that they were already in the time of trouble predicted for the end of the age. In correcting this misapprehension, the apostle assures them that it is impossible that they already should be in this period because certain things must occur first. He, therefore, exhorts them: "Let no man deceive you by any means: for that day shall not come, except there come a falling away first, and that man of sin be revealed, the son of perdition; who opposeth and exalteth himself above all that is called God, or that is worshipped; so that he as God sitteth in the temple of God, showing himself that he is God" (II Thessalonians 2:3, 4). He reminds them in II Thessalonians 2:5 that he had instructed them concerning this when he was with them at Thessalonica. He goes on to state further that they already know what is hindering the revelation of this person (II Thessalonians 2:6). The apostle then repeats what he had previously preached to them: "For the mystery of iniquity doth already work: only he who now letteth will let, until he be taken out of the way. And then shall that Wicked be revealed, whom the Lord shall consume with the spirit of his mouth, and shall destroy with the brightness of his coming: even him, whose coming is after the working of Satan with all power and signs and lying wonders, and with all deceivableness of unrighteousness in them that perish; because they received not the love of the truth, that they might be saved" (II Thessalonians 2:7-10).

This passage has given rise to a number of interpretations because it is not entirely clear what is meant by the restraint of iniquity. Probably the most popular interpretation is that this refers to human government which holds wickedness in check, and may refer specifically to the Roman government. Another suggestion has been made that true restraint of sin stems from God rather than man and what is referred to is the ministry of the Holy Spirit in this present age. In the upper room, the Lord had revealed to His disciples that He was going to send them the Holy Spirit (John 14:16, 17). The present age beginning with the Day of Pentecost has been called by many the dispensation of the Spirit. In this age there is an abundance of ministry of the Holy Spirit in the church in that every individual is indwelt by the Spirit, baptized into the body of Christ, sealed by the Spirit, and given new life by the Spirit.

The fact that the Holy Spirit came on the Day of Pentecost has suggested that the Holy Spirit will depart at the time of the rapture. This would be parallel to the coming of Christ who, though omnipresent in the Old Testament, came as a babe and dwelt among men for the period of His early life. Then He ascended into heaven and the state of things was restored to what had been before the incarnation as far as His personal presence is concerned. In like manner, the Holy Spirit came on the Day of Pentecost in a special sense, though He had been omnipresent for all eternity past. His special ministry having been completed in the earth during this present age, He will then be taken out of the world with the church and the situation will be restored to that which was true before Pentecost. This seems to be a reasonable approach and in keeping with numerous Scriptures bearing out the doctrine of the Holy Spirit.

The Holy Spirit is revealed to be the One who restrains the manifestation of sin. Even in the period before the flood, God had said, "My spirit shall not always strive with men for that he is also flesh" (Genesis 6:3). The ministry of the Spirit in the church not only ministers to the church as such but constitutes a restraint of sin upon the whole world. If the church is to be raptured as the pretribulationist holds, it would constitute a major removal of restraint of sin.

In II Thessalonians 2, the restraining of sin is revealed to continue until "he be taken out of the way." Only then "shall that wicked be revealed," referring to the man of sin of II Thessalonians 2:3. The person being removed is a reference to that which restrains sin, namely, the Holy Spirit of God. The chronology thus set up would be that the Holy Spirit must be revealed first, then the man of sin would be revealed and with it the falling away of the apostasy in the time of tribulation. Inasmuch as the man of sin is probably to be identified with the ruler of the revived Roman Empire, his disclosure would come early in the period and would presume that the rapture would precede the beginning of the seven-year covenant which he makes with Israel.

Another explanation has been offered in that the expression, "a falling away first," actually is a word meaning, "departure." Some have taken this to refer to the rapture itself, making verse 3 read, in effect, that the coming time of trouble cannot come except there come a departure first, namely, the rapture of the church. Though this interpretation has attracted the interest of pretribulationists, and has some justification in usage, inasmuch as the text does not explicitly indicate the departure of the church, it cannot

be proved positively that this is the correct view. Whatever evidence, however, is found in II Thessalonians 2 is
in favor of the pretribulational position in that it seems to
set up a chronology of events which places the rapture of
the church first, to be followed by the revelation of the man
of sin.

FULFILLMENT OF EVENTS BETWEEN THE RAPTURE
AND THE SECOND COMING

The pretribulational view of the rapture of the church
also allows for certain problems which are left unresolved
in the post-tribulational position, namely, that a number of
events seemingly follow the rapture and precede the second
coming of Christ. The events on earth, of course, are those
which characterize the tribulation period. Certain events,
however, will also take place in heaven, namely, the judgment seat of Christ and the marriage of the Lamb. While
these events would not constitute in themselves an insuperable problem to post-tribulationists, they fit so naturally in the pretribulational point of view that they constitute supporting evidence.

THE CONTRAST BETWEEN THE RAPTURE
AND THE SECOND COMING

One of the most dramatic evidences for the pretribulational point of view is the sharp contrast between the
revelation concerning the rapture and the revelation concerning Christ's return to the earth. In the major passages
on the rapture such as John 14:1-3; I Thessalonians 4:13-
18; and I Corinthians 15:51-58, the marvelous hope of the
return of Christ for His own is unfolded. The revelation
indicates that the event will take place in a moment and
apparently that the earth and its inhabitants are left undisturbed. The Scripture does not use the term "secret
rapture," and there is no sure evidence what the world
will see and hear at the time of rapture. On the other hand,
the Scriptures do not give any indication that the rapture

will be subject to observation by the world as a whole. According to John 14:1-3, at the time of the rapture the church will be taken to the Father's house to the place prepared by Christ and the destiny of the saints will be heaven rather than earth.

The chief characteristics of the rapture accordingly may be summarized as including the factors that the saints will meet the Lord in the air, that living saints will be translated, that the dead in Christ will be raised, that the Lord will return to heaven with the saints, that the rapture will occur before the day of wrath, that it concerns only the saved, that it may be viewed throughout the church age as imminent, and that its promises relate only to the church.

A survey of the major Scriptures dealing with the second coming reveal an entirely different picture than the rapture. In Matthew 24, it is indicated that the second coming of Christ will fill the heavens with glory and will be "as lightning cometh out of the east and shineth even unto the west" (Matthew 24:27). Preceding the second coming in the tribulation time, the sun will be darkened, the moon will not shine, and the stars will fall from heaven. It is specifically predicted, "Then shall all the tribes of the earth mourn, and they shall see the Son of Man coming in the clouds of heaven with power and great glory" (Matthew 24:30). In contrast to the rapture, the second coming will be a visible event which both saved and unsaved will see.

A similar revelation is given in Revelation 19:11-16 where Christ is revealed to come from heaven on a white horse clothed with a vesture dipped in blood followed by the armies of heaven also on white horses and clothed in white linen. He is declared as coming with a sharp sword which proceeds out of His mouth with the purpose of ruling the nations with a rod of iron and inflicting "the fierceness and wrath of Almighty God" (Revelation 19:15). At His coming to the earth the armies of men which have

opposed Him are destroyed and the beast and the false
prophet are cast alive into the lake of fire. His return is
followed by His millennial kingdom.

In both of these major passages of Matthew 24 and
Revelation 19, no word whatever is mentioned of the rapture of the living saints. It is a time of judgment upon
a wicked world. Zechariah 14 indicates that His coming
will be to the Mount of Olives from which He had ascended
at the close of His earthly ministry and that when His feet
stand upon the Mount of Olives it will be divided in two
and a great valley will replace the present site of the
mountain (Zechariah 14:4).

There is little that is similar about the two events
except that both are referred to as a coming of Christ
from heaven to the earthly sphere. In contrast to the rapture, the second coming is a return to the Mount of Olives,
precedes the establishment of His kingdom, and is followed
by Christ remaining on earth for His earthly reign. It is
a time when sin is judged, it will follow the prophesied
signs such as the tribulation, and will deal with both saved
and unsaved. The second coming will affect not only men
but will result in Satan and his hosts being defeated and
Satan bound. In view of the decided contrast between
the coming of Christ at the rapture and His coming to establish His earthly kingdom, the burden of proof that these
are one and the same must rest with the post-tribulationist.
The facts would certainly point to the conclusion that these
are two events as different as any two comings of an individual could possibly be.

THE APOSTATE CHURCH OF THE TRIBULATION

Pretribulationists agree that while the church, the body
of Christ, is raptured before the tribulation, those in the professing church who are unsaved continue on the earth and
enter the tribulation time. They form the apostate church
of that period. The Scriptural revelation of this is found in
Revelation 17 where the apostate church is viewed as a

harlot and given the title, "MYSTERY, BABYLON THE GREAT, THE MOTHER OF HARLOTS AND ABOMINATIONS OF THE EARTH" (Revelation 17:5). Expositors of all classes have agreed that this is the apostate church of the tribulation time. It was customary in the Protestant Reformation to refer this specifically to the Roman Church and even modern expositors have had a tendency to return to this interpretation. It seems, however, that the apostate church is not only that of the remnants of the Roman Church but includes all Christendom as well as other religions, the whole united as a result of the trend toward a world church into a great superchurch. In the time of tribulation those who turn to Christ in faith remain outside this church rather than in it.

The apostate church is viewed as having evil association with the kings of the earth. The church will be in a dominant position as symbolized in the fact that she sits upon a scarlet colored beast which has seven heads and ten horns. This beast pictured earlier in the book of Revelation (Revelation 13) is to be identified with the revived Roman Empire. It is apparent that the revived Roman Empire and the apostate church work together to promote each other's power. The time comes, however, when the beast turns on the woman. According to Revelation 17:16; "The ten horns which thou sawest upon the beast, these shall hate the whore, and make her desolate and naked, and shall eat her flesh, and burn her with fire." This dramatic turn of events symbolizes the beginning of the great tribulation when the ruler who had previously dominated the Roman Empire rises to become the dictator over the entire world. Simultaneous with this assumption to political power, he demands that the whole world worship him (Revelation 13:8). As this conflicts with the demand of the world church, it becomes necessary to destroy the world church in favor of the new form of religion which will dominate the period of the great tribulation and be judged by Christ as His return.

Taking these factors into consideration, it is true in one sense that the church enters the time of the tribulation, but it is the apostate church composed entirely of those who are unsaved rather than the church, the body of Christ, which is raptured before these events take place. If the viewpoint of the pretribulationists be correct, the church will be in heaven during the time of the final struggle upon earth and will return with the Lord at the time of His second coming and will share with Him responsibility in the millennial kingdom. The prospect for those living in this generation who are in Christ is for His imminent return with all the blessings which this represents. For the world the sad prospect is that it will move into the end time with its unprecedented tribulation.

CHAPTER IX

THE CHURCH IN HEAVEN

After the rapture of the church, while the period of trial and trouble culminating in the great tribulation unfolds in the earth, the church is represented as being in heaven in the presence of the Lord. The Scriptures relating to this theme are supporting evidence for the pretribulation rapture inasmuch as the presence of the church in heaven is required in order to fulfill these prophecies. Scriptures relating to the church in heaven are occupied with two important themes: (1) the church as the bride of Christ in heaven; (2) the judgment seat of Christ. Of the various figures used to relate Christ to the church, the bridegroom and the church as the bride is the only one that is specifically futuristic and prophetic in character, contemplating as it does the future coming of Christ for His bride.

The Bride of Christ

The figure of marriage is often used in Scripture to represent spiritual reality. In the Old Testament, Israel is represented as the wife of Jehovah untrue to her marriage vows but destined to be restored in the future kingdom. In the New Testament, the church is presented as the bride of Christ not yet claimed by the bridegroom but waiting as a virgin for the coming marriage union. This concept is presented by Paul in II Corinthians 11:2, "For I am jealous over you with godly jealousy; for I have espoused you to one husband, that I may present you as a chaste virgin to Christ."

The use of the figure of a bride to represent the church in her relationship to Christ has in mind the oriental pat-

141

tern in which marriage is contemplated as having three major steps: (1) the legal marriage often consummated by the parents of the bride and the bridegroom in which the dowry is paid and the young couple are formally married in a legal sense; (2) subsequent to the legal marriage, the bridegroom according to the custom would go with his companions to the house of the bride to claim his bride for himself and to take her back to his own home; (3) the bridal procession would be followed by the marriage feast which would often last for many days as illustrated in the wedding at Cana (John 2). In the oriental marriage, there was no ceremony such as is common in western civilization, but the legal marriage was consummated by the parents in the absence of the bride and bridegroom.

Taking this figure as a spiritual picture of the relationship of Christ to His church, it is evident that for individual Christians, the marriage as far as its legal character is concerned is consummated at the moment an individual puts his trust in Jesus Christ as Saviour. In the case of the Christian, the dowry has already been paid in the sacrifice of Christ on the cross, and the bride has been purchased and claimed in a legal way by the Bridegroom. The church is, therefore, already married to Christ as far as the technical relationship is concerned. The day will come, however, when the Bridegroom will come for His bride and this is fulfilled in the rapture of the church. At that time the Bridegroom will claim His bride and take her to His Father's house. This is the background of the statements in John 14:2, 3 where Christ said: "In my Father's house are many mansions: if it were not so, I would have told you. I go to prepare a place for you. And if I go and prepare a place for you, I will come again, and receive you unto myself, that where I am, there ye may be also." This passage contemplates that Christ in the present age is preparing a place for His bride. When this is complete and the bride is ready, He will come to take the bride to her heavenly home which will be accomplished by the rapture and translation of the church.

Further light is cast upon this concept in the Scripture in Ephesians 5 in the exhortation to husbands to love their wives, "even as Christ also loved the church, and gave himself for it" (Ephesians 5:25). This, of course, refers to the death of Christ on the cross in which the price was paid and Christ demonstrated His love and made the necessary sacrifice. This past work of Christ is the foundation for His present undertaking presented in Ephesians 5:26 where Christ is represented as engaged in a work of preparation for His bride, "That he might sanctify and cleanse it with the washing of water by the word." The present work of Christ, therefore, relates to the sanctification of the church and her purification in preparation for the future marriage. This will be accomplished by "the washing of water by the word," best understood as referring to the teaching of the Holy Scriptures and their application to the hearts and lives of believers. The traditional view that this refers to water baptism is contradicted by the present tense of the verb. This is not an event, but a process, and one that continues throughout the life of the church on earth.

The ultimate purpose is stated in Ephesians 5:27, "That he might present it to himself a glorious church, not having spot, or wrinkle, or any such thing: but that it should be holy and without blemish." When Christ comes for His church, the transformation will be complete and the church will be a glorious church, that is, will reflect the perfections of Christ Himself. It will not have a spot, that is, any uncleanness or wrinkle, referring to the corruption of age in decay or anything of this character. Instead, the church will be holy, that is, perfectly conformed to the righteous standards of God, and without a blemish, i.e., without any natural disfiguration. In I John 3:2, the ultimate transformation is compared to being like Christ, "Beloved, now are we the sons of God, and it doth not yet appear what we shall be: but we know that, when he shall appear, we shall be like him; for we shall see him as he is."

The church which is made perfect by the grace of God will be delivered from the earthly scene and presented to the heavenly bridegroom on the occasion of the rapture of the church. The marriage union thus contemplated will result in the church being forever with the Lord (I Thessalonians 4:17), and it will fulfill Christ's declared purpose "that where I am, there ye may be also" (John 14:3). The Word of God pictures the relationship of Christ to His church as the most beautiful of love relationships in human experience and contemplates unbroken fellowship throughout all eternity as the church enjoys the immediate presence of their loving Lord.

Further confirmation is given that this is an event fulfilled in heaven rather than on earth in the millennium is the declaration in Revelation 19:7-9, at the time of the return of Christ to the earth to set up His earthly kingdom. The church is pictured as already the wife of the Lamb and as already arrayed in fine linen. The marriage of the Lamb is declared to have already come and now the invitation is extended to those outside the church, the body of Christ, to participate in the marriage supper (Revelation 19:9) which seems to be a spiritual representation of the millennium or at least its inauguration. As the marriage feast is the final stage, it should be clear that the Lamb has already come for His bride and claimed her previously in the rapture of the church. The marriage (Gr. *gamos*) is actually the entire ceremony subsequent to the coming of the bridegroom for the bride. In this marriage ceremony is the marriage supper (Gr. *deitnon*) which is the meal or supper proper.

The evidence taken as a whole confirms the pretribulational approach to this aspect of the future of the church and contemplates the consummation of the love relationship between Christ and the church in the symbol of holy marriage in heaven. The wedding feast which is the final stage is contemplated by some as occurring in heaven but is probably better related to the events which follow the second coming, especially in view of the fact that the announcement of the coming marriage supper is made at the very time that Christ is returning to the earth.

THE CHURCH REWARDED

One of the major features of the period during which the church is in heaven is the distribution of rewards for faithful service to the church at the judgment seat of Christ in II Corinthians 5:9-11. The fact of this judgment is declared to the Corinthian church: "Wherefore we labour, that, whether present or absent, we may be accepted of him, for we must all appear before the judgment seat of Christ; that every one may receive the things done in his body, according to that he hath done, whether it be good or bad. Knowing therefore the terror of the Lord, we persuade men; but we are made manifest unto God; and I trust also are made manifest in your consciences."

Here, as many other times in the Pauline letters, the church is challenged to labor for Christ in view of the necessity of ultimately giving account to the Lord after He comes for His own. It is a judgment which relates to Christians only and has to do with the matter of rewards for faithful service. Paul declares in II Corinthians 5:9 that this is a worthy motive for labor for Christ that "we may be accepted of him," or better translated, "that we may be well pleasing to him." The fact is stated that all Christians must appear before the judgment seat of Christ that they may receive a just recompense for what they have done in life. The basis of the judgment will be whether their deeds were good or bad.

It should be clear from the general doctrine of justification by faith and the fact that the believer is the object of the grace of God that this is not an occasion in which the believers are punished for their sins. All who are in Christ Jesus are declared to have "no condemnation" (Ro-

mans 8:1). It is a question of sorting out the good from
the bad, the bad being discarded but the good being subject to reward. Paul mentions, however, in II Corinthians
5:11 that he is impelled by "the terror of the Lord" to continue in his task of persuading men to believe and serve
the Lord. The terror which Paul mentions is not that of the
possibility of being lost or unsaved, but rather the terror
of coming before his Lord with a wasted life. In that day,
when grace has brought him to the privileged place of being with the Lord in heaven, the thought of having to present a life that has not been properly spent in the Lord's
service fills him with terror. It was this fear that drove him
on in his service for the Lord.

The truth of the judgment seat of Christ, declared in its
main principles in II Corinthians 5, is presented elsewhere
in the Pauline letters under three different figures. One of
the basic presentations is that of the believer's life as a stewardship. The child of God is pictured as having been en-
trusted with a responsibility which he must discharge on
behalf of his master. On the basis of this stewardship, believers are exhorted not to judge others but rather to judge
themselves. In Romans 14:10-12 this truth is presented,
"But why dost thou judge thy brother? or why dost thou
set at nought thy brother? for we shall all stand before the
judgment seat of Christ. For it is written, As I live, saith
the Lord, every knee shall bow to me, and every tongue
shall confess to God. So then every one of us shall give
account of himself to God."

Inasmuch as each believer must give account to God,
it is presumptive for a believer to attempt to judge his
brother especially in areas where doubt exists as to what
the will of God may be. This does not mean that the
preacher of the Gospel is not called upon to rebuke sin or
to reprove those who are outside the will of God, but it
does require a recognition of the fact that our judgment is
not the final one. Ultimately our main question is not
whether someone else is serving the Lord, but whether we

ourselves are properly fulfilling God's stewardship as committed to us. The principle is plainly laid down, however, in verse 12, that everyone will have to account for his life at the judgment seat of Christ.

The thought of stewardship is reinforced and given further explanation in I Corinthians 4:1-5, "Let a man so account of us, as of the ministers of Christ, and stewards of the mysteries of God. Moreover it is required in stewards, that a man be found faithful. But with me it is a very small thing that I should be judged of you, or of man's judgment: yea, I judge not mine own self. For I know nothing by myself; yet am I not hereby justified: but he that judgeth me is the Lord. Therefore judge nothing before the time, until the Lord come, who both will bring to light the hidden things of darkness, and will make manifest the counsels of the hearts: and then shall every man have praise of God."

Here the Christian is especially reminded that he is a steward of the truth of God and that as such he is required to be found faithful. As in the Romans 14 passage, it is made clear that the main issue is not what man may think about it as there are limitations in our evaluation of our own life. Paul states that the Lord Himself is going to judge him and that therefore we should not attempt to evaluate our stewardship prior to that time. In judging the stewardship of a believer, God not only examines the act itself but the hidden motive and counsels of the heart which prompted it. Paul concludes with a note of expectation, "Then shall every man have praise of God."

A second important figure is used relative to the judgment seat of Christ in picturing the believer's life as a building built upon the foundation which is Christ. In I Corinthians 3:11-15, the foundation is described as already laid, which is Jesus Christ. Upon this foundation, each man is called to build a building or a life which will stand the test of God's final judgment. Paul writes the Corinthians: "Now if any man build upon this foundation gold, silver, precious stones, wood, hay, stubble; every man's work shall be made manifest: for the day shall declare it, because it shall be revealed by fire; and the fire shall try every man's work of what sort it is. If any man's work abide which he hath built thereupon, he shall receive a reward. If any man's work shall be burned, he shall suffer loss: but he himself shall be saved; yet so as by fire" (I Corinthians 3:12-15).

In using the figure of a building, attention is called first of all to the fact that it must be built on the proper foundation, namely, salvation in Christ. Everyone who appears at the judgment seat of Christ will meet this qualification as a person who has put his trust in Christ and has been accepted in the Beloved. Upon the foundation of our salvation in Christ, it is necessary for us to erect our lives. The materials mentioned are typical of what may be incorporated. The gold, silver, and precious stones represent that which is precious and indestructible, whereas the wood, hay, and stubble represent that which is unworthy and subject to destruction. As the passage makes plain, the building will be tested by fire and that which abides after it is tested by fire, namely, the gold, silver, and precious stones which by their nature are fireproof, are going to be made the basis for reward. Christians are assured, however, that even if their building be burned, they will be saved as far as their eternal destiny is concerned but they will be stripped of reward. This is stated in I Corinthians 3:15, "If any man's work shall be burned, he shall suffer loss: but he himself shall be saved; yet so as by fire." Comparing this to I Corinthians 4:15, it seems evident that every Christian will have something commendable about his life, but relatively speaking some will have a life mostly wasted, composed of wood, hay, and stubble, in contrast to those who have lived for eternal things as represented in gold, silver, and precious stones.

Many suggestions have been made concerning the typical meaning of these six building elements. The wood, hay, and stubble clearly represent three degrees of worthlessness as far as eternal values are concerned. Wood obviously is the best construction of the three and may represent temporary things in our life of a necessary nature as scaffolding in the construction of a building. However, when tested by fire the wood is destroyed even though it may be constructed well and be beautiful in its appearance. Hay represents that which is much more transitory, useful for animals but not fit for human consumption. Stubble represents that which is completely worthless. All alike, however, are reduced to ashes.

By contrast, the gold, silver, and precious stones, though much smaller in size and more difficult to obtain, are able to survive the fire. Gold in Scripture is typical of the glory of God and the perfection of His attributes and may represent that in our lives which is Christlike or which reveals the perfection of God's handiwork and grace. Silver is characteristically the metal of redemption and may speak of personal evangelism and of efforts in the extension of the Gospel. Precious stones are not identified and probably purposely are not related to any particular stone. This seems to refer to all other works of God manifest in the life of believers offering a great variety of beauty and color and illustrating that believers may serve the Lord in many different ways. The gold, silver, and precious stones, however, have this one important characteristic, that they are able to survive in the fire.

Taken as a whole, the figure of a building is a reminder, first, of the necessity of building upon Christ the foundation as the only true preparation for eternity. Second, our lives should be lived in such a way that they will have eternal value, and the time and effort extended will be worthy of reward by the Lord at the judgment seat of Christ. It is a reminder that the only real values in life are those which are eternal.

A third figure representing the issues raised at the judgment seat of Christ is used in I Corinthians 9:24-27 where the believer's life is compared to the running of a race or of contending in a fight. The apostle writes: "Know ye not that they which run in a race run all, but one receiveth the prize? So run, that ye may obtain. And every man that striveth for the mastery is temperate in all things. Now they do it to obtain a corruptible crown; but we an incorruptible. I therefore so run, not as uncertainly; so fight I, not as one that beateth the air: but I keep under my body, and bring it into subjection: lest that by any means, when I have preached to others, I myself should be a castaway."

According to this passage, the objective in running the race of life is to receive the prize from the Lord at the end of the race. We are to be guided in our life by this objective. Just as an athlete must apply self-discipline and be self-controlled in all areas in order to win the race, so also the Christian must make all things conform to the ultimate goal of pleasing the Lord at the judgment seat of Christ. Competing athletes, as Paul reminds us, do this to obtain a corruptible crown, that is, a crown of laurel leaves such as were commonly given at the races in Greece. By contrast, the Christian is looking forward to an incorruptible crown, that is, a crown which will not decay quickly like a crown of leaves.

With this incentive, the apostle declares that he himself runs not in an uncertain manner and that he fights not as one that is simply going through the motions. Instead he keeps under his body, literally, "beats it black and blue," thereby bringing it into subjection to his will. The apostle fears that having preached to others to dedicate their lives to the Lord and serve Him, he himself may be a castaway or one who is disapproved or disqualified. The reference to being disapproved does not relate to salvation, but to reward. It is a picture of an athlete who by breaking the rules is disqualified from winning the race. The figure makes plain that a Christian should bend all his efforts to living in such a way that he will not be ashamed when his life is reviewed at the judgment seat of Christ.

The concept of winning a crown or a victor's wreath at the end of the race is spoken of elsewhere in the Scriptures. In II Timothy 4:8, the Apostle Paul declares, "Henceforth there is laid up for me a crown of righteousness, which the Lord, the righteous judge, shall give me at that day: and not to me only, but unto all them also that love his appearing." Here the reward is viewed in a general way as recognizing Paul's righteous life at the judgment seat of Christ symbolized in the victor's crown. Paul does not claim to have a peculiar right to such recognition but declares instead that a similar crown will be given to all who love the appearing of Christ.

The eternal life which will be the possession of all true believers is likewise called a crown in James 1:12 and Revelation 2:10. James writes, "Blessed is the man that endureth temptation: for when he is tried, he shall receive the crown of life, which the Lord hath promised to them that love him" (James 1:12). This passage does not teach that some Christians will have life and others will not, but rather that the very possession of eternal life and its enjoyment in heaven is one of the forms of compensation which the believer will have for his life of service on earth, even though it is based upon the grace of God and the sacrifice of Christ rather than upon his own attainment. The same is true of the mention in Revelation 2:10 where the promise is given to the faithful martyrs, "I will give thee a crown of life." Those who suffer a martyr's death will all the more enjoy the freedom in glory of life in heaven which is their heritage.

The idea of a crown as a symbol of reward is also mentioned in I Peter 5:4 where the statement is made, "And when the chief Shepherd shall appear, ye shall receive a crown of glory that fadeth not away." The crown which is a symbol of reward is described here as a crown of glory that does not fade away, and in I Corinthians 9:25 it is mentioned as an incorruptible crown. It will be a glorious day for the saints when the Lord rewards His own.

Their recognition will not be transitory like the successes of this life, but will continue forever.

The various crowns mentioned in Scripture taken together are a symbolic representation of the recognition by Christ of the faithful service of those who put their trust in Him. II John 8 adds a word of exhortation, "Look to yourselves, that we lose not those things which we have wrought, but that we receive a full reward." While salvation is entirely by grace, rewards are related to faithfulness in Christian testimony and it is possible for the Christian to fall short of the reward that might have been his. Though there is a just recognition of attainment in faith and life, the saints in glory will nevertheless recognize that it is all of grace and that apart from redemption in Christ Jesus their works would have been unacceptable before God. This is brought out in the worship of the four and twenty elders in Revelation 4:10 who cast their crowns before the throne and say: "Thou art worthy, O Lord, to receive glory and honour and power: for thou hast created all things, and for thy pleasure they are and were created" (Revelation 4:11). If the four and twenty elders represent the church, as many believe, the fact that they are rewarded at this point in the book of Revelation is another indication that the church will be in glory following the rapture and translation while the tribulation unfolds in scenes of earth.

The final triumph of the church in relation to being in heaven with Christ will come at the time of His second coming to the earth when the church will accompany Him to the earth. Some find reference to this in I Thessalonians 3:13 in the phrase, "at the coming of our Lord Jesus Christ with all his saints." This phrase, however, may refer to the arrival of the church in heaven rather than the return of the church to the earth. More specific is Jude 14, where the prediction is recorded, "Behold, the Lord cometh with ten thousands of his saints." The church may well be numbered with the armies of heaven mentioned in Revelation 19:14 in the triumphal return of Christ to put down the wicked and to claim the earth which is rightfully His. In view of the imminent return of Christ, the prospect of the glory of the church in heaven is an ever-present one to saints of this generation, and the events which now are prophecy may become a reality very suddenly. Prophecies relating to the church in heaven, however, are only the beginning of a sequence of events which will carry the church into the eternal state.

CHAPTER X

THE CHURCH IN ETERNITY

Comparatively little is revealed concerning the church in
eternity, but sufficient facts are given to provide at least
an outline of the hope of the church. All conservative expositors agree that the church will have its place in the
eternal state. Premillenarians also find the church associated with Christ in His reign on earth during the future
millennium. Allusions to the state of the church both in
the millennium and in eternity to follow indicate a blessed
state for those who have entered by grace into the church,
the body of Christ.

THE CHURCH TO BE WITH CHRIST

One of the significant prophecies relating to the future
state of the church is the fact that believers in this present
age are promised to be "with Christ." In the preliminary
announcement of the rapture of the church in John 14:3,
Christ promised, "And if I go and prepare a place for you,
I will come again, and receive you unto myself; that where
I am, there ye may be also." Just as the church is promised
to be with Christ in heaven in the period between the rapture and the second coming to the earth, so the church
also accompanies Christ in a subsequent activity in the millennial reign and in the eternal state. Other Scriptures
bear testimony to this same concept. In connection with the
revelation of the rapture in I Thessalonians 4:17 the prediction is made, "Then we which are alive and remain shall be
caught up together with them in the clouds, to meet the
Lord in the air: and so shall we ever be with the Lord."

In the figure of the church as the body of Christ in Ephesians 5:25-33, the marriage figure itself indicates that the church will be with Christ even as a wife with her husband. Colossians 3:4 indicates, "When Christ, who is our life, shall appear, then shall ye also appear with him in glory." From these various passages and other allusions of similar nature, it may be concluded that the church will be in the immediate presence of the Saviour throughout eternity to come. The church is specifically mentioned as related to the second coming of Christ in Revelation 19:7-9 and is seen in the new Jerusalem in the eternal state as represented by the twelve apostles (Revelation 21:14).

THE CHURCH TO REIGN WITH CHRIST

In connection with the predictions concerning the future kingdom Christ told His disciples prior to His death and resurrection that they would join with Him in His kingdom and judge the twelve tribes of Israel. As recorded in Matthew 19:28, Christ said to His disciples, "Verily I say unto you, that ye which have followed me, in the regeneration when the Son of man shall sit in the throne of his glory, ye also shall sit upon twelve thrones, judging the twelve tribes of Israel." Further light is cast upon this in Paul's word to Timothy recorded in II Timothy 2:12, "If we suffer, we shall also reign with him." The fact that Christ promised His disciples that they would rule over the twelve tribes of Israel and promised to faithful members of the body of Christ a similar position of honor of reigning with Him, constitutes a confirmation of the premillennial concept that there will be an earthly kingdom between His second advent and the inauguration of the eternal state. These predictions imply a mediatorial kingdom in which Christ is the ruler and in which His followers will share responsibility. This, of course, is in keeping with the many predictions of the Old Testament.

In confirmation of this, Revelation 20 states that saints will join with Christ in His reign over the earth for one thousand years. This privilege is not only afforded the church but is also extended to saints who died in the great tribulation as martyrs. According to Revelation 20:4, John writes, "I saw the souls of them that were beheaded for the witness of Jesus, and for the word of God, and which had not worshipped the beast, neither his image, neither had received his mark upon their foreheads, or in their hands; and they lived and reigned with Christ a thousand years." These martyrs who are put to death by the beast in the time of the great tribulation just preceding the second coming of Christ are raised from the dead and participate in Christ's reign upon the earth. If this prediction is taken in its normal and literal sense, it teaches unmistakably that saints will reign with Christ and adds to previous revelation the fact that not only the church but also these noble souls will have part in the government of the millennial kingdom.

A further word is added in Revelation 20:6 where it is stated, "Blessed and holy is he that hath part in the first resurrection: on such the second death hath no power, but they shall be priests of God and of Christ, and shall reign with him a thousand years." This passage seems to go beyond previous predictions and includes all those who are in the first resurrection. From this sweeping prophecy, it appears that resurrected beings will have part in the government of the millennial earth and, though details are not given, it is evident that their resurrection is with a purpose that they may serve the Lord in this capacity.

Some dispensationalists have interpreted these passages as teaching that only the church, the body of Christ, has part in the millennial reign and that other resurrected saints will not have this privilege. This conclusion seems to be contradicted by Revelation 20:4-6. It is probably more accurate to say that the church will reign with Christ in a different sense than saints of other ages. An illustration is afforded in the book of Esther in the relationship of Esther and Mordecai to Ahasuerus. Esther, the queen, reigned with Ahasuerus as his wife and queen while Mordecai reigned with

Ahasuerus as his prime minister and chief administrative offi-
cer. Both Mordecai and Esther reigned with Ahasuerus but
in different senses. It is possible that there may be a similar
distinction observed in the millennial reign of Christ in that
the church will follow her typical position as the bride of
Christ while other saints will have other responsibility in the
government of the millennium. There is no real need, however, for a sharp distinction between the church and saints
of other ages in the eternal state, though the Scriptures seem
to indicate clearly that each group of saints will retain
its identity throughout eternity.

THE RELATION OF RESURRECTED TO NON-RESURRECTED SAINTS

The Scriptures reveal that the citizens of the millennial
kingdom will be formed of those who survive the tribulation
and who are still in their natural bodies. These, composed
of both Jews and Gentiles, will be occupied with normal life
on earth and be the subjects of the millennial reign of
Christ. They will plant crops, build houses, bear children
(Isaiah 65:21-23), and in other ways have a normal life
under the ideal circumstances of Christ's millennial reign.

The fact that these will still be in their natural bodies
has raised a question as to the relationship of resurrected
saints to those who are still living ordinary lives on earth.
The problem has been magnified out of proportion by amillenarians who have attempted to show that a millennial
reign of Christ is an impossibility.

It should be observed first that the relationship of
spiritual beings with those in their natural bodies is not
an abnormal or a strange one as illustrated in the present
ministry of angels who are unseen and who do not have
physical bodies. Angels do not have homes on earth and
do not occupy themselves with ordinary affairs of life.
Nevertheless, the Scriptures indicate that they are in the
earthly scene even today and have part in the divine government and outworking of the providential will of God.

Further light is cast upon the relationship of resurrected beings to those still in their natural bodies in the post-resurrection ministry of Christ. Though this posed some unusual situations, such as Christ entering a room with the doors being shut and appearing and disappearing at will, there were actually no real complications. Christ was able to talk with His disciples and they were able to talk with Him. They were able to see Him and feel Him, and His presence was just as real in His resurrection body as it was prior to His death and resurrection. Though admittedly the complications of millions of resurrected beings is a larger one than that of one person as in the case of Christ, the fact that Christ was able to mingle freely with His disciples on earth makes clear that there is no inherent problem which cannot be solved by divine wisdom in such a situation. Here as in many other cases, the Bible does not stoop to our curiosity, but expects us to accept by faith that which the Scriptures reveal even though it is quite foreign to our ordinary experience. It is far more honoring to God to accept what His Word has indicated concerning the ministry of resurrected saints, even though it leaves some problems unsolved, than it is to challenge what the Scriptures reveal as impossible of belief. After all, it is entirely reasonable for Christ in His resurrection body to be King of kings and Lord of lords and head the government of an earthly situation such as is pictured in the millennium. It should not strain our faith to believe that other resurrected beings could share with Him in such a government. Some further light is cast on this problem, however, in the study of the Scripture revelation concerning the New Jerusalem.

THE CHURCH AND THE NEW JERUSALEM

In Revelation 21-22, a comprehensive prophecy is given concerning the New Jerusalem described as "the holy city, the New Jerusalem, coming down from God out of heaven, prepared as a bride adorned for her husband" (21:2). A wide variety of interpretation has been offered by expositors concerning the nature and significance of this revelation. Some have preferred to regard the New Jerusalem as purely a symbol and not actually conforming to the reality of a future physical city. Others, however, have preferred to consider the prophecy in somewhat a more literal sense as the dwelling place of the saints. They have differed only as to whether the main thrust of the passage is to describe a millennial situation or the eternal state.

From a comparison of the dimension and situation of the heavenly city of Jerusalem with the characteristics of the millennial earth in relation to the Holy Land, as for instance indicated in Ezekiel 40-48, it seems clear that there will be no city on earth such as the New Jerusalem during the millennial kingdom, as its dimensions far exceed the possibilities of placing it in the Holy Land.

It has been observed, however, that the New Jerusalem is not said to be created at the time of the end of the millennium and the beginning of the eternal state, but is rather described as coming down out of heaven as if it had been previously created and in existence for some time. Though the Scriptures are by no means clear on many of the important factors which would enter into such a decision, attention is called to the fact that, in John 14, Christ promised that He was going to heaven "to prepare a place for you." Some have interpreted this as being a specific reference to the creation of the New Jerusalem in heaven as the dwelling place of the saints.

If this interpretation be admitted, there is no particular reason why the New Jerusalem should not be in existence throughout the millennium and suspended above the earth as a satellite city. Though this is foreign to our present experience of material things, such a concept is not beyond the realm of possibility. If the heavenly Jerusalem is hovering over the earth during the millennial reign, it would be a natural dwelling-place not only for Christ Himself but for the saints for all ages who are resurrected or translated and therefore somewhat removed from ordinary earthly affairs. Their position thus close to the earth would permit them to carry on their functions in earth in connection with the millennial reign of Christ and yet would remove them as far as residence is concerned from continuing or mingling with those in their natural bodies and would solve the problem of lack of reference to a dwelling place for resurrected beings on earth during the millennium.

Though some have attempted to limit the inhabitants of the New Jerusalem to the church, the body of Christ, Scripture seems to indicate that while the church will be present, the saints of all ages will also be included. According to Hebrews 11:10, Abraham "looked for a city which hath foundations, whose builder and maker is God." Further, in regard to the saints of the Old Testament who died without receiving the promises fulfilled, it is stated, "They desire a better country, that is, an heavenly: wherefore God is not ashamed to be called their God: for he hath prepared for them a city" (Hebrews 11:16). Their hope of a city should not be confused with their hope of the land. The possession of the land promised to the nation Israel was to be realized by those still in their natural bodies who survived the tribulation and who were on earth at the time of the return of the Lord. The hope for the city, on the contrary, is for resurrected beings of the Old Testament as well as the New.

The inhabitants of the heavenly city are enumerated in Hebrews 12:22-24, "But ye are come unto Mount Sion, and unto the city of the living God, the heavenly Jerusalem, and to an innumerable company of angels, to the general assembly and church of the firstborn, which are written in heaven, and to God the Judge of all, and to the spirits of just men made perfect, and to Jesus the mediator of the new covenant, and to the blood of sprinkling, that speaketh better things than that of Abel."

Listed in the heavenly Jerusalem and included as its citizens are the angels, the church, God, Jesus, and the "spirits of just men made perfect." It would seem that this last phrase refers to the saints of the Old Testament as well as tribulation saints who with the church will form the resurrected company who will inhabit the heavenly Jerusalem during the millennium and the eternal state.

The New Jerusalem is given detailed revelation and is described in general "as a bride adorned for her husband" (Revelation 21:2). The figure of marriage is used for the church, for Israel, and here for the city in which the saints of all ages will dwell. The fact that the marriage figure is used for more than one entity in Scripture should not be considered confusing, nor should the city be identified specifically with the church. It is rather that the New Jerusalem has all the beauty and freshness of a bride adorned for her husband. In Revelation 21:3-8, it is revealed that the New Jerusalem will be a place of indescribable joy where there will be no tears, no death, no sorrow, no crying, nor pain. This is comprehended in the declaration of Revelation 21:5, "Behold, I make all things new."

In the further description of the New Jerusalem given unto John beginning in Revelation 21:9, John sees the city described as "that great city, the holy Jerusalem, descending out of heaven from God, having the glory of God." The general appearance of the city is described as that of bright light compared to a precious jewel with its major structure being of a clear substance "like a jasper stone, clear as crystal" (Revelation 21:11).

The Apostle John gives in considerable detail the dimensions of the city which is described as being foursquare with the length equal to the breadth and measuring 12,000 furlongs on each side and being a similar distance in height. The tremendous size of the city clearly eclipses anything known in human history, for 12,000 furlongs measure 1342 miles. Such a city would be larger in most dimensions than the Holy Land itself at its widest extent and clearly indicates that the city is not to be represented as being on earth in the millennial reign of Christ. Various suggestions have been made concerning the dimensions of the city, some viewing it as a tremendous cube, others as a pyramid, and still others as a sphere. In any case, the city is of sufficient size to provide a proper base of operation for the saints throughout all eternity.

Though the city may be suspended in space during the millennial kingdom, it seems clear from the narrative that with the beginning of the eternal state following the millennial reign of Christ, the heavenly city comes to rest upon the earth. This is substantiated by the description of the twelve foundations in Revelation 21:14 which contain the names of the Twelve Apostles of the lamb. Foundations intimate that the city will rest on them. Here the city recognizes the presence of the apostles representing the church, the body of Christ, and the fact that their names are inscribed upon the foundation symbolically indicates that the church itself is related to this heavenly city.

On the foundation the wall of the city rests, which is described as "a wall great and high" (21:12) having twelve gates, three on each side, with the wall itself measuring 144 cubits or over 200 feet in height (21:17). If these figures be understood in their literal sense, it would indicate that the wall is of sufficient height to constitute a genuine barrier to all who are not qualified to enter and at the same time is dwarfed by the size of the city inside the wall which is, of course, much higher. The gates have inscribed on them the names of the twelve tribes of Israel (21:12) which shows that not only the church, but Old Testament saints will be included in the heavenly city. The gates themselves are guarded by angels which is another confirmation that angels are included in the heavenly city as previously indicated in Hebrews 12:22.

A dazzling description is given of the beauty of this city and of its materials in Revelation 21:18-22. The wall itself is made of jasper previously described as like a beautiful jewel clear in color. The city as a whole is pictured as "pure gold, like unto clear glass." The gold of the heavenly city is different than the metal of gold common to our present life and may refer to the city being golden in color rather than composed of the precious metal. Whatever its substance, it is transparent and at the same time is gold in appearance.

The foundation of the wall of the city is decorated with twelve precious jewels described in Revelation 21:19, 20. These jewels represent every beautiful color of the rainbow and present an image of indescribable beauty fitting for this city which is the masterpiece of God's wisdom and power.

The twelve gates are said to be twelve pearls, each gate being composed of one gigantic pearl. The streets of the city in Revelation 21:21, like the city as a whole, are compared to pure gold transparent like glass.

In the subsequent description, various aspects of the city are mentioned. Revelation 21:22 mentions that there is no temple in the city in contrast to the temples of earth and the temple of the millennial kingdom. God Himself dwells in the city, and it is declared, "I saw no temple therein: for the Lord God Almighty and the Lamb are the temple of it." Because of the presence of God in the city, there is no need for natural light. According to Revelation 21:23, "The city had no need of the sun, neither of the moon, to shine in it: for the glory of God did lighten, and the lamb is the light thereof." This city will know no night (Revelation 21:25) being lighted by continued radiance of the glory and presence of God.

Into this city, according to Revelation 21:24, the nations of them which are saved shall walk and the kings of earth will bring their glory into it. The reference to "the nations," literally, "the Gentiles," indicates that in the eternal state the racial and spiritual background of different groups of saints will be respected and continued. Old Testament saints will still be classified as Old Testament saints, the church will still be the body of Christ, and Israelites will still be Israelites as well as Gentiles Gentiles. Just as there will be corporate identity, so will there be individual identity. The notion that all identities will be lost in eternity is not sustained by careful examination of this description of the eternal state.

The blessing of entering the city, however, is limited to the saints and it is plainly stated that no one who does not qualify by being written in the Lamb's book of life is permitted to enter the city. It is a gracious provision for those who are the objects of God's grace. Those who have spurned His grace in time will not know His grace in eternity.

In Revelation 22:1, a description is given of "a pure river of water of life, clear as crystal, proceeding out of the throne of God and of the Lamb." If the city be considered a pyramid and the throne of God at its top, the river can be pictured as wending its way from the top down to the lower levels. Though it is difficult to reconstruct the exact image that is intended by the Scripture, it is clear that this pure river of life, though it may be a real and material river, is nevertheless symbolic of the abundance of spiritual life which will characterize those who are living in the eternal state. In Revelation 22:2, it is revealed that there will be the tree of life in the heavenly city bearing twelve kinds of fruit, yielding fruit each month with its leaves providing for the health of the nations. The reference in the Authorized Version to "the healing of the nations" has been taken by some as proof that this refers to a millennial situation rather than the eternal state. In a proper translation, however, the word "healing" is rather "health" and implies that the leaves of the trees are for the well-being of the nations, but does not necessarily indicate that healing is involved. The whole context, referring as it seems to do to the eternal state, would seem to rule out any thought of necessity of healing in a physical way. This is confirmed by Revelation 22:3 where it is stated, "There shall be no more curse; but the throne of God and of the Lamb shall be in it; and his servants shall serve him." Their blessedness before His presence in that they will "see his face" and enjoy His presence is indicated as their possession throughout all eternity.

The revelation is concluded by the statement that the things herein revealed are about to come to pass and will proceed in logical succession subsequent to the return of Christ to the earth. In view of the blessedness of this situation, Revelation 22 concludes with the invitation, "And the Spirit and the bride say, Come. And let him that heareth say, Come. And let him that is athirst come. And whosoever will, let him take the water of life freely" (Revelation 22:17). John himself, as he contemplated the glory of the future, breathed a prayer, "Even so, come, Lord Jesus" (Revelation 22:20). Though many details are not revealed, the glory and wonderful prospect of the saints is given sufficient description to provide substance to our hope and a glorious expectation for all who put their trust in Christ.

CHAPTER XI

SIGNS OF THE APPROACHING END OF THE AGE

Prophecies as they relate to the church take on new significance when viewed from the world situation of the second half of the twentieth century. Though the rapture of the church is presented in Scripture as always imminent, that is, as possible at any moment, the present world situation provides many indications that the rapture itself may be very near.

Strictly speaking, there are no specific signs of the rapture, as Scriptures uniformly relate signs of the end of the age to events which will follow the rapture. If it can be demonstrated, however, that the present world situation is in fact a preparation for events which will follow the rapture, it may safely be concluded that the rapture itself may be very near. The signs of the approaching end of the age are not incidental or obscure factors in the current world situation, but rather stem from major events and situations which are comparatively recent. The combination of many such indications has tremendous significance, and it is safe to say that never before in the history of the church has there been more evidence that the end of the age is at hand.

THE REVIVAL OF ISRAEL

One of the most striking situations from the standpoint of Biblical prophecy in the current world situation is the remarkable revival of the nation Israel and their return to their ancient land. Students of prophecy, especially those who are premillenarian, have long recognized that God's program for Israel is one of the major revelations of Scripture. Beginning as it does with Abraham early in Genesis, its prophecies continue and have their culmination in the last book of the Bible, the book of Revelation. That God is beginning to move once again in the nation Israel after centuries of no apparent progress is a clear indication of the approaching end of the present age and the beginning of events which will bring history to consummation.

The revival of Israel and the formation of the new state of Israel on May 14, 1948, is set in the context of the growing importance of the Middle East. This area of the world which formed the cradle of human civilization as well as the setting of the early history of Israel is important for many considerations. The geographic location of the Holy Land is at the hub of three major continents, namely Europe, Asia, and Africa. It is indeed the middle of the earth and the center of God's dealings with the human race.

Because of the fact that the commerce of the world flows through the Mediterranean and the Suez Canal, the Middle East is of great importance economically and the nation that controls this area of the world is in a strategic economic location. Though for centuries this area has been poor in its economic wealth and development, modern events seem to have brought a shift in this respect and are indication that the Middle East will again become important in an economic way. This is illustrated by the economic development of Israel itself and the tremendous chemical and oil reserves which are found in that general area.

It has long been recognized that the Middle East is also important from a military standpoint. One of the primary objectives of both World War I and World War II was the control of the Mediterranean and the Middle East. It is obvious that any country which desires to play a major role in world affairs must have influence in this area, and every world conqueror has recognized the importance of the Middle East.

From a religious standpoint as well, the Middle East is important inasmuch as it is the cradle not only of Christianity, but of Judaism and of the Moslem faith. No area of the world has been more important in its influence upon subsequent culture, religion, and human thought than the Middle East.

From a Biblical standpoint, the Middle East is most important because it contains the land which was promised to Israel. In the covenant which was originally given to Abraham, he and his seed were promised the land as recorded in Genesis 12:7, "The LORD appeared unto Abram, and said, Unto thy seed will I give this land." This promise is subsequently repeated in Genesis 13:14, 15, and its exact dimensions are outlined in Genesis 15:18-21, where it is confirmed by a solid oath including the shedding of blood. The promise of the land is further given an everlasting and perpetual character in Genesis 17:8 where God said to Abram: "I will give unto thee, and to thy seed after thee, the land wherein thou art a stranger, all the land of Canaan, for an everlasting possession; and I will be their God."

Abram died, however, without possessing the land and the same was true of Isaac and Jacob. When famine overtook the promised land, Jacob took advantage of Joseph's invitation and with his family moved to Egypt. This was a striking fulfillment of prophecy given to Abram many years before in which God had predicted not only that the children of Israel would go to a land which was not theirs, but that afterwards they would come out with great wealth and possess the Promised Land. This prophecy as recorded in Genesis 15:13, 14, reads, "Know of a surety that thy seed shall be a stranger in a land that is not theirs, and shall serve them; and they shall afflict them four hundred years; and also that nation, whom they shall serve, will I judge: and afterward shall they come out with great substance." Embedded in the promise of the land to Abram therefore is the prediction of the first dispersion into Egypt and the return of the children of Israel with great wealth to possess the promised land. Both the sojourn in Egypt and the return to the land were literally fulfilled as recorded in Exodus and subsequent books of the Old Testament.

In return to the land, however, Israel failed to possess all of it, and, though for a time under Solomon much of the land was put under tribute, the prophecy of its ultimate and everlasting possession was never fulfilled in the Old Testament. Instead, after Solomon, the kingdom was divided into the kingdoms of Judah and Israel, and subsequently the people of Israel were carried off first in the Assyrian captivity in 721 B.C., and later in the Babylonian captivity beginning in 606 B.C. The prediction that they would be carried off into captivity because of their sins was the theme song of the prophets in the preceding generations and only after Israel failed to heed the Word of God was the promise fulfilled.

In the midst of the wreckage of Israel's culture and civilization, which included the burning of the city of Jerusalem and its beautiful Temple, Jeremiah nevertheless predicted that Israel would come back to the land after seventy years. According to Jeremiah 29:10, God promised that they would return to the land, "For thus saith the Lord, that after seventy years be accomplished at Babylon I will visit you, and perform my good word toward you, in causing you to return to this place." Both the promise that they would be carried off into captivity and that they would return to the land were literally fulfilled. In keeping with this, it is recorded in Daniel 9 that when Daniel contemplated the prophecy of Jeremiah which somehow came into his hands in a faraway Babylon, he set his face to pray to the Lord and asked the Lord to fulfill his promise (cf. Daniel 9:2 ff). In keeping with the prophecy and in answer to Daniel's prayer, Zerubbabel led 50,000 pilgrims back to their ancient land of Israel and subsequently the Temple was rebuilt and under Nehemiah years later the city and the wall were restored. Once again the principle of literal fulfillment of prophecy is illustrated in the fulfillment of prophecies concerning the captivity and the return of Israel to the land.

Not only were the dispersions into Egypt and into

Babylon and Assyria predicted, but according to Moses himself the sins of the children of Israel would result in their being scattered over the entire earth. According to Deuteronomy 28:63, 64 Moses warned the children of Israel, "And it shall come to pass, that as the LORD rejoiced over you to do you good, and to multiply you; so the LORD will rejoice over you to destroy you, and to bring you to nought; and ye shall be plucked from off the land whither thou goest to possess it. And the LORD shall scatter thee among all people, from the one end of the earth even unto the other; and there thou shalt serve other gods, which neither thou nor thy fathers have known, even wood and stone." The significance of this prophecy goes far beyond the other predictions in that in this revelation it states that the Lord would scatter the children of Israel "among all people." This was subsequently literally fulfilled following the rejection of Christ by Israel. In A.D. 70 the city of Jerusalem was destroyed, fulfilling Christ's own pronouncement in Matthew 24:2 and other references to the destruction of Jerusalem, and later the land of Israel was made desolate and the children of Israel scattered to the four winds. This condition of Israel scattered over the entire earth has continued for almost 1900 years and no significant reversal was witnessed until our generation.

Though dispersed among all the nations, the Word of God was miraculously fulfilled in that the nation Israel was nevertheless preserved. In keeping with Jeremiah's prophecy that Israel would continue as long as the sun and moon endure (Jeremiah 31:35, 36), Israel has been preserved as a distinct people in a situation in which any other race or nationality would have long since been swallowed up. Because of their distinctive religion, culture, and heritage, they longed to go back to their ancient land. In our generation the beginning of such a movement has already been witnessed. At the beginning of the twentieth century, there was not a single Jewish village in all of their ancient land and only approximately 25,000 Jews could be found scattered here and there in the area that once belonged to their forefathers.

The Zionist idea of a new state of Israel in the Middle East advanced by Theodor Herzl in 1897 began to take form only gradually. It received some encouragement when the Balfour Declaration was issued in 1917 indicating that the British government was favorable to the establishment of a homeland for Israel. This action, however, was nullified by the British government after World War I was over. By 1939, when World War II began, the number of Jews had increased in the Holy Land to approximately 400,000 and once again the idea of a Jewish state was looked on with favor. In spite of many betrayals and reversals, the new state of Israel was finally proclaimed May 14, 1948, and since that date has been a reality.

Though its first year was spent in war with its Arab neighbors and heroic measures were necessary for its survival, the state of Israel has made steady progress since, till now it is a well recognized and established nation among nations. Its economic development has astounded the world as land has been cleared, terraced, and irrigated, millions of trees planted, crops of all descriptions produced, as well as substantial industries. Large cities such as Tel Aviv and Haifa have sprung into being as well as the new city of Jerusalem as capital just west of the ancient city which is still outside the borders of Israel. Most important, however, is the fact that now approximately two million Israelites are back in their ancient land, constituting the biggest movement of the nation since the Exodus from Egypt some 3500 years ago.

From the standpoint of Biblical prophecy, the formation of the nation of Israel is of tremendous significance, for what is now being witnessed by the world seems clearly to be a fulfillment of prophecy that there was to be ultimately a complete and final regathering of Israel in connection with the second coming of Christ. According to Jeremiah 23:7, 8 Israel was to be completely regathered immediately after the return of Christ to reign on the earth. This prophecy states: "Therefore, behold, the days come, saith the LORD, that they shall no more say, the LORD liveth which brought up the children of Israel out of the land of Egypt; but, the LORD liveth, which brought up and which led the seed of the house of Israel out of the north country, and from all countries whither I had driven them; and they shall dwell in their own land." As the prophecy makes evident, the regathering in view here is distinct from all previous historic regatherings in that it is an assembly of the children of Israel from all the nations of the earth.

Further light is cast upon this in Ezekiel 39 where it is indicated that when the regathering of the children of Israel from all the earth is complete, not a single Israelite will be left scattered among the heathen. Ezekiel wrote, "Then shall they know that I am the LORD their God, which caused them to be led into captivity among the heathen: but I have gathered them unto their own land, and have left none of them any more there" (Ezekiel 39:28). It seems highly probable that the regathering of Israel, which has so significantly begun in the twentieth century, will have its consummation and completion after Christ comes back and all Israel is assembled in the Holy Land. This concept is repeated many times in the major and minor prophets and constitutes one of God's unfulfilled prophetic purposes.

Further light is cast upon this fulfillment in the prophecies of Amos 9:14, 15 which read, "And I will bring again the captivity of my people of Israel, and they shall build the waste cities, and inhabit them; and they shall plant vineyards, and drink the wine thereof; they shall also make gardens, and eat the fruit of them. And I will plant them upon their land, and they shall no more be pulled up out of their land which I have given them, saith the LORD thy God." In connection with this significant prophecy, it is noted that the children of Israel returning to their ancient land will build their waste cities, plant vineyards, and drink the wine, as well as make gardens and eat the fruit.

This is graphically being fulfilled already in the present restoration of Israel and will have future fulfillment also in the millennial kingdom. Of great significance, however, is the climax mentioned in verse 15 where it indicates that once God has regathered them and planted them on their land, "They shall no more be pulled up out of their land which I have given them, saith the LORD thy God." In contrast to the regathering from Egypt, which later was reversed in the Babylonian and Assyrian captivities, and the regathering from Babylon which again was subject to dispersal in the first century A.D., the final regathering from all nations is never going to be reversed, but the children of Israel will continue in their land throughout the millennial kingdom as long as this present earth lasts.

The force of these prophecies is illustrated by their literal fulfillment. The dispersion and regathering from Egypt was literal; the dispersion and regathering from Babylon was literal; the dispersion to the entire world is literal and the twentieth century is witnessing the beginning of the final literal return to the land. It is a proper conclusion that Israel back in the land is a preparation for the end of the age.

According to the interpretation followed by many premillenarians, Israel's consummation will involve a covenant for seven years with a Gentile ruler in the Mediterranean area. This covenant anticipated in Daniel 9:26, 27, is between "the prince that shall come" and the "many," referring to the people of Israel. It is transparent that in order for such a covenant to be fulfilled, the children of Israel had to be in their ancient land and had to be organized into a political unit suitable for such a covenant relationship. Prior to the twentieth century, such a situation did not exist and tended to support unbelief on the part of some that Israel would never go back to their ancient land and could never have such a covenant. The fact of Israel's return and establishment as a nation has given a sound basis for believing that this covenant will be literally fulfilled as anticipated in Daniel 9:27. If the rapture occurs before the signing of this covenant, as many premillennial scholars believe, it follows that the establishment of Israel in the land as a preparation for this covenant is a striking evidence that the rapture itself may be very near. Of the many signs indicating the end of the age, few are more dramatic and have a larger Scriptural foundation than the revival of Israel as a token of the end of the age.

THE RISE OF RUSSIA

One of the great phenomenons of the twentieth century has been the rise of Russia to a place of international power and importance in the mid-twentieth century. At the end of World War II, Russia was a broken nation with its major cities destroyed and the flower of its manpower lost in war. There seemed little likelihood at that time that within a few years Russia should be in a position to become a world power. In the years following World War II, however, just this has occurred. Though its ultimate military strength and potential may be debated, it is unquestionably true that the United States and Russia are today the most powerful nations of the world and that Russia is at the peak of its power in its entire history.

The rise of Russia is a significant factor in the end of the age due to prophecies that relate to an invasion of Israel from the far North. Two long chapters found in Ezekiel 38-39 are devoted to this prophecy. Though not identified with Russia by name, the prediction is given of an invasion of Israel in which the invading army is completely destroyed by an act of God. The time of the invasion is declared to be "in the latter years" or "in the latter days" (Ezekiel 38:8, 16) at a time when Israel has been regathered to their ancient land. Israel is described as dwelling in "unwalled villages" and "dwelling safely" (Ezekiel 38:11) after having been "gathered out of many people" (Ezekiel 38:8). The situation in Israel is pictured as one of rehabilitation of places formerly desolate in rebuilding of cities and the establishment of new wealth and power (Ezekiel 38:12, 13). Such a situation and battle does not fit any historic context, but with the return of Israel to the land in our modern day a condition is created which in many respects corresponds to the context of Ezekiel's passage.

One of the areas which Russia would very much like to possess is the Middle East with its tremendous reserve of oil and chemical deposits. The importance of the Middle East is growing in modern affairs and Russia probably desires this territory to the south more than territory in any other direction. An invasion of Israel in the twentieth century by Russia seems a likely development in the end of the age. The fact that Russia has risen to such power in our day sets up a situation which, coupled with Israel's return to the land, establishes the basic conditions set forth by Ezekiel for the fulfillment of its prophecy.

Though all the factors are not yet fulfilled and it can hardly be said that Israel is dwelling safely in their land at the present time, the rise of Russia coupled with the return of Israel to the land puts two major component parts together in a prophecy which would have been impossible of fulfillment prior to the twentieth century. The situation of Israel dwelling in unwalled villages is a modern situation, not true in the ancient past. Never during a period when Israel was in the land was Israel threatened by an army from the far North. Though the passage contains a number of unresolved problems such as the return to antiquated weapons and other details of the prophecy, the general picture unmistakably corresponds to the modern situation. The rise of Russia therefore is another factor in the contemporary situation in which the stage is being set for the final drama of the end of the age.

THE RISE OF COMMUNISM

Another important aspect of the rising power of Russia is a spectacle of the world-wide sweep of communism. Never before in history has a new ideology swept more people into its fold in less time than communism has accomplished since World War II. Approximately one billion people are under communistic government throughout the world and the penetration of communistic ideas in other lands is obvious.

The rise of communism is peculiar in many respects because never before in history has an atheistic philosophy gained such a wide footing in any generation. While in the past many nations were pagan and worshiped heathen deities and idols, it is unprecedented for a great nation such as Russia to embrace atheism as its official religion. The spread of atheism to China, as well as many other nations, has greatly enlarged its influence and future potential.

The significance of an atheistic system such as communism in the end of the age fits into the prophetic picture with remarkable precision. In Daniel 11:36-45, an absolute ruler is described who will "magnify himself above every God, and shall speak marvelous things against the God of gods" (Daniel 11:36). This king is represented as disregarding all the deities of his forefathers and exalting himself to a place of deity in their stead. In Daniel 11:38 he is further described as one who honors "the god of forces," literally, the god of military forces. This expression makes clear that this absolute ruler who regards himself as God is completely atheistic in his approach as reflected in his disregard of all deities and in his exaltation of military power as the only entity to be feared. It clearly identifies him with materialistic and atheistic philosophy. It would be difficult to define in simple terms the communistic philosophy more accurately than by the description, atheistic and materialistic, and as respecting only power in war. The false religion which will be epitomized in this ruler is therefore akin to communism in all its important principles.

According to Scripture, the false religion which this king forces upon the world is the final form of blasphemy and false religion which will characterize the world at the end time prior to Christ's return to establish His kingdom.

If this king is to be identified with the beast out of the sea of Revelation 13:1-10, as many expositors do, this ruler is the same as the one who was given power over the entire world and of whom it is predicted, "all that dwell upon the earth shall worship him" (Revelation 13:8).

The significance of communism, therefore, is that of a preparation or forerunner of this future false religion. Millions of young people in communist lands are methodically being trained that there is no God and are taught to respect only military power. Such a preparation is an obvious one for this future world ruler, and the communistic ideology, though not identical in some respects to this future false religion, is nevertheless its counterpart religiously and constitutes an evident preparation for the world-wide sweep of this false religion. The fact that communism has such a wide following today and has made such impressive gains in our generation is another major factor in preparing the world for its climatic end at the second coming of Christ. While Russia as a nation will never conquer the world, communism apparently will embrace all people except those who in that day turn to Christ.

The Growing Power of the Orient

One of the important developments of the twentieth century is the rising power of Oriental countries such as Red China, Japan, and India. The release of these major countries from foreign domination and their growing importance from the military and economic standpoint has reversed a trend of many centuries. It is obvious that in future world affairs, the Orient will increase in importance. Its multiplied millions of souls, its large territorial area, and its potential for economic and political development are obvious to all observers.

From the standpoint of Biblical prophecy, the Orient is important because of certain prohecies which indicate its participation in events at the end of the age. In the Scriptures which describe the final world conflict, including a gigantic world war, one of the military forces is described as coming out of the East. The ruler of Daniel 11:36-45 is troubled by "tidings out of the east," apparently an indication of rebellion against him and military attacks from the East. This is given further light in the book of Revelation where in chapter 9 in connection with the sounding of the sixth trumpet an army is described as coming from the East from the great river Euphrates numbering 200 million and capable of slaying a third part of the earth's population (Revelation 9:15, 16). A later development of this matter is given prominence in the sixth vial of Revelation 16:12-16 where it is predicted that the Euphrates River will be dried up "that the way of the kings of the east might be prepared."

While many explanations have been given of this difficult prophecy, the most logical is that it refers to an army which comes from the East led by its rulers. Subsequent verses indicate that this army will proceed to the Holy Land and form a part of the military force to participate in "the battle of that great day of God Almighty" that will have its center at Armageddon which is properly identified as the Mount of Megiddo on the southwest rim of the valley of Esdraelon. This is the final great world battle which is under way at the very moment Christ comes back in power and glory to establish His earthly kingdom.

The evidence that a great army will come from the Orient and participate in the final world war conflict is a natural conclusion, and the extraordinary size of the army is in keeping with the tremendous population of this area of the world. The fact that the Orient is rising in power and in military significance in our day seems another development in keeping with the prophetic description of the end of the age and therefore constitutes a sign that the coming of the Lord may be near.

THE TREND TOWARD WORLD GOVERNMENT

One of the dramatic developments of the twentieth century is the rise of world government in the formation of the United Nations. Though students of political science have long dreamed of a world empire and conquerors of the past have hoped to achieve a rule over the entire earth, no government has been able to embrace the entire population of the world. The twentieth century, however, has witnessed the effort to unite nations in a form of world government with the purpose of averting international strife and warfare between nations.

The League of Nations which was formed after World War I proved to be premature, and without the support of the United States was soon doomed to failure. The rude reminder of World War II that war is not the best way to settle international government problems set the stage for a program which would provide a medium for discussion of international difficulties. Thus came into existence the United Nations following World War II which today embraces more than one hundred nations of the world and almost every prominent nation.

The rise of world government is especially significant from a prophetic standpoint because of plain Scriptures which predict that in the days immediately preceding the second coming of Christ a world government will be in operation. Early intimations of this are given in the prophecies of Daniel where in chapter 7:23 the final ruler and his empire is said to "devour the whole earth." The world government thus predicted is to be followed by the kingdom of Christ which will be brought into being at His second coming. Confirmation of this concept is found in Revelation 13, where the world ruler of that day is described as having power "over all kindreds, and tongues, and nations" (Revelation 13:7). This is obviously a government of far greater sway than any of the previous empires mentioned in Biblical prophecy such as that of Babylon, Media-Persia, Greece, or Rome. These empires, to be sure, embraced much of the civilized world but did not actually rule over "all kindreds, and tongues, and nations."

The significance of the formation of the United Nations

is probably not that of being an earlier stage of this world government. It is rather that the formation of the United Nations indicates an acceptance on the part of millions of people of the principle of world government as the only effective way toward world peace. Apart from Christians who entertain the hope of Christ coming as a means of bringing peace to the world, those outside the Christian faith have no alternative but to accept world government as the only way to peace. Millions of intelligent people today believe that the only hope of averting atomic suicide is to accept some form of international control in which individual nations will surrender some of their sovereignty in favor of international control. Though the rise of nationalism and independence of many small nations has for a time tended to fragmentize rather than unify the world, the weakness and interdependence of nations is even more apparent today than ever before. In a world brought close together by rapid means of travel and weapons of destruction which can reach any portion of the globe, the significant fact is that for the first time in history the concept of a world government has seized the minds of large masses of people. The world situation with its scientific improvements has developed to the point where such a world government becomes a necessity if future world conflicts should be avoided. The rise of the United Nations, therefore, is another apparent sign in progress toward preparation for the end in that millions of people are already prepared to accept such a world ruler when he rises in the last days. Trend toward centralization of power as manifested in all areas and as predicted for the end time is supported by the formation of the United Nations and its evident trend of increasing power in the world.

THE RISE OF THE WORLD CHURCH

The history of the church since apostolic times has been one of multiplication and division. Though a semblance of unity was achieved in the fourth and following centuries, division soon became characteristic of the church. The Eastern and Western churches divided in the eleventh century and further division took place in the Protestant Reformation. Within Protestantism itself, hundreds of denominations arose as well as thousands of independent churches. The process of further division and schism continued until the twentieth century.

In the last thirty-five years, however, a new development has come into being, namely, a trend back toward unification of the church. The desire for ecumenicity or a world church had long been discussed but did not take tangible form until preliminary meetings were held in 1925 and 1927. Out of this came the Temporary Ecumenical Council in 1938 and finally the World Council of Churches was formed in 1948. Since then, millions of church members have become party to a movement which is intended to bring together all branches of Christendom into one gigantic church including not only Protestantism, but the Roman Catholic and the Greek Orthodox branches.

From a prophetic standpoint, a world church of this character has unmistakable significance, because of predictions which anticipate just such a move at the end of the age. Apparently subsequent to the rapture of the church, a world church will emerge depicted in the uncomplimentary terms as a wicked woman in Revelation 17. This has long been held to represent a revival of the Roman Church and may well describe its course in a time when Protestantism and the Eastern church has rejoined Rome. Though all details are not supplied in the prophecy of this chapter, the woman who is labeled as "Babylon the Great" seems to represent the world church in the period immediately following the rapture of the body of Christ. The world church thus depicted will be superseded by the materialistic atheism which will characterize the great tribulation that will destroy the world church and replace it according to Revelation 17:16, 17.

The formation of a world church in the twentieth century from a prophetic standpoint, therefore seems to be a preparation for end-time events. The ecumenical movement as it is constituted today undoubtedly includes many genuine Christians. These, however, will be raptured at the time Christ comes for His own, leaving the organization bereft of any regenerated believers. Such a church will rapidly go into apostasy as the Scripture indicates, and prepare the way for the final form of blasphemy which will characterize the great tribulation.

While not a determinative sign in itself, the formation of a world church, added as it is to other signs that seem to speak of the end of the age, supports the concept that the rapture of the church may be very near.

THE TREND TOWARD APOSTASY

One of the sad notes of prophecy as it relates to the end of the age is the prediction that instead of the church becoming better as the age progresses, it will grow worse and end in utter apostasy. As Paul wrote Timothy in II Timothy 3:13, "Evil men and seducers shall wax worse and worse, deceiving and being deceived." The extended passages of Scripture dealing with apostasy, such as I Timothy 4:1-3, II Timothy 3:1-13, and II Peter 2-3, combine in a testimony that the age will grow progressively farther from the truth and will justly deserve the judgment of God at its close.

Any observer of the theology of the contemporary church will recognize the drift which has been apparent in the twentieth century. A large portion of the church no longer subscribes to the inerrancy of Scripture, the eternity and deity of Christ, His substitutionary atonement, and His bodily return to the earth. These and other great doctrines of the faith have been rejected by the modern mind and replaced with a new theology. The present trend toward apostasy, according to the Scripture, is only the beginning and will have its ultimate form in the period after the church, the body of Christ, has been raptured. The presence of the true church in the world, containing as it does thousands of evangelical believers, has tended to stem the tide for the time being. But once believers are removed from the earth, there will be nothing to hinder the progress of false doctrine and the rejection of that which has characterized Christianity since its beginning. The change in the theology of the church is, therefore, another sign that the age is progressing to its prophesied climax and that the coming of the Lord may be very near.

When all the evidences relating to the end of the age as they exist in the contemporary scene are summed up, they contain an impressive list of events and situations which are peculiar to the twentieth century and especially to the post-World War II period. The revival of Israel, the rise of Russia, and the extensive power of communism, the growing power of the Orient, the development of world government, the formation of a world church, and the trend toward apostasy are major signs that the end of the present age may be very near. If so, prophecy as it relates to the church is headed for its consummation and the glorious promises which constitute the hope of the church may be fulfilled in the not too distant future. The devout soul, while striving to be "always abounding in the work of the Lord," with the Apostle John can sincerely breathe the prayer, "Even so, come, Lord Jesus" (Revelation 22:20).